LOST
HONOR

John W. Dean III

𝔖𝔱𝔯𝔞𝔱𝔣𝔬𝔯𝔡 𝔓𝔯𝔢𝔰𝔰
LOS ANGELES

DISTRIBUTED BY
HARPER & ROW
NEW YORK

For all those who read *Blind Ambition,*
this is the rest of the story.

"The horror of that moment," the King went on, "I shall never, never forget!"

"You will, though," the Queen said, "if you don't make a memorandum of it."

Through the Looking-Glass
Lewis Carroll

"If way to the Better there be, it exacts a full look at the Worst."

"In Tenebris II"
Thomas Hardy

Contents

Preface
xi

Myths and Realities
1

CHAPTER ONE
Smelling Like a Rose
7

CHAPTER TWO
The Fox and the Hedgehog
27

CHAPTER THREE
Living in the Past
47

CHAPTER FOUR
Everything Is Different Now
77

CHAPTER FIVE
What If
99

CONTENTS

CHAPTER SIX
The Scene of the Crime
135

CHAPTER SEVEN
Kansas City Blues
159

CHAPTER EIGHT
When You Kick the King
185

CHAPTER NINE
Hiding and Seeking
221

CHAPTER TEN
Through Others' Eyes
249

CHAPTER ELEVEN
The Resurrection
267

CHAPTER TWELVE
Looking for Woodward's Friend
311

Epilogue
355

Acknowledgments
359

Index
361

Preface

When I was still Counsel to the President of the United States and was meeting regularly with Mr. Nixon in the Oval Office, Dick "Red" Moore dropped by my office one morning for a chat. Dick's red hair had turned pure white long before he came to work at the White House, and his grandfatherly appearance added clout to the advice he parceled out to the younger aides like myself.

During the course of one of our conversations, back in March of 1973, Dick had said, "John, you really should keep a journal to record your meetings with the President. What's being said in those meetings is history."

"Dick, what's being said in those meetings I wouldn't want to put on paper," I answered. He shrugged and nodded in resignation. If he didn't understand then, he certainly does today.

Dick Moore's advice was not lost on me, and often I thought about his suggestion when I realized how important those conversations were. When I was writing my testimony for the Senate Watergate committee—still unaware of Nixon's taping system—I certainly wished I had followed his advice. After my appearance before the Senate, I thought again of his suggestion, and I decided to start a journal, not for the sake of history, but to keep a record of the events affecting my life. I purchased a handsome, leather-bound diary and began writing.

Soon I discovered that my discipline as a diarist left much to be desired. Some days I didn't feel like writing, and often, when the mood did strike, the diary was not at hand.

After a few weeks of on-and-off jottings, I read what I had written and became concerned that some zealous investigator or prosecutor might try to subpoena my rather intimate reflections and observations, since Watergate was still very much alive. The thought of anyone's knowing my vulnerabilities and weaknesses horrified me. The entire project seemed potentially embarrassing, so I abandoned the diary.

Nonetheless, I had written enough to realize that recording events gave them perspective, that writing about chaos in my life gave it stability, and that articulating fears made them more manageable. Soon again I found myself keeping a record. But not as originally planned.

When I felt like writing I would simply find a piece of paper, from old envelopes to airline stationery, and wherever I might be I would write. At first I wrote notes, or letters, to be mailed later to my wife, Mo, or to my lawyer, Charles Shaffer. I felt this would protect the contents from investigators, since it was privileged communication. But within a short time I dropped this paranoid pretense. What I was writing, and continued to write, was about the impact that Watergate was having on my life.

After six years of keeping this journal, it had grown to twenty-seven thick file folders of dated notes. Sometimes I would reduce a day, week, or month to a single handwritten sentence on a scrap of paper; other times I expanded an encounter of a fleeting moment to a dozen or more typed pages. Occasionally the entries were erratic, but usually very regular. It is clear that when I was down, troubled, or bored I wrote more, and more often. But when I was busy, happy, and at peace, I had little to say, even to myself. The journal was a place to share thoughts and feelings, to note events and discoveries, a friend and confidant and, at times, even an enemy, for the journal was me.

My journal is the basis for the story that runs through this book, and throughout the book I quote directly from it.

The fact that this book is autobiographical may suggest that I am a hopeless narcissist, since no experience in my life could have the historical impact of the events I have already recorded in *Blind Ambition.* But the story in *Blind Ambition* did not end, for Watergate did not end. I have written autobiographically because it is the only way I know to explain what I have discovered, uncovered, and experienced about the effects of Watergate on American politics, the presidency, Congress, the courts, the news media, and the public— and upon those of us who were directly involved.

In exploring the consequences of Watergate, I have traveled throughout the country, and I have read enough books, articles, and documents to start a small-town library. But this is certainly not the book of a historian or reporter, rather someone who was deeply involved in one of our country's most shameful and far-reaching scandals, who wanted to know for himself what it all meant.

I have tried to look honestly and objectively at the information I have gathered, because it is important for me to know what really happened. The most difficult task has been looking at myself. All of us know how much of our lives we live inside our heads, and it is a life unknown to anyone except ourselves. This life exists apart from the acts and words by which others judge us. It is this life that I often recorded in my journal, and, in drawing from those writings, those voyages to my interior life and most private thoughts, I have learned that the line between self-analysis and self-indulgence is dangerously thin.

Equally precarious is the line between exhibitionism and honest confession. Aware of this, I have asked friends, editors, and even a few foes to tell me if they think I'm too close to shoals of false modesty, self-service, or indecent exposure. If I have not steered clear it is my fault, not theirs.

A story as personal as the one I have told in this book is not told to just anyone; rather, throughout the telling I had in mind those people I've met in lecturing, those who have read *Blind Ambition,* or watched it on television, and those who have written, or personally asked, the questions which this book attempts to answer. For you, this is the rest of the story.

Myths and Realities

I was uncomfortable. It was hot, muggy, and edging toward oppressive—and it was not just the mid-June Washington weather that made it feel that way. I had decided to revisit my past, and I had come to the nation's capital to do it.

The walk from the Fairfax Hotel, nestled along Massachusetts Avenue's embassy row, to a favorite nearby Connecticut Avenue bookstore/newsstand to pick up *The New York Times*, *The Washington Post*, *Time*, *Newsweek*, *The New Republic* (and anything else I spotted that had devoted time and thought to the current resurrection of Watergate), brought back a lot of memories.

Once this city had been the most exciting place in the world to me. Its pulse had been mine, and I'd relished every beat for over a decade. I'd gone to graduate school here, law school, and then become a part of the very machinery that makes the city run. I'd first come to the city filled with ambition and hope to make it big, to become one of its powerful people—for nowhere in the world was there more power. But I'd left Washington in shame and disgrace. Now, I hoped that this visit might help refurbish a bit of my tarnished self-image, and even restore a part of this man's lost honor.

JUNE 17, 1982—Washington, D.C.

Ten years ago, on this day, the word *Watergate* came to mean much more than a luxury hotel and office complex on Virginia Ave-

1

nue in Washington, D.C. It became an epoch, an era. Today it is history, a date commemorative of political infamy. For on this day, in this city a decade ago, a stillborn plot of presidential skullduggery ended in what would become a shameful and public political abortion. It was on this day that the discovery of a White House-commissioned "third-rate burglary" gave birth to a first-rate national scandal.

Today the fever of revival has peaked in the heat of Washington, although the temperature began rising months ago. For the past five months, at least, I have been receiving calls and letters from reporters, magazine editors, and network television news producers, all requesting interviews or appearances in connection with their plans to reexamine Watergate from a ten-year perspective.

I have turned down all except John Lindsay of *Newsweek*, Hays Gorey of *Time* magazine, Larry Meyer of *The Washington Post*, and an appearance on NBC's "Today" show. I talked to these reporters because I respect them, and I agreed to do the "Today" show because it is covering my costs in returning to Washington— the only place to be if I wish to begin wrapping up my own Watergate investigation.

I think I have read, or watched, everything of any significance in connection with this tenth-anniversary reprise, and, while I don't know why I thought it might be otherwise, the quality of the analyses has been very disappointing. Now, more than ever, it is clear that Watergate has had no lasting effect, has brought no real changes in government, and has had little impact on the people of the country. It was, and clearly always has been, a political-cum-media event.

Being here this week has enabled me to confirm what I have long suspected, that Watergate has become little more than a symbol. While symbols are important, inevitably they come to eclipse the greater meaning inherent in the events they represent.

These few days in Washington have enabled me to do more work on the Deep Throat question, as well.* The developments in this area have taken on a disturbing quality. I had always assumed that unraveling the Deep Throat mystery meant little more than

*In the unlikely event that a reader needs reminding, "Deep Throat" was the name given to the "reliable source" who supplied Bob Woodward and Carl Bernstein of *The Washington Post* with important inside information during their investigation of Watergate.

locating the answer to a Watergate trivia quiz. Never did I attach importance to this enigma, yet each step of my investigation has raised increasingly important questions. If I am correct about the identity of the man I am now pursuing as the top candidate, it could produce a surprisingly different view of Watergate. I thought I knew all there was to know about the entire mess, but the Deep Throat investigation has opened several dark passages I had neglected to look down before.

Because I am so visible, and would be recognized even in the darkest of corridors in Washington, I have made arrangements with Hays Gorey to help me. Hays has spent many long hours for *Time* magazine trying to unearth Deep Throat. I trust him.

Hays and I met almost surreptitiously at the home of a former neighbor in Old Town, Alexandria, Virginia. My friend was out of town, so I was confident of our privacy. As we pulled chairs from the dining table, Hays acknowledged the wisdom of our seclusion.

"No sense in stirring up any rumors," he observed, "and your being spotted with a *Time* reporter would certainly make people in this city wonder what we were up to."

When I told him what I was doing, and that I needed some help, Hays said that he'd like to know what I had uncovered, so that he could better determine whether he could help, and how best he could do so. Hays said another reporter at *Time*, John Stacks, had also been working on this question with varying degrees of intensity over the years. While he didn't say so, Hays was probably doubtful that my own research could have outperformed the impressive resources of *Time*.

It took about forty minutes to present to Hays a capsulized summary of my investigation. He sat mesmerized as I proceeded step by step, until I reached the point where I moved from the general to the specific, telling him precisely whom I believe all the evidence points toward, and why. Hays was speechless.

"You've done an amazing job of pulling it all together," he said, finally. Then he sat silent for another few moments, digesting all I had told him, his eyes twinkling as he quickly sorted back through the evidence I had given him. He was visibly excited by what he had just heard, since he had, himself, spent so much time thinking about it. When he spoke again, he was slightly out of breath. "Well, John, you're really onto something here."

Hays stood up, not to go anywhere, but because his adrenaline was running. "I have only felt this kind of excitement about a story—or, I should say, learning the truth about a story—on one other occasion," the seventeen-year veteran of *Time* told me. "And that was when I learned what really happened at Chappaquiddick with Teddy Kennedy." Hays said that he would like to work with me; that, indeed, given the significance of what I had discovered, "there is no way I could not help."

As I moved about Washington that week, the shallowness of the hype surrounding the tenth anniversary continued to irritate me in a way I had not expected. As one of the participants in Watergate, it is likely assumed that I am among those least equipped to see it or evaluate it objectively. Thus, my analysis would be considered inherently faulty. Not to belabor this assumption, which I feel is incorrect, I must say that an accurate analysis of the legacies of Watergate is of far greater importance to those of us involved than to most others, since we must live with this history. Die with it too.

A problem in coming to grips with the significance of Watergate is the notion that most people have: that, because it was a significant event in our nation's history, it must have significant and lasting meaning for the nation. But if there is such an important lesson in Watergate, why is it so difficult to discern? Why is it not evident to all, and what is it?

In reading and watching the news media's coverage of Watergate's tenth anniversary, I discovered several recurring points: that Watergate was revealed because of the vigilance of the press, which cracked the case; that Watergate confirmed that "the system works"; that, in the balance of powers, the presidency was held accountable; that the threat of an "imperial presidency" was ended; that higher ethical standards were brought to government; that Watergate alienated countless numbers of citizens from government; and that Watergate made most of those involved rich and famous.

These, according to the experts, are a summary of the legacies and lessons of Watergate. For me, they are myths.

I have long wanted to know what it all has added up to, because this event has become so intertwined with my life and my reputation. And, while I wish I could accept much of what has been written and said about Watergate now that ten years have passed since it all began, I know that what is being said is often wrong. Over the years since Watergate I have collected too much information that is contrary to the current media synthesis to remain silent.

I did not plan to follow Watergate's continuing impact, but, since it has both directed and followed my life, the choice has not always been voluntary. In truth, I thought that Watergate had ended on that glorious day in January 1975, when I was released from prison.

CHAPTER ONE

Smelling Like a Rose

I stood at my window looking for the last time at the big maple tree on the other side of the chain-link fence, a fence the other inmates said was to keep people out rather than in, since this was a protective facility and not a prison. The tree was now nearly bare. I was sure I had counted the loss of almost every leaf as fall had turned to winter. That old tree had been a silent friend who had shared my time. And now, if I wasn't dreaming, it would soon become the only pleasant memory of this crummy little room in which I had existed for the past four months.

I don't remember how long I stood at the window, what else I looked at, or if I had any thoughts other than the one I kept repeating over and over, until, finally, I said it aloud to give it reality: "The nightmare is over!"

When I turned from the window, I wiped small tears from my eyes and cheek. Actually, I was surprised to find them. They should have been tears of joy, but they were tears of relief. It was true; it really was over. I could feel all the pressure of uncertainty that had accumulated in my life suddenly vanish; like a man snowbound in a forest, spring had miraculously arrived. There was no joy of victory, nor satisfaction of surviving. Just relief that it was over, that I could stop worrying about the uncertainty and do something about it.

I had told myself that Watergate would end when I was out of prison. Although technically I had not been in prison, I now knew

7

that "cells" or "walls" did not make a prison, but loss of freedom did. I had lost my freedom on September 3, 1974, when I set foot in that little room in a battered BOQ built during World War II on a since-deserted army base called Fort Holabird, outside of Baltimore, Maryland. It was a "witness protection facility" operated by the U.S. Marshal's Service.

Now I was free. More accurately, I was returning from a brief visit to that state of shock I'd been in ever since my lawyer had called a few moments earlier to tell me that Judge John Sirica had reduced my sentence of one to four years, for my involvement in the Watergate cover-up, to "time served." I felt emotionally drained, yet physically charged with excitement. I began to plan everything from how to start packing and making flight reservations to what I would do with the rest of my life now that it was mine again. The mental wheels were spinning, but the cogs were not engaging. I had to sit down for a moment on the edge of the bed and collect myself.

I heard a minor commotion outside my door. It was my former White House colleague, Jeb Magruder, charging down the hall, shouting, "Holy shit, I can't believe it! I'm free!" I leaned into the hallway and one of the other prisoners stopped and congratulated me. I had said nothing, but word of freedom spreads fast in prison. Others hope it's contagious, and it was. I learned that, in addition to Magruder and myself, Herbert Kalmbach, another of the "Watergate guys,"* as we were called by the other prisoners, also had been released by Judge Sirica.

"How about Chuck Colson?" I asked the inmates who had gathered at my door. Colson had not been freed, I was told. Poor Chuck, I thought, it's going to be rough. He had been taken to Washington earlier that day to testify and, when he returned, he

---

*The "Watergate guys" who shared the Fort Holabird facility with me were:

Charles W. Colson, the former special counsel to President Nixon. A political adviser and White House overseer of the 1972 re-election campaign, Colson served seven months for obstruction of justice.

Herbert W. Kalmbach, Nixon's personal attorney and a GOP fund-raiser. Kalmbach served six months for violation of campaign-contribution laws.

Jeb Stuart Magruder, formerly an aide to H.R. (Bob) Haldeman and later deputy director of the Committee for the Re-election of the President. Magruder served seven months for his participation in the Watergate break-in and cover-up.

would find us freed. Damn tough, I thought, putting myself in his place. I did not get a chance to see him before I left, but I placed a note of encouragement in his room. We'd renewed our White House friendship, which had become strained during Watergate, and had enjoyed some good conversation together at Holabird.

The compound was soon buzzing with excitement. Jeb and Herb and I all congratulated each other, all began packing and frantically making necessary arrangements. Then I was out of the place, using a back exit of the army base to escape the gathering of newsmen and television cameras that had already assembled at the main entrance.

Pete Kinsey, who had worked for me at the White House, took the afternoon off from his job at the U. S. Senate and drove out from Washington to pick me up and take me to the airport. The minute Pete's car reached the main road I felt it. I really felt like a free man. The claustrophobia of incarceration was gone. The emotions controlled in confinement were suddenly unleashed. As we passed in front of the base, where the press was clustered, I opened the window and shouted at the top of my lungs: *"God bless old Judge Sirica! I love the bastard!"* But they were too busy waiting for me to come out the gate to hear my farewell.

Within twenty-four hours of this sudden and unexpected release from prison on January 8, 1975, everything about my life seemed to change for the better. Freedom completely turned my world upside down. I was starting my life over. It was an unreal and very heady time, particularly when I returned home to California, where I was greeted by two unexpected but very seductive strangers named glory and greed.

Glory first leered at me across the tarmac as my flight touched down at Los Angeles International Airport. There, jostling each other in a familiar dance, were nearly fifty news reporters, thirty photographers, and a half dozen television camera crews—the kind of media festival that inevitably generates a crowd of several hundred curious onlookers.

It had never occurred to me when I made my flight reservation that United Airlines would announce my arrival time to the world and arrange a press conference at the airport. I wasn't ready for such a conspicuous homecoming, nor did I want it.

Of course, they parked the airplane a sufficient distance from the arrival gate to ensure that the television cameras had the United Airlines corporate emblems—and me—in focus. By the time the United executive stopped me at the bottom of the ramp, I was fuming. I had no intention of making a public spectacle of my reunion with my wife and friends. I wanted my privacy.

"Mr. Dean, please wait," shouted the man from United, approaching me on the run. "Where is Mrs. Dean?"

"How the hell would I know!" I answered with all the disgust I could put in my voice. "What's this circus all about?"

"Well, the press is very anxious to speak with you," he offered with obvious understatement. "And we've set up a room for a press conference. If you'll just follow me."

"Sorry, but I'm not interested." I decided to ignore the horde and go home. Ignoring the press was a subtle but permissible tweak of their collective nose, and that was exactly what this outrageous invasion of my privacy made me feel like doing. I restrained myself from sticking out my tongue or giving them the Bronx cheer.

Walking toward the waiting crowd I looked for my wife, Mo, or for some familiar face. When I saw our friend Gene Adcock, whose six-foot-four-inch frame made him easy to notice, I knew that Mo had undoubtedly spotted the mob and had been wise enough to send Gene.

As I hit the edge of the crowd, a cacophony of questions and comments engulfed me:

"Over here, Mr. Dean, for a press conference."

"Welcome home, John."

"How's it feel to be free?"

"What are your plans for the future?"

"Where's Mo?"

"Will you stop for some pictures, please?"

"How do you feel about Richard Nixon, who didn't go to jail?"

"How seriously did Watergate hurt the presidency, do you think?"

Ignoring the interrogative barrage, I plunged toward my friend. "Hi, Gene. Let's get the hell out of here, fast."

"Follow me," he said and, turning and lowering his shoulder to the crush, began pushing his way through.

"Is that your chauffeur, John?"

"Aren't you going to hold a press conference?"

"Has Mo left you?"

"Did the country learn anything from Watergate?"

"How do you feel now that it's all over?"

"Mr. Dean, can Watergate happen again?"

Slowly, Gene made his way, while I followed, shaking my head and saying, "Sorry, but I've nothing to say." Finally we reached the top of an escalator, and the noisy crowd gradually faded away. Gene said Mo was waiting in the car on the lower level, and we descended in silence.

As we rode down the escalator I thought about the absurdity of what was happening: these news people acted as if they expected Mo to come bounding across the airport toward my open arms like a girl in a Clairol commercial; then they expected me, eyes filled with tears of joy, to pause and explain to the television cameras, in a fifteen-second burst of lucidity befitting the time for a news clip, why Richard Nixon was The Undisputed and Honest-to-God All-American Son-of-a-Bitch. What I had to say consisted only of what I told Mo as I hugged her in Gene's waiting car: "Boy, am I glad to be home!"

Waiting at the gate to our driveway we discovered a smaller bevy of reporters and another camera crew. Again, I told them I had no comment. While we waited for the electric gate to swing open, one of the reporters came over with a stack of telegrams.

"These were delivered to the house," he said, passing them through the car window. "Can I ask you why Mayor John Lindsay sent you a wire?"

The top telegram on the stack was from John Lindsay, a *Newsweek* reporter who had covered Watergate, but not the former mayor of New York. Unable to resist the opportunity, however, I answered, "Well, I suspect Lindsay's very happy I never implicated him in Watergate."

"What?"

"I'll tell you, off the record, that John Lindsay knows as much about Watergate as Nixon himself, maybe more." The gate opened and Gene pulled up the drive, leaving a very confused and slightly dismayed reporter at the bottom.

The moment I walked into the house that Mo and I had bought

nearly a year before, I toured every room, touching the walls and furniture to reassure myself I was home. By the time I reached the master bedroom I felt absolutely giddy. I took a flying leap onto the bed and somersaulted back to my feet on the floor. I was home again! I was truly free to move and breathe and think again. That night, when I couldn't sleep, I wrote what I thought was my last journal entry, for the experience of the past four months was still crowding my thoughts.

JANUARY 9, 1975—Los Angeles.

Prison is loss of freedom. It is a devastating loss. Everything you have taken for granted is gone. You have no control over your life, no choice. Others decide when and where you wake, eat, work, and sleep. Your life is tied to rules and regulations that discourage individuality and disregard normal impulses. You accept the rules and adjust, just as you accept the crowded quarters, body odor, lack of privacy, standing in lines, and boredom.

Doing time is not a matter of physical survival, but of emotional survival. So, regularly, you check your feelings, reactions, and disposition. At first there is fear, but it is unfounded because you are not threatened. Self-pity comes and goes, a waste of emotional energy. Anxiety is constant, but of a low-voltage variety.

Doing time is like climbing a mountain wearing roller skates. You compute how long it will be until you are eligible for parole. You count the days; when really bored, you compute the hours, and they drag. You fight depression with an outpouring of letters to friends and loved ones to assure them all is well.

You're coping pretty well, when you get one of those painful reminders of your situation. Either one of two events occurs, or recurs. You learn of a family problem that demands your presence to handle, and you understand the meaning of helplessness. The problem would be nothing if you were not in prison, but in prison it seems enormous because you can't deal with it.

The other event is visitor's day without a visitor, which is the definition of loneliness. That makes you think a lot about home, loved ones, friends, the world outside. You remember little things you did before.

Constantly you are thinking, thinking, thinking. It happens while you are mopping floors or performing other "robot" tasks you've been assigned, or as you lie awake at night wishing the escape of sleep. The layers of your character are slowly being peeled away, like the skin of an onion.

Yesterday the interminable ended. It was the best day I ever had in prison: the last day. A chapter of my life has closed, punctuated with the exclamation that *I'm free!* But exclamation points pass quickly, and mine is followed by questions I cannot answer easily or hurriedly: What about the future? What do I do now?

I must answer soon.

The joyous reverie of homecoming and freedom was constantly interrupted by telephone calls beginning the moment I arrived home. Carl Stern of NBC was the first to call to request an exclusive interview, saying, "I haven't seen an airport arrival like yours since Frank Sinatra was at his peak of popularity. I watched it live back here in New York. We piped it by cable across the country hoping you'd stop for the cameras." I told Stern I was not sure I wanted to be interviewed. He asked me to think about it, and I said I would. His call was followed by countless other calls from friends and acquaintances who wanted to say "hello," or wish us well, or invite us out, plus hundreds of telegrams from strangers with thoughtful wishes, and from more reporters requesting interviews.

I began to feel strangely like a hero being welcomed home, instead of a released prisoner. While I tried to shrug it off, I liked the attention, particularly the flattery of the repeated job offers—and each day brought another one. These bolstered my self-confidence tremendously, and it needed the bolstering.

I appreciated the offers to work for law firms, but to work without a license to practice, as one firm suggested, would make me a high-paid law clerk, which was not for me. To seek readmission to the bar, as another firm suggested, would involve a public embarrassment I was not ready to handle. I doubted that there was a bar association in the country with the guts to readmit me, though I was probably more qualified to practice now than when I was first admitted. And I certainly had grown more sensitive to legal ethics after what I had been through. When you've been burned as badly as I'd been, your ethical sensitivity is much greater than most of those who are routinely admitted, because for them the ethical questions are academic. For me, they had become very real and consequential, and I wasn't about to make the same mistake again.

I was most interested in a job offer from the head of a large multinational corporation, who repeatedly assured me that he wanted me, not because of my notoriety, but because of my future potential. He suggested I initially work for one of his company's European or South American subsidiaries, until Watergate was forgotten. I was tempted, because accepting his offer would have meant financial security, but I couldn't ask Mo to start packing up to leave the country. She loves living exactly where we live and I was sure she did not want to leave.

The most important immediate factor in my thinking was the health of Mo's mother. Irene was close to both of us and had been a stable adviser and supporter throughout the Watergate days. Recently, her declining health had taken a turn for the worse, and it was vital to both of us that we be nearby to support her and to provide help. It was impossible for us to leave the country under these circumstances.

Not all the offers were flattering. In fact, I was distressed by a call from a gentleman in New York who claimed he had the "perfect job" for me. I listened with amazement, nay, at a loss for words, as this total stranger introduced himself by saying, "You are at an echelon, John, and so am I, where people know lots of people, all over. I was sure that I knew someone who would know someone who knew you. I was so sure that I bet a guy a hundred bucks he could pick at random any ten names from my personal phone book and, from one of those names, I'd come up with your phone number, which is unlisted, right?"

"Right. I guess your theory was good. What can I do for you?"

He ignored my question and, in a continued effort to be friendly, explained more than I was interested in hearing about how he knew the someone who knew me. Finally he got to the reason for his call.

"There is big, big money, John, I mean it, in making and marketing what I call 'sexually explicit' movies for home television. There are more new gadgets coming on the market than you'd believe—things you plug into your TV to watch prerecorded programs and movies."

"I'm sorry, but. . . ."

"Wait! Hear me out. I'm not talking about those stag films you used to watch in the fraternity house. I'm talking about classy stuff, big-budget movies—a couple of million—with pretty people. But we've got to get the law in tune with the times, so people can buy these movies without feeling it's wrong, or against the law. You know what I mean?"

"I don't know if I know or not. But I'm not interested in being involved with anyone or anything connected with 'porno' movies, so I think we should end this conversation right here."

This man not only sounded pushy, he was. I was insulted, but he pushed on. Then he nearly knocked me over by an offer of a quarter of a million dollars annual retainer. For part-time work, no less! That was extraordinary enough to make me roll my eyes, and several times. But I kept my head and just listened as he explained that he wanted me to lobby before Congress and state legislatures for changes in the so-called obscenity laws, to appear on radio and television talk shows to help the cause, and to write magazine and newspaper articles as well. I decided he must be connected with the Mafia, because no one else could throw around that kind of money. When he finished, I abruptly answered, "Sorry, I'm not interested." And I hung up.

While I managed to sound firm, I didn't feel it. This call bothered me because it made me think about how others saw me. I knew the estimation must be low or I would not have received such a call. But his offer helped me make a decision. As I looked down at the now silent telephone, there was no doubt in my mind that, if I were to do anything greedy, it would be respectable.

David Obst trafficked in both glory and greed—in what seemed to me a very respectable manner. So I decided to let him handle me. I had once been told that, if there were a disaster in Washington, Obst would own ten percent of it. David was a literary agent and he "owned" a good hunk of Washington, including Bob Woodward and Carl Bernstein—the *Washington Post* reporters who authored *All the President's Men* and *The Final Days*.

David arrived in California a few days after my release, and, still reeling from my conversation with the fellow who wanted me to pimp for pornographers, I let him take charge of my future. I was not sure what he would do on my behalf, other than to make certain that his ten percent of me was worth something.

The first thing David did when he arrived was to organize a press conference, in our driveway, not because he thought it a good way to handle all inquiries, but because "it will make publishers want your book all the more when they see what hot copy you are." He had commenced his negotiations. When I suggested giving an exclusive interview to NBC and Carl Stern, David replied, "You gave at the office; no more charity," and he began negotiating with Stern for payment.

He also suggested that I consider lecturing, which had not occurred to me. David announced, with typical enthusiasm, "I've got a man in Boston who'd love to arrange a tour for you. He's the best in the business. He handles Woodward and Bernstein. You could pick up some fast dollars and get some good exposure that would help book sales."

If all this was crass and crude exploitation, David made it seem like normal operations, and, other than some minor twinges of discomfort, it didn't trouble me. Rather, it seemed that at least I was making the best of the bad situation I'd put myself in. Within a few days David managed to tie my life up with a lovely green ribbon, bow and all, and hand it over to me.

By the end of my first week home, David phoned, announcing, "All finished. The deals are done and it's absolutely fantastic. I'm on my way over to tell you all about them."

As he came through the living room he jumped on the sofa and, as if he had just won a tennis match and crossed triumphantly over the net, declared, "Celebration time!" David was wearing what he called his "tennis garb," but his worn sneakers, torn shorts, and old shirt looked like he'd been the last in line for handouts at Goodwill Industries. David was not one to wear his success, obviously.

He sat on the sofa smiling. In fact, David couldn't stop smiling. "As soon as Mo comes back in, I'll tell you all about it," he whispered teasingly to me.

Mo, carrying a tray of strawberry margaritas, which David had suggested as a celebration beverage, entered the room and passed out the drinks. Obst got right to the point. "Here's the bottom line: I've got you a guaranteed three hundred thousand over the next cou-

ple of years for your book. You'll get an immediate seventy-five
grand when you return from your vacation and sign the contract;
then next year, when you finish the book, another seventy-five; and
then another seventy-five when they publish it. The rest will come
when they do the paperback, which will be about two years from
now. How's that sound?"

"Good," I said.

"We sure can use it," Mo added.

David took a sip of his margarita, leaned back on the sofa, and
noted abstractedly, "It's not bad, is it?"

"What? The drink or the deal?" I asked.

"Both."

"I haven't tasted the drink. I'm afraid it might flatten me, not
having put my lips to alcohol in over four months. But the deal's
amazing, especially since neither they nor I know what I'm going to
write about."

"You'll figure out something, I'm sure. You've also got whatever
comes in from the lecture tour," Obst added as he licked the salt on
the rim of his glass. "That should be pretty terrific, too. Walker (Bob
Walker, president of the American Program Bureau) told me you're
the hottest lecturer he's ever handled. I'll call you and let you know
how he's doing."

"You can't call us," I said. "There's no telephone on the island
where we're going."

"Oh, well, you'll just be that much more surprised to find out
how rich you'll be."

"I'll drink to that," I said, raising my glass for a toast, and
added, "and to the fact that you've made the future look a lot
brighter than it has for some time. Thanks, David."

"Don't thank me, thank Richard Nixon for making this all possible." David laughed and we all raised our glasses a bit higher.

"To Richard Nixon!" we toasted in chorus.

The next morning, as Mo and I boarded a plane for Miami en
route to a little island in the British West Indies, we felt ebullient.
Mo's mother was feeling and looking better than she had in months
and, for a change, our future seemed certain and bright. When our
plane took off out over the Pacific, and then gently began banking
back east over the Long Beach harbor, Mo turned to me and said,

"Remember our boat ride with Senator Goldwater last fall? It seems like it was years ago now."

I agreed, as the pleasant memory of that afternoon floated onto my mental screen. I had developed a friendship with the Goldwater family that dated from the days when Barry, Jr., and I were roommates at military school, and I had always enjoyed visiting with them. On this occasion, Senator Goldwater had taken us for a cruise on his yacht, the *Toh-Be-Kin*, from Newport Beach to Long Beach harbor. It had been a delightful excursion, with his grandchildren oohing and aahing at the dry-docked *Queen Mary* as we motored alongside it.

Heading back to Newport, Mrs. Goldwater and I were talking on the upper bridge about my going to prison, when the Senator turned to me to say, "I've been thinking about your situation, John. I know it doesn't look very good to you now, but you're going to come out of this whole mess smelling like a rose. Believe me, you just wait and see." At the time I thought the Senator was wrong. Now, after only four months in prison, and the welcome home from both friends and strangers, I thought maybe he'd been right.

When the seat-belt sign went off, I got up to take off my jacket and noticed the *Los Angeles Times* on the lap of the man in the seat in front of me. Obst had been at it again. A front-page banner headline read: DEAN BOOK DEAL 300 THOUSAND. I was about to ask the man if I could borrow his paper and show it to Mo, when he picked it up and started jabbing at the headline with his finger, saying to the passenger beside him, "Isn't that disgusting, just disgusting?" Quickly I sat back down, thinking the guy must be a Nixon-lover.

Sour grapes, I thought, and dismissed this man and his conversation. I felt the deal Obst made was fair, and, not being a writer, I knew I would have to work hard for every cent. While I felt no compulsion to tell my story, I wanted to write a book because I did need time to figure out what to do with the rest of my life, and a book about Watergate, I thought, would help me sort out my life while paying the mortgage.

I had turned down employment opportunities during Watergate so that I could meet the full-time demands of the countless investigators and prosecutors who had wanted and needed my help. For eighteen months I had volunteered my time. During that time, when I was stone broke, I had been offered a minimum guaranteed quarter-of-a-million-dollar contract to write a book about Watergate, which I'd discussed with the staff at the Watergate special prosecutor's office; they asked me not to sign a book contract until Watergate was over, and I had not. Cooperating with the government had wiped me out financially, not to mention emotionally. I felt it was all right to write a book now.

JANUARY 22, 1975—Grand Turk Island, British West Indies.

It's truly relaxing here; at least it is for me. The island is beautifully primitive; our hotel isn't luxurious, but comfortable; the weather is endless clear sunshine. But, best of all, there are no people. I have discovered I have a real problem with people. I don't want to see people because I'm embarrassed—even, at times, ashamed—to be who I am, or to be who they think I am. I really don't know how to deal with these feelings.

I understand now that we judge ourselves, to a greater extent than I've ever before admitted, through the eyes of others. I know it is difficult for any person to consider himself evil, or greedy, or stupid, since he must live with himself. Yet the mirror of my identity is partly in the eyes of others, and I find I keep checking to see how I look.

For a while I thought I looked pretty good. Although I've always known I would have to wear the "scarlet letter of Watergate," as I once described the stigma I felt to a newsman, I didn't think it would be for very long. I had a plan that I thought would solve that problem, and, until these past few days, I had been confident it would work.

The plan had been simple, and I had fallen into it rather than plotted it. I had decided to testify fully, openly, and honestly about the worst days of the Nixon administration for a host of reasons—ranging from saving my own neck, which was about to be sacrificed by my former friends and associates, to my true disgust in knowing what I knew and being part of it. Once I had made that decision, I believed it was the right thing to do, and what others said became irrelevant.

Soon I found I was totally occupied testifying. Literally every day related to giving testimony, or preparing to give it. That was when my plan started to fall into place for me. Not only would I testify for anyone and everyone, I would be the best witness they'd ever had, for I was sure that this would transform my image, as well as my very soul, from bad to good.

The euphoria of my freedom has evaporated in the last few days and, oddly, I feel like a man who was forced to retire before he was ready. My release from prison was also my release from testifying. No longer will the prosecutors be calling on me, since the trials are over and they have exhausted my knowledge, my usefulness. No longer does my life really have a focus or, in fact, a purpose. Writing a book or giving a lecture is not the same as sitting on the witness stand, where your words have a unique, and unalterable, significance.

I also suspect that this newfound discomfort I have with strangers is some kind of subconscious announcement that my plan to transform myself through all that testifying has failed.

It's amazing. It took me just a few months to screw up my life. I wonder how many years it's going to take to straighten it out.

The days of our vacation passed like those invisible air currents I watched the seagulls ride on, seemingly motionless in the clear blue sky high over the beach. We measured time not by our watches, which we stopped wearing, but by the sun. With no newspapers, radio, or television on the little island of Grand Turk to remind us, time flowed by unnoticed. No longer was I counting days, as I had for the past four months in prison, and this felt even better to me than the warm sun that we basked in by day and the tropical breezes that lulled us to sleep by night.

Mo and I had talked and walked and loved a lot, laughed and played again, and rediscovered our relationship. It had changed, and I had changed, because of what we'd been through together. And, on a walk that would turn out to be the last of our vacation, I told Mo how she and our marriage had changed me—and, perhaps, history.

I had entered our marriage a lifetime noncommunicator, having grown up in a family where I was never encouraged, and seldom permitted, to express my real feelings. This inability to communicate had made a disaster of my first marriage, in which I had been, instead of a husband, little more than a roommate, primarily interested in my career as a Washington lawyer. Watergate ended not only that career, but my silence.

History would never record that Maureen Elizabeth Anne

Kane, a.k.a. Mo, had been responsible for the downfall of the Nixon presidency, but I knew she'd had a major role. Back in the summer of 1974, while I was in the office of the Watergate special prosecutor, one of the lawyers had said, "You know, John, as long as you were interested in pursuing the cover-up, it worked. A lot of us think that, if you hadn't changed your mind, the cover-up might have succeeded." If that is true, and I feel there is something to it, Mo was responsible for my change of heart.

Within a month of our marriage, the cover-up had started to fall apart. The reason: my marriage proved what I had long suspected—that I was a lucky bastard who had married an incredibly good and decent person, a beautiful lady both inside and out, an honest, loving, thoughtful, intuitive, and intelligent soul who deserved better. This woman made me go straight, so to speak, because I wanted to be the honorable and admirable person she thought she had married. The decision to break rank had turned out well, and, from the negatives of Watergate, I had discovered the positives of love.

From the day my dreams of success disintegrated into ashes of false pride, through each phase of the Watergate crisis that became our daily lives, I found myself listening and talking with Mo—with increasing candor and openness—about everything. I had learned how to communicate.

"I think that communication is the most important thing in a marriage," I finally explained to Mo as we walked along our favorite stretch of beach. "It's more important than sex or friendship or even love, because none of those things can survive without it."

"I agree," she answered. She said nothing more as we proceeded along the water's edge, hand in hand, each with our own thoughts.

That evening at dinner we informed our host, Lance, that it was time for us to return to reality. Mo was worried about her mother, a concern I shared. I began thinking about my lecture tour, which loomed in the near future. More important, we knew that we had found our harmony again. Lance said that he would arrange to have an airplane pick us up by noon the next day. Our concerns eased, the dinner conversation turned to my proposed lectures.

"What are you going to talk about?" Lance asked.

"Well, I've given it about three seconds of thought and decided that I'll talk about love."

"You've got love on the brain," Lance said, alluding to an earlier conversation in which I'd suggested that he should give marriage another try.

"One thing is certain. You can't talk about love in the days of the Nixon White House," Mo observed, "because if there was any, it's the one thing Nixon successfully covered up."

"I'm sure Nixon loved his job, loved his daughters . . ." I began.

Mo cut me off. "But that's not the kind of love I'm talking about. How did he love his wife?"

"Occasionally, and only if it was necessary for some public or political reason," I surmised.

"Exactly. And do you think Watergate would ever have occurred if Nixon and the rest of you had gone home to your wives and shared what was really going on? Do you think Pat Nixon would have approved of break-ins and dirty tricks? For that matter, do you think that men who really know what it means to love, to trust another person and care about another person, could have done the thoughtless and 'public be damned' things that went on in that White House?" Mo answered her own question. "No way. You were all a bunch of cold fish, selfish and loveless."

"Whew!" Lance exclaimed, then smiled and asked Mo, "Would you like me to see if the hotel has a soapbox?"

"No, I'm serious. I think that if John had felt then the way he does now about how important love is to living, and had he experienced love then, he would not have been so self-centered and thoughtless."

"Mo's right," I said. "And maybe that's central to Richard Nixon's problem. Obviously, the way a man loves a woman is influenced by all those hang-ups he starts acquiring as a child. But I can tell you from firsthand experience that a good woman can, with sustained love, break down the barriers."

Mo smiled. Lance put his hands in his face. I continued nonetheless.

"I'm sure Nixon has a true affection for his wife, but I wonder if he truly loved her when he was president. I'll never forget one of the first assignments I was given to handle; it was some Nixon family business, and I was admonished that under no circumstances was I to discuss it with Mrs. Nixon. The President didn't trust her."

"The few times I saw them together, I always got the impression," Mo injected, "that they were miles apart, living different lives in the same forced world. And I am sensitive about that sort of thing."

"Well, maybe Watergate changed that for the Nixons, too. I hope so."

JANUARY 23, 1975—Grand Turk Island.

It's amazing how well our marriage has survived the ordeal of Watergate. There's no doubt in my mind that the glue that's held us together is our unabashedly romantic feelings toward each other, plus the reciprocated respect and trust that has developed and continues to grow. The marriage was a bastion for us both during Watergate, a special part of our lives that held together when all else fell apart.

Mo has taught me a lot about love, not just romantic love, but the attitude of selfless sharing and concern about people. It's part of her makeup, the way she is, naturally. She works from the assumption that everyone is good and is deeply distressed when they prove themselves otherwise. I was always fairly ambivalent toward my fellowman and never surprised to find evil lurking within, but always pleased to find good. Mo can befriend people instantly. It takes me time, but I'm learning.

Watergate has taught me one lesson very clearly. Those friends who stayed closest to us, worried with us and about us and our future, were not, with a few exceptions, my friends. The people I had thought friends, people whom I had gotten to know, either because of what they could do for me or what I could do for them, vanished when the trouble started. Those people that we met through Mo, people we loved and respected and trusted, people who asked nothing of us, nor we of them, but friendship—they were solid. For true friendship is but another form of love, I now know.

The last night of our vacation I couldn't sleep. When I finally did doze off, Mo was soon shaking me awake because I was talking loudly and incoherently. I had been dreaming I was still in prison and, when she woke me, it took several long seconds before I realized I was not. The distance from prison still felt very short, and, while my body had escaped, my head was still struggling to break free.

As I lay awake in bed, I thought that it was absolutely weird that I had been in prison. Me! Honest, careful, cautious, righteous, basically moral person. I certainly was not a criminal.

I looked over at Mo, who was sleeping soundly. I wondered if she thought of me as an "ex-con," a felon no less. Of course not, I decided, because she knew me and what I really was. But I knew, too, that to the rest of the world I was someone who had "done time." I began thinking about what it might mean.

The trivial occurred to me first, such as wondering if people would shun the Deans. I felt I could avoid that embarrassment by moving cautiously, carefully selecting the company we kept. Then I remembered a reality I'd never taken into account, one of those facts I learned while working at the Department of Justice: Many states take away the civil rights of convicted felons, often with a blanket suspension that removes the right to vote; to hold public office; to drive a car; even to have a fishing license. Startled by this realization, I thought I could have some really serious problems.

I sat in the dark, on the edge of my bed, numbed by the vision of these horrible consequences. Somehow, and quickly, I knew I would have to find out what the law was in California. Sleep was impossible now. I crossed the moonlit room to a table, turned on a small lamp I was sure wouldn't disturb Mo, found a tepid beer I had been sipping earlier in the evening, and sat down at the table with a cigarette. As I listened to the waves pounding on the beach below, I knew I had been deluding myself in feeling that I had come through Watergate unscathed, smelling like a rose; and, if I further fooled myself about the seriousness of what I had been involved in, and that I was once a criminal, I would only compound my problems.

I thought about a conversation I had had with Joey a few days before I was released from prison. Joey was a Mafia hit man who had forced himself into retirement by becoming a witness for the government. I enjoyed talking with him because he liked to discuss books, and he was extremely well read.

It seemed like yesterday that I had been walking past the television room, a mere cubicle with two disheveled-looking easy chairs, a battered table between them, and an old black-and-white television set someone had salvaged. A voice from the room had shouted, "Anyone for dominoes?"

"Why not," I had answered. Anything that passed a little time really was worthwhile. The game began with idle chatter but, at one point, Joey turned off the television and began telling me about a day when he had made three "hits" and thirty thousand dollars. His matter-of-fact discussion about killing prompted me to ask, "Didn't it bother you to kill someone?"

"Shit, no. It never troubled me. I wasn't paid to have feelings. I was paid to be a soldier."

"How about the first time you knocked off someone? How'd it feel then?"

"The same," he said flatly, then laughed. "The first job, John, you and the rest of this fucking country sent me on, 'cause I learned to kill in Vietnam. Those gooks were after my ass, so I felt that them mothers were nothing but skinny bags of shit. Actually, I had good feelings killing gooks."

"You're a Catholic, right?" I asked, pointing to the crucifix on the chain around his neck.

"Damn right. Hail Mary," he said, as he grinned and crossed himself.

"Seriously, Joey, have you ever thought about what God may think of your killing other people?"

"You're starting to sound like Colson,* and he's on my case real good. But Chuckie's okay; that son-of-a-bitch was a Marine like me. He understands."

"It really doesn't bother you to kill?"

"Nope. But I ain't doing no more. I'm out of that business now, for good."

"How many hits have you done?"

"Hey, listen, the government don't even know that, man. But they know about twenty-eight of 'em; how's that for starts?"

"Amazing."

He reached across the small table between us, slapped me on

---

*Colson had become a "born again" Christian while in prison and later founded the Prison Fellowship to further the cause of Christianity among convicts.

the back, smiled, and asked, "How's come you're asking me all these questions, Counselor?"

"Curious is all, I guess." Then I decided to confess. "Actually, we've never talked about your being a professional killer. I was interested in how you felt about yourself, since I've been thinking, or trying to work out in my mind, about my own crime. . . ."

"Shit, man, Watergate weren't no real crime, that was politics," he interrupted, and the thought made him burst into laughter again. "Hey, Deano," he finally continued, "don't be no Raskolnikov, okay, 'cause you didn't hurt no one." He was referring to a long and late conversation we had had a few nights earlier about Dostoevski's *Crime and Punishment*.

"Stop this," I told myself, as I hit a mental switch that interrupted my reminiscences and put Joey in a freeze-frame close-up. This picture of his angular and marred face, dark, Vitalis-shiny hair, and deep-set black eyes, which seemed to peer hungrily out of caves, ready to leap at passing prey, hung for a moment like a wall poster plastered on my memory.

I didn't want to think about the past anymore, particularly about Joey's insensitivity, his near-blindness about himself. Could it be that I was as blind and insensitive about Watergate and my involvement? But I abandoned that question. I didn't want to think about how I felt about my involvement in Watergate. What I wanted to think about was nothing, so I began listening again to the waves crashing, rolling, and returning to the sea on the beach below our cottage—reassuring sounds.

I looked across the room at the comforting picture of Mo, sleeping like a child, and soon flicked off the table lamp and returned to bed. I lay awake for hours pondering if I were better off or worse off because of Watergate. And what about the country? Was it better or worse because of Watergate? I didn't know the answers.

CHAPTER TWO

The Fox and the Hedgehog

"Hello, this is Joe Schwinn," I said. I could hardly believe my own voice as I assumed this telephone identity. But I didn't have the courage to use my own name.

Mo and I were on our way to Washington from our Caribbean idyll, and a stopover in Miami afforded me my first opportunity to call the U.S. probation office in Los Angeles to obtain what I feared would be bad news.

Continuing the impersonation, I said, "I am a Miami attorney. I have a client in California who is about to be released from federal prison after serving a term for obstruction of justice." I took a deep breath.

"What can we do for you, Mr. Schwinn?" a friendly-sounding man responded.

"Can you tell me what the collateral consequences are for a felon under California law? For example, does he lose the right to vote? Can he have a driver's license? Are there any other practical problems?"

Joe Schwinn, mythical lawyer for John Dean, bit his lip while waiting for the answer. The wait felt interminable as the man double-checked with a colleague. Finally, he answered, "Except for some professional groups who are licensed by the state, such as doctors and lawyers, there really are none."

"No blanket suspensions?"

"No, sir."

My mental indigestion was relieved, but not for very long. That morning, the Miami newspapers were reporting that Boston University students had voted to cancel a lecture by Ron Ziegler, Nixon's former press secretary, because they questioned "the morality of helping the chief spokesman of the Watergate cover-up profit from his actions." That is going to be trouble for me, I thought, as we headed on to Washington and my own upcoming lectures.

In the next three days I watched a small critical mass grow into a chain reaction, with the news media serving as the catalyst. Soon it seemed that, if I tried to lecture, I would be smack in the middle of a media holocaust. Ron Ziegler's one appearance was quickly forgotten, and my lecture tour became the new focus of angry statements. *The Washington Post* reported that protest meetings were being held and petitions of opposition were circulating on campuses to block my scheduled appearances. When I heard myself called "a moral degenerate whose indecent public exposure should be stopped to show that crime doesn't pay," on a radio news editorial, I decided that I had had enough. I called David Obst.

"I don't need this criticism. The lecture tour is off," I told him flatly.

"Just hold on, John. Let's not do anything hasty. I'll fly down to Washington this afternoon and we'll talk about it."

"There's nothing to talk about. I'm tired of being pilloried by the press, so the hell with it. I don't need any more grief. I've had enough to last a lifetime."

Three hours later Obst walked into the house Mo and I were visiting and immediately reached for the telephone.

"John, the best way to prove that you are wrong is to talk to Bob Walker yourself. Okay?"

Bob Walker came on like a steamroller of enthusiasm, telling me that there had been problems on only a few campuses, very few, and that the press had pumped them into a big deal. On most campuses the issue had not even arisen.

"You know, John, you're doing most of these schools a favor. I mean it. Most of these schools are charging admission to attend your lecture. At your first stop, the University of Virginia, they have already sold over 4500 tickets, at prices ranging from $1.50 to $2.50. That auditorium down there has six thousand seats. They've told me they'll even sell out the standing room. Your appearance will raise a couple of thousand bucks for them, instead of costing them money. The stupid press isn't going to write that you're helping these schools, but you are. I really mean that."

Obst took the telephone from the dining room table where I was sitting and went into the kitchen, where he spoke with Walker in hushed tones for another few moments. Then he returned with a clincher. He explained the situation in which I had placed Bob Walker. Acting as an agent on my behalf, Walker had represented to the schools that I would appear on the given dates. Based on that representation, the lecture committees at many of the schools had prepaid a lease on an auditorium, printed posters and tickets, spent money on radio and newspaper ads, and had already presold tickets.

"If you cancel, Walker is liable for the money that the schools have already spent, which figures roughly between five and ten thousand dollars. Technically, those expenses are yours. . . ."

"Bullshit, they're mine!"

"Hey, you gave me the okay to go ahead with the lecture tour." David sensed from my expression that this could get nasty. He quickly added, "Don't worry, though. I've handled everything. Walker thinks that if you show up Sunday night in Virginia, even just to read a statement that you are canceling, it will get him off the hook with the other schools. That's the least you can do."

I had boxed myself into a "no win" situation. If I didn't go, it would cost me money I didn't possess; if I did go, it could cost me a public embarrassment I didn't need. I could visualize the crowd booing my arrival and applauding my cancellation.

"I'll go with you and tell Polish jokes to warm them up if the crowd looks hostile," Obst quipped.

Most of the next day I spent drafting the statement I would read at the University of Virginia explaining why I was canceling the tour. While working on the draft, I tried again to imagine what my audience might be like, and wondered if indeed they might be hostile. I had given little thought to the possibility that I might be subjecting myself to danger.

It could happen, I realized. Some nut might think he could make the world a better place by shooting me. And what better setting than a crowded auditorium? Thus far, I'd been lucky. The death threats I'd received during Watergate had been serious enough that the government had insisted I be protected, and special arrangements had been made to protect me even while I was in prison. My lawyer, Charlie Shaffer, told me that the government had offered to continue its protection when I was released from prison. Maybe I had been foolish to turn it down, and was being even more foolish now by opening myself to the risk. I tried, without success, not to think about it, and the dinner that David Obst had arranged that night with Bob Woodward and Carl Bernstein helped.

The publication of *All the President's Men* in 1974, during the waning days of Watergate, had made Bob Woodward and Carl Bernstein national figures, unanimously lauded for their "brilliant" investigative work on Watergate. With the publication of their book the press could not resist the provocative invitation to speculate about their secret sources, most notably, of course, the mysterious "Deep Throat." There was an aura of romance surrounding this intriguing informant that provoked even veteran reporters to lapse into florid prose when forced to describe him, as witnessed by the *Time* magazine piece [April 22, 1974] that accompanied the release of the book:

> Foremost among [Woodward's and Bernstein's] sources was a man whom the authors still tantalizingly refuse to name. They called him "Deep Throat" and report only that he was a pre-Watergate friend of Woodward's, a trusted and experienced Executive Branch official with "extremely sensitive" antennae that seemed to pick up every murmur of fresh conspiracy at the capital's power center.

"Who is Deep Throat?" became an Establishment parlor game. Clues to his identity, in the form of descriptive habits and furtive practices, had been littered throughout the text of Woodward's and Bernstein's book, and a new cult began hungrily to amass them. Who was this man who smoked cigarettes and drank Scotch, who insisted that Woodward move a flower pot on his balcony as a sign that he needed to talk to him, who would draw the hands of a clock on page 20 of Woodward's morning paper to indicate what time he would meet with Woodward, and who then would meet with him in an underground garage or in a bar, one secret, the other public?

Many names were tossed into the public till, and it was inevitable, I suppose, that mine would be among them. In May of 1974 an article appeared in *New Times*, a magazine that, cashing in on the new craze for "investigative journalism," represented itself to be, in glossy, bi-weekly form, relentlessly that. (The magazine has since folded.) While the writer allowed that it was only "remotely possible" that I was Deep Throat, he suggested that I might be double-agenting my way out of the mess I was in because I knew the story was bound to come out anyway and figured I might "legitimatize" my own information by having it appear in the *Post*.

I considered some of the names of the other candidates in the *New Times* article to be as silly as my own: L. Patrick Gray, Melvin Laird, Henry Petersen, Richard Kleindienst, Fred Fielding, even Richard Moore. None of these men, some more knowledgeable than others, appeared on the surface to fit into the mold that Woodward and Bernstein had fashioned.

I had met Carl Bernstein fleetingly during the Watergate investigations, when he had wanted to interview me. He still looked more like the manager of a rock band than my concept of a *Washington Post* reporter. Bob Woodward was Carl's opposite, from his short hair and soft midwestern voice to his slight shyness and droll sense of humor. Also at the dinner were Bob's new wife, Fran, a very attractive and intelligent reporter for the *Fort Worth Star-Telegram*, and Scott Armstrong. I had met Scott when he worked for the Senate Watergate committee, and now he was working as a research investigator for Carl and Bob on their new book, *The Final Days*.

We bantered cocktail conversation until Obst—who had sequestered us in a private dining room at The Empress, his favorite Chinese restaurant in Washington—dazzled us by ordering our dinners in Chinese. Carl chidingly accused him of faking it, and the jokes that followed carried us into the dinner.

There was not much hope of the dinner conversation's amounting to more than a pleasant display of David Obst's star clients, since Woodward, Bernstein, and Armstrong were working on *The Final Days*, and I was about to start on *Blind Ambition*. The dialogue was guarded, to put it mildly. Here sat about as much knowledge on the subject of Watergate as you could gather in one room without including Nixon, and we were treating our tidbits of information as carefully as children in a card game.

There was, of course, some conversational probing, with an occasional question such as I asked Carl: "Are you guys going to try to interview Nixon?" To which he answered: "Do you think we could?" I responded: "Have you tried?" Not to be outmaneuvered, he parried: "Who would you ask about getting an interview if you were us?" So it progressed: all questions, no answers.

All this time I had the impression that Woodward had been studying me, deciding how he felt, for although he was sitting beside me, he had almost avoided talking. When at last he did start a conversation, it felt as if he had lowered a barrier he carried around himself.

"I'm glad that you are going to lecture, John. I think you can do a lot of good," Bob said quietly, as the others talked. I felt he meant it, too, for he did not sound like a man given easily to idle chatter. He told me briefly of his own experiences in lecturing, lest I had the impression it was easy work. He made it clear that it is mentally demanding, emotionally taxing, and physically exhausting.

"Just out of curiosity," Woodward soon asked, although I doubted it was the casual question he was dressing it as, "what did you think of our book?"

"I liked it, but I confess that for me it was a little different to read than for most people. It was more like a compendium of old *Washington Post* stories that raised a lot of unpleasant memories."

Bob laughed gently. "I guess that's right."

Others were not listening to our conversation, so I decided to have a little fun. In a voice that the others might hear, I said: "I must say, however, that there's no mystery to me about your sources of information."

"Right on," said Obst from across the table, clapping his hands.

"In fact," I continued, "I'll bet on it."

"How much?" Scott Armstrong asked, volunteering to hold the money.

"How about this wager: I'll read through *All the President's Men* and footnote every single unidentified source—there must be a couple of hundred—and for every one I get right, you owe me a dollar. For every one I get wrong, I'll give you a dollar."

"You really think you know?" Woodward asked, cracking a wide, Cheshire-cat smile.

"Watch him, Bob," Bernstein cautioned with feigned alarm. "I think Dean is as clever and devious as we are in smoking out a story. If we have to pay him the full amount, we've confirmed he was right, and we've also revealed all our sources. No deal. But nice try, John."

The dinner ended with a ritualistic reading of our fortune cookies. It is interesting how these inane phrases, written by secretaries, batter mixers, and salesmen at the cookie factory, actually make people pause and think. Everyone laughed at mine: "Even the longest day has an end." I forced a smile. Only the others knew why they laughed, but I knew why I didn't. I was thinking about how the next day might end.

FEBRUARY 1, 1975—Washington, D.C.

I had the extraordinary feeling that Bob Woodward was challenging me to discover the identity of Deep Throat. Obviously, he couldn't, and wouldn't, come right out and encourage anyone to expose a source. But he is a bright guy with the kind of complicated mind that has already set up this little cat-and-mouse game, and he knows that I'm probably the best-informed person on the flow of information about Watergate, simply because I was often the conduit for such information. If he and Carl have been honest concerning the clues and tidbits they have dropped about Deep Throat, this could be a fascinating challenge to take on.

And I can't kid myself: I would love to meet the only snitch in the world more famous than myself. Yes, I would! I would like to know his motives, his reasons for the peculiar information he leaked in peculiar ways. Why he gave it to Woodward. I can't think of a single leak in all of Washington who doesn't have a personal motivation for divulging information to the press. Either they hate their boss, or they feel their department's budget is being squeezed, or the Republicans are no damn good, or some such thing. My own motivations as a snitch certainly were complicated. Everything from my wife's love to my lawyer's intuitions, from personal disgust to my very sensible fear of prison, had me blowing the whistle. But never is the noble "news source" just a person coming forward in the interests of truth, justice, and the American Way. Can Deep Throat be different?

As I think about it, there are several "why" questions concerning Deep Throat and his information that I would like to answer. My first reading of *All the President's Men* was a shocker—not because of what Deep Throat knew, but because of what he didn't know.

Woodward and Bernstein skated along on some very thin ice, thinner than I realized at the time the articles were appearing in *The Washington Post*. Not only was Deep Throat's information inadequate at times, but sometimes he was just dead wrong about matters that Woodward and Bernstein treated as fact. And they have never owned up to these mistakes.

The search for Deep Throat could prove to be not just a good mystery puzzle, but a way of putting in proper perspective the real contribution of *The Washington Post*. I do not think Deep Throat alone had enough information to bring down Nixon. If the Nixon White House had had to contend only with *The Washington Post*, the Watergate cover-up probably would have succeeded. But they had other problems—myself among them.

Woodward joked with me about my Watergate obsession. Because Deep Throat is the biggest unanswered question about Watergate, I have a feeling that he could easily move into the center of it.

"You're really in a nasty mood, aren't you?" Mo said when I tossed the Sunday *New York Times* on the kitchen counter the next morning.

"Vile. I really don't want to go down to Charlottesville tonight."

"I don't blame you. Frankly, I wish you wouldn't; it scares me."

"Me, too. Some nut may decide he's found a perfect opportunity to save the world by blowing my head off, and if. . . ."

"Don't even talk about it, please, John."

"All I was going to say is that I think that Obst and Walker are wrong. They think that if I go down there and tell the assembled mass that I'm canceling my lecture, that I'll find people want me to talk and they don't really care about the fact I'm being paid." I was sure the opposite would happen, and that I would make a fool of myself by appearing before a hooting, booing, angry crowd.

My tension built throughout the afternoon. Never, not even during what I had thought to be some rough experiences in the past few years, had I felt as much anxiety. I knew it wasn't stage fright, for I had long since worked out that fear. As a child I had appeared often before groups large and small, young and old, as an amateur magician, a hobby I'd discovered could earn me far more than mowing lawns. Before I was old enough to think about being afraid of public appearances, I had learned there was nothing to fear—a facility that later helped me in law school and then in working my way up in government.

As we drove to Charlottesville, Obst sensed my tension and tried to engage me in diversionary, idle conversation. But I was too depressed, feeling that, at best, I was about to suffer disastrous public embarrassment, and, at worst, I was walking into a death trap.

We met the chairman of the University of Virginia's speakers' committee, a young law student named Andrew, at a prearranged place near the auditorium. We followed him to the rear of the building where we were met by a small group of security people. I realized that others were concerned about my living through the night, too.

"We've sold out the auditorium," Andrew reported as he led us through a corridor to the backstage area. But he seemed even more enthusiastic that "all the television networks are here, plus a lot of Washington news reporters."

"That's terrific!" Obst chimed in. I was thinking the opposite, for my worst fears were being realized.

The backstage corridor led past doors that were open to the auditorium. Uniformed police officers were guarding the doors, but not well. As I glanced through the door to see the crowd, several students spotted us, pushed past the officers, and came running toward us. They wanted autographs.

As I signed autographs, Obst talked with the students, obviously enjoying himself, as he kept repeating, "Terrific! That's terrific!" When we finally got to the room backstage, Obst said to our host, "I hope you've got a good seat for me." He looked at his watch: "It's five minutes to eight. Maybe I'd better get out in front."

"I've held a front-row seat for you," the young law student assured David, and instructed one of the security people to show him where it was located.

"Break a leg," David said as he headed toward the door. "I'll be right in front if you need any help." Then, turning to the security man, but speaking for my benefit, he said, "I've got to have a good seat in case someone shoots Dean. I want to be able to get to the assassin fast and sign him up for a book. If you lose an author, you've got to replace him."

"You sadistic bastard, get out of here," I said, and smiled for the first time all day. Obst giggled and waved goodbye.

Andrew went over the introduction he planned to give. It bordered on being flattering. He also explained that, after my talk, the two of us would sit in large chairs, where I would be given a small microphone and could answer questions from the audience. When I hinted to Andrew that this would be my first and last appearance, he said, "I think that would be a mistake. I've talked with some of the other schools. They're as excited as we've been that you're doing this tour."

Minutes later we walked into the auditorium, and up onto the stage. The crowd erupted with applause, whistles, and shouts. I listened for negative sounds, but heard only a thunder of enthusiasm at my arrival. Maybe I was wrong, I thought, as the audience quietly listened to Andrew's introduction.

Enthusiastic applause greeted me again at the podium. When it subsided, I quipped, "I guess you know who I am. I am E. Howard Hunt wearing my John Dean disguise." When the audience laughed and applauded this lame humor, I began reading from my prepared statement:

"In the interval since the arrangements for my lecture tour were made a few weeks ago and tonight, things have changed. I am not sure the climate is conducive to our having the kind of discussion of Watergate and the Nixon years that I had hoped we could have. Now, the issue is not the substance of my speech, but rather the fact that I am exploiting Watergate or, as some put it, 'making crime pay.' "

Impulsively, I abandoned my prepared text. I would let the audience decide my fate. For the next few minutes I explained as honestly as I could that I couldn't afford to lecture for free, I was broke, but that if the audience thought it wrong, or immoral, that I be paid, I had no intention of continuing. Finally, with my tongue feeling like pressed cotton, I put the matter to the audience for resolution.

Their response left no doubt. They wanted me to continue and talk about Watergate. Because I had not given any thought to speaking, I didn't know exactly what to say. Yet I had to continue, so I just started talking.

The pattern was set that night at the University of Virginia. Throughout the country varying amounts of controversy would precede my lectures, and each time, like a man who didn't quite believe what he was hearing, for I did not, I would begin my appearance by asking the audience if they objected to my talking about Watergate for a fee. Each time, the almost unanimous response encouraged me to continue.

Nervous, despite my promise to continue as long as the students wanted to hear me, David Obst had practically refused to leave my side for the first four days of the tour. Mo had returned home to California.

"If you write your book the way you have been lecturing, you'll have a surefire bestseller," Obst said as we settled in for the night at a vintage 1940's motel cabin in Roanoke, Virginia. The first three lectures had gone exceedingly well; I was loosening up, and opening up to the audience.

"Let's have a drink," I said, noticing the bottle of Scotch that had been placed on the bureau by our host.

"I'll mix. You're the star, so please, Mr. Dean, make yourself comfortable."

"David, how many days have you been wearing the same clothes?" I inquired as he took off his jacket and vest. I knew David had not planned to travel with me beyond Charlottesville, but had continued along in spite of his early plans. Fortunately, I had carried my suitcase, thinking I would be headed back home to California.

"If you promise never to tell my mother," he said, sniffing the air, "I think this is the fourth day. I'm not sure. Not bad, huh? And it's terrific for crowd control. If you haven't noticed, nobody comes near us when I'm with you."

"Someone once told me you were one of the strongest agents in the business. Now I understand."

"Damn right. Have client, will travel. Here's your drink."

David and I chatted for a while, and, after a few drinks, I decided to go to bed. I assured David I would continue with the tour,

since it had gone so well so far. I also assured him I could make it
without his uplifting spirits and guiding hands.

"I'm not so sure I should go back to New York; you may need
my hands," he said, as I parted for my bedroom. "You know what
those students asked me tonight when they dropped us here at the
motel?" I nodded my ignorance. "They wanted to know if I was
your bodyguard.

"I said, 'See these hands?'" He was holding them as if he
might salute himself with both. "I said, 'These are deadly weapons.
I'm a karate expert hired to protect John, and I use these because
it's so difficult to carry firearms on airplanes. But they are just as
lethal.'" Suddenly he began flailing his hands in the air.

"Goodnight, David."

"Kiillllllllll! Kill! Kill . . . ," I heard through the wall as I un-
dressed and climbed into bed. I would miss David on the tour.

FEBRUARY 5, 1975—Roanoke, Virginia.

My life has become so very odd. When I went to the White
House as a young lawyer, I never dreamed that it would lead to a
stint in prison. When it became clear that, because of what I had
done in the White House, I would go to jail, it would then have
seemed even more ludicrous that my misadventures would result in
a lucrative book contract and a lecture tour to discuss my crimes.
Yet, here I am: the former Counsel to the President, the felon, the
ex-con author with my young, bearded agent in a cabin in Roanoke,
Virginia, on tour. I'm going to pinch myself to be sure this isn't
some Scotch-induced delusion.

Why *am* I baring my soul publicly? Is it just the money? Or
am I some sort of exhibitionist, displaying parts of my most private
thoughts for some kind of perverted self-gratification? Do I enjoy
getting emotionally naked in front of a crowd? I guess it is not so
surprising that audiences sit there in silence, transfixed by this psychological striptease act.

No, no, no, that's not it at all. You're being a clever fellow,
John. You have learned that to blow the whistle on yourself is less
painful than having someone else blow it on you. You are trying to
take the venom out of your audiences by sticking it to yourself before they have the opportunity to stick it to you. You have found

that redemption must be preceded by honest confession, and you are campaigning for your atonement in the public confessional. Good luck, fellow.

"Irene is dead."

I had traveled to Cleveland, given another lecture, and taken an urgent phone call en route to a luncheon reception. Mo's voice came through the telephone as if she were being forced to repeat a rumor she didn't believe. Silence confirmed the terrible reality, and she broke down. "I need you, John. Please come home fast."

Within an hour of her call I had arranged my flight home, postponed my lecture tour, talked with a nasty reporter from the Cleveland *Plain Dealer*, made it from downtown Cleveland to the airport, talked again with Mo, and was airborne for Los Angeles. Mo's last words, before I rushed to board my flight, were, "Say a prayer for Mother." I did just that as we taxied toward the runway for takeoff.

I loved Irene for the way she loved her daughter. I had watched Irene and Mo grow closer even in the short time I had known them together, and Mo had told me that her relationship with her mother had become more meaningful to her each year as they had both grown older. Now, Irene was gone, and the void that she would leave in our lives was uncomfortable, painful to contemplate.

When the airplane reached its cruising altitude, which the captain announced was 33,000 feet, I looked out the window. The heavy cloud cover had cleared, and below I could see the snow-dusted fields of February blanketing the rural Midwest, hiding it under a gray and colorless quilt. I squinted to sharpen my focus, and for several minutes was carried into a deep private meditation on the landscape below.

We find identity in our lives, I thought, as I looked at the pencil-thin roads and clusters of indistinguishable buildings below, through our membership in a family, neighborhood, community, church, race, and citizenship in a state or nation. But the significance of life, its quality and meaning, or lack thereof, is found in our minds, those mysterious meeting places where our hereditary instincts, emotions, and powers of intellect mesh with the living experiences unique to each of us. There we develop the feelings, beliefs, and habits we call personality and character.

I sat back in my seat, closed my eyes, and waited for a swarm of unanswerable questions to go away. "Why am I feeling so lost?" "Why has Irene's death left me with such a feeling of emptiness?" "What am I looking for?" "How can I redirect my life?" I pretended I was punching the questions into a computer. The answers would come to me after a scan of the memory bank. But I waited again, and nothing happened. No printout appeared. I opened my eyes to the nearly empty first-class cabin.

A flight attendant was sipping coffee in the forward galley. I watched her munch on a roll and shift her weight with the rocking of the airplane. "She's an animal," I mumbled to myself. "We're all just animals." Not that she was unattractive or ill-mannered—to the contrary, she was a very pretty brunette with a petite figure and a delicate, porcelain face. She's the kind of girl who carries an umbrella in the sun, I decided. But, fundamentally, she's an animal.

This bizarre stream of thought seemed a relief from my own anxieties, so I allowed my mind to wander further. As I watched her move about the galley, I began mentally to strip the clothes off this young flight attendant to see her animal body. My thoughts were not sexual, but very clinically detached.

I watched her breathing, an average of sixteen breaths a minute, which I estimated was a consumption of seven to eight quarts of air per minute—an incredible million gallons per year. As she continued to sip and munch, I calculated that an average meal, including liquids, weighs approximately two pounds, which adds up to about forty-two pounds of food each week, or a ton of food and drink each year.

That pretty young woman is a monster. She's nothing but a digestive tract with teeth that will devour several wheat fields, countless coops of chickens, a herd of cattle, patch upon patch of lettuce (she looked like a salad eater), and she'll swallow enough water to fill several swimming pools. Is that life? Just animals breathing, eating, digesting, defecating?

Suddenly the mini-skirted monster looked down the aisle, directly into my rudely fixed gaze. Immediately, I gave her back her clothes and smiled politely. She wiped the crumbs from her mouth, finished her coffee, and headed toward me. I was sure that she knew I had been watching her. Mo once confided to me that all women have a sixth sense which tells them when a man is watching. Flustered, I felt as though she knew what I had been thinking.

"Can I get you something?" she asked as she approached my seat. I shook my head, relieved that my peculiar thoughts had not been transmitted. "Mind if I sit and talk to you for a minute? It gets boring standing around on a flight this empty," she added.

"Sure, have a seat."

"You look a little bothered about something. If you don't mind my asking, are they being a little rough on you? I mean, your lecturing and all that?"

Obviously, she had recognized me. But I was surprised that my emotional stress was so apparent to her, since I usually masked my emotions well. I explained the reason I was flying home, and she expressed sympathy. "Actually, my lecture audiences have been a delight. From time to time certain members of the media enjoy chewing on me, but I can understand why."

"I wondered how you felt about that. I have to tell you something," she said with an embarrassed look. "My husband is one of your biggest fans. He's in medical school at Case Western Reserve and he watched all of your testimony during Watergate. The other day the Cleveland *Plain Dealer* had an article about you that wasn't very nice. It outraged Wally, my husband, and he wanted to write a letter to the editor because he thought what they wrote about you was unfair."

"Thank Wally for his support," I replied.

"Doesn't it bother you when they write that stuff? Don't you feel like giving them a piece of your mind?"

"Sure, sometimes I feel that way, but then I recall the story of 'The Fox and the Hedgehog,' and I decide that it could be worse."

"I don't know that story."

"Actually, it's a story that came to my attention during the darkest days of Watergate, when my life was at a low point. An old and dear friend had called. He, like Wally, was bothered by news stories about me that he knew to be untrue or distorted. He was a man of considerable influence and he felt he could help by personally admonishing certain editors and reporters at various publications. When he called, I had just finished rereading *Aesop's Fables*. Reading is a way of escaping reality for me."

"For me, too."

"Anyway, I declined his offer by reminding him of the story of 'The Fox and the Hedgehog.' "

"Tell me the story," she insisted puckishly, curling her legs beneath her in the seat as a child might.

"Okay. Once upon a time there was a fox who was trying to swim across a very rapid river. He became caught in the force of a current which carried him down the river and deposited him in a deep ravine, where he lay injured, sick, and unable to move. Sensing an ill and helpless animal, a swarm of hungry, blood-sucking flies landed on him. A hedgehog passing by saw his anguish and asked if he could help the fox by driving away the tormenting flies. 'By no means,' replied the fox, 'for these flies which you see are full of blood, and sting only a little, and if you rid me of these, which are already satiated, others more hungry will come in their place, and will drink up all the blood I have left.' "

FEBRUARY 12, 1975—Los Angeles.

We have buried Mo's mother. And alongside all the history-making events I have witnessed, the love and bravery of Irene Kane seems awesome. She died painfully and slowly, over a period of years, from the degenerative process of bone cancer. Yet, she did it nobly. When she saw her daughter and her son-in-law in trouble, she rallied, she refused to succumb to the cancer until she knew that we would be all right. Without that peace of mind, she couldn't die.

I talked with Irene almost every day I was in prison. Despite being allowed only a precious few calls, I found no call more important, for I drew strength from talking with her, and I hope she found some comfort in talking to me. She had always felt that Richard Nixon was a crook and regarded Watergate as "just politics"; she couldn't understand why her son-in-law should go to prison. But she wanted to see Mo and me survive it.

Upon my return to California, I went immediately to see Irene at her modest home in Mar Vista. She was not about to die in the sterile, impersonal environment of a hospital. She was going to die in her own bed. During that visit, she asked to speak to me alone.

"Promise me that no matter what else happens you will always take care of Mo." She looked me straight in the eyes with a strength born of long, hard years of raising her children while working on the assembly line at Hughes Aircraft, as though all the power in her dying body was being summoned up in that look. She was too frail for me to hug her in assurance, but I gave her my promise. When she closed her eyes it was as though she had been given permission to end the struggle.

Mo is going to join me on the lecture tour. She feels getting away for a while will be good, and I agree. It's important we be together and sort out what is really important to our lives, and nothing is more important than our simply being together.

It added up to nine solid weeks that I criss-crossed the country. John Dean and his Electric Kool-Aid Watergate Confessional Drag-and-Stomp, Plus Wife on Occasion. Through fifty-two colleges and universities, the ritual is repeated over and over.

The plane is always late, overcrowded with people who recognize me no matter what disguise I have devised. I arrive in the airport tired, aching, and still trying to digest the mystery meat served on the flight. The lecture-committee chairman (usually a political science major or law school student) has brought along his girlfriend and perhaps several of the lecture-committee members or his fraternity brothers. "Did you have a nice flight?" I am asked *ad nauseum.* "Of course, I'm alive," I think to myself.

They want to be pals and buy me a drink at a terrific local saloon where I can reveal to them what was really on the missing 18½ minutes of tape. When I decline, they settle for a half hour of idle chitchat in the back of the committee chairman's 1966 Chevrolet en route to the hotel. There, more chitchat with the manager, who personally guides me to a suite that is cold, too large, and contains nothing to eat except a grotesque basket of fruit wrapped in yellow cellophane. The phone is already ringing and doesn't stop when I try to lie down for ten minutes to collect my thoughts. Despite a carefully stated policy of no interviews, the lecture committee has generously provided the local press with my room number. If I can get room service, they send up a club sandwich that makes the airline food seem bearable in memory.

If I am lucky, there is no time for a meal before the lecture. But, more often than not, the chairman of the political science department or dean of the law school has assembled a few of his stalwart faculty members and "best students" for a little dinner at the faculty club or a favorite local restaurant. They don't want to be my pals; they want to show me how knowledgeable they are about Washington and Watergate; they want to tell me, ever so politely, that I have a bad moral odor and that I have made it tough for them to teach their students ethics. They drink too much and can't understand why I grimly nurse my Scotch-and-water and keep checking my wristwatch.

Finally I get to the auditorium or gymnasium and I'm greeted by the half-dozen pickets from the Young Peoples Socialist League or the Young Americans for Freedom, who are carrying the usual signs: DON'T MAKE CRIME PAY—BOYCOTT JOHN DEAN, or WATERGATE CRIMINAL GO HOME. Their pleas are being ignored by the thousands streaming past them, and they seem cold and unhappy. Actually, I begin to empathize with my boycotters, although I wish I could explain to them that the lecture fees that I am earning still don't pull me out of the debts incurred during two years of testimony and incarceration. Probably they wouldn't care.

Backstage, more campus dignitaries, more autographs, more chitchat. Security is always lax and the halls are full of hand-shakers and Instamatic-poppers. The lecture-committee chairman wants me to hear his introduction, which he delivers in a nervous monotone. For a few seconds I am left alone, as the litany of my life and crimes drones over the public address system, and then: "Ladies and Gentlemen, Mr. John Dean." The roar of applause, the adrenaline pumping through my nervous system, and suddenly three thousand faces are staring up at me. I'm on. They've come to see the John Dean Show, and I had better make it good.

I never wrote out lecture notes, so each night I would stand there and be mildly curious about what I would have to say. Unless there was a particular event in the headlines that seemed relevant to Watergate (and during those weeks a great deal of news about

Watergate continued to break in the press), I would simply tell the story of my early experiences in the White House, the basic outline of the Watergate events, my decision to testify, and then I would open the evening to questions fom the audience.

The questions were an eye-opener, because a large segment of the general public would also be invited to attend the college-sponsored lecture, and the audiences were comprised of quite a cross-section of ages and occupations. No matter where in the country I was speaking, the questions from the audience generally revealed how little the public understood of Watergate. The facts were unclear, the characters intermixed, the meanings confused. Many matters were reduced to questions of absurd simplicity:

Q: "Mr. Dean, if you knew about the break-in in the summer of 1972, why did you wait until the spring of 1973 to contact the prosecutor's office?"

A: "Well, the reason I didn't rush over to report it to the prosecutor's office is that I was busily engaged in covering it up."

Q: "Will the CIA ever reveal what really happened in Watergate?"

A: "While there was no bonfire on the South Lawn of the White House to burn the Watergate tapes, I suspect that there was a mighty conflagration in suburban Virginia, where the CIA is headquartered. I doubt that anyone will find much in the CIA files."

Q: "Did you just go along with the illegal activities in the White House out of loyalty to Richard Nixon?"

A: "I did the things I did because I was looking out for John Dean. I knew what pleased my superiors and I did my damndest to please them. In retrospect, I would have to admit that I was blinded by ambition."

Some of the questions were actually too comical to answer: "Mr. Dean, were you one of the good guys or one of the bad guys?" Or: "Should the Republican party have been charged with the crime, too?"

Obviously, these questions presumed the appropriate answers and evidenced considerable misunderstanding of the facts—none more so than my favorite of all time, a question asked in dead earnest: "Whatever happened to Rose Mary Wood's baby?" (This, of course, was a reference to a syndicated cartoon which had parodied the concept of a "Devil child" being born to Mia Farrow in the movie, "Rosemary's Baby." In the cartoon, the baby was Nixon.)

Amidst the more amusing aspects of my lecturing were some genuine insights about how Watergate had been perceived by the public and how the event had affected them. Without a doubt, the two issues that had most upset them, and continued to do so, were that President Gerald Ford had pardoned Nixon, and that tax money was being given to Nixon for his office and staff and would be given him the rest of his life.

I was surprised to discover a fair number of Nixon supporters showing up at my lectures, and I later calculated that over 300,000 attended during this tour. The vast majority of the audience, however, was overwhelmingly filled with hatred for Richard Nixon. While this was not a surprising fact, the intensity of that hate was, and I realized it would be a long time before the man would ever regain public acceptance.

In collecting the statements and viewpoints of my audiences, I began gradually to create a collage of impressions for myself about Watergate. But nothing was as impressive as the comment that was repeated to me almost daily—in airports, after lectures, in faculty clubs, on the streets—and always in the same words: "I really enjoyed your show on television." As if Sam Ervin and his Select Committee had been some kind of soap opera! As if we had set the government teetering on the brink of disaster just for the nation's viewing pleasure!

For many people, perhaps a majority, Watergate was a television event; it was theater, an electronic entertainment more interesting for its theatrics, drama, and treachery than for its impact on the nation. The real question that lingered in my mind was whether anyone, including myself, had really learned anything from this "show."

CHAPTER THREE

Living in the Past

Natchitoches, Louisiana, was sweltering when I arrived on May 1, 1975, for a final lecture before settling into work on my book. During the ride from the airport to Northwestern State University, I enjoyed the southern charm of a faculty member who briefed me en route on everything from crawdaddy fishing to Cajun cuisine.

"Listen, John," my host said just before we arrived on campus, "a lot of people here want to know who that Washington reporter's source was. You know, the one they call 'Deep Throat.' "

"Really?" I chuckled.

"You know who it is?"

"Well, I've given it some thought," I replied cautiously. I had been asked the question before, that first night at the University of Virginia, and I had said then that I thought Deep Throat was a literary device, a fictional composite of several people. My speech had been reported by the media, and David Obst had informed me that Woodward had been upset by my statement. Through Obst, Woodward reasserted that his source was a single, real person. He requested that I please stop saying publicly that Deep Throat was a fictitious character, and I did.

Since then, however, I had had a very interesting private conversation with one of the lawyers in the Watergate special prosecutor's office about Deep Throat's identity. The occasion had been a visit to the prosecutor's office when my lecture tour had taken me

47

back to Washington. The prosecutors were still investigating peripheral matters within their jurisdiction and naturally turned to me as a source of testimony. I had nothing new to offer them, and, besides, I was not particularly interested in testifying at another trial, so my session with the prosecutors soon turned into a bull session.

One of the prosecutors said he had read my statement about Deep Throat's being a fictitious character, a multiple source. He confided, on the promise I not say publicly where I had heard what he was going to tell me, that he and several of his colleagues felt they had figured out Deep Throat's identity. They were pretty certain it was Earl Silbert, the assistant United States attorney in Washington who had originally handled the Watergate investigation and prosecutions. What made them feel certain was somewhat persuasive.

The prosecutors had read a secret diary that Earl Silbert had kept, detailing his handling of the case. Silbert had not confessed to being the leaker to Woodward in the diary because, according to my prosecutor-friend, Silbert was not dumb, and, if he'd written about giving Woodward information in the diary, he would have been confessing to a crime. It's a crime to disclose grand jury testimony, and it is incredibly unethical for a prosecutor to talk with the press about his investigation.

Silbert was no fool. And Deep Throat was no fool. What was apparent from the diary was that Silbert knew much of what Deep Throat knew, when Deep Throat knew it. The very keeping of a diary suggested that Silbert had the kind of self-protective thoughts when handling the case that might result in a man's befriending a journalist like Woodward—and a newspaper like *The Washington Post*—who together could come to his rescue should he ever need them.

I could not disagree, or with certainty agree, with this conclusion, because I had not seen the actual diary. But several weeks later, deep in the bayou, when I was asked, I thought it a chance to explore the question. I named Earl Silbert.

As I expected, the newsmen in the front row of the auditorium were scribbling furiously in their notepads. I thought that naming Silbert would provoke other reporters to take up the investigation. Because I was not certain, I decided that I had to soften the blow of my accusation. So I added, "Silbert's going to be very unhappy with me for naming him. And I must say I'm not absolutely sure. If I'm wrong, I expect a strong denial. On the other hand, if I'm right, I expect some bobbing and weaving in Washington."

The next afternoon when I returned home to Los Angeles, Mo was laughing. "The phones have been going crazy," she said, and gave me a long list of reporters who had called. She also gave me a wire service story that another reporter had dropped off in the mailbox. As I read the story of Silbert's denial, Mo said, "The reporters want to know if you think Silbert is bobbing and weaving, or do you accept his denial?"

"No comment," I said to her with my best wise-guy grin. I was surprised at the extent of media reaction to my naming Silbert, and, as I looked over the list of reporters who had called, I realized how irresponsible it had been for me to name him without any personal investigation, even though I'd had a very good source—which I couldn't reveal.

I decided not to respond to any of the press inquiries. They would want to know why I thought it was Silbert, and I could not betray the confidence of those who had told me it might be Earl. Answering the inquiries could only get me burned for my own irresponsibility in naming him. I resolved at that moment never again to name anyone I might think was Deep Throat unless I had conducted my own investigation.

MAY 4, 1975—Los Angeles.

I am dismayed by the awesome power of "the media." Often they have been arbiters of American morality, but since Watergate they've become the moral guardians of the nation. In town after town where I've lectured, from Natchitoches to East Lansing, and from Providence to San Diego, I noted that virtually every newspaper and local television station has recently installed "investigative reporters" on their staffs—media bounty hunters in pursuit of evil doers. I wonder if there is enough evil to go around for them all.

The power of these new investigative journalists is not only that they report news, but that they make news, too. They have become a new police force of the nation, augmenting (and at times replacing) criminal and regulatory investigators, prosecutors, grand juries, courts, judges, and legislative committees. They certainly aren't bogged down by any sort of process or procedure, and they can indict, prosecute, and convict anyone, as long as they have a story that sells papers or attracts viewers.

Before Watergate, that kind of reporting was "muckraking"; today it is "investigative journalism." It is the single hottest area of interest on campus; journalism classes and schools are filled, and countless young people are standing in line to get such jobs with papers and television stations.

Today I had a telephone call from Obst, who asked if I'd be interested in becoming an "investigative journalist" for *Rolling Stone* magazine. I told David I would have to think about it, and obviously I've got some time to do so, for I can't do anything until I complete the book. But my initial reaction is that it would be a wonderful irony: from Watergate criminal to junior "Woodstein!" Also, it could be a wise thing for me to do next. As frightening as I find some types of investigative journalism, I realize that I would be working in the ranks of the "good guys."

Initially, the work on *Blind Ambition,** my book about Watergate, was enjoyable; both the novelty of being a writer and putting my past in order were pleasant new experiences. I was not sure where to start my story, so I thought about how my audiences had reacted to the things I had said at my lectures. Always there had been the greatest silence, and the most attentive faces, when I had talked about my personal experiences, as opposed to the more "historical" facts and information surrounding Watergate. Frequently I had been asked in lecture halls, or by reporters, how I had ended up as Counsel to the President at age thirty-one. It was not a question I had ever answered in any depth, but it seemed like a logical place to start a book about my years at the White House. Yet what I started doing was thinking, not writing.

For the first time, I thought about how I had ended up in the nation's capital, and at the White House, no less. I found myself

---

*On February 15, 1975, the *New York Post* had run a picture on the front page, and without any accompanying article, of a lecture I had delivered the previous evening at Syracuse University. The caption below the picture noted I had talked about my "blind ambition," and several people at Simon & Schuster who saw the *Post* said, "That's the perfect title." I had to agree.

looking back at the path I had traveled and the reason I had traveled it. I had examined much of my life at the Nixon White House while in prison, but now I was looking at those first fascinations and early emotions that fired and fueled the ambition that would later betray me. I found myself sorting through both pleasant and unpleasant memories.

My first visit to Washington, D.C., had been on a gray, cold, and drizzly day in January 1957, when I had gone to march in President Dwight D. Eisenhower's second inaugural parade as a cadet from Staunton Military Academy. I was fourteen years old and a proud member of the Howie Rifles, a precision drill team composed of fifty-five Staunton cadets, all honor students.

The president had always been one of those unreal, larger-than-life characters for me, until that parade. We had begun the march along the traditional route from the Capitol down Pennsylvania Avenue after what seemed an interminable wait in the staging area. Despite our warm uniforms, we all thought we might freeze to death before we began, but the march warmed us up a little. I was oblivious to the crowd because you always look straight ahead in precision marching. Yet, as we reached the end of Pennsylvania Avenue, I could see the reviewing stand off in the distance.

Our cadet commander, Art Stern, shouted out over the music of the band, "Clean up those lines," which signaled we would soon be under the eyes of the President of the United States. I was marching on the far left column, which meant I would pass right in front of President Eisenhower. Suddenly my heart began to beat faster. What if I tripped, or dropped my rifle when we went into the rifle salute? My hands were numb with cold and my feet were tired. I'd die if I messed up, I thought.

"Present arms," came the next command, and I moved my rifle without dropping it. "Eyes left," shouted Stern, and fifty-five young Staunton cadets snapped their heads toward Dwight David Eisenhower. There he was, right in front of me—black overcoat, white silk scarf, and black homburg. I wasn't fifteen feet away from the President of the United States.

The General gently raised his arm in salute to us, then, rather than return his hand to his side, he lowered his arm and formed an "O" with his finger and thumb, in what I was sure was a personal greeting to me. Then a wonderful smile crossed his face. If he had leaped from the reviewing stand and embraced me, it would not have surpassed the thrill of being so close to this great man.

As we passed in review, I took a fleeting look at the man standing beside Eisenhower. While the President seemed to be enjoying his parade, his Vice President, Richard Nixon, looked as though he was finding the day a wearying experience. I took a last look at Eisenhower and wished, "Boy, some day I want to have a chance to be close to the president." I could not have known that the president I would eventually be close to was standing next to Eisenhower.

Later that same day I went with my military-school roommate to visit his father in his offices in Washington. Senator Barry Goldwater of Arizona was already one of the most distinguished members of the Senate. Although I had no real understanding of what the Senator actually did, I was dazzled by his presence. I had seen his picture in newspapers and on television. And now, here he was in the real-life circumstances of the Senate chambers, exuding charm and importance. He was the first celebrity I had ever met—a famous face amidst a city of impressive buildings and beautiful monuments—and I was star-struck.

Although that glittering first impression of Washington changed nothing in my life at that time, a seed had been planted. Until that day I had harbored the notion that I was going to be a doctor and help people. It was a career that I had rebelliously decided upon in order to be different from my father. He was a business executive, the president of a manufacturing corporation that made toys, and, quite naturally, he thought that his son would follow in his footsteps. But I was equally determined not to. Medicine seemed sufficiently remote from business.

Early in life I recognized my gift of a phenomenal memory, or the ability to concentrate and pay close attention when I wished. Unfortunately, I used it mainly to coast through school as a lazy and indifferent student who could cram quickly for exams without the drudgery of studying. I was also a fast reader and developed a voracious appetite for newspapers and magazines in lieu of my texts. The trip to Washington further stimulated my interest in national affairs, and—although my family was basically apolitical—I began to fancy myself a conservative Republican in the mold of Senator Barry Goldwater. As editor-in-chief of my prep-school paper, I began cranking out conservative political editorials on major issues.

From Staunton I went to Colgate University in upstate New York, a school I selected because of its swimming coach and a strong swimming team, but I quickly tired of being at a school without women. (I confess that I have always liked women and always will. I've even lusted in my heart a bit.)

When I informed my father that I wanted to transfer to another school—"a coed school, please"—he introduced me to one of his friends, who was an active alumnus of a small school in Ohio called The College of Wooster. According to this man's glowing descriptions, all the girls at Wooster were gorgeous, and they partied all the time. I believed him and was enrolled. I guess you could tell a kid from an all-boys school almost anything in those days.

Although Wooster was not exactly as advertised, as an English major I was one of only two males in the department, and that ratio kept me entertained through an entire semester of classes. One day, as restless urges were beginning to propel me again, I saw a notice on the door of the political science department announcing the "Washington Semester Program," which enabled students to attend American University for a semester and get a taste of government in action at the same time. Well, this sounded pretty good to me. I could get to Washington without actually leaving Wooster, and my father wouldn't think I was an academic dilettante.

There was one small hitch: the program was open primarily to political science majors. But I wanted to go very badly, and my newspaper and magazine habit enabled me to discuss politics and world affairs as well as any political science major, so the department agreed to sponsor me as a candidate for this program on the condition that I carry a double major—English and political science—when I returned.

I would have promised to study nuclear physics. In fact, the faculty advisers made my double major rather pleasant. During my senior year, I completed an independent-studies project that would satisfy both departments. I was amused to read in one magazine profile written about me during the Watergate hearings that my thesis had been "Ethics in Government." It was nothing quite so ironic; prosaically enough, the title had been "Verisimilitude in the Political Novel." I surveyed American political novels from *Uncle Tom's Cabin* to *Advise and Consent*, comparing the material the novelists wrote with actual history and real situations. Most of the novels were not very realistic and the exercise left me with a strong distaste for political novels—with the stunning exception of Robert Penn Warren's *All the King's Men*.

During that semester in Washington, my political consciousness blossomed. I became fascinated with the excitement of power on Capitol Hill and with the world of government. In fact, I can recall the moment when I made the decision that I would have a career there. As a spectator, I attended a reception and parade at which President Eisenhower welcomed President Charles de Gaulle of France. I had found myself a place to stand that was right across from Blair House and in front of the Executive Office Building. It was also right next to the Marine Corps band. As Eisenhower and de Gaulle drove by, and the band struck up the national anthem, I found myself in a patriotic frenzy. All my earlier glamorous visions of Senator Goldwater and my adolescent fantasies about Washington were cemented in that moment. I knew that I would not only work there, but I would rise to the top.

I began to eat, breathe, and sleep politics. I made friends and connections who were active in government, already living the exciting life I envisioned for myself. I found myself beginning to understand the tortured processes of legislation and power brokering in Congress.

When the semester was over—all too quickly—I tried to get a summer job working in my congressman's office. Because my father was prominent in our area of western Pennsylvania, he was able to arrange an interview for me. When I arrived at my congressman's office, I found him dead drunk, throwing Eagle pencils at the fanny of one of his better-looking secretaries. I decided in that instant that I did not want to work for that congressman, but I did want to get a lot older a lot faster so that I could run against him for his seat in the House of Representatives. I managed to stay in Washington working as a lifeguard, and my enthusiasm for politics remained undampened.

Upon my return to Wooster for my final year, I decided to run
for school president, which was absurd since I had been on campus
for only one semester and could not recall having stayed on campus
for a single weekend in my entire student life. Naturally, I lost. The
experience taught me something valuable, however. I determined
then that my life in government would not be sought through the
egomaniacal competitiveness of elective politics, but through the ap-
pointive route. I wanted to move high in government based on my
merits, not on my ability to give crowd-pleasing speeches.

When I returned to American University the following year as
a graduate student with a fellowship in political science, I quickly
realized that all I could really do with a graduate degree would be to
teach. I had higher aspirations. It was becoming clear to me that the
highway to important posts in Washington, D.C., was law, so I entered Georgetown Law School and emerged in 1965 not only with an
LL.B., but with a lot more friends and contacts in government. It
was the first time that I had ever behaved like a serious student, and
I had ranked ninth in my third-year class.

During graduate school I had married a senator's daughter. At
the height of the Watergate hearings I was fascinated to hear that
my father-in-law had been responsible for my meteoric rise in government. Ironically, I had never met the man; he was a Democrat
and I considered myself a Republican; and, more decisively, he had
died before I and his daughter had met.

For all my contacts, energy, and ambition, I still could not find a
decent job in government when I came out of law school, so in 1965
I went to work as an associate at Welch & Morgan, a law firm that
specialized in broadcast law. Finally, through a broadcast economist
who was a consultant at Welch & Morgan, I developed a relationship with Jerry Schiappa, a congressional aide, who told me that the
job of minority counsel was coming open in the House Judiciary
Committee.

Jerry's boss, Congressman William Cramer of Florida, was a
member of the committee. After passing muster with him, I was
interviewed by all the senior Republican members of the committee,
down to the man to whom I would be reporting directly, William
McCulloch of Ohio, the ranking minority member of the committee.
As luck would have it, McCulloch had gone to Wooster; he needed a

lawyer and a man who could write speeches for him; and he liked me. Voilà! My first job in government.

"Dean is willing" became my personal calling card. No matter what little service a member of the committee required, I was ready. I wrote speeches, prepared hearing briefs, cross-examined witnesses, prepared amendments for the floor, covered legislation before sub-committees, briefed new members of Congress on procedure, ghosted two books, and did favors for everyone and anyone.

I discovered that the patronage system was alive and well on Capitol Hill. Politicians have long memories and don't forget their friends. I would regularly scour the halls and stop in various congressmen's offices to collect work, and they remembered that I did it efficiently. I never dropped the ball. It was a simple formula, but it worked.

I never doubted for a second that I was going to the top. It was only a matter of how long it might take; I was restless to get there. I had a sense of confidence that permitted me to take on any assignment with the feeling that I was going to do it exactly right. And I did.

There were other elements that helped me. I fashioned a studious, conservative image for myself, a Brooks-Brothers look that made me appear already successful and older than my years. I was good at quick evaluations of people and able to sense what pleased them. Undoubtedly this was born of my childhood insecurities, my need always to be liked. I never knew who might help me at some point, so I sought to have everyone like me. Also, I was socially adept. Growing up in an upper-middle-class family, you learn how to make charming dinner conversation at the country club, and how to handle a variety of social situations.

But most of all, I worked hard—very hard. My work at the Judiciary Committee did not go unnoticed. I had helped Republican Congressman Richard Poff prepare a revised version of the criminal-code-reform bill and to get it passed over a similar piece of legislation proposed by President Lyndon Johnson. It was one of the few Republican bills passed during the Democratic administration of Lyndon Johnson. At any rate, when Poff was appointed to the National Commission on the Reform of Federal Criminal Law in 1967, he arranged for me to brief the entire commission on the background of the revised criminal-code-reform legislation that, essentially, I had written. No one knew more about the subject than I did, and in the briefing I was able to demonstrate just that. The next day, I had an offer to be associate director of the commission.

While my energy, work, and ambition were paying off in my career, my home life was deteriorating. Through a peculiar stroke of fate, my wife had inherited several million dollars from a wealthy stepuncle. We ceased to be a struggling young lawyer and his wife, trying to make ends meet. Suddenly, we left our apartment and moved into a large house in a fashionable neighborhood. Money no longer a problem, my wife could not understand why I would want to continue the arduous pursuit of a career in government when I could comfortably set up a small private law practice and ease immediately into semiretirement. I was not about to be semiretired from anything, and my appointment to the commission gave me a taste of the success I had worked so hard to achieve. I felt emasculated by her money, and she felt alienated by my work. The marriage was dissolved by our differences.

Plunging into work for the commission, I became well known on the Hill as one of several young guys who could cook up legislative proposals to make political points on America's crime problem. Actually, I was anything but a criminal lawyer, but I was imaginative, and the crime problem was a major issue of the 1968 campaign. Early that year I had been invited to join the Nixon presidential campaign as an adviser on crime issues, but I had declined. I had begun to feel that there would be more potential for me working in the inner power circle of lobbyists and advisers. It seemed as though I was headed out of government proper and into a lucrative and powerful part of the private sector where I could utilize my expertise in understanding how Washington really worked. Then Richard Nixon was elected.

Almost immediately, John Mitchell and Richard Kleindienst were visiting with people in Congress who recommended me for an appointment in the new administration. After various feelers and telephone conversations, Mitchell and Kleindienst asked me to meet with them in New York on December 31st. It didn't matter much to me, anyway, I thought with a certain self-pity, since I was already in the process of a divorce and had no plans for New Year's Eve. So on

the last day of December 1968, I attended a meeting with the future
attorney general and deputy attorney general that would result in
my going to the Justice Department as associate deputy attorney
general of the United States.

I realized, at the time, that I was hired at Justice because I was
knowledgeable about the legislative process and because I knew the
congressmen and senators on the committees that the Justice Department dealt with. I became the lobbyist and liaison man with
Congress for all Department of Justice programs. And I enjoyed the
power brokering, the behind-the-scenes manipulations, and the ability to influence the decisions of the mighty.

If I had planned it, I probably would not have made it to this
high-level position at the Department of Justice, a position that I
discovered one day when reading a top-secret contingency plan for
the department in the event of nuclear attack, made me the thir-
teenth man to become attorney general in a 30,000-employee department. Yet, there I was, just barely thirty years of age and five
years out of law school, and destined to be in the White House only
a few months later.

When I eventually did move over to the White House, I wondered, was this really me, John Wesley Dean III, the kid from
Emma Avenue in Akron, Ohio, here at the right hand of the president of the United States? It was not only an amazing feeling to
have risen that high in government, but I also felt confident that I
had made it to a point where I could only go higher.

I realized quickly that there were a lot of fish in the Washington, D.C., pond. I wasn't a minnow, but my White House job
didn't make me a trophy fish, either. Curiously enough, although the
job was important and it was an impressive title, very few people in
Washington knew who the Counsel to the President was. It was nice,
however, to be able to take out that little leather folder with my
White House identification in it and get instant service when I
needed to cash a check. I was known within the government power
structure, but not to the public.

The trappings of success at the White House level were more
than peer and power recognition, however. The self-congratulatory
feeling of those first days dissipated soon in the labors of the job. The
first-class treatment tended to seem irrelevant when one's mind was

consumed by one crisis after the next, for the White House is the crisis center of government. No corporation could ever provide the perquisites that come with a job in the White House, but no corporate chief, nor his staff, deals with such vital and important matters.

The limousines and helicopters and weekends at Camp David were only the most visible part of the "perks." For example, the best restaurant in Washington was the White House dining room. Actually, there were two: the regular staff dining room and the "executive" dining room. The latter was accessible only to the Vice President and a few of the senior staff members. It was a plush private eating club with navy Filipino chefs and waiters. Of course, if you were foolish enough to want to eat outside the White House, the best tables at the swank establishments awaited you.

Travel as a White House staff member was a total pleasure. Mysteriously, the best first-class seats on overbooked airplanes would become available. Sold-out hotels would somehow discover an exquisite suite for you, even without reservations. In foreign countries, the American embassies were far better than the most exclusive travel agent you could find. Everywhere I moved outside of Washington, it seemed as though I was a celebrity: deferential treatment and red carpets were offered in every area. Whenever I had the opportunity to get away from the office, I took advantage of the situation and traveled anywhere, including around the world in twenty-one days.

Being a bachelor in Washington had certain perquisites of its own. I met a lot of beautiful women who were smitten by the idea that every time my beeper went off, it was the President calling with urgent matters of state. And my beeper went off a lot; though it was usually only my office calling, it didn't hurt my love life.

Just as I had learned from the top-secret memo how highly ranked I had been when I was at the Justice Department, I discovered my rank at the White House in a different way. Before the second inauguration, the staff was given District of Columbia license plates. The Vice President receives "1," and on down according to rank. I was "13" in the administration. By that time, however, there was already more shame than pride in being at Richard Nixon's side. I never put the plates on my car.

Curiously, it was during that second inauguration of Richard

Nixon that I was to fulfill my childhood dream, born at the
Eisenhower inauguration, of standing behind a president for the cer-
emonies. But on the day that I was invited to stand behind Richard
Nixon, I didn't want to. I was uneasy about everything he stood for.
I was going to work each day thinking that I might actually prefer
the strain of going to jail to the strain of continuing to report every
day to the White House.

Since the assignment of presidential protection had passed from
Alexander Butterfield* to me, I proffered the excuse that I was too
busy overseeing the security operations to participate in the cere-
mony. This was not true, but I sent Mo in my place. When I was at
the highest moment of my career success, I had reached the bottom
of my feelings about myself. The situation had ceased to be bit-
tersweet; it had turned sour.

As I worked away at *Blind Ambition*, I looked over the totality
of my days in government. I knew that there were more good days
than bad ones. The sweetness of the successes I experienced had not
been totally bittered by what had happened. But I realized that no
one wanted to hear about all the things we did at the Nixon White
House that were good, right, wise, in the best interests of the nation,
unselfish, and thoughtful. And I suspected it would be a long, long
time before anyone would bother to look.

As the weeks progressed into months, the novelty and enjoy-
ment of working on *Blind Ambition* wore off. Reliving the worst of
the past by thinking about it, then writing about it, became unpleasant. For days on end I would find myself brooding about decisions I
had or had not made. At night I would dream about the days gone,
as if they were the present. While I did feel good about some of the
things I'd done, the embarrassment of my ambitious mistakes over-
powered the comfort I might find in the brighter moments.

My life had moved into the past tense. I seldom bothered to
read the newspaper or watch television, and I asked Mo to turn

*Alexander Butterfield was the former presidential aide who first disclosed
the existence of the White House taping system to the Senate Watergate committee. In early 1973, Butterfield became the head of the Federal Aviation Administration.

down social engagements. I wasn't visiting my past, I was reliving it, mentally. I was unceasingly wading through the details, the minutiae, and the assorted flotsam and jetsam of my Watergate experience that I hoped would add reality to my book.

I began measuring time by how many pages and chapters I had completed, and, eight chapters into a working outline that called for fourteen, I surfaced long enough to realize what I had been doing to myself. My now trusted friend and agent, David Obst, called to say that he was coming out to California and wanted to read what I had written thus far. Great, I thought, but what have I written?

I estimated that I had poured out roughly 100,000 words, and, other than my typist, who had cleaned up my rough drafts, no one had seen the material. David's call caused me to conjugate life from past to present and read what I had written with all the distance and dispassion I could muster. Some of it was good, most of it was very uneven. At times I was clearly pouring ashes on myself, and at other times I was totally self-serving. My typewriter had become something between a confessional and an advertising agency.

Reluctantly, I let Obst read my manuscript. He was encouraging, "Great, just continue to get it all down, in case someone shoots you," he playfully chided in his normal blasé fashion. "Say, by the way, I've got another client coming to L.A. this week who'd like to meet you," he said matter-of-factly.

That client was anti-Vietnam-war activist Daniel Ellsberg. David wanted me to meet with Dan, because Dan appreciated my testifying that his rights had been infringed by the Nixon White House. I'm not sure what I expected from our meeting, but I did not expect what I got.

I had only a newspaper knowledge of Dan Ellsberg, the man who leaked the "Pentagon Papers," a government study of the Vietnam war which showed the government's ineptness, callousness, and deceitfulness in fighting that Asian battle, to *The New York Times*. I knew, as he knew, that the criminal charges the government brought against him were largely fueled by Nixon's pique at his leaking these documents, even though they did not directly affect Nixon. The case had been dismissed against Ellsberg, in part because I had reported to the federal prosecutors information about the break-in by Gordon Liddy and the others at Ellsberg's psychiatrist's office.

Dan Ellsberg, I discovered, is an intense fellow. Barely had he seated himself on our living room sofa than he turned to me and asked offhandedly, "Nixon planned to have me killed, didn't he?" This kind of opening line can catch your attention.

"No," I answered, shaking my head with dismay and as an emphasis of my annoyance. This "Nixon the Killer" type of question bothered me. I'd been asked it by probing reporters and investigators, and always it had made me uncomfortable. People assumed, wrongly, that I knew all there was to know about Nixon's presidency. I never heard of any murder plots, although nothing would surprise me about Nixon. For a long time I had worried that murder, too, would be included in the "Watergate mentality" ascribed to all of us who had been there.

"You never heard a word, not even a rumor, that they were out to bump me off?" Ellsberg persisted, evidencing a degree of disbelief, even distrust in my answer.

"Dan, I think you should know by now that anything and everything I knew about the Nixon presidency I have testified to in one form or another. Believe me, if I had heard about any murder plots, I'd have talked about them, if for no other reason than to protect myself from being associated with those who had been involved in such crap."

Ellsberg's cool, blue eyes studied me for a moment. I wondered what he was thinking. I decided, when he finally turned to Obst with a smile, that he believed me. Yet he had not discarded the potential of his having been the target of a Nixon murder scheme.

"I guess John really doesn't know," he told Obst, as if I'd suddenly left the room. As he talked, it was clear he wore this imaginary murder plot as a badge of honor, that he'd been so hated and so important that the President had wanted to kill him. Clearly, his ego would not accept anything less than such a likelihood.

The more Ellsberg talked, the more bored I became with our conversation. Rather than listen closely, I merely nodded occasionally, for he reminded me of an assistant professor testing the thesis of his doctoral dissertation on a captive audience of students.

"They created the 'Plumbers' Unit' with Howard Hunt and Gordon Liddy because of me," he observed at one point.

"Well, Dan, I think it happened before you started leaking government documents, but I'm not sure."

"No, you're wrong. It happened when Hoover refused to interview my father-in-law, Marx, who was a pal of Hoover's—used to send him toys. . . ." As Dan went on, I nodded and drifted off into my own thoughts, thoughts about how important this awful time in Dan Ellsberg's life had become to him. He was still living the worst moments in his anti-Vietnam-war crusade, even though the war was long over.

At another point, Ellsberg caught my attention with the remark, "I think what I did was really, when you analyze it, the cause of Watergate." The way he said it sounded as though he might like to take the credit for it. Yet he'd raised an interesting point.

I offered that I had two theories that explained Watergate, although I would write about neither in *Blind Ambition*. They were carefully considered opinions, based on facts as I had seen them firsthand.

"If you ask me," I said, "the mentality that produced Watergate was not one of pure evil or of wanton disregard for the law; rather, Watergate was the product of a Cold War mentality that resurfaced during the Vietnam war."

"What?" Obst protested, emerging from his silence and sitting upright on the edge of the sofa. Ellsberg said nothing, as if assimilating the intrusive observations of a student.

"Remember," I continued, "it was during the Cold War years that men like Howard Hunt and Gordon Liddy were trained by the government to spy. From their point of view, they were doing things for which men were once given commendations—when the target was a suspected Communist."

"That's certainly no justification for their actions today," Ellsberg noted.

"We're not talking about justification. I'm talking about explanations. Why it happened. In the broadest sense. And Hunt and Liddy weren't the only ones with that cold-warrior mentality. Richard Nixon became 'Tricky Dick' Nixon because of the Cold War. Nixon pursued Alger Hiss when he was a congressman and continued pursuing 'Commies' in his campaign against the 'Pink Lady,'

Helen Gahagan, as he fought for his seat in the Senate. He was one of the earliest cold warriors."

"That's all true, but what does it have to do with Watergate?" Obst asked.

"Vietnam resurrected that mentality. Regardless of what you both might think, I felt then, when I was at the White House, and I still feel, that Nixon did his damndest to end the war in Vietnam. He couldn't buy the demonstrators' approach, because he was sincerely worried that to just pull out would endanger strategic locations in Southeast Asia, as well as cause serious loss of confidence here at home. He was afraid the attitude would develop: 'Well, we lost the war, so we're not as great a nation as we think.' "

"Bullshit," Obst interrupted.

"No, let John finish. I've always wondered how their minds worked at the White House," Ellsberg said calmly, with a patronizing smile.

"Well, all I wanted to say is, whether you agree or not with Nixon's thinking, that's what he thought. He was convinced of his own good intentions."

"What's your other thesis?" David asked, since he and Ellsberg obviously didn't want to accept the first.

"It is simply that most of Watergate can be explained by pure stupidity. I met a fellow in prison who was fairly high up in the Mafia. One day Joey said to me, 'Let me tell ya something.' He sounded and looked tougher than he really was. Anyway, he said, 'I used to really respect Richard Nixon. He was my kinda president, you know—tough, a no-bullshit type of guy. But then, when I saw what a lousy criminal the guy was, I realized he was stupid. Ya gotta have brains and real guts to be a good criminal.' Well, Joey was right. We were lousy criminals. We were stupid about these things, and that's why it became such a mess."

"Very possibly true," Dan said, nodding his agreement.

"I'm convinced," I continued, "that Nixon and Mitchell and Haldeman, the whole bunch of us, would rather admit to a crime than admit to being stupid. But down deep in our souls, we knew we screwed up because we weren't as smart as everyone figured. It's interesting that people who write about Watergate keep looking for deeper, darker motives, or the fine hand of the CIA, or some other secret conspiracy at work. The public can't believe that everyone in the Nixon White House was as stupid as the record indicates we were. But we were, and, as soon as you understand this, you come to a better understanding of Watergate."

Both Ellsberg and Obst were now wriggling and restraining themselves with their questions. "I certainly didn't have the impression that you thought Nixon was stupid from the way you described your meetings with him," Obst noted in a mildly challenging manner, referring to what he'd read in my manuscript.

"True, from reading *Blind Ambition*, people won't have that impression, because I'm recounting those conversations from the point of view I had at the time. I was convinced that Nixon was cleverly manhandling me—that he knew all and had heard all. But when I began to write those sections, I reread all the transcripts of Nixon's conversations, and my fresh perspective gave me a different view of the man. I thought about the many other transcripts of his statements I've been given to read over the years by the House impeachment committee and the Watergate prosecutors. What is evident to me now is that Nixon didn't have any damned idea of what was really happening. He couldn't remember from day to day what he was being told, who was involved, or how much they were involved. So it is not much wonder he made such bad decisions. Nixon should have been impeached for stupidity, not high crimes and misdemeanors."

"You're serious, aren't you?" Obst asked.

"I couldn't be more serious. He certainly wasn't a fool. But he wasn't the quick study of complicated and unfamiliar facts that everyone thought he was. No one ever put down on paper for him, as we did with everything else, exactly what had happened. He was told about it piecemeal, in passing remarks, and he never did get all the necessary details in his head to understand its meaning. What he did know, he rationalized and justified through that Cold War mentality I mentioned."

"Tell me about Kissinger, and the wiretaps that he authorized, or targeted, or whatever he claims he did," Ellsberg asked, moving the subject much closer to his own personal interest.

"I don't have anything to tell you that you don't already know." I could see that look of disbelief again. But I was speaking the truth.

I had little knowledge of the so-called Kissinger taps, one of which had picked up Ellsberg and consequently resulted in the dismissal of the criminal charges against him.

The conversation with Dan Ellsberg stayed in my head for several days. It had made me think about several things I had not recently thought about, such as the day *Time* magazine had called the White House for comment on an article they were then preparing about wiretaps on newsmen, i.e., the "Kissinger wiretaps," as they later became known. My tracing this leak had led me very close to uncovering Deep Throat, who had reported these wiretaps to Woodward early on.

It had started on February 23, 1973, when Nixon's press secretary, Ron Ziegler, had called me, looking for guidance. Was it in fact true, he wanted to know, that the White House had ordered wiretaps on newsmen? I knew the story was true, but felt I must check with John Ehrlichman to advise Ziegler on how he should respond.

Many months earlier, I had heard that Ehrlichman had requested White House aide Jack Caulfield to undertake such an operation. And indeed Caulfield had tried, starting with an effort to wiretap syndicated columnist Joseph Kraft's residence. But, in the tradition of most such White House operations, it had been an unprofessional and unsuccessful, though undiscovered, fiasco. Caulfield had tried to enlist the aid of the Secret Service, which turned him down.

Nixon finally assigned the task to a reluctant J. Edgar Hoover, who successfully carried out the assignment but proceeded to hold the White House ransom for his job when they later talked of retiring him as director. Most of the evidence of the taps was destroyed by former deputy director of the FBI, William Sullivan, whom Hoover had instructed and entrusted to see that the taps were installed. But Bill Sullivan kept one set of records and, when he and Hoover had a falling-out that forced Sullivan from the Bureau, Sullivan had passed his set of records along to his Justice Department friend, also a friend of John Mitchell, and then assistant attorney general, Bob Mardian. It was Mardian who had told me that he had passed the wiretap records on to John Ehrlichman to prevent Hoover's ever using them as blackmail.

I wasn't supposed to know all this. It had been dribbled to me in bits and pieces, first by Caulfield, then a few more facts from Ehrlichman's assistant, Bud Krogh, and finally I got the rest of the story from Mardian himself, during one of our many late-night drinking sessions, when we did some hand wringing together over the nasty problems of Watergate.

To Ehrlichman's surprise, I confronted him with my knowledge when I called to ask how he wanted Ron Ziegler to handle the *Time* story. At first he denied knowing anything, but soon he knew he couldn't bluff me on this one. I pressed him for what he wanted Ziegler to say. Finally, Ehrlichman angrily blurted, "Just tell Ziegler to deny it, period."

"Deny it?" I repeated, to make certain he was certain.

"Deny it!" he repeated, and added, "It sounds like your friend over at the FBI, Mark Felt, has been talking again. If he hasn't, someone sure has. Why don't you see if you can find out who's doing all this chatting?"

Ehrlichman's question was my command in those days. So I began a little detective work. First I called Mark Felt, who played his cards very close to his chest. Felt had long been suspected by the White House as a major leak at the FBI (and many later figured he was Deep Throat). I played dumb and asked Felt if it were true or not that such wiretaps had been in existence.

"You really want to know?" he asked in a smug tone. Not so much as a "boo" about whether or not I was authorized by the White House or National Security Council to know. In fact, he was anxious to tell me, and quickly responded to my "Yes," with, "Then ask Bill Sullivan." That's when I called Sullivan and requested that he come over to my office as soon as possible.

While I waited for Sullivan to arrive at my office, I thought about how I might approach him about the *Time* leak. He would be a foxy old fellow, much more experienced at such a session than I. I pictured in my mind the man I'd seen twice. He looked like a man of many secrets. His face was old, wrinkled, and unsmiling, and his eyes said they had spent many sleepless nights.

He arrived at my office on that February 23rd afternoon, to my surprise, wearing the same suit he'd been wearing the past two times I'd seen him. Coincidence, I thought; I might be wearing the same suit, as well. But his suit was special, that's why I'd remembered it. It had the look of those G-men in the 1940's movies: double-breasted, big shoulder pads, and a steely blue sheen.

As I greeted him, his eyes cased my office, and he selected a seat people seldom took, one not in front of my desk, rather way off to one side. Actually, it was an extra chair that I would bring up to the desk when more than four in front of the desk were necessary. No one would easily bug this ex-counterintelligence officer, I thought to myself, as I pulled my chair around so we could talk.

Pleasantries were dispensed with quickly. I cleared my throat, pulled my chair a little in his direction, and looked him square in the eyes, in silence for a moment.

"Bill, the White House learned this afternoon that you leaked to *Time* magazine about the wiretaps on newsmen and White House staffers."

Sullivan never blinked, nor swallowed, nor cleared his throat. Not a blush or flush. No visible reaction preceded his unsmiling, matter-of-fact response. "Well, the White House has learned wrong."

"You know about those taps, and what I'm talking about," I continued in a prosecutorial tone.

"Well, what I know and what I feel at liberty to speak with you about are not the same thing." His tone was defiant. Even with a hint of anger.

Cagey fellow, I thought. He's turned this into a situation that makes me look like I'm trying to get some national-security information out of him. I backed down, turned friendly, and told him that I had been asked to uncover the leak. I revealed that I knew all about the wiretaps, and that Mark Felt had pointed the finger at him. But I assured him I did not believe Felt for a second.

"Why the hell would I leak it? That's the dumbest thing I've ever heard," he exploded. "If you thought it through, you would know I am one of the last people in the world who would want that story out." I assumed he was referring to his own role in the matter, but he wasn't about to volunteer details when I probed.

It took a while, but eventually our conversation became quite relaxed, and Bill began to open up. He outlined what had happened: how Hoover had placed him in charge of the operation; how Al Haig, Henry Kissinger's aide, had come to his office with the "targets," which was a new little tidbit for me. Sullivan then told me he had handpicked FBI agents from the Washington field office, "the finest and most trusted only," and that he had controlled the summaries and logs of the taps.

He confirmed how he had all the evidence of the operation destroyed at the field office, which had infuriated Hoover, for it had taken away hard evidence that Hoover could have used to blackmail the White House, and that he had given the one set of logs he had personally kept to Mardian when he left the FBI.

Then Sullivan began to lecture me on how to uncover a leak by determining everyone who had access to the information, then eliminating them one by one. For some reason known only to him he'd decided to initiate me. His entire tone changed, his rigid position in the chair became more relaxed, and he actually scooted his chair a bit closer to my desk. Suddenly, I'd become a confidant.

"Listen, John, I'd really like to assist in any way I might, to help you all here find out who did leak it. Leaking is a dirty business, and I've had to deal with those spineless little snakes that exist in the bureaucracy for many, many years."

Then he moved closer to me and lowered his voice. "The only way I think the story could have gotten out," he observed in a confidential manner, "was because Hoover told Pat Coyne,* who I understand told Nelson Rockefeller. And Rockefeller probably told Kissinger. Hoover was that kind of leaker, you know, did it indirectly, so that the White House would know that the old man was doing a little chatting."

Hoover had blown the whistle, softly and in a trusted ear, on the FBI. The old man was brilliantly devious. He was letting the White House know that, if he was forced to do their dirty work, there would be a price. And to have the threat of leaked information come through Kissinger, who would know J. Edgar was sending his mes-

---

*I would later repeat Pat Coyne's name to Richard Nixon. I had (and have) no idea who this man was, although Nixon seemed to recognize the name.

sage with this little whistle, was an extraordinary touch. I tried to conceal my amazement, but it was unnecessary, as Sullivan was abruptly ready to leave. He had a parting message for me.

"This damn Watergate thing has certainly gotten blown out of all proportion," he said in an off-the-cuff manner, as he rose from his chair and hiked his belt line.

"Sure has," I noted.

"For chrissake, what other presidents have done, as opposed to what Mr. Nixon has supposedly done, well, I'll tell you, Mr. Nixon looks like a saint. And, believe me, I know what I'm talking about."

"What do you mean?" I asked, as we walked across my office and stood before the door.

"Listen, Franklin Roosevelt used the FBI for anything and everything. So did Lyndon Johnson, for that matter."

Bill Sullivan didn't have to draw a picture for me. It was clear he was offering a little *quid pro quo*. He had information that could help the Nixon White House soften the impact of Watergate. We could help Bill Sullivan by bringing him back into government to chase spies again. I gently pressed for more.

"I've not thought about those things for a long time," he said. "I'll tell you what. I'll really give it some thought. I'll talk to some of my old colleagues and compare notes and memories. And you give me a call in a few days," he said, sticking his hand out to bid farewell.

On the afternoon of March 19, 1973, Bill Sullivan returned to my office. He was still wearing the same blue suit.

"Have you figured out who leaked that story to *Time* yet?" he asked.

"Not for certain, but I followed your suggestion, and I've got a good idea where it might have come from." In the intervening days I had traced knowledge of the wiretaps to about five people on the White House staff, the Secret Service, the FBI, and the CIA. I had eliminated all candidates, except the FBI, the Secret Service—and Al Haig. I didn't know what to think about Haig, but several people on the White House staff suspected he could be the "leaker." The Secret Service did not seem a very likely source, since they had not actually carried out the taps, but had only turned down Caulfield's request to them. Most likely it was someone within the FBI, so I pursued this with Sullivan.

"Let me tell you something about the Bureau, John. Sure, these guys leak stories to the press. In fact *The Washington Post* has a line into a couple of guys in the Washington field office, and that's where that fellow Bernstein and his partner (Woodward) are getting some of their information about Watergate. We know who the leakers are, but they don't have very much information. I can tell you they didn't know about the taps I handled."

Sullivan spoke with total conviction about his knowledge. If what he was saying was correct, and he was very believable when he assured me that since our last meeting he had spoken with every agent and security man who knew of "his taps," as he called them, then the only places the leak might have come from were the Secret Service and the White House staff. It just didn't fit, however. I'd have to retrace it all to be certain. So I turned to the other reason Sullivan had come to visit.

"I must tell you, Bill, I've told the President about your offer to give us some information about past presidents and their use of the FBI. He's very interested, to put it mildly," I added with a laugh.

Sullivan wasted no time commencing a diatribe against Hoover and the FBI. The information he was disclosing was everything I'd always suspected, but couldn't believe anyone would ever admit, or even be in a position to talk about. I made some notes on a pad on the sofa beside me, hoping an occasional fast jot wouldn't bother him. It didn't. After his departure, I translated what he had related to me. I was sure I had captured the essence of what Sullivan had said.

The FBI was doing dirty political work for every president that Sullivan could remember. But the Democrats were far more active in this regard than the Republicans. Hoover would talk directly to the president, not go through his attorney general or any other subordinate, although FBI subordinates talked to White House subordinates about such things.

No records were kept on these doings between Hoover and a president, unless a president made some formal request. Then Hoover used these requests for leverage over a president. The requests were done on "pink memos," which meant that they would end up in a special file in Hoover's office, or be destroyed at Hoover's instructions.

The presidents who used the FBI for political purposes the most were Franklin Roosevelt and Lyndon Johnson.

Examples of FDR's uses of the FBI included investigating the background of his opponents to major legislation, like his Lend-Lease legislation; he had newsmen investigated who were writing negative articles about him or his proposals. Even Mrs. Roosevelt used the FBI to check out both her friends and enemies. Sullivan named names, but I did not recognize them. For example, FDR turned the FBI off several background investigations of people he wanted to appoint, because he didn't want derogatory information arising about them. Sullivan mentioned Sumner Welles, who Hoover had learned was homosexual.

Lyndon Johnson's uses included a lot of very specific examples, as if Sullivan had files in his possession documenting them, like Johnson's putting Anna Chennault* under physical surveillance in 1968, and the details of a special FBI squad that Johnson had assembled for the Democratic convention in Atlantic City in 1964.

Sullivan said this "special squad" did everything from bugging Johnson's opponents to stealing documents to infiltrating the news media. Sullivan grew very agitated in talking about this operation, saying, "If the truth were known about what Johnson did in 1964, it would make Watergate look like child's play." Sullivan also noted that, "there was never before, nor since to my knowledge, anything quite like this FBI operation."

Apparently, the Kennedys did not use the FBI. As Sullivan put it, "Jack and Bobby didn't trust Hoover for a second. They were afraid of him." Sullivan suspected that the Kennedys' distrust originated back in the early forties, when Jack Kennedy was a young lieutenant in the navy, and very much a man about Washington. Apparently, at that time Hoover had surveillance on a very attractive

---

*Anna Chennault, Chinese-born widow of World War II hero General Claire Chennault, and an active Nixon fund-raiser, allegedly persuaded South Vietnamese officials not to negotiate with Lyndon Johnson just before his 1968 election. It was said that the "Dragon Lady" was an agent in preventing Johnson from obtaining peace in Vietnam.

lady who was suspected of being a Nazi spy. During the course of this surveillance it was discovered that Jack Kennedy was sleeping with the woman, and Hoover related this information to Kennedy's father, which resulted in Kennedy's being transferred out of Washington.

Bill Sullivan offered very little on Republican presidents, probably in appreciation of his audience. He did note that Hoover thought the sun rose and fell when Tom Dewey got out of bed and retired at night. Hoover was sure that Dewey was going to be elected president and defeat Harry Truman, whom Hoover hated. Truman apparently had a similar feeling toward Hoover, and Truman did not use the Bureau as other Democratic presidents had.

Dwight Eisenhower, to Sullivan's knowledge, never asked Hoover for anything. But Hoover volunteered information to Ike, whenever he had something of a gossipy nature he thought might interest him, like the fact that Ike's 1955 opponent, Adlai Stevenson, was divorcing his wife and was involved with another woman.

"One thing you might keep in mind," Sullivan cautioned me when I asked him if this information about prior presidents could be "leaked," "other things could come out, things about the Nixon White House."

Sullivan then proceeded to tell me a story, suggesting it as an example. He said a high official at the Nixon White House, whom he didn't name, had expressed concerns to Hoover about homosexuals flocking to Washington to take government jobs. As Sullivan described it, it was "like the colored people, back in the thirties, forties, and early fifties, who came to Washington because there was no job discrimination here." The White House had expressed concern that the gays could make Washington the gay capital, because of the current hiring policy regarding homosexuals.

Sullivan indicated that the Nixon White House was most immediately concerned with the State Department, "where the fruits and nuts have nearly taken over the place." The White House wanted the Bureau to find out any facts that it could, and Hoover assigned a couple of key staff people to do this.

"That's hard for me to believe, Bill," I said, expressing my doubts.

"Well, try this. How do you think this story would read?"

Next, he proceeded to recite an even more bizarre tale of how the Bureau had learned that a high judicial appointee had been forced to resign by the Nixon Justice Department. The basis for the forced resignation, according to Sullivan, was the fact that the Bureau had found out that this man had been engaged in homosexual activity. Apparently, the information had first been discovered by the District of Columbia police, then the Bureau, and, when the Nixon people learned it, they had used the information to force the resignation.

I felt disgusted. What the hell was I doing with these people? I was most anxious to get Bill Sullivan out of my office. I suspected he might be setting me up, and placing himself in a position where he would not be asked ever to testify about his knowledge—or to leak it. As far as I was concerned that was fine. But I did feel that the President was entitled to know what Sullivan had reported to me, so I pushed him to write me a memo.

"Type it up yourself, Bill. Just give me some rough notes," I insisted. He at first resisted and finally agreed.

And now here I was, three thousand miles away from Washington, three years away from Bill Sullivan's handing me the document I had just reread, and again I felt the same despicable feelings.

Yet, rereading the Sullivan memo, I couldn't help thinking that what he told me was proof positive that Watergate did not represent something new to government, that Nixon and staff were not original sinners. Indeed, most every modern president had committed abuses of a similar nature.

There was a basis for Nixon's apologists to claim that "it didn't start with Watergate," and that the difference between Nixon and his predecessors was simply that we "got caught." Future historians who honestly address the issue will see that an *ex post facto* morality judged Richard Nixon, and, in this sense, he was held accountable for the sins of all the presidents before him.

Those who work at the White House know it, even some journalists know it, but it is not well known publicly that a surprising degree of communication occurs between the past and present administrations. The presidents have confidential talks, the White House staffs mingle and exchange information, and, most of all, the bureaucracy that serves the White House freely passes on useful information, as well as gossip, about prior activities in the Oval Office.

This fact was apparent when I showed the Sullivan memo to Haldeman and Ehrlichman; they merely shrugged, saying, "What's new about that stuff?" There is little doubt in my mind that the activities they condoned and often initiated were, to them, nothing more than business as usual in the White House. Yet, what Nixon and his staff—including myself—did was in excess. It was the arrogance of power running wild. From placing the White House guards in Bavarian-style uniforms to spending countless millions to refurbish and refurnish the White House Executive Office Building and Camp David, to Watergate itself, Nixon was never happy with just a small abuse. While the abuses themselves happened under other presidents, they never happened as a matter of standard operating practice; and they never occurred on such a grandiose scale of power flaunting.

I had caught myself rationalizing, wanting to believe Watergate was no worse than what had gone before. Sullivan's memo and the memories of his visits had made me uncomfortable. Both in lecturing and now in writing my book, I had sought to avoid such thinking. My task as an author, not unlike what I did in my Senate committee testimony, I felt, was to give the facts of what had happened. Not apology, but information. The book would be different from my testimony because I wanted to explain the interrelationships of people and personalities—information that was irrelevant in hearing rooms and courtrooms, but vital to understanding what had gone so radically wrong at the core of our government.

I pushed the Sullivan memo away from me in disgust and looked out the window. All the old emotions had returned, and I was reliving those unpleasant scenes with a guilty perspective. I felt anger at myself, and at all of us in the Nixon White House, for the stupidity of what we had done.

JUNE 25, 1975—Los Angeles.

Well, John, you think Ellsberg is crazy and pathetic for living in the past. What do you think you are beginning to do?

I do nothing but sit around and think about what I did and

where I was, rather than where I am or where I'm going. It is unhealthy. And for Mo, I am sure, I am becoming the all-time great bore.

Enough. If writing this book requires that I live in the past, it's a great mistake. I should be able to jump back and forth. I'm treating the book like I used to treat my job, with an all-consuming devotion. I've got to stop this, and find another approach.

I'll start tonight, by taking my wife out for a change, and tomorrow I'll give further thought to investigating Deep Throat's identity, for that was fun. Sifting back through the leads that I'd once uncovered while pursuing the leak of the "Kissinger taps" might provide the key to the mystery.

CHAPTER FOUR

Everything Is Different Now

"One problem with the movie business is that they always publicize the actors and shoot the movies, instead of vice versa," I announced, and began chuckling at my wit. We were driving to Warner Brothers' Burbank studios. Mo forced a pained smile.

"Is that supposed to be funny?" she asked.

"Just a little joke for Robert Redford."

"Relax, dear," she said sweetly. "Stick to politics and don't try to be a comedian."

We had been invited to visit the movie set for "All the President's Men." It would be my first glimpse into the making of a movie, a real behind-the-scenes peek at Hollywood. I was already intimidated into nervous jokes by the prospect of meeting the formidable duo who would be our guides: Robert Redford and Dustin Hoffman.

At The Burbank Studios lot we were met by David Obst, who had conceived this visit as publicity for all his clients: Woodward, Bernstein, Dean, and Dean (he also represented Mo, who had just finished her book). David led us onto a sound stage that had been designed as a replica of the *Washington Post* newsroom. It was an incredible reproduction, down to such details as old *Washington Post* newspapers on the desks.

We arrived on the set during a break in the shooting, and Redford and Hoffman were there to greet us. While we shook hands, photographers appeared out of nowhere. I hadn't expected them. They clicked, and we all produced our best plastic smiles. Redford, who was also the producer, sensed my discomfort and quickly shooed them away.

Talking to these Hollywood heavies was not that easy for me. So I strolled around the set looking at the IBM typewriters, trying to appear as if I knew what you do when you visit a movie set. I am sure I looked as helpless as the poor soul shopping for a new car— who kicks the tires, sits behind the wheel, listens to how the door slams, and avoids the salesman. Mo, with her customary ease, was deep in conversation with Dustin Hoffman. Later, she confided that he had said to her as we were having our pictures taken: "John's a little uptight right now, isn't he?"

"A little, I guess," she had answered.

"It's neat, the way you stay right beside him," said Hoffman. "That's what my wife does when I'm uptight or uncomfortable."

I was "uptight," but also fascinated, even if this was a standard Hollywood publicity stunt. Political movies, like political novels, usually miss the mark in capturing reality. Yet, here I was, standing in the middle of verisimilitude, if I'd ever seen it. This was a very expensive set, and I was impressed.

Redford returned from his conversation with the photographers he had ushered out, obviously giving some instruction like, "Have those pictures in my trailer as soon as possible." I asked him, "What do you do with all this stuff after the movie?"

Redford smiled. "Well, fortunately, we've made an arrangement with a company that is opening new offices to buy all the desks and typewriters and chairs and other office furnishings. The rest of the set, I don't know yet." (I later heard that the set would become, with slight modification, the set for the "Lou Grant" television series.)

"You bought the movie rights to this story early on, didn't you?"

"Well, I didn't buy them until the book was finished by Carl and Bob, but I told them I thought their story could make a good movie. Actually, I went back to your old city, Washington, while they were still reporting on Watergate, and I spent some time with both of them. I followed a similar process with the movie 'The Candidate,' when I actually went out on the campaign trail to get the feel of it. Even before the outcome of Watergate was clear, I thought there was a good story in how Carl and Bob were investigating Watergate."

Dustin Hoffman explained that he had to do some script studying, and he excused himself. Redford took us for a complete tour of the newsroom set, showing us how the pillars, which looked like steel cast in concrete, were merely white paper and could be moved for the camera angles. He was properly proud of this set and explained the technical moves the cameras could make around the newsroom, following people, giving the newsroom a feel of constant action, or any other mood that was necessary.

"Did you know Dwight Chapin very well?" Redford asked me casually, as our tour was coming to its end. For him to ask about Chapin was an extraordinary coincidence. That very morning I had received a letter from Dwight, saying that, since the Court of Appeals had affirmed his perjury conviction, he was going to go ahead and begin serving his sentence (of ten to thirty months), while his lawyers appealed his case to the Supreme Court. With Redford's question, I flashed on Dwight's less than optimistic thoughts:

> (The appeal) will take many months, if not years. Ninety-five percent of the cases seeking review by that court are turned down. I have taken into account that I am thirty-four, and this problem has been part of my life for three years. It has become time to bring the matter, as it affects my daily life, to a conclusion.

I was judging my response to Redford's question, for I wasn't sure what had prompted it, when he said, "I went to high school with Dwight Chapin." He looked me square in the eyes with his big blues, as though he were talking about someone who had departed. He was.

"Sad to say, Dwight is on his way to prison. Your question surprised me. It's ironic, because I just got a letter from Dwight today, telling me he had decided to more or less toss the towel in and get his prison term behind him."

Redford was slowly shaking his head, for it just didn't fit to have Dwight headed for prison. He wasn't the kind of person anyone would have pegged for that fate. At least, that's what Redford's face and expression were saying to me, so I returned to his question.

"I can't say that I know Dwight all that well. We weren't social friends at the White House, nor did we work closely. Yet I always felt that we had a really good rapport; we communicated through all the bullshit that existed back there, if you know what I mean. I've always thought of him as a special sort of person, and feel terrible about what's happening to him."

Redford apparently agreed, nodding understanding, so I asked where they had gone to school. I didn't really know where either of them had grown up.

"Out here, in the San Fernando Valley." He said nothing for a moment, locked in thoughts of high school, I assumed. "Dwight was a hell of a nice guy, a really fine person. I can't believe he got himself mixed up in all that mess," Redford said softly, slipping his hands in his pockets and slumping his shoulders.

"Nor can I. I think Dwight was the victim of an angry government. The fact that he was indicted, convicted, and is on his way to jail is proof that the government can get anybody, if they want to. Even you!"

Robert Redford chuckled easily and gave a nod of appreciation. I added, "Dwight doesn't deserve to be thrown in the same stew with Mitchell, Haldeman, Ehrlichman—or me, for that matter."

Everything that occurred was being lumped under the "Watergate" label. Most of the activities did not belong there, but the word had become a symbol, as much as an event. The public's confusion about the misfeasance, malfeasance, and nonfeasance of the president's men was the result of sloppy reporting, combined with a clear effort to "get Nixon" and his staff. Indeed, Carl Bernstein and Bob Woodward had relied on the "toss them all in the same Watergate basket" stratagem in reporting their stories, and in writing their book. The hard facts, as opposed to information from "reliable sources close to the investigation," show this was unjustified.

Maybe not too subtly, I was trying to give Robert Redford a message about his movie. But David Obst told me, as we departed from the set, that very few people really knew what was in the final script, since it had been constantly rewritten. We'd all have to wait and see.

Back home, I found Dwight's letter on the kitchen counter

where I had left it. No one will ever make a movie about this side of the story, I thought. Movies need heroes, because the world needs heroes. Real-life stories seldom have them, unfortunately.

Dwight Chapin had been an advance man for Richard Nixon during the 1968 presidential campaign, a young protégé of the campaign's top advanceman, Bob Haldeman. During the '68 campaign, Dwight had learned what it was like to be on the receiving end of "dirty tricks," and had seen some of his carefully orchestrated advances become near-disasters because of the "pranks" of Nixon's opponents. In 1971, he decided that it was time to attack, instead of defend. Dwight was appointments secretary to the President and, as such, in charge of advancing presidential trips, including everything from China to those of the forthcoming '72 campaign.

Dwight felt it only fair that the Democrats be given a little of the medicine they had made him taste, so he proposed to his boss, Haldeman, that a "political prankster" be hired for the campaign. The man he had in mind was an old undergraduate chum from USC, Donald Segretti. Haldeman approved, but insisted that such activities be untraceable to the White House. Segretti was hired and Dwight gave him some examples of the "pranks" expected, such as having a train pull out of a station while a candidate was still talking, and distributing false baggage calls at a candidate's hotel to cause staff confusion. Dwight told Segretti to do as little as possible personally, to use false names, and to make sure his work wasn't traced back to the White House. His general goal was to cause as much confusion as possible among the Democrats and make them think that they were doing it to each other.

Segretti was more ambitious and imaginative than Chapin could have expected. In addition to false campaign literature, bogus pickets, press conference hecklers, and much media misinformation, Segretti devised some unusual stunts. He began with phony orders for room service, liquor, and limousines that were charged to various Democratic candidates; and then, he became still more inventive. He paid twenty dollars to a University of Florida coed, whose job it was to run naked in front of Muskie's Gainesville hotel, screaming, "Senator Muskie, I love you."

Without Chapin's encouragement, Segretti's enthusiasm soon

edged over the line from sophomoric humor into unfortunate slander. He wrote a bogus letter, on Citizens for Muskie stationery, accusing Senator Jackson of being a homosexual, and Senator Humphrey of cavorting with prostitutes at the expense of lobbyists. (That "prank" cost him four and a half months in the slammer.)

Many of the "dirty tricks" stayed within the parameters of activities generated by pranksters like Dick Tuck (who played tricks on the Republicans on behalf of the Kennedy organization in 1960). But, like so many Nixon operations, the "dirty tricks" became excessive. Segretti created more and more bizarre schemes to embarrass the Democrats as the campaign progressed, and reported these to Chapin after the fact.

From the moment of the Watergate break-in, Dwight was worried. Chapin had nothing to do with Watergate, nor did Segretti, but with the FBI rumbling about the country and newsmen looking for anything and everything improper about the campaign, he was concerned that Segretti's activities might be discovered. To my knowledge Dwight had committed no crime, although he certainly had not been performing as the public would like to believe young White House aides should perform.

The "dirty tricks" were discovered quickly, both by the FBI and Carl Bernstein. The FBI had no real interest in Segretti, or his activities, since they were unrelated to Watergate. Carl Bernstein had discovered Segretti through an anonymous phone call to *The Washington Post* that reported how Segretti had traveled about the country to recruit other "pranksters" to work for him. Actually, Carl was far ahead of the FBI in learning about the extent of Segretti's activities. Indeed, the biggest scoops that Carl and Bob got on their Watergate-related stories concerned Segretti; then, with the benefit of leaked information, they nailed Chapin for his connection with Segretti.

It had been the coverage of *The Washington Post* that had forced the prosecutors to continue to pursue Chapin. Dwight had committed no crime in his role with Segretti. Although his association was not criminal, the prosecutors kept pressing him for more and more information about Segretti's activities. Dwight was most worried about revealing Bob Haldeman's approval of the program, not to mention the extent of his own knowledge of what Segretti had been up to. As the prosecutors pressed, Dwight made some serious errors. He pretended not to remember, when, in fact, he did. He, like Haldeman and Nixon, believed you could not be guilty of perjury if you said, "I don't recall." He was wrong.

When he returned from the grand jury to the White House, he sought out Dick Moore. He realized that he'd made a mistake, that he'd played a dangerous game with the prosecutors in saying he could not recall. He felt he should call them and recant his statement. Moore agreed. The call was placed, and the prosecutors, Earl Silbert, Seymour Glanzer, and Donald Campbell, were delicately approached on the matter. But it was for naught. They had Chapin, and they knew it. He was now indictable and, in fact, soon was indicted. I wondered how Redford's movie would portray all this.

AUGUST 15, 1975—Los Angeles.

Robert Redford and Dustin Hoffman will make Bob and Carl living legends. They're entitled to great credit, but how accurately will their roles be portrayed? The movie's impact should be major, and anyone who happened to miss what "Woodstein" and *The Washington Post* did during Watergate will, I suspect, have one hell of a vision. The public already believes that *The Washington Post* uncovered Watergate almost single-handedly. They didn't. But who am I to say so?

Today I discovered that someone has finally done the necessary work to right this popular misperception. The observations of Harvard and MIT political science professor Edward Jay Epstein, soon to be part of a book, arrived yesterday in the mail.

Professor Epstein has surveyed the Watergate horizon dispassionately, and, in his book, *Between Fact and Fiction: The Problem of Journalism*, he argues that the press did not uncover Watergate. He shows how it was not the work of enterprising reporters who pierced the veil that shrouded the misdeeds of the Nixon presidency. Rather, it was the government's investigation of itself. First the prosecutors, and then the congressional investigators, unraveled the tangled knot of interrelated events, plots, and cover-ups. And then, those with information leaked it to the media.

Epstein credits Carl and Bob with their work on uncovering the Segretti operation. But he feels that they were "diverted to the trail" of Segretti, and that they mistakenly assumed "that this was

all an integral part of Watergate." Epstein makes a special note of
this diversion and suggests: "The behavior of the officials who
steered Bernstein and Woodward onto this circuitous course makes
in itself a revealing case study." The main "official," as the professor notes, was "Deep Throat."

But Epstein finds "perhaps the most perplexing mystery in
Bernstein and Woodward's book is why they fail to understand the
role of the institutions and investigators who were supplying them
and other reporters with leaks."

I doubt if the movie will add much to the understanding of
this role. This is all the more reason to pursue Deep Throat, whose
motives and actions might show the connections among various institutions of government.

Shortly after my peek at movie making, a true introduction to
the people who run the industry that dominates the city where we
live came via an invitation to Hugh Hefner's Playboy Mansion West.
I was surprised when we were invited by Hefner to a party, but delighted, as most men would be.

The day after the party, I described the place to my mother:
"It's a beautiful old Victorian-style mansion, with high-ceilinged
rooms, great marble-floored halls, all surrounded by rolling lawns
and immaculate gardens." Which is not quite the way I described it
to an old friend: "I'll tell you, Fred, I've never seen so much nice-
looking stuff per square inch in my entire life"—and I wasn't describing furniture.

Hef's Place, as the regular visitors call it, is a modern man's
fantasy castle, which the founder-publisher-editor of *Playboy* has
made a reality and shares with his friends—and the friends are
many. Not since F. Scott Fitzgerald's imagination created *The Great
Gatsby*, with his lavish parties, has any host entertained so consistently with such extraordinary style.

Hefner invites a remarkable flow of intellectually stimulating
people who stop by to mingle with the constant supply of beautiful
people, and it is a great mix. From the small gatherings on Sunday
nights for a screening of a newly released movie, to the huge bashes
that are thrown periodically in flawlessly decorated tents covering
"acres" of lawn, the Mansion parties are a nice place to meet people.
Mo and I found ourselves meeting many, and, in doing so, noticed an
interesting phenomenon.

The process of getting acquainted, among so many so-called celebrities, had never been easier. You know them, they know you, you all know what it's like to be a public person. Instantly you have a common bond. You feel safe, and realize that they do too, since being a public person means losing a degree of privacy. You instinctively know, as they do, what to talk about. There is none of that "what do you do" conversation, so together you can leap right into real conversation. Everyone understands that being a public person doesn't make you any different from anyone else. Certainly, they are not intimidated by talking to you, nor you by them. The situation was entirely comfortable and led to many new friendships for both Mo and myself.

Hef's Place, and the ease and pleasure with which we met new people, made me more interested in exploring the world we lived in called Beverly Hills. I was still at work on *Blind Ambition*, but my work was becoming increasingly difficult. I would tinker with what I was writing during the day, and, rather than relive more of the past by night, I felt it was healthy to get out and experience the here and now, start putting distance between past and present.

While working on *Blind Ambition*, I wondered if and when I would feel what I had expected eventually would come: the catharsis. That expunging of guilt, that discharge of pent-up emotions, that cleansing of spirit by transferring my life to paper had not yet happened. I had written enough to suspect that it never would. What had been achieved, however, was perspective. Reducing yourself to paper gives you a picture of yourself that is in far sharper focus than all those thoughts about your life that rumble loosely in your head.

Seeing myself on paper made me realize that, in many ways, I had not changed. Yet I wanted to change, particularly to break the old habit of working all the time instead of playing from time to time. The White House workaholic was pictured clearly on the pages of *Blind Ambition*.

In my effort to change, Mo and I became new riders on the cocktail-and-dinner circuit in Beverly Hills. The Deans were fresh blood, different types, something unique for a hostess to mix and match. I could talk politics and government with an intimacy and authority that could hush a room. The people in the movie business are very interested in politics, but only for a while. They are most interested in the movie business, so I never had to perform very long for our dinners. Actually, I did far more listening than talking. Then I began asking questions about the business of making movies and television shows and records.

New friendships were developing with people in this entertainment mecca and, recognizing my lack of knowledge about what was going on, who was the head of this studio or that one (since they play musical chairs with each other's jobs), or who was about to star in what upcoming thirty-million-dollar project, I decided to subscribe to "the trades." I began reading *Daily Variety* and *The Hollywood Reporter* each day, as I had once studied *The New York Times* and *The Washington Post*. A new education had begun.

DECEMBER 30, 1975—Los Angeles.

Our recent social whirl has made me feel a bit more reassured. No one cares about the fact that I have been in prison. My concerns about this social stigma may have been an overreaction, just as now my lingering uneasiness about how people view my role in Watergate may be overwrought.

The people I meet fall into two categories: those who "thank" me for my testimony, which is certainly pleasant; and those who say nothing at all. It is the latter group that I wonder about.

I would prefer to have people say, "Oh, you're the bastard who blew the whistle on Nixon," or something worse, rather than invoke a mysterious silence. Silence is the food of paranoia. It causes me to wonder whether these people have any feelings about Watergate. Are they so shocked and appalled to find me in their midst that they are speechless? Are they being polite and trying not to embarrass me with old memories?

In the course of an evening I can often become comfortable with these silent ones. If they engage in pleasant conversation, I assume they are merely being polite in not raising Watergate. If they avoid me during the evening as if I were an escapee from a leper colony, I decide in my mind that what they are saying across the crowded room is not very nice. Even paranoids have enemies.

There is a positive aspect to my situation, however. I have absolutely nothing to hide. The worst mistakes and misdeeds of my life have been made public, and even a few sordid skeletons were invented to put in my closet. My childhood, prep school and college days, my personal life, my finances and tax returns—anything and everything I have ever done has been examined by government investigators and news reporters. I am a man with no hidden past left to reveal, and without a worry that someone will stumble upon something that I would prefer remain unknown.

The chance to meet with the people who populate the movie industry has been a useful opportunity for a man who is uncertain about what he could and should do with the rest of his life. Actually, it is impossible for me not to note, and draw comparisons between, this newfound world and my old one.

Surprisingly, there are more similarities between Washington and Beverly Hills than there are differences. Most striking is that both are one-industry towns, both are very social, and both are filled with public figures. Also, both cities are melting pots, drawing people from the rest of the country—to Beverly Hills for stardom and money, and to Washington for public service and power. The turnover rate is high in both, and transients form the core, but there are always the "old" crowds and the "new" ones.

It was difficult for me to tell if I was getting away from Watergate and old memories by going out, meeting new people, and talking more than government and politics. This change of pace in socializing three or four times a week was, I hoped, giving me some perspective on writing *Blind Ambition*. Yet I wasn't sure, so I typed up a little reminder and scotch-taped it to my typewriter. It was a quote attributed to Ernest Hemingway, and one I thought appropriate for an autobiographer who wanted to avoid writing an "alibiography": "The most essential gift for a good writer is a built-in, shock-proof shit detector."

On an afternoon in late January 1976, I was reading through a stack of material that I had been working on with my "detector." I had red-penciled vast amounts, and was feeling very uncertain about what I should or should not include in *Blind Ambition*, when I was interrupted by the telephone. A vaguely familiar voice asked: "Is this John Dean?" I confirmed and the caller continued, "Forgive me for bothering you, this is Marlon Brando."

Sure it is, I thought. Someone was pulling my leg and I was about to call his bluff with a "Bullshit, there is no Marlon Brando. He's been captured by the Indians." But then the caller explained: "I hope you'll excuse the liberty of my calling. I got your unlisted number from my agent, who knows you." It was Marlon Brando's voice, unmistakably.

I assured him, "There's no problem."

"Say, John," he said in a whispered voice right out of "On the Waterfront," "would it be possible for us to get together sometime soon? I'd like to talk with you about something."

"Sure, when would you like to get together?" I was very curious to know what he wanted to talk with me about.

"How about now?"

Twenty minutes later, a four-wheel-drive Jeep was rolling up our driveway, and Marlon Brando jumped out, after struggling for a moment with his seatbelt.

"These damn belts saved my life once. I always wear them, even though they're a bit tight right now."

As we shook hands and I invited him up to my office, I realized it had probably been about three years since I'd seen Brando in "Last Tango in Paris." Walking behind me up the steps to the office, he volunteered, "I've put on this weight, John, since I quit smoking. I guess you noticed."

"You're smart, the weight is easier to control than the cigarettes, so that's terrific you've licked them. You can always get the weight off."

"Yeah, I guess that's right," Brando mumbled.

The mystery of his call was resolved quickly when he explained that he was considering producing a movie about the Indians at Wounded Knee. Back in 1973, the American Indian Movement occupied the trading post and church at the site of the 1890 massacre of the Sioux Indians by the U.S. Army cavalry. The takeover of Wounded Knee was to draw attention to grievances of today's American Indians, but the government almost had a second massacre on its hands.

When the Indians refused to leave, the troops were brought in, this time the U.S. marshals (and FBI agents). Soon shots were being traded between the marshals and the Indians, then it very nearly erupted into a mini-war, with some thousands of rounds of ammunition, armored cars, and even two Phantom jets buzzing the little village. The 250 Indians were again outnumbered, and after seventy days, gave up. Brando was still annoyed at the heavy hand of the government, which seemed totally uncalled-for, and he wanted to learn more about who had been giving the orders.

At the time of Wounded Knee, Watergate was busting at the seams. I knew little of what had happened, other than remembering a few of the people at the White House who were consulting with the Justice Department about the problem. I told Brando what I knew, and suggested whom he might talk with, including John Ehrlichman. But Marlon was way ahead of me.

"I visited with John Ehrlichman, down in New Mexico," Brando observed as he puckered his lips, unconsciously imitating John Ehrlichman.

"Oh!"

"Ehrlichman seems like a fairly decent fellow. I liked him. Is he okay?" He asked the question as if we were old friends and he wanted my feelings about my former colleague.

"John's a decent guy. No doubt about it. He's bright, charming, and I understand that he sees his life very differently today than he did in the old days at the White House."

"I got that impression, too," Brando added. It was uncanny; like a theatrical chameleon, Brando had assumed Ehrlichman's tone of voice, his mannerisms, right down to the peculiar arching of the eyebrows when Ehrlichman looked over his glasses. Brando had taken on Ehrlichman's personality!

I soon discovered, as our conversation proceeded, that whomever we were talking about, Brando subtly assumed that personality, from Nixon to Kissinger, and a very easy slide from Kissinger into Nietzsche. The conversation drifted from Indians and began leaping time and geography. At one moment we'd find ourselves talking about how Jews had influenced his life in acting, and next we were discussing the real basis of power in America.

Had darkness not told us of the passing of time, we might have gone on for hours more. But, with darkness, we were into books. I asked him if he had read *Escape from Evil*, by Ernest Becker.

"Should I?" he queried.

"It might be worth your time. I just discovered the book when browsing the other day. Bookstores and hardware stores are the two stores that are important in life to me. I found the Becker book and finished it yesterday. I'd like you to read it."

The book was down by my bedside, in the house, so I suggested we go visit with Mo for a few minutes and I'd get the book.

Often I find that giving someone a book makes an important statement much better than I can in conversation. *Escape from Evil* makes such a statement. The author, Ernest Becker, has distilled with dazzling synthesis much philosophy about the nature of human-kind, and he makes a very strong case that the roots of man's evil are found in an innate and all-encompassing fear of death that plagues each of us. From anthropology to existential philosophy, from psy-chology to contemporary history, Becker marshalls evidence that our efforts to transcend death produce our evil actions. As despairing as this might sound, I hoped that Brando might discover what I had in this extraordinary book, and feel the encouragement of understand-ing Becker has given to humankind's darker impulses and drives.

After we had had a glass of wine and some conversation with Mo, Marlon clutched *Escape from Evil* in hand and headed for home. It had been an unusual day, a delightful surprise for me.

"John, I've got a book I'd like to share with you, too," he said, just before climbing back into his Jeep. And three days later, when he arrived for some of Mo's beef stew—the best in Beverly Hills—he brought with him a copy of *The Gentle Tasaday*, by John Nance.

Just as I was making a statement with the Becker book, so did Brando with his. The Tasaday are a very small group of primitive people who were discovered living in the rain forests of the Philip-pine Islands in 1971, and John Nance's book recounts the discovery of these gentle and loving people. The book tells of the great effort to protect and preserve these people, to leave intact their native ways, to save them from both the well-intentioned and the curious, and to permit them to live as they have for centuries before being dis-covered. Marlon could only hope, I assume, that our government might be as thoughtful of the American Indian.

The Gentle Tasaday also shows that there is hard evidence that man is not, by his very nature, evil. Here were a people that had no hate, no need for weapons of war; in fact, not even a word in their language for "enemy" or "war." Here were men, women, and chil-dren who still lived in caves, but had advanced beyond any other society, in peace with one another and in balance with nature. If, perchance, these are relics of our common caveman ancestors who have made it into the twentieth century untouched by what is called civilization, then it is civilization, and not human nature, that needs examination.

I find it more enjoyable to read books than to write them. And my writing problems were greatly relieved with a trip back to New York and a visit with David Obst, and then my editor, Alice Mayhew. She was happy with what I had done, but not fully satisfied. Alice said she understood my quandary over how much or little of some things to include, which was the basic dilemma I was having with *Blind Ambition*. She approved a plan I had developed with Obst to get editorial assistance from journalist and writer Taylor Branch. With Taylor's help, I was sure I could finish *Blind Ambition* in a short time.

Taylor soon arrived at Los Angeles International Airport, sporting a handsome red beard which gave an impressive maturity to his youthful and freckled face. Before assisting him in finding a suitable hotel accommodation, I suggested he drop by our house to meet Mo. It resolved his hotel search, for both Mo and I formed an instant fondness for him, and his Georgia gentleman's charm, quick wit, and sensitive manner.

Taylor was a delight to be around, and Mo insisted he stay at our home in the guest bedroom. I don't think Taylor was in our house more than nine hours when those final barriers which separate strangers were shattered and all hell broke loose. Thus began what can only be described as a work festival—with a lot of fun thrown in.

Each day Taylor and I managed a hefty output of work. Taylor studied my draft chapters, prepared questions, and then asked me to fill in information he felt was important. At first I felt uncomfortable, but I soon realized I was talking to a friend who was genuinely curious to hear my story.

Quickly, I loosened up, for Taylor would howl with laughter as I would tell him one anecdote after another. One evening, I was trying to remember some facts Taylor felt should be added to a chapter, but they weren't coming back with ease. Taylor said, "Hey, try this." He reached into his shirt pocket and brought out a marijuana cigarette.

"You've got to be kidding! Me? A joint?"

"Try it, you may like it," he intoned in a sing-song manner with a great smile across his face.

"Why not?" I thought. I took a hit and waited for the flashes. There was nothing. I tried another puff. Still nothing, although it was sure rough on the windpipe. Finally, I took a huge drag and waited. I still felt virtually nothing. Or, that is what I thought. In a few minutes I was back at my typewriter, producing what I thought was coherent prose. Here is what came out:

UNDATED —

I know now that Watergate was really the nasal spray of the American presidency—it cleaned all the dirty boogers out. But that's unimportant, for I must report faithfully my first encounter with the famed cannabis bush, and say that the flowers of fantasy, the willows of wisdom, the herbs of insight—well, it flopped for me! Too much control!!!!

(AUTHOR'S NOTE: *Next, there appear in this journal entry several undecipherable sentences that have been obliterated by a series of "xxxxx's." The discernible text picks up as follows.*)

The toaster far exceeds the waffle iron for raw ingenuity, and could be ranked with the wheel and safety pin on mankind's achievement scorecard. (*Again, the entry is unreadable and, when I first noticed the next morning what I had done, I wondered how so many non-word words had made it to the paper. On analysis, I realized that my fingers had been on the wrong keys and I clearly had paid no attention to what was ending up on the paper. Obviously, the joint had bent my mind more than I had thought at the time.*)

From the typewriter, I do recall, I soon moved to the refrigerator, where I devoured half a can of chocolate sauce that was richer than Howard Hughes. Within two hours of my token tokings, I was fast asleep on the sofa. This was my first, and last, experience with the devil weed. It makes me too hungry, and too sleepy, to be my drug of choice. I prefer Scotch, thank you.

A few evenings later, I found myself on a trip of a far different nature. I was invited to the Directors' Guild theater to see a screening of "All the President's Men." I slipped into the Sunset Boulevard theater unnoticed by the pack of paparazzi in the lobby looking for

Hollywood luminaries, and I wasn't comfortable until the lights were dimmed.

Although I had lived the other side of the story, I enjoyed the movie. It was good drama, but terrible history. In truth, it had little to do with what actually had happened in those days past in Washington, yet it did sketch in broad outlines the story of Watergate. It was mostly fiction, blended and confused with facts.

I left the theater, as the credits for the movie were rolling, relieved—relieved that not once had my name so much as been mentioned in the movie, although I had played a prominent role throughout the latter chapters of the book, *All the President's Men.* I was curious about this conspicuous omission (and have never been able to get an answer from Woodward, Bernstein, or the screenwriter, William Goldman).

The movie also stirred my curiosity, as it did almost everyone's, about the identity of Deep Throat. For several days I found myself replaying one scene over and over. It was the scene in which Deep Throat was first mentioned in the movie, and it differed in its dramatic presentation considerably from the book.

In the book Woodward's first contact with Deep Throat is referred to merely as his calling an old friend for some information about what happened in the early stages of the Watergate investigation. But, in the movie, Woodward's first contact with Deep Throat is a very dramatic little scene. The scene opens in the newsroom, the one that Mo and I had visited at The Burbank Studios with Redford and Hoffman. Woodward (Redford) and Bernstein (Hoffman) have just been chewed out by their *Washington Post* editor, Ben Bradlee (Jason Robards), about one of their early Watergate stories. Bradlee won't accept their story and tells them, "Get some higher information next time!"

Woodward decides to do just that, and suddenly we see him on the street in Washington at dusk. Actually, it appears that the scene was shot across from the Executive Office Building on the corner of 18th and Pennsylvania Avenues, where there suddenly appeared a phone booth. In reality, there's no such phone booth and, in fact, this is more than a mile from the office of *The Washington Post*, which would have made a very long walk.

Then there is a close-up on the phone booth. The dime is dropped by Woodward. Seven dials with his finger. A voice answers, "Yes?"

"This is Woodward," he says flatly.

Silence on the telephone.

Woodward continues, "I want to talk to you about Watergate. I know . . . ." He's interrupted by Deep Throat.

"I'm not going to talk about that subject," a mysterious voice says adamantly.

"But we talked about Wallace," Woodward pleads.

"But this is different."

Woodward pushes a little harder. "That was about the shooting of a man running for president!"

"But this is different."

"How?"

"Not about this story. Don't call me again."

Woodward does call again and eventually makes face-to-face contact. A very dramatic vision of Deep Throat emerges in the movie, an image I kept visualizing: the shadowy face (played by Hal Holbrook) who meets Woodward in an underground garage in eerie shadows of fluorescent lights somewhere in Washington.

It was this mental image, plus the latest revelations from Woodward's and Bernstein's second book, *The Final Days*, that caused me to raise the subject with Taylor Branch.

"Do you think I should uncover Deep Throat's identity?" I asked Taylor.

Taylor nearly dropped his beard and, when he closed his mouth enough to speak, he remarked, "Are you serious?" His eyes blinked with the excitement of a child on Christmas morning.

"Well, I've got some thoughts about how we could smoke him out, but it would delay the book a couple of months."

As we talked it over, I realized I couldn't do what I wanted to do in the remaining time. Alice Mayhew, my editor at Simon & Schuster, was coming from New York for a last session on the manuscript. Alice wanted to take back the final draft with her.

Maybe I would divulge to Taylor the name of one of the prime candidates. This was a tip I had gleaned from a conversation with former White House colleagues who had survived Watergate and who had remained at the White House through the final Nixon days and on into the Ford presidency.

Several White House insiders felt they had solid information that narrowed the Throat down to Woodward's Yale classmate David Gergen, who had worked as a speechwriter at the Nixon White House. I decided to give my insider's tip to Taylor, who was delighted, for, according to journalistic rumor, Deep Throat "on the hoof" was worth ten million dollars. All I asked of Taylor was that he keep me posted on his investigation.

During the six weeks that Taylor was with us in California, we had totally edited the manuscript. Alice arrived from New York and returned with almost all of the manuscript in hand. All that remained to be done was the editing of some journal entries that would compose the last section. But, still, I needed an ending for the book.

What I really need, I thought, as I looked at my copy of the nearly completed manuscript, which was stacked almost a foot high at the upper left corner of my desk, is a transition from the past to the present, from the there and then of Watergate to the here and now.

As I sat chewing on the stem of my eyeglasses as if they were licorice, my thoughts were interrupted by the buzzer on the telephone intercom from the house. It was Mo, who had been showering when I'd bolted down my breakfast cereal and hurried on up to my office over the garage. We had talked the preceding evening about her giving me some help in tidying up the office.

"Can you use a good filing clerk up there now?"

My desk was cluttered with papers and files, and strewn with broken pencils and empty soft-drink cans. Truly, the entire office was in such post-cyclone chaos there wasn't a chair or sofa to sit on, because they were filled with books, magazines, newspaper clippings, and mail.

"Thanks, dear," I said, looking at the situation, "maybe in a little while, but first I want to think about how to end the book."

"Thought you worked that out last week."

"I did, but this morning I woke up with second thoughts. The reason I think they agreed that my story began when I went to the

Nixon White House and ended with my release from prison, sort of the truth and consequences of my ambition, as Alice put it, was that the last journal entry I let them read was my last day in prison. I don't think that gives any idea of where I am today, and I need a transition up to the present."

"They don't have to read your journal," Mo interrupted. "All they have to do is go up to your office to see that you've become a human hamster. I thought you were up there cleaning up that mess."

"Not yet," responded the hamster. I enjoyed the mess about my office, just as I did the fact that, although it was midmorning, I hadn't bothered to shower, shave, or tuck in my shirt. To me, this was not degeneration, but a sign of regeneration. For too many years I had kept the slob in me closeted, pretending to the world to be impeccable Mr. Meticulous because I was insecure and self-conscious. I seriously believed those old bromides: "Clothes make the man," and, "A tidy office shows a tidy mind." Now it was clear to me that such thinking made good fertilizer for roses. Roses were on Mo's mind, too.

"Well, what about the roses?" she asked.

"When I finish this, I'll be happy to help plant them."

"When do you suppose that will be?"

"Probably tomorrow, okay?"

"John, I think you'd better think about the roses, too, when you're through reading your journal."

"What do you mean?"

"You once told *Time* magazine that when Watergate was over you planned to spend a lot of time smelling the flowers. Well, we didn't have any flowers when you worked at the White House, and we still don't have any flowers. Think about it."

I did think about it. Mo had a point. I thought that I had changed a lot since my days at the White House. Watergate had been an incredibly maturing experience. I had reexamined my values and priorities in life and felt I had decided what was important. I had tried to look at my mistakes honestly and learn from them. But Mo's remark gave me a nagging feeling that maybe I hadn't changed as much as I'd thought.

In my search for an ending, I began plowing through files and reports, and I set aside information that I believed I should look at.

Soon I had a collection that included the report of the Senate Watergate committee, a report from the Rockefeller commission that had studied intelligence activities, the House impeachment report, and a stack of recommendations for changes in government as a result of Watergate. Then I flicked through old copies of the *Congressional Quarterly* and placed paper clips on recommendations for legislative changes. To this I added various newspaper clippings from my files, suggesting other reforms, until I had a voluminous stack.

While I was studying the recommended reforms I received a call from David Obst. "Now that you've finished your book," David said, "how would you like to write a movie?"

"What do you have in mind, 'The Blind Ambition Story'?" I chuckled.

"Not your movie, but a movie you'd write. I was talking with this friend of mine, Howard Rosenman, who's a hot young producer. I told him that you could write a great movie about what would have happened if Nixon hadn't been caught, if there'd never been a Watergate. What do you think? Brilliant idea, huh?"

"I'm not sure I know what would have happened," I began, when David cut back in.

"Sure you do, or you could figure it out, and, anyway, it's fiction. So I've told Howard to give you a call, but it will be a couple of months, since he's working on another project. That'll give you some time to think about it. So start thinking, kid."

I had a lot of other things to finish thinking about first, like what had in fact happened, and in front of me were about 150,000 words of it, with a long list of reforms that were being urged because it all had happened. David had pulled my thoughts away from the task at hand. I paced about the office, thinking about his call. Then I looked out the office window and saw Mo weeding the flower bed to make it ready for roses. I paused and looked at my disheveled self in the mirror on the armoire where I stored office supplies. I looked around my office at the mess, and then I looked again at the lengthy reforms list in my hand. It hit me. I was different. The government was different.

"Everything is different now." I typed it on a sheet of paper, and put it on the bottom of the manuscript. Then to make it a reality, I went out into the sunshine to help Mo.

CHAPTER FIVE

What If

It had been a long time since the news media had bothered me with one of their "urgent" messages. That was until the doorbell rang on Tuesday evening, April 27, 1976, and Western Union delivered a message: PLEASE CALL BRIAN WELLS OR DICK SAXTY, NATIONAL ENQUIRER, COLLECT AT 305/568-1111 URGENT.

Ugh, the *Enquirer*, I thought. Then the word *urgent* caught my attention and triggered a sudden rush of unpleasant anxiety, the kind I wanted to shelve now that I had finished my book. Urgent bulletins used to come over the AP and UPI wire-service machines down the hall from my White House office, tapping out unpleasant stories with me in the middle. But this couldn't be such a story, I reasoned as I returned to the den with the telegram.

Moments earlier, I had been enjoying the Arts and Leisure section of the Sunday *New York Times* after a day of planting roses with Mo. I handed Mo the wire, as she looked up from a book.

"The *Enquirer*! What do they want?"

"Who knows," I shrugged.

"Are you going to call them?"

"I don't know." I looked at my watch. It was seven o'clock. I studied the wire again. Area code 305, I was pretty sure that was Florida. It would be ten o'clock there, but it said "urgent." Maybe they were still in the office waiting for me to respond. "What do you

99

think I should do?" I asked her, but she was gone, engrossed in her book, and didn't hear me.

Damn it, wouldn't the press ever leave me alone? I didn't like feeling those resurrected anxieties. It annoyed me that this pleasant day was being spoiled by the old jitters that had been a part of daily life during Watergate. Now here I was, the guy with nothing to worry about, no secrets, worrying.

It's dumb to sit here and stew over this for another second: deal with it, I told myself and reached for the telephone. There was no answer at the Florida number, but I felt better. At least it was not so urgent that reporters were waiting for me.

Because I had to fly east in the morning for a final editorial session and several lectures, I decided to check with friends in Washington to see if there were any stories brewing that involved me. Nobody had heard anything. "Hell, I wouldn't call them back," Taylor Branch said when I read him the wire. "You'll never win," he insisted. "They may say that they've learned that you are planning a sex-change operation in Sweden, and then they'll say that the vehemence of your denial convinced them they were right." So I dropped the matter and went on about my business.

MAY 1, 1976—Boston, Massachusetts.

It was as if David Obst had planted the question at the lecture this afternoon as a reminder of the screenplay idea he wants me to be thinking about. A student wanted to know what might have happened if Watergate had never been uncovered.

I answered with my best opinion, but I have never really given the matter very serious thought. I said that I thought there would have been another Watergate someday, and it might have been worse than the one we had, and I believe that is true.

The Watergate Special Prosecution Force Report acknowledged, to my surprise, that Watergate had historical roots which presaged abuses of institutional power—that it represented a "climax" to such trends. I had been aware of those trends even before Bill Sullivan laid them out in specifics, and in answering the question I reasoned that, if those trends had not been interrupted, they would have continued to grow, and the abuses would have been worse later.

Watergate today seems like a great disaster. But tomorrow, when historians start to look back on it, perhaps it will be seen as a blessing in disguise. Happening when it did, it might have prevented even worse things from taking place.

While I had done nothing about the *National Enquirer,* I found that they had done something more about me. As I was having a room-service meal in my Boston hotel, Mo called to warn me that Gerry Hunt of the *Enquirer* had shown up at our house, and he would be calling. "He sounded decent enough, was very polite, and said he was checking information about Richard Nixon that didn't involve you."

I trust Mo's instincts about people, and, within a short time of her call, the *Enquirer* reporter was on the line asking me, "When will you be back in Los Angeles, since I'd rather not talk on the telephone."

His maybe-our-phones-are-bugged approach reminded me of times I would rather not remember; I didn't live in a paranoid world any longer. So I told him, "I'll be back in about five days, but whatever you need to know I can answer on the telephone, now."

"Is there someplace I can meet you before you get back?"

"Not before Seattle, but. . . ."

"Where's Seattle?" That question made me realize I was talking to a foreigner, a man with a British accent.

"It's north of Los Angeles," I answered evasively. "What is it you want to meet about?"

"Well, I'd like you to look at some letters we've come across that purportedly were written by Richard Nixon. We're trying to check on their authenticity. They are handwritten and allegedly were sent by Nixon to a lady-friend. If they are real, he was having quite an affair with her."

Uncontrollably, I burst into laughter. "You have got to be kidding." Nothing seemed less likely. This reporter didn't sound very convinced either, as he was being unusually careful—"purportedly," "allegedly," "if real." The last thing I wanted to get connected with was some trumped-up story about Nixon's having an affair. So I told him I couldn't help him.

"Maybe I could call you later this week? I am going to talk with some of your old colleagues to see what they say. You might be interested in their reactions."

Clever fellow, I thought. Indeed, I wished a camera could record their reactions, for this was comically ludicrous. I gave him the telephone number where I would be in a few days, but he had barely hung up when I realized I had given him the wrong number. "Oh, well, so what," I thought. At least he had given me a good laugh.

Ever since going to prison I had disliked leaving home, and even a week of lecturing seemed long and lonely. No longer did I have the wanderlust for travel. I was happiest at home and with my wife.

Our marriage had been put to a test during Watergate, but it had been put through other tests since. With the exception of my time in prison, Mo and I had been together virtually twenty-four hours a day, every day, since my departure from the White House. No longer did I go off to the office; my office was at home. Seldom did I go out to lunch; rather, I preferred to wander into the kitchen around noon for a snack. While this obviously had to be at times a strain on Mo, I liked it. We had not just survived the proximity, we had flourished in it. So I filled my time on the road much as I had my time in prison: with books, magazines, and lots of thinking.

My lecture audiences—a more even mix of students and adults from the local community—were different from those of the year before. But the differences were subtle.

I could feel when I entered an auditorium that the collective mood of the audience was more subdued. They sat with silent anticipation now, no longer displaying the almost voyeuristic excitement that, during my previous lecture tour, had made me feel like part of a freak show. Clearly, these audiences had come to learn what they might from my visit, while I suspected the earlier audiences had come for entertainment.

From Murray State University in Kentucky to the National Council of Social Studies in Oklahoma, and from a suburban country club in Pikesville, Maryland, to colleges in Boston, Hartford, Chicago, and on to Seattle, I found the audiences had moved Watergate completely into the past as well. They did not want another episode or two of that horrifying and sometimes confusing political soap opera that had gone off the air. Rather, they were looking for perspective, understanding, and, most important, meaning.

The fact that 1976 was an election year influenced many of those who attended these lectures. Republicans Ronald Reagan and Gerald Ford were squaring off in the primary fights, and the outcome was anything but clear. The nationally unknown former governor of Georgia, Jimmy Carter, was leading all the better known Democratic opponents, like Representative Morris Udall, Senators Birch Bayh and Fred Harris, and Kennedy family in-law Sargent Shriver. Presidential politics was on people's minds and in the news.

At my lectures, this concern produced countless questions, such as: "How can we really know what the man we're voting for is all about?" (You can't.) "Are the Democrats any more politically moral than the Republicans?" (I have no way to know.) "Hasn't Ford shamed himself and the Republican party by pardoning Richard Nixon?" (Richard Nixon doesn't think so.)

There were many questions about the Nixon pardon, and much anger at Ford, so often I tried to ease the tension with a quip before explaining that I felt it grossly unfair that Nixon had been pardoned. It was abundantly clear to anyone traveling the country at this time, and meeting with people of all political persuasions, that President Gerald Ford was in deep political trouble, even with his own party, because of the pardon.

This lecture series made me realize that I had previously misjudged the public's understanding of politics and government. After touring the preceding year, I had been dismayed at the ignorance of the public. But that judgment was based on my own limited exposure to a decade of living in the politically intense city of Washington. First as a student, then as an active practitioner, I had lived and breathed politics. Why I ever assumed that others would share the same intensity of interest, I don't know.

Now that I lived nearly 3,000 miles from Washington, I understood why the people of this country might not be able to name their congressman or might not understand what GSA or the Assistant Secretary for Manpower are doing for them—or not doing for them. But they do have a visceral feel for it all.

In hundreds of private conversations and in the formal give-

and-take of lecture halls, my political antennae picked up a very clear signal: The "silent majority," the very people whom Richard Nixon had shrewdly spotted as a constituency worth cultivating, had become disenchanted with government. These people, who believe in the work ethic, who have a quiet, all-abiding pride in this country, who feel there is more right than wrong with America, were now angry with government because Richard Nixon had let them down.

In 1970, when I was working at the White House, this conservative trend had been identified for Nixon by some very able political analysts—men who had spent their lifetimes watching and analyzing political trends; men who talked daily with state, local, and national politicians taking the political pulse of the country. And Richard Nixon himself was extremely astute at such political readings of the public. The consensus of Nixon and the pros around him, a consensus I saw confirmed in some of the most expensive and sophisticated polling ever conducted, was that the country was definitely headed—before Watergate—on a conservative course. With the silent majority at the core, a new conservative majority was clearly emerging. This development had convinced Nixon and his closest political associates that the tide was rolling in favor of their way of thinking.

While I was no longer privy to such political information, or to the assessments of the professional politicians who kept tabs on it, it was apparent to me that Watergate had shattered this conservative impetus—at least temporarily. The recognition that Watergate had reversed a national trend encouraged me to turn my thoughts again to the question of what might have happened "if."

The 1976 election had offered the Republicans a chance for another landslide. After Richard Nixon's resounding victory in 1972, the political sages were already projecting that the GOP would capture Congress with ease. And who would be leading that charge, carrying the torch for the new conservative majority?

The inside word at the White House before Watergate fell apart was that Nixon was grooming John Connally. Connally's influence with Nixon increased each day of his membership in the inner circle. No other adviser—not John Mitchell, Bob Haldeman, Henry

Kissinger, John Ehrlichman, no one—carried the clout with Nixon that Connally carried.

There is little question that, had there been no scandal, John Connally might easily have become the thirty-eighth president of the United States. Not only would Nixon have been leading his bandwagon, but Connally would have had the backing of many of Nixon's political cronies and campaign pros, who shared Nixon's admiration of Connally's ability, toughness, and political savoir faire. Nixon would have been able to transfer, along with his constituency, his own team of experts to assist in the race. If the conservative trend of the public was the first casualty of Watergate, the promise of John Connally's political future was surely the second.

Another "what if " came to mind—the role that Richard Nixon had envisioned for himself, in American domestic and foreign policy, at the end of his second term. Mr. Nixon had no intention, as a former president, of fading into obscurity, or of merely writing memoirs that most people would never read. ("I hate writing books, and believe me I know what it's like," he once told me, referring to his experience in writing *Six Crises*.) Nor would this ex-president sit on the board of directors of America's giant corporations and lend them his good name. ("That's humiliating for a former president of the United States. I did that after I was vice president and it was very embarrassing," he protested.) None of these fates would be Richard Nixon's, for while still president he was actively planning how he would remain a force in politics and an influence in world affairs after he was no longer president.

The Richard Nixon Presidential Library Foundation was at the core of his future plans. The word *library* is a misnomer here, since, unlike presidents before him, Nixon had no interest in such a memorial. The Nixon library would be a working center, a power nucleus for his future, from which would emanate Richard Nixon's influence on the affairs of the world.

About the time that Watergate was pulling the Nixon presidency apart, Nixon was trying to bring together the best minds he could find to plan his future. He was exploring everything from the physical structure and location of this post-presidential center to how he could maintain his impact long after he had departed the Oval Office.

At one point I had been dispatched to California to inspect a large and particularly beautiful hillside tract near Nixon's home in San Clemente. Nixon and his pal Bebe Rebozo had taken a liking to this land, which belonged to the United States Marine Corps, and understandably so. The ocean-view acreage was worth millions.

So plans were made to have the Congress donate this valuable site to the Nixon library. The congressional-relations people were dispatched to talk it over with key members of the House and Senate Armed Services Committees. Much to Mr. Nixon's pleasure, they were amenable to the idea. The location had all but been finalized, and plans were made to move the matter quickly through the Congress, when Nixon's world began disintegrating.

What would have sat atop this prime southern California property overlooking the beautiful Pacific ocean? An impressive edifice, certainly. Back in 1971 Mr. Nixon, Bob Haldeman, John Ehrlichman, and others had been invited to Austin, Texas, for the opening of the Lyndon Baines Johnson Library, and they returned very impressed. "LBJ did it first class, and with a grand style," Bob Haldeman told me. "But we'll do it better, you just wait and see."

Nixon had refurbished the White House and Camp David—upgrading them from LBJ's "nice" appointments to "elegant" and then on to "imperial"—with the use of secret government funds from unaudited budgets and appropriations which the President could call upon. There was considerable searching for funds that might be diverted to the Nixon library. Presidential libraries, by act of Congress, receive enormous amounts. But for what Nixon had in mind, this was peanuts.

Had there been no Watergate, architectural plans and construction of the envisioned complex would have commenced during Nixon's second term. Undoubtedly, untold millions of taxpayers' dollars would have been funneled into the project, not to mention the assignment of countless government-salaried employees to work on it. In this sense, Watergate probably saved taxpayers far more than they now pay for Mr. Nixon's retirement fund and staff support.

Even the multimillions available through open and diverted government funds would not have been enough in the minds of the planners. Nixon was also having conversations about using the political fund-raising talents of Maurice Stans and Herbert Kalmbach to amass more millions for the building and operating funds of the complex. This too, it was felt, should be done while Nixon was still president since, in Haldeman's words, "He still has clout. People don't want to piss off a president; they don't give a damn about ex-presidents." There's no telling how many ambassadorships, government contracts, or other favors might have been subtly sold to fund this elaborate operation.

While it is not perfectly clear—to borrow a term—what else would have gone on inside this base of Nixon's post-presidential operations, it certainly would have housed all the documents and tapes relating to the Nixon presidency. "Lyndon Johnson grabbed every paper and file cabinet in the executive branch, and hauled it all down to Texas," Haldeman once admiringly observed to me, when instructing me to determine what was and was not Nixon's when he left the government.

The reason Nixon wanted everything he could get his hands on was because it had real value—not just historical value, but cash value. I learned this one afternoon when I received an unexpected call from Haldeman, instructing that I get right over to Henry Kissinger's office as fast as I could. "Henry's having a meeting with his personal lawyers, some sort of estate-planning session, and he feels that all his papers are his. But I want you to tell him they're not. They belong to the President." Haldeman was particularly concerned about Kissinger: "I think Henry's gotten wind of the fact that we're going to get the tax laws changed."

Consequently, I was assigned to work with other lawyers whom Nixon had asked to address the problem of how to amend the tax laws. He wanted laws passed to allow all his papers to be used for tax deductions, or for private sales to others without tax consequences. Also, he wanted others to be able to make tax deductions by donating to the Nixon library. As Nixon envisioned the scheme, an old pal like millionaire Walter Annenberg could buy Henry Kissinger's papers for several million dollars, and then donate them to the Nixon library. Annenberg would get a huge tax write-off, and Nixon or Kissinger—whoever owned them—would get several million dollars. Also, Nixon wanted this change in the law so he could put some papers in his own estate and provide an enormous legacy for his children and grandchildren. Sometime before the second term ended, there would have been a concerted effort to so amend the tax laws. Thus, Watergate literally cost Nixon millions of dollars, for, had he remained president, he probably would have succeeded with this plan, and soon after leaving would have become a multimillionaire.

Shortly after Nixon's second inauguration there were meetings of the "trustees" of the future Nixon library. After the formal meetings, the President arranged clandestine second gatherings, since Nixon didn't like some of those people he had selected for public-image purposes. This smaller group of truly trusted friends gathered around the huge table in the Roosevelt Room at the White House. Discussions proceeded on how to assure that Richard Nixon remain a man of influence after leaving office.

As I was juggling several Watergate problems at that time, I moved in and out of these discussions. But I recall bits and pieces of conversation. The talk around the table touched on matters like future meetings of world leaders at the library, signing of peace treaties at the library, controlling all the Nixon papers and controlling use of those papers by historians, the writing of books about the Nixon presidency, and requiring all White House aides and Cabinet officers to sign a contract not to publish anything without the prior approval of Nixon or his representative. Even the making of movies that could be distributed to high schools and colleges, in which the Nixon point of view could be presented, were discussed.

Whatever the future plans called for, it was clear that there would be a massive public relations operation. Taft Schreiber, a long-time Nixon supporter and a director of the entertainment conglomerate, Music Corporation of America, grew astounded toward the end of one of these meetings. Schreiber turned to me after Haldeman subtly suggested that Taft should take over many of these public relations functions, and noted, in words I thought summed up the entire matter, "I think they want me to be a good Goebbels."

As excessive as these plans for Nixon's post-presidential future now appear, they pale in comparison to the plans that were readied for his second term, plans that would have changed the operations of the presidency and entire executive branch dramatically. Richard Nixon wanted to be remembered as a strong and forceful president, and, had he accomplished the restructuring of the presidency he envisioned, the words *strong* and *forceful* might have proved to be understatements.

Nixon's reorganization plans called for a sweeping reform of the entire executive branch, essentially removing independence from lower agencies and departments and giving all policy-making power to a small group of "Counsellors to the President." The counsellors would not be accountable to Congress; they would report directly to the President and would be his handpicked, most trusted assistants. They would maintain control of the federal bureaucracy through policy decisions and funding manipulation. Ultimately, Congress itself would have to bow to the will of the President and his counsellors, as they would effectively control all of the mechanisms of executive government.

Government by this plan was thought to be vastly more effective and efficient—although purists might argue that it would also be a trifle undemocratic. Nixon's plan was nothing less than the full realization of the "imperial presidency."

Development of this plan began as early as 1970, under the direction of John Ehrlichman, with assistance from Roy Ash, the incoming budget director. The work of Ehrlichman's little task force was as tightly held a secret as the Manhattan Project. When I was informed of the executive reorganization plans, the plot had been finalized. My job was to make certain that the plans were, as Ehrlichman and the President believed, capable of being implemented without congressional approval—in short, by presidential executive order or fiat.

The government, particularly the executive branch, has never been structured according to its functions. Rather, it has grown up haphazardly into (at that time) eleven Cabinet departments and several hundred independent agencies, bureaus, commissions, and councils. There is considerable overlap of function, and an equal overlap of competition among all these government entities for power, control, and funds to deal with their interrelated functions.

While it is no secret that the government needed reorganization, the prospects of doing so were always considered dim because it usually takes an act of Congress to do it. The departments and agencies of government are all creatures of Congress, existing subject to their statutory mandates. To amend the laws creating these organi-

zations of government takes a majority of Congress that is difficult
to muster.

Congress doesn't like reorganization. The massive bureaucracy
howls if a power base is shuffled or a feather bed is ruffled—and the
bureaucracy has many friends in Congress. Indeed, on occasion, the
power-base bureaucracy, with its congressional influence, can have
the positive effect of tempering rash or ill-considered White House
directives.

Needless to say, congressmen are also very reluctant to give up
any power of their own, since this is the source of their importance in
Washington, their ability to generate publicity, and, ultimately, it is
the basis of their reelectability back home. A reorganization plan
ultimately costs some members of Congress part or all of their power
and jurisdiction over departments and agencies.

But, the Nixon reorganization plan did not need congressional
approval because it did not disrupt a single department or agency in
a technical sense. Under the plan, all agencies and departments
would remain intact, but there would be four super-Cabinet officers
who also would be regular Cabinet officers, the so-called Counsellors
to the President. There would be a counsellor for each major function area of government: economic affairs, human resources, natural
resources, and community development. These four counsellors, with
their direct access to the President, would have authority over all the
Cabinet officers or agency heads whose functions fell within their
area of concern.

There would also be a "Counsellor for Foreign Affairs," Henry
Kissinger, who through the National Security Council would coordi-
nate the activities of the State and Defense Departments. John
Ehrlichman would be a counsellor, who would dissolve his Domestic
Council and take over the unused office of Inter-Governmental Relations, as a vehicle to provide mayors, governors, and state legislators
a new and direct line to the President.

Countless people who worked at the Nixon White House during
the first term were being placed in key positions and powerful jobs
throughout the executive branch: Egil (Bud) Krogh, Jr., was made
the Undersecretary of Transportation; Edward L. Morgan, from
Ehrlichman's staff, was Assistant Secretary of the Treasury; Gordon
Strachan, who had worked for Bob Haldeman, was appointed the

General Counsel of the United States Information Agency. It is not farfetched to believe that G. Gordon Liddy might have ended up somewhere atop, or even heading, the FBI, and E. Howard Hunt at the CIA, had there been no Watergate.

To make certain that the departments and agencies did not rebel against the control and direction of the super-Cabinet, Nixon commenced a house cleaning, calling for the resignation of every presidential appointee the day after the 1972 election. Anyone and everyone who was unloyal or unwilling to swear their fealty to the White House was out. In their place would be the loyalists.

There is a strong case to be made for streamlined reorganization of some sort, but not necessarily the Nixon plan, which, as everything else, was excessive. Few members of the public, and even fewer members of the Washington press corps, appreciate that the real agony of the presidency is not merely that of weighty decision making; it is the added agony of the daily struggle with federal bureaucracies that frustrates every president. No matter what presidential directives are issued, they must be implemented through a maze of civil service employees, all of whom have unshakable job security. Presidential efforts become stalled by ineptitude, ignorance, disagreement, or, sometimes, outright sabotage.

Sooner or later a president realizes that even his Cabinet and sub-Cabinet have been captured by that bureaucracy, since all top officials, including Cabinet officers, must rely on the bureaucracy to get anything done within a department or agency. Because they develop a close working relationship with the men and women of the bureaucracy, they soon start thinking more like the bureacrats than the White House.

To deal with this situation, a president has to rely more and more on his White House staff to shape policy and ram it through to implementation. To accomplish this, the staff must grow bigger and more complex, and soon the White House itself is handling the daily operations of government. These problems of the resistance of the bureaucracy and inability to implement policy were not new to the Nixon presidency. It is the nature of the system and almost inevitable for any president who wants to do more than be a caretaker.

In the abstract, Nixon's executive reorganization plan appeared harmless. In fact, some of the lawyers from the Department of Justice and a former law school professor of mine from Georgetown, whom I recruited to work on the legalities of implementing the plan—and these were all individuals who were absolutely above reproach, several of whom were not even Nixon admirers—felt the plan was incredibly sound and necessary.

They did not, however, as I did not at the time, fully understand how the plan was keyed to placing spies and White House loyalists throughout the government to make sure that the President's wishes were carried out. The bureaucracy would be kept in line by an aggressive firing policy. Although the totality of the bureaucracy could not be replaced, selected members could be removed, so the stick and the carrot would be out for twelve to eighteen months to get them into shape.

The awesomeness of this reorganization plan, which could have changed profoundly and forever the very nature of the presidency, was brought to my attention by Rupert Wendell, a friend who once taught political science. After describing the plan to this very conservative Republican, who still believes in Richard Nixon, his face turned white. "My God," he exclaimed, "what you have just described is how the Soviets govern through the politburo. It sounds as though Nixon and Brezhnev have talked about more than détente. John, the whole plan is frightening," said a man who is not easily frightened.

If there had been no Watergate, this reorganization would have been accomplished, for it was already being implemented at the time that Watergate caused it to be abandoned. In fact, many congressional observers feel that one of the reasons for the intensity of the Senate Watergate investigation was a reaction to the Nixon reorganization plan. They say that this gave a certain added animosity and inclination to investigate Watergate and to force Nixon from office.

When I arrived at my motel room in Seattle, the telephone was already ringing. It was a most unexpected caller.

"Mr. Dean, Gerry Hunt of the *Enqirer* here. I'm right down the hall from you. Could we get together?"

An hour later a stocky, sandy-haired Britisher was standing at my door. His expression reminded me of a sweet-faced basset I once owned, who ate a neighbor's cat and arrived home with a satisfied, but uneasy, look.

"Gerry, anything I have to say is for background only, and I don't want to be quoted on anything." Not being very comfortable about a meeting with the *Enquirer*, I wanted to establish some rules. I didn't want to be the person to identify these love letters, should they be real.

"I understand, and I assure you that will be the case. You can look at any notes I make," he said, gesturing to the small spiral notebook he had opened. "And I'm not recording this conversation," he assured me, correctly thinking I suspected a hidden recorder.

"Gerry, let me ask you this." I was up and walking about, still feeling unsettled. "If the letters are real, and you publish them, don't you think that'll cause an awful lot of hurt to the Nixon family?"

He didn't have a ready answer, so after a moment's pause, he gave me an honest one. "Yes, I guess they would be hurt, if they're real. That's precisely what we're trying to find out."

Obviously, Gerry Hunt's role was to investigate and he had nothing to say about whether the letters would or should be published. I wondered if my qualms revealed some latent sympathy for Nixon and his family, or if I was concerned about my potential involvement in authenticating the letters. I sat down and began reading the letters he had brought with him (of the eighteen he said the *Enquirer* knew existed).

The handwriting looked a little like Nixon's. The first letter he gave me was dated "10/15."

"What year is this?" I asked.

"October 15, 1973, we believe. The letters you have are not in any order. That's one of the few that's dated."

I deciphered the writing slowly, occasionally requesting his assistance with the particularly illegible passages. While reading, I said nothing about the content of the letters, but I was dumbfounded by their sexual bluntness.

"No way," I said, shaking my head. This was smut, and Richard Nixon had more class.

While I had not seen a sample of Nixon's handwriting in some time, I continued to be struck by what did look like Nixon's writing, or a decent forgery of it. The writing was as inconsistent as the content of the letters, so I finally asked, "Have you had handwriting experts look at these?"

"Yes, but we've only given them a small bit of the letters, only samples for testing. They can't say definitely if it's his writing or not. You're the first person we've let read the letters. But you say, 'no way.' What would you say if Nixon had been drinking?"

"Listen, Gerry, this whole situation makes me very uneasy. My first reaction is that they couldn't have been written by Nixon. There are parts that sound like him, and others that don't. I suppose if a person were drinking, it would explain the difference."

"So what's your reaction, overall?"

"If these are Nixon's letters, they certainly humanize the man. If they're a fraud, whoever did them has been studying him closely for some time or knew him pretty well. I frankly can't tell you whether these are his letters or not. But if I had to place a bet, I'd say they're bogus. Gerry, where did you ever get these letters?"

"We got them from a literary agent in New York, one of the biggest," he added with emphasis.

"Who, might I ask?"

"I can't say," he answered.

I tried to think of a "big" agent who would handle something like this. Who was handling the Judith Campbell Exner book about her affair with John Kennedy? Scott Meredith. When I guessed, Gerry Hunt admitted it was indeed Meredith who was trying to sell the so-called Nixon letters. With this admission, he went on to tell me a bizarre tale of how Meredith had come by the letters—a tale more bizarre than the letters themselves.

Allegedly, Nixon had made an arrangement for a courier to deliver the letters to his lady-friend, who lived in Spain—a contessa, no less. The courier, a fellow named Charles Delane Bruce, lived just outside Washington, D.C., in suburban Maryland. Somehow the courier discovered whose letters he was carrying and their content. When he felt that Nixon's presidency was in trouble, he began making copies of them and later gave the copies to a girlfriend who lived in Alabama. (Hunt would not disclose her name, nor the names of any others involved.)

The courier, Charles Bruce, apparently was killed in an auto accident, and his Alabama girlfriend gave the letters to a California businessman she knew. The California businessman gave them to his twenty-six-year-old son, who had approached Scott Meredith by writing a letter instructing Meredith, if he was interested in the letters, to run an ad in the *Los Angeles Times* classifieds, saying, RICHARD COME HOME, and giving a number to call. Meredith did just that.

After Meredith got the letters, he had several handwriting experts check them, and the experts said they were Nixon's, but couldn't be one hundred percent positive. He then offered them to the *Enquirer*, whose interest was subject to establishing their authenticity. Complex, but simple. However, I hadn't heard anything yet.

"What do you know about this courier?" I asked.

"Well, he lived in Rockville, Maryland. We've checked him out as best we could. Actually, he wasn't killed in an automobile accident. He was murdered."

"What?"

"Right. We found out the man was homosexual, and we've checked with the local police about his comings and goings, but I really don't have all the facts. One of the other fellows on the story is working on those details."

"You mean he was bisexual. You said he gave the letters to his girlfriend," I added.

"That's right, I guess that's true. But she denies it. We've talked to her and she says she never touched the letters. But we're sure she's lying."

"Why are you sure?"

"Well, I'll be honest with you. After we talked to her, we pulled her phone records. Those records show she called her businessman-friend in California. So we tracked him down from numbers on her telephone bill, and we're going to confront him in the next few days."

I had heard other investigative reporters talk about obtaining telephone records as other people talk of taking books from the public library. Apparently it is standard practice.

"Why didn't you just ask the literary agent (Meredith) for all this information, and whom he was representing?" I asked, since that would have been a simple way.

"We did, but he wouldn't tell us. Apparently his client is getting cold feet now."

"I can understand that."

"We've really not been able to establish how the courier even got the letters. In fact, we almost dropped the story after investigating him. We went over the police reports on his murder, and there's nothing to indicate he was a government courier. As best we can tell, he didn't even have a passport. We talked to his parents, who live in Alabama. They never heard him mention he'd ever been out of the country."

"Did you say that he was a diplomatic courier?"

"That's what we were told, that he was some kind of government courier."

"It doesn't sound right to me. I doubt if an official courier would know what he was carrying, particularly if they were letters from a president to his secret lover. I don't think couriers know what's in their pouches. It just doesn't fit."

"I agree," Gerry said, making a brief note in his little notebook.

My thoughts raced ahead of my words. If these letters were real, and they had been secretly opened and copied as described, the President had subjected himself to extortion. Maybe he had been blackmailed!

If that were true, it would be an understatement to say a serious national security issue was involved. An extorted man is owned. The revelations of John Kennedy's incredible risks with Judith Campbell, given her ties to the Mafia, had first raised this issue in my mind. Presidents are different from everybody else, for their vulnerability can affect a nation's fate. But the *Enquirer* had not considered the security aspects of the letters—at least, the reporter with whom I was talking had not.

Several thoughts ran through my mind. It surprised me that people considered me an expert on Richard M. Nixon—for I was still trying to figure out who he was and what he was all about. If these were truly Nixon's letters, they showed a new side of the man, a man far more trusting of others, a man who recognized his emotional vulnerabilities. The letters portrayed a Nixon who openly admitted his mistakes with Watergate and the mess he had made of his presidency and his life. This was not the Nixon I knew. On balance, I felt the letters could not have been authored by Nixon.

Gerry Hunt had been honest with me, and I didn't feel that he would abuse the meeting we'd had. So when he invited me to join him in the motel's disco lounge for a drink, I accepted. As we chatted about politics, life in Washington, and Watergate, the talk eventually turned to Deep Throat.

"It would obviously be a hell of a story to get him," he said, shaking his head.

"Well, I hate to sound boastful, because I may be wrong. But I think he can be identified."

"Why don't you do it?"

"I haven't had the time or money. And it will take both."

"Listen, John, the *Enquirer's* got a million-dollar fund, just for that purpose. If you'd be interested, I'll talk to them."

"Thanks, but no. I've got a friend (thinking of Taylor) who's already doing some preliminary work, which just might resolve the matter very soon. We'll have to see."

"Okay, but I'd be happy to talk to my editors. Give it some thought."

The music started again, blaring louder than before. Gerry and I looked at one another, shrugged our shoulders, downed our drinks, and called it a night. Back in my room, I turned on the television. Johnny Carson's guest was a former professional robber who was telling people how to protect themselves. Interesting, I thought. This man talks about his crime, and everyone applauds his rehabilitation. I talk about mine and I'm accused of "cashing in." I turned off the television, got out my "what if " notes, propped up the pillows on the bed for a back rest, and settled in to think again about the man whose crimes had been pardoned.

Richard Nixon is the most complex man I've ever met. The many facets of his personality make him difficult to analyze. I'm not sure anyone, including Nixon himself, understands his character. Anyone who plays the amateur-psychiatrist game with him might as well be psychoanalyzing the fictional Dr. Jekyll without knowing about Mr. Hyde, because the public Nixon is but a smattering of the real man. The real Nixon is probably unknowable, yet certain patterns in his disposition and character are clear.

The man has an evil streak to his nature. The tapes of his White House conversations forced even his apologists, who had once worked with him and later written books, to acknowledge his "darker side."

My first look, eye to eye, at the panorama of Nixon's dark landscape came on September 15, 1972, the day the indictments were handed down against the original Watergate break-in team. My talk with the President on that day was one of the most embarrassing conversations I had had to recount when writing *Blind Ambition*.

Even now I still shuddered and felt uncomfortable at my approval of Nixon's mean-son-of-a-bitch presentation of what he was going to do with his presidency—how he would exact revenge against his enemies after the '72 election. He was going to attack everyone, from lawyer Edward Bennett Williams, who was representing the Democratic National Committee, to a few turncoat Republican senators. He threatened angrily to unleash the Internal Revenue Service, the FBI, and other government agencies on those who had opposed him. (Someday, the full text of this taped conversation will be released publicly, and historians will get a vivid picture of Nixon's darker side at work.)

There is no question that Richard Nixon was an evil president, and that his staff, myself included, supported him in his immoral actions. Cleaning up the office, after I'd finished writing *Blind Ambition*, Mo had come across a paper that she gave me to file. It was a memo from Bill Safire to Haldeman, written on August 4, 1970:

> According to *Newsweek*, Larry O'Brien (along with Cliff White) will be on the board of directors of an "international consulting firm." Lobbying for foreign governments without the appearance of lobbying, I guess.
>
> Can't we raise a big fuss about this? Insist that he register as a foreign agent, demand to know what fees he will be getting for what work and "to what extent the Democratic National Committee is available for sale to foreign governments"?
>
> We could have a little fun with this and keep O'Brien on the defensive.

This memo was one of my first glimpses of how the White House staff operated. Haldeman forwarded this memo to me with the instructions, "Will you please look into this, find out what the facts are and see what we can do."

Being new at all this, I went to see Bill Safire. I told him that Haldeman had passed his memo along to me, and asked him what he had in mind. "I just thought we should stick it to O'Brien, make his life a little tougher," Safire replied. "The boss (Nixon) likes to do that sort of thing from time to time. We should take a few shots whenever we can get a chance. I just thought this was a really nice opportunity," he said, with a memorably wicked smile.

A few weeks later, after turning White House private detective Jack Caulfield loose, I responded to the Safire memo by recommending that nothing be done. I concluded that there was no evidence that anything improper had occurred. Haldeman agreed. When I saw Safire in the hall one afternoon, I told him the results. "Too bad," he lamented. "Maybe I'll do better for you next time." Everybody, it seems, fed the Nixon paranoia.

MAY 8, 1976—San Francisco.

Oh, my aching head. I'm going to take the WCTU pledge again. En route home, I stopped to meet with (*Rolling Stone* publisher and editor) Jann Wenner to discuss the possibility of my reporting on the GOP convention for *Rolling Stone.* Last night, Jann and I sat up half the night talking politics, drinking Scotch, and driving ourselves to the edge of deafness with his stereo. Scotch certainly helps to resolve the world's problems, and last night we poured a lot of it on the biggest of them. With each glass we became more brilliant. Maybe *that's* why I was accused of being Deep Throat! My Scotch-and-cigarettes habit!

P. S. Agreed to cover the convention. JWD—investigative reporter!

David Obst's producer-friend, Howard Rosenman, and his partner, Renee Missel, came to visit and discuss Obst's proposed movie project. Together we fantasized about the far reaches of an empire ruled by King Richard I that hardly would have needed Machiavelli to make it more sinister.

My problem with writing a movie script based on the "what if" principle was that I was too well acquainted with the realities to push them to the speculative lengths that Hollywood required. I was also concerned that my reputation as an insider in the Nixon White House would lend credibility to a fictional story and further cloud the already murky understanding of Watergate. But these able young producers stimulated my thoughts, and from time to time I would find myself developing screen scenarios in my head.

My plots, given my concern for verisimilitude since studying political novels in college, were always developed out of reality. One such plot development led me into a view of Richard Nixon that possibly provided the best look yet at his character makeup, and possibly the most intriguing "what if" that might have resulted without Watergate.

It all started when I was making notes in my journal about a question that arose while lecturing in Seattle. The question was based on the rumor that Nixon had been talking to pictures on the wall at the White House during his final days. "Was Nixon crazy?" I was asked.

Surprisingly, I had been asked that same question three years before by the special prosecutor's office, and then later by the staff of the House impeachment committee, and they were serious. I answered the investigators with, "I have no idea. But why do you ask?" Never was I given any satisfactory response to my question, but when a subject as serious as a president's going bonkers arises, it's cause for both alarm and thought. Later it struck me as an intriguing idea for a movie.

In my role as Counsel to the President, I had made certain I was intimately familiar with the 25th Amendment to the Constitution, which provides for succession to the presidency in the event a president becomes disabled and "unable to discharge the powers and duties of his office." There always exists the real possibility of a president's being severely injured by a would-be assassin, but never had I contemplated the operations of the 25th Amendment with a president gone mad.

Obviously, Nixon did not go 'round the bend: he handled his seventh, and ultimate, political crisis with the same fortitude with which he'd handled six earlier. Still, the possibility of a president's being unable to perform his duties by reason of a mental disability is real, given the stresses and strains of the job. I thought a story about this could be a doozie of a political-horror-comedy-thriller movie, and my interest in authenticity required that I check the available data on Richard Nixon.

It was during my White House tenure that I learned that the CIA employs psychiatrists to provide "psychological profiles" to help our government better understand both our friends and foes. I was told that these studies can provide invaluable insight into why a foreign leader does something, and what he might do next. That potential had attracted me, back in the summer of 1974, to first read *President Nixon's Psychiatric Profile*, a book by Dr. Eli S. Chesen. Now I was rereading it.

Dr. Chesen was a young practicing psychiatrist who had spent several months observing what Nixon said, analyzing how and why he said it, and the way he appeared as he said it. He reviewed what material he could find on Nixon's background and then wrote his analysis. The book was more a sketch than a study, and I thought the doctor had been cautious in presenting his findings, mindful of the justified outcry that had followed the 1964 presidential campaign fiasco, when many members of the American Psychiatric Association had offered their political opinions of presidential candidate Barry Goldwater disguised as medical opinion.

Dr. Chesen concluded that Nixon was not mentally ill, but had serious hang-ups, like excessive concern with conformity, rigidity, overinhibition, compulsiveness, overconscientiousness, inability to relax, anxiety, and an unrelenting striving for total control. It revealed Nixon in a new light for me.

Several months later my interest was revived when I read an article in *Newsweek* about the preparation David Frost was making to interview Nixon. The article mentioned that Frost had met with Dr. David Abrahamsen, a psychoanalyst who had studied Nixon. The name registered because I'd been sent a book by Dr. Abrahamsen's publisher, *Nixon vs. Nixon: An Emotional Tragedy*, which I'd ignored. I now decided that, if Frost thought Dr. Abrahamsen could be helpful, his book was worth a read.

Dr. Abrahamsen's book says more about Richard Nixon than most people probably want to know. For me, it brought another perspective on Nixon. I had never considered the impact Nixon's youth had had on his character. It was a joyless childhood, filled with poverty, illness, and death. He had a harsh, unloving, and sometimes brutal father and a determined, but often absent, mother.

I doubt if even the most avid of Nixon-haters could find joy in reading of the events and people that made him a loner at a very early age, forcing him to assume undue responsibility, compelling him to compete with—and outdo—his father. He was a child without love, pushed inward to settle for the often unsatisfying gratification of achieving—like mashing potatoes better than his brother, winning the high school debate, or graduating at the top of his class.

According to Dr. Abrahamsen, Nixon's youth left him with deep emotional scars. "The idea that he had to work around obstacles which to his mind other people didn't have . . . gave rise to bitterness, self-pity, manipulation, and suspiciousness, all creating an unresolvable conflict."

As the book moves from childhood to chronicle Nixon's early adult years, it is easy to get caught up in the new revelations of what Nixon did, like breaking into the dean's office at Duke Law School, along with two cohorts, to secretly check his grades. But as a psychoanalyst Dr. Abrahamsen is not interested in the "what" of such an episode, rather the "why": why the young Nixon would risk the loss of his law-school scholarship to check on his scholastic standing, when grades would eventually be given out anyway. "Such actions are those of a man who unconsciously feels undeserving of success and acts in a self-destructive manner," the doctor says.

Throughout the book, Dr. Abrahamsen details and documents Richard Nixon's insecurities and his compulsive need to control everything affecting his life. The facts presented certainly validate Abrahamsen's observation that "Nixon exhibited practically the same mental makeup and behavior pattern just after the early childhood stages as he did when he was a man thirty or sixty years later." When you add Nixon's insecurities and need to control to his self-destructive impulses, suddenly such craziness as the Watergate cover-up, the proposed break-ins at the Brookings Institution and

Daniel Ellsberg's psychiatrist's office, the wiretappings of newsmen to uncover leaks and the like become comprehensible. Clearly, Nixon wanted "political intelligence" because he was insecure and thought the information would give him control. The risk was not a risk, if psychiatrist Abrahamsen is correct. Unconsciously, he hoped to get caught because he felt undeserving of being president.

I've never understood how Nixon could prevaricate with such aplomb, although long ago I concluded Nixon was an excellent actor. Dr. Abrahamsen's research confirms that Nixon could easily have become a professional actor; he has been able to cry on command since his days in his high school drama club, shifting his mood and manner instantly and at will. Theatrically speaking, and psychologically speaking, his denying any wrongdoing as president is quite easy for him.

Abrahamsen says Nixon is not lying, since emotionally he is unable to perceive reality. What he has done is repress his criminal acts to the point that they are, for him anyway, nonexistent. Consciously Richard Nixon feels innocent, according to this psychiatric analysis of his character.

What bothered me about the book was the fact that Dr. Abrahamsen had never met Richard Nixon, yet page after page of his analysis fit with what I knew about him, and I considered myself more than the casual observer. The book's explanations seemed too logical to ignore, and they were far harsher than Dr. Chesen's psychiatric diagnosis. I decided to take a further step. I wanted to know about the author: his professional background; what prompted him to write the book; how objective was his study; how complete was his research? So I called Dr. Abrahamsen and quizzed him at length.

David Abrahamsen, M.D., has impressive credentials. He told me he was seventy-two years old, and a practicing psychoanalyst. I discovered he is a Fellow in all the assemblages important to his profession—the American Psychiatric Association, the New York Academy of Medicine, and the American College of Psychoanalysis. His educational and professional background would fill pages, but most impressive are his associations with the leading mental health institutions in the country, including St. Elizabeth's Hospital (Washington, D.C.), The Menninger Clinic (Topeka, Kansas), Bellevue

Hospital (New York City), faculty membership at the College of Physicians and Surgeons at Columbia University, the Board of Overseers of the Lemberg Center for the Study of Violence at Brandeis University—to mention a few. Dr. Abrahamsen's specialty, the study of the criminal mind, has taken him into countless federal and state courtrooms to testify as an expert psychiatric witness.

Looking for the most obvious bias, when I got him on the telephone I asked about his political persuasion. "Are you a Republican or Democrat?"

"I am a Democrat, but I have voted for Republicans. I have never voted for Richard Nixon, however."

I asked why he had written a book about Nixon.

"It wasn't really my idea. The publisher came to me and asked me to write it. I refused, at first. I told them I couldn't do it without detailed information about Nixon's infancy, childhood, and adolescence. Only when I was convinced I could get the necessary information did I agree because I wanted to see what kind of man Nixon really was. I've tried to be as objective as I could, for it's easy to condemn, but difficult to understand. Being professionally objective was a very fundamental thing to me. And I must say this, a number of psychiatrists have read the book, and most of them agree with my conclusions."

Reading between the lines of his response, I asked, "Are you saying you've been conservative in your analysis?"

"Yes, that's correct. I think my colleagues know me as a conservative. Recently, I gave a talk before a group of psychoanalysts in Toronto. They received the book very well, but several thought I should have gone further than I did. I told them I couldn't because I had no direct evidence, and I'd based my conclusion on the evidence I had. I must tell you, there are a lot of psychoanalysts who believe Nixon has been a very sick man, and still is."

Clearly, he did, too, so I moved to the basis for his conclusion, with a question about how long he had studied Nixon before writing his book.

"Well, like many, I've been watching Nixon for years, but the kind of study necessary to write the book, well, that took me three years."

"Did you try to talk to Nixon personally?"

"Oh, yes. I wrote him even though I didn't think he'd see me, but as a matter of courtesy I wrote. An assistant answered and said that Nixon wasn't giving any interviews, but if he did, I was told I'd be high on the list. I've still not seen him, however."

Restraining my laughter at that response, I proceeded. "Do you think that your conclusions are suspect, since you've never had Nixon on the couch, or in a clinical situation?"

"No, I don't believe my analysis is affected by that at all. As a matter of fact, I don't think Nixon would have been able to provide much information about himself. As you know, he is a man very much turned toward himself, very preoccupied. He's very self-serving and always has been. I don't think he's capable of talking openly about himself, so even if I could have spent time with him, it wouldn't have helped me make my analysis. I must say it was quite hard to get the information I needed. I had to travel all over the country to talk to people who could provide raw information about his emotional and psychological development. It was like being a detective at times, but, in writing this book, I hoped it could serve as a model for psychobiographies."

I proceeded to take Dr. Abrahamsen, almost page by page, through his book as I looked for holes in his research, evidence of his bias, or unsupported conclusions. The fact that I didn't find these things may mean that someone like myself, without psychiatric training, doesn't know the right questions to ask. As our conversation came to an end, there were two questions I felt I had to ask— questions that I felt needed to be put to rest, questions that had circulated about the former president ever since his final days in office.

"Doctor, I know that terms like *insanity* or *being crazy* are imprecise and undefinable, but when I add up some of the precise terms you have used in your book to describe Nixon—well, like. . . ." I could hear him softly laughing on the other end, knowing where I was headed.

"Yes, like . . . ," he said quietly, still chuckling.

"Well, like on page 224, you say, 'his judgment was often faulty,' and on page 226 that he 'exhibited all the signs of a paranoid personality.' Then you talk about 'the impairment of his mind,' and on 228 you say that Nixon belonged to the category of people who, 'intrinsically unhappy, hostile, and therefore depressed, are a threat, to themselves and others.' "

"That's right, yes, that's right," the doctor kept quietly repeating after each citation, so I continued.

"On that same page you say, 'Nixon deviated from the norm,' and on 230 that 'Nixon always suffered from a sense of dejection and was always emotionally unstable.' Then you get even heavier when, on page 231, you conclude that 'Nixon's behavior, most appropriately described as a character disturbance, and possibly of no small order, has lasted since early childhood.' And finally, on page 234, you observe that his 'emotionally crippled state' prevented him from acting in a legal manner. Now, I'm a lay person, but when I read all those labels I said to myself, Nixon's crazy!"

"Yes," he said, as though following the course of my reasoning.

"He's mentally ill! Is that a fair conclusion to draw from your book?"

"Yes."

"Let me ask you, if I might, because I think it's important: Could Nixon be considered not guilty of any crimes in Watergate, by reason of insanity?"

"Oh, god," he groaned, then sighed. The silence that followed suggested he was unhappy with my question. I was surprised he'd not been asked it before, given his background as an expert witness on such matters.

"I mean, if I read the old M'Naghten rule and the Durham rule (relating to criminal insanity) correctly," I wanted to break the uncomfortable silence, "and if I had a bunch of witnesses such as yourself. . . ."

"Well," he began gently, sighed again, and continued. "I've been on the commission which changed that rule, and we made it that, if the person is not able emotionally to appreciate the wrongfulness of his act—and I think that he wasn't able to . . . so he would be declared insane."

I hadn't expected the answer he gave me to my last question. I was stunned. Nixon truly insane! Not guilty by reason of insanity! Were those suspicions or well-founded medical opinions? If Dr.

Abrahamsen was right, and that's a very big *if,* it adds a far different interpretation to history.

"What if" speculation was very much in vogue during those early years following Watergate, as evidenced by a mailgram I received from *The New York Times Magazine,* inviting me to "join half a dozen writers in writing about a thousand words for a symposium on the theme, 'Where Would the Country Be Now if the Watergate Break-in Had Not Been Discovered?' For example, who would have run, who would have won the election? What programs would Nixon have started, what buried? Would Nixon have been discredited anyway? Can be serious or light speculation. . . ."

When I thought about what could have happened, I felt I understood what would, in fact, have happened. I had been there, watching trends and working on the matters that were coming to fruition. I didn't feel my speculation was idle. But who would want to hear all that bad news?

The way to handle the *New York Times* symposium, I decided, was the light approach. I would try to capture what I really believed in a manner that people could brush off. In parody of Woodward and Bernstein's bestselling book, *The Final Days,* I decided that my contribution to the symposium would be about "The Final Day."

I fantasized a transcript of the last secretly recorded conversation of the Nixon presidency, a transcript that one day might have been found in the basement vaults of that planned Nixon library complex. The scene of this last conversation was the Oval Office. The time was moments before Richard Nixon would leave that office for the last time as president and head up to Capitol Hill for the inauguration of his successor.

The *Times* symposium never came together. But this is what my contribution would have been:

The Final Day

THE PRESIDENT: *"Hi, Bob. I was just sitting here thinking that in about an hour I'll no longer be President*

of the United States. I'll miss the place. Of course, every-
body will still call me Mr. President." (Clears throat.)
"Say, Bob, uh, uh, you can call me Dick again at 12:01 ...
if you wish ... but others, I mean like Henry and the peo-
ple who will work for me at the library, I still want them
to call me ..."

HALDEMAN: *"I understand, Mr. President."* (Telephone rings.)

THE PRESIDENT: *"Yes, yes, I'll take the Brezhnev*
call." (Silence.) *"Hello, Mr. President, I mean, Mr. Secre-*
tary." (Silence.) *"Correct. Fine. Sure, I'll see what I can*
do. Nice talking to you, too, and good luck to you, my
friend." (Telephone returned.) *"Bob, you know, all that*
fellow wants to talk about are cars and women. I thought
he was calling because I was leaving office. What he
wanted, however, was for me to pass along that he doesn't
want any more American presidents giving him cars. Then
he asked me, or maybe I didn't understand the Kremlin
interpreter, but what he asked me is to send him a movie,
once I get out near Hollywood at San Clemente, called
'Deep Throat.' Say, Bob, who is Deep Throat?"

HALDEMAN: *"Henry knows. I'll have him handle it."*

THE PRESIDENT: *"That's fine. You know, Kissinger's a*
damned clever fellow. I taught him everything I know,
made him Secretary of State, and then he convinced Con-
nally, who's slicker than a sow's ear, whatever that means,
that's one of Connally's ... anyway, Henry was damned
ingenious convincing Connally to name him as his Vice
President. Henry had the argument that Connally under-
stood. Connally told me about it. He said that since Henry
could never become President because he wasn't born in
the United States, he wouldn't be a walking reminder of
his mortality. God, it's awful having a Vice President, Bob.
Every time I used to look at Spiro, and then when he was
gone, at John Connally, all I could think about was dying.
That's why I never wanted them around."

HALDEMAN: *"Even cleverer for convincing Connally to*
let him serve as Secretary of State while Vice President."

THE PRESIDENT: *"I wish I'd thought of that when I*

was Vice President. I'd have asked General Eisenhower to name me to a Cabinet post. Maybe Secretary of Agriculture, because my mother would have liked that. Bob, it's boring being Vice President and a president should get some use out of his veep. I think that the Connally-Kissinger precedent of putting a Vice President in the Cabinet is going to last for years to come. I wish I'd thought ... oh, what the hell, I've thought of enough other things." (Silence.) *"Let me ... last night I was reading* Six Crises, *which is uh, uh, you know, appropriate to keep the feel. The President has to feel history, Bob. This is a historical moment, right now. Every minute I sit here is historical, I guess. Isn't that right, Bob?"*

HALDEMAN: *"We're going to have to leave for the Capitol pretty soon, Mr. President."*

THE PRESIDENT: *"Uh,* (expletive deleted) *right. Otherwise, old Connally will* (scatalogical reference deleted), *but I've been trying to think of something really historical to do before I leave this desk. And I've got it."* (Unintelligible noises, which sound like desk drawers opening and closing.)

HALDEMAN: *"Here's a piece of paper, if that's what you're looking for."*

THE PRESIDENT: *"These damn desk drawers are full of nothing but those junk cuff links and golf balls and paperweights and tie clasps. ... Here, Bob, take these and pass the damn things out to the staff. It's a bit of history for them. It's good for a president to be thinking of those who have served him, right, Bob?"*

HALDEMAN: *"Better hurry, or you'll be late."*

(Two minutes of silence.)

THE PRESIDENT: *"How do you spell commendable?"*

HALDEMAN: *"Why?"*

THE PRESIDENT: *"I'm writing out a pardon for Agnew. I'm gonna leave it here on the desk. My last act. Compassion, that's good, Bob. Isn't it?"*

HALDEMAN: *"Sometimes."*

THE PRESIDENT: *"We may have been a little tough on Spiro, sticking him with that tax rap."*

HALDEMAN: "You said you couldn't drop him from the ticket, so we had to send him to jail." (Laughter.) *"I've enjoyed reading his novels."*

THE PRESIDENT: "Well, he's been in there three years now, that's enough. Although jail is a good discipline for writing. Okay, done. I like doing things as President, Bob, like sending Howard Baker to the moon last week on Apollo Fifteen, uh, Sixteen, uh ... whatever. It's nice Howard's so small, the trip will help his image. Everybody loves an astronaut. Also, I liked helping Ehrlichman win his seat in the Senate and helping you get your new job as Chairman of the Board of Howard Hughes' World Enterprises. I'd like to do something for Colson, too, but I don't understand him now. He never even calls anymore, since he's joined those Haray, the Ha ... whatever."

HALDEMAN: (Chuckle.) *"Hare Krishna! I had a report from the Secret Service a few days ago that Chuck showed up in front of the White House, with his shaven head and saffron robes, selling copies of the* Bhagavad-Gita.*"*

THE PRESIDENT: (Silence.) *"It's sad. He was such a wonderful hatchet man. Oh, well, what the* (expletive deleted).*"* (Silence.) *"Speaking of hatchet work, I like that picture on the front page of* The Washington Post *this morning. It's a fine newspaper, I must say that it's really turned out to be a damned fine paper."*

HALDEMAN: "Herblock collecting an unemployment check, yeah, I liked that, too."

THE PRESIDENT: "We got 'em good, huh, Bob? After the FCC revoked their television licenses, and the Justice Department forced divestiture of Newsweek, *I thought we had 'em, but I must say that they were tough* (expletive deleted) *over there at the* Post.*"*

HALDEMAN: "The IRS, SEC, Labor Department, and FBI helped with their investigations, but we really broke their backs and forced them into bankruptcy when we threw forty of their reporters in jail for failing to disclose their sources."

THE PRESIDENT: *"You don't think we were too rough, do you, Bob?"*

HALDEMAN: *"Never."*

THE PRESIDENT: *"Good. I think Walter Annenberg's got himself a good investment, and putting Ron Ziegler in charge of all the television stations and making Pat Buchanan editor-in-chief was a blow for fairness in American journalism."*

HALDEMAN: *"Mr. President, it's time to leave for the Capitol, but I've got to know what you want to do about the taping machines . . ."*

THE PRESIDENT: *"What taping machines?"*

HALDEMAN: *"You remember, the one on your phone, and those mikes under your desk, and over there above the fireplace . . ."*

THE PRESIDENT: *"Oh, right, I forgot about those damn little things, but I'm sure glad we got 'em, Bob."*

HALDEMAN: *"I've instructed the Secret Service to dismantle every piece of equipment during the inauguration and . . ."*

THE PRESIDENT: *"No! Listen, Bob, I want that machinery left in place, and I don't want Connally told about it. Today bugs are everywhere. They're necessary. They do it to us, we do it to them. We do it to ourselves. Someday, people will realize all those bugs we've got, and they've got, make us the most open, democratic society in the world. There are no secrets in government or business today."* (Silence.) *"But I'd like to have that fellow, Jim McCord, the guy we hired to be the library security chief, double check the library again, because . . . (Unintelligible) . . . Kissinger . . . (Unintelligible) . . . and tell CIA Director Howard Hunt . . . (Unintelligible) . . . since FBI Director Liddy said . . . that alcoholic fellow Dean, we sent off to. . . ."**

*On later rereading this transcript, I realized that the same law that prohibits a foreign-born American from holding the office of president would also prohibit his holding the office of vice president. I hope the reader will indulge this satirical tampering with Constitutional law.

MAY 27, 1976—Los Angeles.

I wonder how Nixon feels when people probe everything from his sex life to his psyche, and poke fun at his presidency. It must hurt. He's a man of great pride, and maybe he has been punished the most severely by being denied what the proud seek most—respect and honor.

These thoughts are prompted by a call today from *Enquirer* reporter Gerry Hunt. He said he realized that he'd never called back to tell me what they'd done with the Nixon love-letters story. "It's dead," he said. They couldn't prove the letters were authentic.* Nor did the *Enquirer* editors think the story had any appeal. "The public has no interest in Richard Nixon's love life," Hunt told me. "They wouldn't care if he'd been carrying on with a gorilla!"

Gerry Hunt also asked me if I was interested in talking with the *Enquirer* about revealing Deep Throat. In fact, I think that is the real reason he called. He hinted, again, that they had lots of money for such projects.

The Deep Throat story would lose its significance if I gave it to the *Enquirer.* Whoever this individual is, he must be keeping his identity a secret for a good reason. If he's in the FBI, he'd probably get fired. If he's in the Justice Department or U.S. attorney's office, he might be prosecuted for divulging secret grand jury information. These are the most obvious places for such a source—if there is a Deep Throat.

There is a growing school of thought that there is no Deep Throat, that I was right in saying he was a composite. Possibly, this is why Woodward reacted so strongly to my making a public statement to that effect. Could it be that they had a good source, but that source had only half the story, and they had to convince Bradlee (the *Washington Post* executive editor) that they were on stronger footing than they really were?

Alice Mayhew, my editor at Simon & Schuster, who also edited Woodward's and Bernstein's book, watched the manuscript of *All the President's Men* develop from version to version, and helped cook up the whole detective-story approach of the book. She says

---

*The chief postal inspector, at Nixon's request, investigated the attempted sale of the alleged "Nixon love letters" to determine if a fraud was being perpetrated. In a report issued on November 19, 1976, their handwriting experts concluded that the letters had not been written by Richard Nixon. No fraud was found, because the true author was never discovered.

she doesn't believe there is a single source who was Deep Throat. Alice should know.

Taylor Branch, who also worked on Woodward's manuscript, doesn't believe there was a Deep Throat, and Taylor has given it a lot of thought lately. He recently reported that he had completed his investigation into my tip, Dave Gergen, Woodward's old Yale friend who worked at the Nixon White House. He said he brought Gergen to tears in his accusation. But Gergen absolutely denies being Deep Throat, although he certainly says he knows Woodward. Taylor is writing up his investigation for *Esquire*.

Hays Gorey has been working on Deep Throat for *Time* magazine. He says he met with Woodward, and Woodward insists there is a single source. Hays says emotionally he believes Woodward, but mentally he's having trouble buying the single source.

Now is probably the best time for me to get down to having a hard look at this question. My head is still filled with Watergate, having just finished *Blind Ambition*. Also, my files are not yet in storage. But the thought of taking my head back to those days is more than I can bear. Also, I've got this uncomfortable feeling that, as much fun as such an investigation might be—and it's the only thing connected with Watergate that now appears like fun—it might become very unpleasant.

If I were to prove that there was no Deep Throat, it would be a disaster for Woodward and Bernstein. Not only would they have been caught in a lie, but a fraud that produced a Pulitzer Prize for their newspaper, and all kinds of honors and awards for them. I like them both. For me to show them to be little more than blindly ambitious young journalistic hucksters would place my motives in doing so in question. In fact, in a "Q and A" column that appeared in *Time* recently (May 3, 1976), Woodward told Hays: "I don't think reporters trying to identify other reporters' sources is the noblest kind of journalism." So I think you could say that Bob is a little touchy on the subject.

No, I must nurse this along, and look for the right time and place, and reason, to unravel the best mystery, maybe the greatest "what if," of Watergate.

CHAPTER SIX

The Scene of the Crimes

My life as a fledgling political reporter began on June 1, 1976, when Jann Wenner, the editor-in-chief and publisher of *Rolling Stone*, announced that "a unique observer of Republican politics" would be assigned to cover the 1976 Republican National Convention in Kansas City, and the ensuing presidential campaign. Aware that I had gained this opportunity because of my peculiar fame, I was pleased to learn that Jann had mentioned that "Dean is a good writer with an extraordinary recall of detail. He knows exactly what power politics is like when the stakes are high." No one laughed.

In fact, to my surprise, the announcement was carried by the media as a straight news item with little or no commentary. This initially lulled me into believing that I might actually be allowed to work as a reporter without myself becoming a story. I knew that a low profile would be important in obtaining access to the people involved in the campaigns.

Reaction to the announcement made it clear, however, that there would be no magical transformation from Watergate felon into news reporter. "It might be tough, John," cautioned one ex-colleague. "You're not a very popular fellow with many Republicans and you might find yourself listening to a lot of phones being slammed down."

"Be careful, knuckle sandwiches don't taste good," offered another cheery observer.

I determined to proceed with caution, and decided to return first to familiar turf in Washington. My planning, along with reading and clipping background news articles, was delayed, however, by a thick, two-volume, 815-page report I received in the mail: the findings and recommendations of the Senate Select Committee on Intelligence. The documents mesmerized me and completely diverted my attention for days.

The report was a devastating review of White House sanctioned abuses of the CIA and FBI throughout history. The long litany of activities placed Watergate, and the Nixon White House abuses, in a clearer context—less original sin and more standard malpractice. But particularly interesting, as the media coverage of the release of the report had noted, was that the abuses had been instituted or condoned by some of our most respected political figures, from Franklin Roosevelt and Harry Truman to Robert and John Kennedy. And none of them expressed the slightest qualm about such practices as slipping LSD into drinks, breaking into houses and offices, theft, bugging, wiretapping, subverting foreign governments, or even planning assassinations.

Summarizing this attitude for the Select Committee was none other than my old friend, William Sullivan of the FBI: "Never once did I hear anybody, including myself, raise the question: 'Is this course of action . . . lawful, is it legal, is it ethical or moral?' "

Watergate had provoked the congressional inquiry into these abuses, although Congress had known for years that such activities were taking place and, before Watergate, they had been largely ignored. Why, I wondered, had Watergate engendered so judgmental an attitude about what was right or wrong, acceptable or unacceptable in government? Why had investigative journalists ignored these matters before Watergate? Why, before Watergate, had the public been unconcerned about such abuses and illegalities? Why, even now, did the public almost yawn at these historical revelations, yet still feel such outrage over Watergate itself?

Obviously, scandal is not new to Washington, particularly not new to Congress. It was Mark Twain who observed in *Following the Equator*, "It could probably be shown by facts and figures that there is no distinctly native American criminal class except Congress." Congressional scandals were accepted as a way of life, and no one was shocked or even interested very long in such scandals. It is the White House that stirs intense interest and produces the scandals that history records with prominence.

The scandals of the Nixon administration were succinctly characterized as a new form of trouble, in the spring of 1974, by Vermont Royster. Royster wrote (in *The American Scholar*) about both Vice President Spiro Agnew's misconduct and Watergate, "The two affairs were different in kind. Mr. Agnew's was a simple case of bribery and kickbacks, an all-too-familiar felonious behavior among public officials. What has come to be subsumed under the single word Watergate was of another order, an attempt to use governmental power to subvert the political process in the broadest sense of that term."

In searching for other White House scandals that might give me some perspective on what had occurred at the Nixon White House, I found Royster was right. Misconduct of financial corruption, various kinds of greed involving money, were "all too familiar" in the White House.

President Ulysses S. Grant, whose memoirs I had read while in prison, endured one scandal after another during his administration (1869–1877). Although few can tell you what the phrase means, the "Teapot Dome scandal" marked the presidency of Warren G. Harding, just as Watergate will surely mark the presidency of Richard M. Nixon. Before Watergate, Teapot Dome stood alone as an American presidential scandal, yet actually it did not involve Warren G. Harding himself.

Teapot Dome was the name of an oil reservation in Wyoming that the Secretary of the Interior, Albert B. Fall, leased to oil tycoon Harry Sinclair in exchange for a bribe of a herd of cattle and almost a quarter of a million dollars. The Interior Secretary also leased a second reserve to oil entrepreneur Edward Doheny at Elks Hill, California, for a one-hundred-thousand-dollar bribe. Mr. Fall had the dubious distinction of being the first member of a president's Cabinet to go to jail. John Mitchell, I guessed, was the second.

For sheer magnitude, Teapot Dome is the only scandal close to Watergate for its scope and lasting historical significance. While the scandals that plagued the Truman presidency were many, they had no lasting effect.

Richard Nixon always was particularly rankled that Truman himself had escaped any charge of corruption. On several occasions he angrily told me, disgust dripping from his voice, "Truman was involved in things far worse than anything we've done." Another time he noted, "Truman covered it up, believe you me he did, 'cause I was sitting up on one of those committees trying to get information out of the White House in those days. We tried to nail him, but they pulled the rug over everything." What Nixon was talking about were the so-called tax-fixing charges involving high Truman officials. The Truman administration was forced to remove some sixty-six people because of this scandal, but, to Richard Nixon's dismay, Truman could never be directly implicated.

When I was in prep school, I had read about a scandal that brushed the Eisenhower White House involving the White House chief of staff, Sherman Adams. He was accused of accepting an oriental rug and a vicuna coat from industrialist Bernard Goldfine, in exchange for improperly intervening with regulatory agencies. Adams denied any wrongdoing. Dwight Eisenhower defended him to the end. But when Goldfine refused to answer a congressional investigation, Sherman Adams was forced to resign. I remembered how Richard Nixon would occasionally allude to Sherman Adams during Watergate. I think Nixon decided to emulate Eisenhower by first defending his friend, John Mitchell, and later Bob Haldeman and John Ehrlichman, when they became entangled in the web of Watergate.

The Nixon White House staff was even more fascinated by a scandal of the Lyndon Johnson administration: the Bobby Baker affair. Baker had become a friend of LBJ's while Johnson was still Democratic majority leader of the Senate. Baker became the secretary of the Senate majority, and was the subject of much press coverage for his incredible ability to compile a multimillion-dollar fortune on a modest Senate employee's salary. By the time Lyndon Johnson moved on to the White House, Baker's shady dealings had caught up with him. Baker was indicted and convicted for tax evasion, larceny, fraud, and conspiracy. Lyndon Johnson was tarnished, but never touched directly.

"Lyndon Johnson was involved with Bobby Baker up to his elbows," Deputy Attorney General Richard Kleindienst told me shortly after I arrived at the White House. Kleindienst had had a chance to talk to some of the personnel in the criminal division of the Justice Department. He said he had always suspected it, and, indeed, it had been a rumor in Washington for a long time, but now Kleindienst seemed to have hard evidence. During a late-evening gin game in his Justice Department office, one of his favorite pastimes when the working day was completed, Kleindienst said to me, shaking his head, "I've heard stories about Lyndon Johnson's badgering and bullying the FBI and the Justice Department that you wouldn't believe. He made damn sure that no one was going to put him in jail."

These facts were known to John Mitchell, Bob Haldeman, John Ehrlichman, and, although I never heard him say it, I assume they were known to Nixon. The fact that Lyndon Johnson had guided the Justice Department away from his footprints in the Baker affair gave justification to Nixon's efforts to control the FBI and Justice Department in its pursuit of Watergate. The Nixon attitude was: It has been done before, so why shouldn't we do it now?

Because these prior scandals had indirectly affected the handling of Watergate, I realized that the way Nixon and the White House staff had handled Watergate would, in turn, affect future presidents. We had written the book on HOW NOT TO HANDLE A WHITE HOUSE SCANDAL. The lesson was clear: Take your losses fast, and take them openly. Sir Walter Scott had made the point succinctly: "Oh, what a tangled web we weave, When first we practice to deceive!"

The only historical precedent I could find for something the nature of Watergate, a misuse or abuse of power for political purposes, as opposed to bribery and misuse of funds, I discovered quite by accident.

The closest public library to our home is the Beverly Hills Public Library. A library card is as important to me as my driver's license, and I headed out to get both on the same day. I stopped first at the library. While waiting at the desk for one of the librarians, who was on the telephone, I browsed through the books she had stacked on the return desk. One of them caught my attention: *The Coming to Power: Critical Presidential Elections in American History*, edited by Arthur M. Schlesinger, Jr.

I opened the book at random and discovered I had turned to a discussion of the presidential election of 1876, between Rutherford

B. Hayes and his Democratic opponent, Samuel J. Tilden, which sounded like it was out of the Watergate handbook. Hayes had stolen the election by fraudulent means. I had never read of this election fact, so I decided to check out the book, once I got my card.

Unfortunately, I didn't get my card. Because we do not live in the city of Beverly Hills proper, rather live in the Beverly Hills postal zone, which is actually Los Angeles County, I was given an application to fill out and, with the payment of a small fee, would be given a card.

I began filling out the application. At one point it requested the names of two friends who lived within Beverly Hills. While I knew people who lived within the city limits, I was undecided about whom I might put down, for fear they would be hassled if I should—as I sometimes do—end up with a stack of overdue books. I wouldn't want them bothered, I thought. I couldn't decide whom to put down, so I said to the librarian, "What if I don't have any friends in Beverly Hills?"

"Then you can't get a card."

"Well, when I get two friends, I'll come back," I said, looking at my watch and realizing I'd have to really hustle if I were going to get to the Department of Motor Vehicles before it closed.

Later that evening I received a call from another of the Beverly Hills librarians, who began an apology that I didn't understand immediately. "Oh, I'm so sorry, Mr. Dean, that you didn't get your card. Several of us here at the library thought we recognized you. And we want you to know, Mr. Dean, that the Beverly Hills Library is your friend. So if you come back down, we'll issue you a card."

Wasn't that nice, I thought. They'd clearly thought I'd been serious about being friendless. She had been so thoughtful, I didn't have the heart to explain I was "putting on" the other librarian. That was a mistake. A few days later, a wire-service story ended up in newspapers throughout the country, reporting as a straight story that "John Dean has no friends in Beverly Hills."

With a head that was filled with thoughts of scandals past, I jetted off to Washington to have a first look at the impact the Watergate scandal had had on the city. But my primary purpose was to look at presidential politics, so en route I began making notes about why I was returning to Washington to start covering a convention that would be in Kansas City. I thought that visiting the presidential-primary states, or states that selected delegates in state conventions, was really an exercise in futility.

Presidential politics begins and ends along the shores of the Potomac. It is here that the political parties and the presidential candidates themselves maintain their national headquarters. It is here that one can find knowledgeable political observers and analysts with a national political perspective. The capital city is by far the best political-rumor mill in the world for someone interested in presidential politics. It was the only place to start to understand what would happen in Kansas City six weeks later.

My old political passport into the world of Republican politics had been canceled, and I was sensitive to earlier admonitions about my popularity with members of the Grand Old Party. So, I started background-information gathering with a trusted friend, Senator Lowell P. Weicker of Connecticut. He asked me to join him for lunch at the Senate.

Senator Weicker, of course, had been a member of the Senate Watergate committee, and I thought he might be making a mistake in being seen with me, even in semipublic. So, when I arrived in his office at the Old Senate Office Building, I said, "Lowell, if you'd rather have some sandwiches sent here to the office, it's fine with me."

"I'm not embarrassed to be seen with you, not for a second," he boomed in a voice that his entire office could hear. "No, sir, I think what you did for the country, as I've told you before, took a lot of guts. Listen, John, I've already taken plenty of static, believe me, for buying your house. I assure you it didn't bother me for a second. In fact, it was a great house."

When Mo and I had moved to California, Weicker had acquired our house in Alexandria. He had made a good purchase, but it had cost him the outrage of several of his home-state newspapers. After living in the house for a year and a half, he had sold it at a hefty profit. I assumed the sale had come because of pressure from those state newspapers, plus the fact that it was publicly rumored that he might be under consideration to replace Nelson Rockefeller as President Ford's running mate in the vice-presidential spot.

The walk from the Old Senate Office Building to the Senate

dining room in the Capitol building was, for me, the retracing of a familiar path. The Senate dining room has always suggested the elegance of another era. The square tables sport crisp white linen tablecloths, the damask chairs are worn but regularly reupholstered, the ornate walls are always freshly painted, and the carpet is constantly replaced. Care is taken to maintain the room's original turn-of-the-century flavor and feel. While their numbers have dwindled, there are many white-jacketed waiters who are as hospitable and gracious as Pullman-car porters once were. At lunchtime in the Senate, this small dining room, a short distance from the Senate chamber, buzzes with activity as senators visit over a meal with their constituents, lobbyists, newsmen, and each other.

"Before you ask me any questions about the convention, or the campaign, let me raise a subject I think is damn important," Weicker said, taking his glasses off, then rubbing his eyes.

"Damn it," he said, staring intently at me, his voice rising, "do you know that, in over two years since Watergate, the Congress hasn't done a damn thing to prevent another Watergate from occurring? John, you stuck your neck on the line. So did I. Lots of people did. Don't you think somebody should be doing something up here?"

"Frankly, I am a little surprised that there hasn't been more done," I said as softly as I could.

"Well, let me tell you this, my friend," Weicker immediately rejoined, "except for finally passing some election reform that had been sitting around here for years, there hasn't been one single new law written as a result of Watergate. How does that strike you?"

"Amazing!" And I truly was amazed. Considering the noise that had been made about Watergate, and the perennial congressional desire to show the folks back home that they're doing something, I would have thought new legislation would already be in blossom on the Watergate graveyard. Maybe it was understandable, however. After all, there were ample laws in existence to prevent a Watergate from happening before it did happen. Congress knows as well as anybody that you can't legislate morality.

In the course of my preconvention investigating I had had no trouble getting behind the scenes of the Reagan campaign. Both Paul Laxalt and John Sears had been more than accommodating.

But President Ford's campaign operation presented a problem—who was doing what?

The week before I arrived in Washington, there had been a reference in *Newsweek* to Bill Timmons. It suggested, but didn't say, that Timmons had become Ford's key nomination strategist. To get more information, I arranged a lunch with *Newsweek* reporter John Lindsay.

Lindsay talks like a seasoned Washington journalist, but his gruff and gravelly voice belies a gentle manner. While he speaks in metaphors of the extreme, what he says is more cynical than what he really believes. He is a reporter who has seen it all and loves the action best when he is wading through the worst.

"By God, we miss you guys," he said, when we greeted each other for lunch. "Your former leader is the best thing that ever happened to newsprint, at least since the printing press."

"Pretty slow, is it?"

"Slow? It's worse, it's like being in withdrawal. It's painful. You know, most of us got hooked on Watergate, like junkies. We were mainlining with a couple of mind-blowers at least every twenty-four hours. Now, a lot of us just wander around this town looking for a fix, and end up going back to our offices and sniffing glue pots, trying to patch together something that will work. You guys really treated us right," he said, laughing. And we ordered our lunch.

During lunch we discussed Ford's pardon of Nixon, which was felt by the media to have been a colossal blunder. The Washington press corps would never forgive him, Lindsay thought. While John didn't say it, buried between the lines was a hint that many of the press corps were annoyed that they had been robbed of all this wonderfully gory coverage.

Lindsay himself had a certain sympathy for Nixon. He told me how he had been dispatched by *Newsweek* to try and interview the former president in San Clemente. He described how awful Nixon had looked; how Ron Ziegler, who was still in good health, was equally pathetic in his inability to accept the reality that Nixon was no longer president. Lindsay thought that Nixon was now back on the road to recovery, although his golf game certainly hadn't improved any, and that Ford had probably saved his life by granting him the pardon.

When the talk turned back to Washington, it was evident the

city had changed since I had been in government. Not necessarily
for the better. "Everyone is suspicious of everyone and everything
now." That did not please Lindsay, either, who added, "People in government suspect that we in the press are out to nail them, and we in
the press think they're lying all the time. It's really gotten a bit ugly,
living here in the aftermath."

"Is there really something called 'post-Watergate morality'?" I
asked him at one point.

"Yeah, it's called fear!" he quipped. "Fear of getting caught at
doing anything anyone else can accuse you of doing wrong."

I learned from my conversation with John Lindsay that I still
had many contacts in high places. President Ford had retained virtually the entire Nixon Cabinet and sub-Cabinet when he came to
office. Although there had been inevitable shifting from job to job at
the middle level, many of the players were old acquaintances, even
friends.

For me to contact these people was a delicate matter (and
would continue to be so, for many would, five years later, join Ronald
Reagan's White House). As a "special correspondent" for *Rolling
Stone*, I found myself in the position of having to promise I would
protect their anonymity.

During my White House years, I had grown to have a low regard for any news stories that cited "reliable" but "unidentified"
sources. But, as I proceeded to visit with old friends in my new role, I
began to realize that anonymous informants are often the only
means an outsider has to get inside information. Clearly, protection
of sources is an essential *modus operandi* for the reporter.

However, I didn't feel much like a reporter, as I commenced on
this brief detour from the road to Kansas City. Because of requests
by those I was seeing to meet at their homes after work or at some
remote restaurant, I felt at times like a KGB agent trying to determine if the American government had been measurably weakened
by Watergate. At other times, because of the nature of my inquiries,
I felt like a political scientist examining theories against practice, or
comparing concepts with reality. As these friends and acquaintances
took me below the surface of Washington with their insights, a different picture of the city emerged.

The most striking difference had been the change in the relationship between the presidency and the Congress. By Constitutional

design, the two were equals, designed to check and balance one another. By practice and tradition, the executive branch had grown to
be the more powerful of the two branches, by far. With Watergate,
that imbalance of power appeared at least to have begun tilting
again, for Congress had been prompted into exerting itself.

While Congress had, as Lowell Weicker stated, done little to
implement major Watergate reforms, I found that there was a growing accumulation of little-noted changes. Collectively, they evidenced the real response that Congress had made to Watergate, all
the rhetoric aside.

"The Congress is going right for the president's strong suit, his
greatest powers. First they started firing the heavy artillery, then
they sent in the commandoes for a little rape and plunder," an aide
to the National Security Council told me. He explained how, in the
fall of 1973, during some of the darker days of the Nixon presidency,
when Richard Nixon was being bombarded with questions, demands, and decisions about Watergate as a result of the Senate
Watergate hearings, Congress had passed the War Powers Resolution. "As far as I'm concerned, that was a clear signal, the beginning, and it's been clear ever since that Congress is playing a new
game with the presidency. Just a few years ago Congress would not
have dared to tamper with the president's foreign-policy powers and
war-making prerogatives. Watergate has changed the presidency."

The War Powers Resolution forces the president to report the
circumstances and to justify the commitment of armed forces to any
foreign hostility within forty-eight hours. And, unless Congress ap-
proves, he must withdraw those forces within sixty days. In effect,
the Congress had forced its partnership with the commander-in-
chief. Without a Watergate-weakened president, this would not have
been possible.

By no means is this law the most significant change. Even more
pervasive is congressional entry into the domain of presidential bud-
geting for the executive branch. According to the Constitution, Congress has exclusive powers over the federal purse strings, but the
presidency—with the president as the chief economist of the nation—has become the guardian of the purse itself.

In the wake of Watergate, Congress reasserted its grip on the
federal budget. The implications of the 1974 Congressional Budget
and Impoundment Control Act will be felt by presidents for many

years to come. Under the powers of that law, the Congress can virtually neutralize the president's budgetary powers, as well as strip him of his option not to spend. Richard Nixon's frequent use of this fund-impoundment power had particularly rankled the Congress.

One of President Ford's men in the Office of Management and Budget, which used to be the only budgetary show in town, said, "Federal spending may change tremendously as a result of congressional budget reform. Congressional influence can only grow as they learn how to use the powers they have given themselves."

Among those powers is the power to gather information. In the aftermath of Watergate, Congress has strong attitudes about the executive branch's withholding information. "The Congress is damn near ready to throw Cabinet officers who withhold information in jail, or maybe even lock them in the basement of the Capitol," a Ford aide said. "They're playing hardball on the Hill these days." He was referring to an incident in 1975, when the House Oversight and Investigations Subcommittee issued a subpoena demanding that Secretary of Commerce Rogers Morton provide them with the names of all U.S. companies that had joined in the Arab boycott of Israel. Morton refused and, only under the very real threat of being voted in contempt of Congress (a jailable offense), did he relent.

Part of the congressional demand for information is related to the new budgetary functions. But there is also a new effort to exercise oversight of the departments and agencies of the executive branch. Since Watergate, I discovered, congressional oversight is everything. No longer are there forbidden grounds, such as the CIA and FBI. Those previously "untouchable" agencies are now subject to a scrutiny unlike any supervision in their histories.

These changes in the daily operation of government seldom make headlines. Thus I suspect that few realize the tilt toward increased congressional power. While the change certainly does not signal a diminishing of the president's powers, it does suggest a balance, a renewal of the checks. After Watergate, Congress was forced to admit that it had allowed too much to go on in the White House for too long.

Lowell Weicker was right that the recommendations of the special prosecutor's office and the proposals of the Senate Watergate committee had been ignored. Yet other things had changed. As I moved about Washington each day, I discovered additional bits and pieces that showed at least a short-term effect that Watergate had had on the government.

I had not forgotten the purpose of my visit to Washington in the midst of my post-Watergate research. Everywhere I went, I got into discussions of the campaign, adding background for the article I would write for *Rolling Stone*. While most were not prepared to go on the record, some were. It had been confirmed that Bill Timmons, who had once been in charge of congressional relations at the Nixon White House, had moved into active involvement with Ford's campaign. So I paid him a visit.

Bill Timmons's offices, now that he had departed the ranks of government, looked surprisingly like an annex to the Nixon White House. The handsome office complex was decorated in that same elegant Williamsburg motif. Bill did not look like a retired government employee; yet six years at the House of Representatives, six years as a staffer at the Senate, and six years at the White House, plus his military service, made him a pensioner at forty-five. The worried look of years past was gone, but so was that mood of excitement. Clearly, Bill didn't want any more of that excitement. His new business, lobbying Washington for corporate clients, was prospering.

"I didn't really want to get involved in the election this time around," Timmons said. "I've been fighting it. In fact, some of my clients don't like it very well, either. But, when the President asked, I couldn't tell him no. I think you know how it is."

I did. The conversation turned to people filling the key positions at the convention and talk of strategy. But soon Watergate wound its way into the discourse.

Timmons, sensitive to Ford's phobia about anything that appeared to be like what Nixon had done, confessed, "Despite whatever else they say about Haldeman and Ehrlichman, those guys could get things done for the President. They ran the place. A guy like Cheney (Richard Cheney, Ford's chief of staff) certainly can't keep Kissinger in his place, or put down Don Rumsfeld (Secretary of Defense), who was his old boss."

"Has Watergate changed campaigning?" I wanted to know.

"I'll say it has, it's not half the fun it used to be." Timmons too stressed the atmosphere of suspicion that existed because of Watergate, an atmosphere that made everyone uncomfortable.

As the interview was concluding, he asked me to whom I was

talking. I told him those with whom I had met, and some with whom I was planning to meet. I mentioned my upcoming appointment with Senator McGovern. "That's wonderful," Timmons laughed, enjoying the irony of the fact that I would be meeting with Nixon's 1972 opponent, the target of many of the Watergate abuses.

The ease with which I was moving through the corridors of power in my new role as reporter gave me confidence that I might as well also conquer the hottest story in this city at the time. Everywhere I had been in Washington, people were talking about the latest congressional scandal involving Representative Wayne Hays (Democrat–Ohio) and his nontyping secretary, Elizabeth Ray. Why not interview Miss Ray for *Rolling Stone*? Her book, *The Washington Fringe Benefit*, had just been published and was creating a strange stir. One had the feeling that a lot of mattresses had suddenly been emptied behind Washington's closed doors.

After getting the number from a friend and placing several calls from my hotel, I found Elizabeth was very reluctant to be interviewed. She'd been burned by the press and wasn't talking to any reporters. She had never heard of *Rolling Stone*, although she did know who I was, which gave me an opening. "Listen, Liz, no one knows better than I do what it's like to have newspeople trying to do a number on you."

"I guess that's right," she responded in a less hostile tone, evidencing more of her southern accent.

"Maybe I can do an article that will straighten out some of the misimpressions about you." That old newsman's ploy had been used on me many times. No longer did I buy it, but it still worked on the uninitiated.

The next afternoon, after discovering a message at my hotel giving me the lady's okay, I was off to Elizabeth Ray's apartment. First, however, I called Mo to tell her what I was going to do. If another reporter spotted me entering Liz Ray's apartment, assumed a tryst, and wrote something titillating, it might be difficult to explain at home. There didn't appear to be any reporters watching her building, but, for propriety's sake, I carried my notepad and tape recorder conspicuously.

The apartment was almost uncomfortably neat—no books,

magazines, pictures—nothing other than basic furniture. From the living room I could see the now famous bedroom, with its sofa, white bedspread, and neatly folded comforter, a room that had seen many of Washington's powerful smile on sleepless nights.

Liz was wearing blue jeans and a tight red sweater that accentuated her best features. Her long blond hair looked like it had just been washed, and the soft fresh tresses fell over her shoulders. She was pretty. Barbara Walters might not be happy to hear it, but Elizabeth Ray looked like she could be Barbara's daughter.

Jann Wenner had insisted that the interview be taped, but Miss Ray was reluctant to be recorded. I found a solution. I placed the recorder between us on the sofa, and told her she could turn it off any time she didn't want an answer to be part of whatever article I might write.

I proceeded gently with the questions, starting with those I knew she would be quite comfortable answering, ranging from where she had grown up (in Alabama) to how she had arrived on Capitol Hill as a secretary who couldn't type (she smiled and batted her eyes to that one). Finally, it was time to get into the nitty-gritty of what she had been a part of in Washington—sex and power.

"You were very much, in your own way, connected with that thing in Washington called power. And you were one of the pawns in the power game." Liz realized we were getting into serious business. She nodded and murmured, "Uh huh," like a small child. I continued.

"Without naming names, I'm curious about the mechanics of how it worked. You made indirect references in your book to how you were asked to sleep with somebody to help on a crucial vote on a piece of legislation." I was getting right to the point, and she looked away, obviously embarrassed to be talking about her sexual exploits.

"Uh huh," she murmured again, looking down at the floor.

"You didn't elaborate very much on that in your book. Was there a reason?"

"I'm not sure I understand exactly what you mean."

"Okay, let's. . . . "

"You mean why power was so important to me?"

"No, no." I was becoming distressed. Maybe I should pose the question more bluntly.

"You mean other girls in Washington?"

"No." She was trying to follow me, but, as she had admitted earlier in our conversation, she was not the brightest child. Yet, without coaching, she got the gist of what I was asking.

"We had a whole chapter on that, but it was cut out," she said proudly, but disappointedly. "It was basically how girls—wives and girlfriends—and women in Washington get used."

"And what were some of the examples you had?"

"Oh, well, the wives are also used, you know. Like you know we had a chapter about a couple of wives of congressmen, and how unhappy they were; no names, of course. The drinking problems, the husband away from home and running around, you know. We had some chapters about that which got cut." It was beginning to sound as if the best parts of her manuscript had ended up on the editor's floor.

"Did you see more of Republicans or Democrats?"

"I didn't see any Republicans. In fact, I don't really know any Republicans."

"You know, you've gone through something that's an experience I understand, Liz," I said, with genuine empathy. "It's being a whistle-blower. It's a situation I had to wrestle with for a long time, and deal with and solve. How do you feel about that?"

"Well, some articles were written about me as 'Tattletale Liz,' and the like. . . ."

"Does that hurt?"

"Of course it does," she said, and her voice and face told of that hurt. She paused for a second, then added, "But I can't really let it get to me. I have to live with it, and ignore it."

"But you feel you've not told all, and that you've been very protective of people."

"I tried not to hurt people. Unfortunately, some people feel wronged." She reported that she had truly feared for her life when she told reporters about Wayne Hays, who had told her what the Mafia could do to little girls who caused problems. Liz did not think she had blown the whistle, as much as she had told her story for self-survival.

I was curious to know the impact her activities had had on her once extremely active social life. "Is it tough now to date people?"

"Yes." She looked sad with the answer. "Still, there are a couple of people I consider friends; there's one person who is still around to take me out, Duke Zeibert (the Washington restaurateur), who doesn't mind if I use his name. I mean, everybody else is ashamed to be seen with me, but he's not. He's my true friend."

Liz said that, other than Duke Zeibert and her girlfriend Carol, who was staying with her, everyone was gone. "It's very funny," she said. "I mean, no one is around to hold me and to talk to me. I've had to buy friendship. Well, not friendship, but—the nurse-secretary combination woman you saw leaving. I'm paying for that."

"Do you know why you got involved as you did?"

"Sometimes I've wondered if I was really stupid or what. I've tried to analyze this, to see if I was the dumbest girl in the world to get into what I did. But I didn't think I had any choice. I was used for going out with other men, I mean, I was used in every kind of way." Her look left little to the imagination.

"So, if you had to advise other girls. . . ."

"I would tell them to try not to get into that kind of situation, like I was. I'd tell them that it's not glamorous like I thought it was. It's not that way at all. You know, you pay for every minute of the glamor. You really pay, emotionally and physically, you pay for every bit of the excitement of power," she explained with more feeling, more pain than anything she had expressed.

Liz knew she was used, but always felt she would find a Prince Charming who'd save her. She searched but didn't find him. There were no princes on Capitol Hill, she had decided.

It was time to leave. She had talked for almost two hours, and I barely had the seed of a story. As I began to pack my tape recorder, she asked, "Would you like to see my pictures?" She batted her eyes coquettishly. I must have blushed, because she sighed and added, "You don't have to, of course. I just thought you might like to."

"Sure."

She disappeared into the bedroom and reappeared with a ten-by-twelve-inch living-color photograph of herself, nude. "This is the one I think *Playboy* is using," she observed. "Do you like it?"

"Why, yes," I said, feeling my face flush. Her body was lovely, sensuous and soft-looking. Mo wouldn't be too keen on this phase of my visit, I thought, as my embarrassment and guilt started vying to see which would push me out of the door first.

"How about this one? Actually, I like it better," she said, pulling another revealing picture from her folder.

"You certainly photograph beautifully," I said, now visibly nervous.

"I'm glad you like them."

"Thank you, Liz. I've really got to get going. It's late. I've got a dinner engagement," I lied. I thought she was teasing me, suddenly finding that I'm really shy.

I thanked her again, and, closing the door, I didn't think I would ever see or talk with Elizabeth Ray again in my life. I would not pursue the story. I felt an empathy for her. To do the story I had in mind I would have to "use" her, and she had been used enough.

I don't have the killer instinct that's necessary to be a good journalist, I thought, driving back to town. That bothered me. Why should I have any feelings about Elizabeth Ray? Because I've been where she is. But maybe she's not a survivor. I would just tell Jann that there simply wasn't a story that hadn't already been printed.

It was an early evening for me. I made notes of questions I wanted to ask Senator McGovern, and others, and was asleep by 10:30. Out of the black the telephone rang.

"Hi. I hope I'm not bothering you," a voice that took me a moment to place began. It was Elizabeth Ray. This time, libido and ego were vying for my attention. "I just thought I'd give you a call to ask if you knew when my article will run."

"Gee, I really don't know," I replied.

"Oh, well, did you get everything you needed?"

"Yes, thanks again." Suddenly my male ego told me that this girl was lonely; obviously, she wanted company. My perception of the situation undoubtedly was influenced by my imagination, which had been stimulated by reading her very explicit book. I suspected that I was about to be either subtly seduced or blatantly propositioned. How should I handle it, I wondered? See what she says next, I told myself.

"I just called, John, because, well, I wasn't really sure I should, but you seemed so nice, uh, uh. . . ."

"Yes, what is it, Liz?"

"Well, my attorney told me to call and find out the publication date. So I did. I'm sorry if I woke you. Goodnight."

I'm not even sure I said "goodbye" before she hung up. My ego totally shattered, I got back in bed and started laughing. "You fool," I said aloud to myself.

JUNE 28, 1976—Washington, D.C.

Even though everyone likes to talk about the Elizabeth Ray–Wayne Hays scandal, no one takes it very seriously. There are other Liz Rays in Washington, everyone knows that. There are Liz Rays in every business and in every city. We even had a couple at the Nixon White House. So it's really no big deal.

As for Congressman Wayne Hays, he, like Richard Nixon, appears to have had an almost bottomless reservoir of ill will to draw upon. Most of his congressional colleagues are delighted he was caught with his pants down. But had there been no Watergate, had no poison-tinged atmosphere been left behind, Wayne Hays might have escaped trouble. His lame explanation of why he had a non-typing secretary on his payroll might have slipped through and been forgotten.

Thanks to Watergate, however, Wayne Hays didn't have a chance. His colleagues had no choice but to jump on him, and to make certain their own payrolls were in order. Even the Department of Justice could not ignore this matter, about which, in years past, they would have said that public disgrace is sufficient punishment for a congressman. While it is doubtful that Hays violated any criminal laws, Congress will have to go through the motions of investigating, or be subject to attack for failing to check. John Lindsay is right. Washington is not a very pleasant place in the aftermath of Watergate.

Unlike their Constitutional co-equals in the White House or federal courthouses, members of the United States Senate do not have lavish quarters. Most Senate offices are cramped and crowded with staff, furniture, and files—and a feel of disorganization. Senator McGovern's office suite appeared comfortable, orderly, and organized, I thought as I arrived. From his reception office I was led to a small inner office where the Senator was waiting. As we shook hands, I could not but think how much stronger his personal presence was than the image captured by television. With his well-tailored, dark blue three-piece suit, his white mane razor cut, and his tanned, strong countenance, he looked, I decided with surprise, like a man who could be president.

The Senator invited me to the seating area, where he seated himself in a shiny black rocking chair. As I sat on the sofa, I said, "Senator, I understand you're going to be working as a commentator for ABC news at the convention. What kind of commentary are you planning?"

"I don't know. Do you have any thoughts or ideas?"

"Well, uh," I hadn't expected this, but I gave it a shot. "Maybe you should tell people what's going on behind the scenes, like, say, selection of the vice president—how that's done, things like that—since you've been through the experience."

The Senator laughed. "I'll say I've been through the experience. There's no doubt in my mind that our effort at the presidency was mortally damaged by the Eagleton affair. It was rough, John. I'd not even considered Tom Eagleton as a running mate. Then, after I was nominated, I offered the vice-presidential spot to Ted Kennedy. But he wouldn't give me an answer." Neither McGovern's voice nor face concealed his disgust at the treatment he had been given by Senator Edward Kennedy. "He kept us waiting and waiting and waiting. It wasn't until two o'clock the next day that Kennedy finally turned me down. After that, it seemed everyone said no, which surprised me."

We talked about Jimmy Carter, and McGovern was not very enthusiastic. "Carter's platform seems to be winning the election. Then, once he's president, he'll figure out what to do. But Carter will have a rough race against either Ford or Reagan." I could tell he wanted to change the subject, for he'd stopped rocking.

"John, let me ask you something. You're the first person from the Nixon White House I've had a chance to ask this. I've always wondered if Nixon took my candidacy seriously."

I assured the Senator he had been taken seriously, citing, among other examples, the efforts of G. Gordon Liddy to break into his campaign headquarters, plus strenuous efforts by the White House to confront him on the issues. Yet I had to admit to him that both public polls and the secret White House polls showed Nixon a sure winner. Thus, the concern was more one of making sure the President won by a large margin. Since we had strayed into the past, I tried to connect it with the present. "Do you think Watergate will be an election issue, assuming that Ford gets the nomination?"

"No," he answered flatly, turning his chair more in my direction. "Let me tell you something about Watergate. I knew that my chances of beating Nixon in '72 were slim, but I thought my candidacy could help raise important issues facing the country. While I didn't have any idea about the dimensions of Watergate, still I knew something was wrong. So I repeatedly raised it during the campaign. Do you know what happened? Every time I did raise Watergate, people on my staff would say, 'Senator, no one cares!' They were right, because no one did care. If I couldn't use it in 1972, I assure you it can't be used this year."

"You're not saying Watergate didn't have an impact on Republican politics, are you?"

"I don't know what it did to Republicans. But I do know it certainly had an impact, after we learned what was really going on. I just got back this morning from Canada. Last night I attended a dinner in Winnipeg for the Queen of England, who's up there visiting. Toasts were being made at one point in the dinner and, because I was there, a toast was offered to the United States, specifically to our president." The Senator looked directly at me, with his eyes slightly squinted, a hard look for this gentle man, when he said, "It upset me, what happened when that toast was offered—a titter of laughter went around the room. The president is a joke."

"You mean Ford?" I asked.

"No," he answered abruptly. "The toast was made to the president, to the office, not to a particular man. I've never had anything like that happen to me before, and it's upsetting. Since Nixon brought shame on the office, it's not viewed the same. Nobody would have laughed when Eisenhower or Kennedy or Johnson was president. I think Watergate has caused that sort of disrespect."

From this disparaging analysis of Watergate's world impact, the conversation moved to the fact that the Senator had, during his bid for the presidency, raised many moral issues relating to government, issues that were initially buried by the Nixon landslide, but now had been resurrected in the wake of Watergate. I wondered if McGovern felt vindicated by what had happened.

"No, not really," he said thoughtfully. "But I think that, since

Watergate, the presidency has been made more accountable, to the public, to the Congress, and even to itself."

As I departed Senator McGovern's office a few minutes later, I felt that he had pinpointed the major change in the office of president since Watergate—accountability. From the recommended reforms of the Senate Watergate committee and the special prosecutor's office to the actions of Congress in passing the War Powers Resolution and the Congressional Budget Act, there was an effort to put reins on the presidency. Even the remaining widespread feelings of suspicion in the Washington press corps could be translated into a demand for accountability.

JUNE 30, 1976—Los Angeles.

My trip to Washington, the conversations with both old friends and new people, and the material I have been gathering for my *Rolling Stone* piece suggest a new awareness and interest in the powers of the president since Watergate.

President Ford has never been able to get a grip on those powers, and has been governing largely through the negative authority of veto power. He has vetoed countless acts of Congress, which, given his short time in office, is far in excess of his predecessor. His opponents in the race for the White House, Jimmy Carter and Ronald Reagan, have been pushing a very anti-Washington theme, recognizing the post-Watergate public sensitivity to presidential powers.

Like most historical events, Watergate did not produce immediate and radical change. But the Watergate experience has caused modified attitudes, different perspectives, reappraisals, sharpened consciousness, and a concern that history not be repeated. The changes in government since Watergate have been more in attitude than in new laws, new codes of ethics, new rules and regulations, or in the restructuring of operations. Frankly, I had expected that more legislative action would be taken.

Gerald Ford, as the first post-Watergate president, has done far less to change the presidency than I had anticipated. His changes are only a cosmetic difference in style, rather than any substantive alteration of the presidency he inherited. President Ford is merely operating the Nixon presidency in the absence of Nixon.

Ford has a phobia about doing anything that even resembles Nixon's actions, but, if Richard Nixon woke up tomorrow and found himself back in the White House, other than a few new faces, he could pick up where he left off. I am not too sure Nixon's old Cabinet officers would be so happy to see their old boss back, for President Ford has given them more access to the Oval Office and has ended the Nixon practice of letting the White House staff push them around.

Under Ford, apparently both by design and by the disposition of the man, the departments and agencies have been given far greater independence. Indeed, that fact, the new assertiveness of Congress, and the new suspiciousness and outright hostility of the Washington press corps mark the most significant changes in Washington since Watergate.

The institutions of government that appear to have been most affected are not the White House and Department of Justice, as I would have thought. Rather, the intelligence-gathering agencies like the CIA and FBI have had to weather lingering efforts to exorcise government of "Watergate-type" activities. The full impact on these agencies cannot yet be measured.

One of the areas of the new post-Watergate morality that I became aware of on this trip, a matter I was generally cognizant of but had given little thought, is the ripple effect that Watergate has had on American business. It began because of illegal and improper campaign contributions, then spread into illegal bribes of foreign officials as a part of doing business overseas, and has continued into other areas from antitrust to tax investigations and government contracts. Because of Watergate, investigative agencies such as the SEC have a new attitude about pursuing their powers. American business has been affected by Watergate.

While I had many conversations during my visit about the "morality" of Washington today, and while this subject is on my mind, I have been very restrained. I don't want to sound as though I "got religion" because of Watergate, because I am not sure I did. What I feel and what I do five years from now will answer that question. It will probably be that long before anyone will know if Washington got religion because of Watergate.

My room at the Jefferson Hotel in Washington had a large bookshelf, and actually had been filled with old books, a charming touch. I assumed that the hotel didn't worry about guests' pilfering these books that might have cost five cents apiece at a used-book store. One of the books I happened to thumb through during my visit was a bound, tattered set of old *Saturday Evening Post's*. Back in 1960, the magazine had run a series of articles entitled, "Adventures of the Mind," in which eminent thinkers gave their views on current topics. I enjoyed reading several of these lengthy articles, particularly one by Telford Taylor, who had been the American chief counsel at the Nuremberg war-crimes trials. Mr. Taylor, who had spent his life moving in and out of government service and the practice of law, addressed the question of ethics in public office. I jotted down several things he said, and the crux of it all is, "Historians, philosophers, and sociologists have debated for centuries the question whether Homo sapiens behaves more or less virtuously in his public than his private capacities. But they have always observed that political morality is a social phenomenon. The lapses of public officials do not reflect merely their characters as individuals, but rather the structure and customs of the entire community."

Translating what Mr. Taylor wrote, I guess the question is not only what impact did Watergate have upon Washington, but upon the country at large? Because what happened in that larger community will determine what will happen in the long run in Washington. I don't know the answer to that question—yet.

CHAPTER SEVEN

Kansas City Blues

As I prepared for my trip to Kansas City, I felt like a disinherited cousin planning to crash a family reunion. I was not too comfortable, plus I was troubled by ominous premonitions. I had become especially sensitive to these inner signs, after having paid a high price for ignoring my intuitions during my days at the White House.

I recall vividly those nightmare flashes from my subconscious in the pre-Watergate era. Even on days when a seamless, thick carpet of deception appeared to be neatly containing the illegal activities and dirty plots, I would be visited with fantasies of the entire scheme's collapsing in a national scandal that would bring us all disgrace and, perhaps, even jail. Oh, my prophetic soul!

Years later, it was clear that I had been given glimpses of my own future. These premonitions were the work of a subconscious mind that had put together the pieces I had been unwilling to consciously assemble. I had dismissed these thoughts as too horrible to think, and had thus denied myself the benefit of my own intuition. Ignoring my feelings had brought to fruition my own worst fears.

This time I knew I should examine these feelings, even though they were still fragmented and developing. The least clear of the premonitions was that by going to Kansas City I would be embarrassing myself, even subjecting myself to ridicule. How, or why, was still unclear, for the intuition was inchoate, merely a haze of visions. The second was the more perceptible of these loose thoughts which

159

the calculus of my subconscious had delivered up for my awareness. I fantasized I would end up being more of a news story myself in Kansas City—by the very fact that John Dean was attending these high rites of the Republican party—than any story I might cover as a reporter.

These barely defined concerns were very much on my mind when I finally arrived on Sunday, August 8, 1976, in Kansas City. As I walked from the airplane through the nearly empty Kansas City airport, I had a strong urge to get on the next flight back to Los Angeles and repay *Rolling Stone* for my expenses to date. Instead, I took a taxi to my hotel.

Rolling Stone could not exactly compete with all the television networks, wire services, national magazines, major newspapers, and foreign press for the best available hotel space. In fact, the hotel manager told me when he formally welcomed me to his hotel, *Rolling Stone* had been lucky to get two rooms anywhere.

"Two rooms?" I asked.

"Yes, one for you and another one for Mr. Steadman from England."

So Ralph Steadman was being sent to illustrate my article. I had seen Steadman's drawings, and they were bizarre at times. But then, anyone who worked with the notorious gonzo journalist Hunter Thompson had to have an altered consciousness. We would be a curious pair in Kansas City, I thought.

The next morning I started out early on the business of covering the convention. I picked up my press credentials at the convention center and went to the press room in the basement. There, the daily press releases detailing schedules, announcements, background information, and other tidbits for reporters could be found.

John Lindsay of *Newsweek* greeted me as I was leaving the area with a stack of press releases in hand. We talked for a moment, and I was about to move on when he asked, "Where did you find all the information?" I pointed, he nodded and started off, then stopped. "Say, John, what about your giving me an interview? Maybe we could get a small piece or sidebar out of what it's like for you, being here reporting on this convention." I felt I shouldn't do an interview, so I begged off.

A few minutes later I found myself escaping from this building filled with newsmen, as every one of them had the same idea. No less than twelve other reporters had stopped me to request an interview. In self-defense I found myself fleeing back to my hotel room. I sensed the trouble materializing already. How could I be an observer if I were going to be constantly observed?

Back at my hotel, I found four more messages from reporters. When the telephone in the room rang again, I was happy to hear it was not another reporter.

"Hello, this is Ralph Steadman. I just thought I'd ring you up and introduce myself, let you know I'm here in Kansas City, since we're both here working for *Rolling Stone*."

"Hi, Ralph," I answered with relief. "Welcome to the United States." After some small talk to get acquainted, I suggested he come up to my room and visit.

Within moments, Ralph was at my door. Steadman wasn't what I expected, but then I didn't know what I was expecting. Viewed from one angle, Steadman bears a striking resemblance to Marlon Brando, but, from another, one of his own illustrations from *Alice's Adventures in Wonderland*—the Mad Hatter. Little did I realize at this moment that I would discover in time that he could be either, or neither.

I had been crouched over my typewriter, an IBM electric that the hotel had supplied me at *Rolling Stone's* request. It was broken. The hood of the machine was on the floor.

"Something wrong with your typewriter?" he soon asked, spotting the dismantled machine.

"It seems to be spinning its gears."

Ralph had apparently decided that I was a man who had no idea how machinery operated, so he offered to repair it. I happen to be an innate mechanical wizard, I immodestly confess, and can repair anything from a broken toaster to the latest model of automobile. Yet Ralph was so sincere in wanting to help that I let him proceed. We talked about the problem and soon he had put the small rubber belt, which had slipped off the flywheels, back into place.

"Thanks, Ralph. I'm not quite sure how I could have fixed it without your help."

The phone rang and Ralph answered. "It's a reporter from the *Kansas City Star*. He wants to know if you're available for an interview. What should I say?"

Shaking my head, I asked Ralph to tell him I was tied up.

Back on the phone, and with a perfectly straight face as he looked at me, Ralph told the caller, "I think you've got the wrong number. This is Ralph Cholmondeley of the London *Telegraph* and, to the best of my knowledge, John Dean is still in jail, so I don't think you'll find him here in Kansas City. Cheerio."

I'd liked Steadman from the moment we met.

"Ralph," I said, "I don't think we can cover this convention, at least I can't, unless I get a feel for the city. Conventions are more than meeting and voting and bunting and bugles and all that shit." This was also an excuse to avoid other reporters.

We decided to check out Kansas City. First we inspected the Kemper Arena convention hall. Our tour was thorough but quick, from the bottom of the podium to the top balcony seats. Handsaws sang across the empty arena as workmen readied the hall.

Next it was the Kansas City stockyards, about five hundred yards from Kemper Arena. Why not? We started off toward them but ended up at the West End Bar. Ralph wanted a beer and whiskey first; I was ready for an iced tea. The radio in the bar reported it was the hottest day of 1976 in Kansas City—105 degrees. A nice day to visit the stockyards.

"Stand back there, fellas!" A man as wide as he was tall, dressed from toe to head in khakis much too clean for a stockyard, was shouting at us. "Those bulls will shit on your shoes!" Ralph and I moved back from the pen. This man's spotless clothes marked him as a voice of expertise.

"Where's your abattoir?" Ralph asked a weathered cow-handler lounging in the shade. The man had no idea whether Ralph was looking for a bathroom or speaking a foreign tongue. He stared blankly and said nothing. I translated. "Is there a slaughterhouse here in these yards?"

"Nope, not anymore. They're outside the city now."

"I'd really like to see an abattoir," Ralph said as we walked toward the feed pens.

I now understood where all those violent but appropriate drawings he was famous for came from. But I was not up for blood. "I don't know, Ralph; I'd like to try some Kansas City beef first."

"You're probably right," he said.

Inside a large concrete building with rows and rows of cattle pens, Ralph stopped. "Listen!" The cattle were bellowing in a syncopated rhythm. Low notes sounded like foghorns, the high ones like a clarinet with a split reed. "And look at those faces. I love cow faces," Ralph said. He studied them silently, then spoke again. "I say, John, you know what I see? Those are delegates. Delegates are nothing but cattle."

He was right.

Ralph took out his pad and began sketching.

Suddenly I heard hoof beats. Jesus! Not twenty feet away was a herd of cattle being driven straight at us. I climbed a fence and shouted at Ralph. The cowboy driving the cattle merely nodded as he passed, whirling a sawed-off baseball bat with six feet of leather, obviously disappointed we had not been trampled. "Looks like he also beats his wife and kids with that bullwhip," I shouted as Ralph rushed over, all smiles.

"Did you see that one cow that wouldn't get into the pen? She wouldn't follow the others, didn't know which way to turn; she was blind in one eye. That's an uncommitted delegate!" Ralph had found something. So had I. I enjoyed Ralph's company and his brutal objectivity about our politics.

Back to the West End Bar, which looked like a replica of a set from a western movie, where Ralph ordered another whiskey and beer. He needed fuel. "What the hell is a political convention really all about?" he asked.

Ralph wasn't interested in any textbook definitions, so I tried to quickly separate the chaff. "Well, of course, it's a device for a political party to nominate their candidates for president and vice president. Actually, it's much more and far less. It's a party, a chance for conventioneers to have a good time, you know, fellowship with a lot of like-minded souls. It's a chance for the hierarchy of the political party to make a lot of absolutely unimportant people feel very important by assigning them positions on committees to decide on the platform, or rules, or whatever, or give them exposure on television. Also, it's a chance for the news media to spend a lot of money covering it, even though very few people give a damn about watching or reading all the details that will pour out of here. But what it actually is, I guess, is one of those rituals in American life that make people feel good, like praying in church instead of in a bedroom."

AUGUST 10, 1976—Kansas City.

During our travels, I ran into a couple of Secret Service agents advancing President Ford's trip to the convention. We had a very pleasant visit, sitting on sawhorses in the middle of the floor of the empty convention hall, drinking soft drinks. I decided it was an opportune time to do a little probing on the Deep Throat question, for, even though it was doubtful, it wasn't impossible he could have been in the Secret Service.

"Bill, what kind of problems does the Service have with leaks?" I asked the senior of the two.

"Why," he snapped, "now that you're a reporter, you want us to give you an inside story?" We all laughed, and played with this potential in jest, until I got the conversation back on track.

"What I had in mind was, back while I was at the White House, during Watergate, there was a lot of leakage, so to speak, and it could have come from the Service."

"I'll say there was leakage," he immediately rejoined, "but it wasn't from the Service. Or at least I don't think it was from the Service. Let me tell you something about the Secret Service, John. We don't exactly have the best relationship with the press, so we avoid them as best possible."

"Why do you have a bad relationship?"

"Maybe *bad* isn't the right word, but just not good. The reason is that from time to time we have to become the heavies for the president, or the presidential candidates, or the White House staff. When they don't want to talk to reporters, we get the word, and often physically remove or block them from access. This can really piss them off, and they blame us. So it's not the best of relationships."

The more we talked the less likely it appeared that the Service could have been Deep Throat's base of operations. The Service takes very seriously its pledge of silence in not talking about what it learns when protecting a president or his family. "If we were known as leakers, it would make our protective duties impossible, because we can't protect unless we have both the trust, and cooperation, of those we're assigned to," this agent told me with a very convincing sincerity.

This conversation has convinced me that I should continue to focus on the Justice Department, and the FBI, despite Bill Sullivan's comments.

I dreaded the first night of the convention. Literally thousands of people who could hate me would be assembled. I was a specter of the Nixon past, about which no Republican wanted to be reminded. My presence forced that ugly legacy to mind.

Although I had accompanied Ralph to more bars than I could count, I had not been drinking. Since prison I had closely monitored my drinking, for the years of heavy consumption during Watergate had worried me that I might become an alcoholic. But the pressure I had placed on myself by coming to Kansas City had to be unleashed. At night I wasn't sleeping; during the day I had unconsciously been clenching my teeth until my jaw hurt. So the last night of that preconvention week, Ralph and I went on a drinking spree that left me damn near catatonic the next day. My head hurt so badly that I stayed in bed most of the day in order to be able to make it to the opening night.

The first night of the convention Ralph and I found our seats in the press section, an uncomfortable focal point, but safe. Being surrounded by several thousand newsmen seemed less a threat than being amongst the delegates and other party faithful filling the hall. Many of the newsmen I knew, most I didn't. My seat was right on the aisle and reporters started stopping by. No interviews, I repeated countless times. I had a stack of requests back at the hotel and had avoided them all, except for a student journalist whom I had decided to give a break (a bad decision I later discovered).

"Let me just ask you this, off the record," one reporter who stopped by insisted. "How come you've become a journalist?"

"Off the record?" I said, and he nodded affirmatively. "Well, I gave it some thought and I felt that journalism was a profession an ex-convict could feel comfortable pursuing." He didn't laugh.

Another reporter sat on the steps beside my aisle seat and, in a curt tone, asked, "How come none of your other buddies from Watergate are here?" To which I answered, "Because they're on parole, which prohibits them from hanging out with disreputable people." He laughed, conveniently missing the point.

Maxine Cheshire of *The Washington Post* slid into the seat beside me and said, "I don't blame you for a second for not giving these reporters an interview," and then talked about how she'd be glad to put me into a nice blind item in her gossip column. She left and Theodore White, author of *Making of the President(s)*, walked by, paused, smiled, and said, "I had a couple of mistakes in my last book, didn't I?" I nodded a slow affirmative, and was glad he didn't stop to ask which one had bothered me the most, since I'd not read his book (*Breach of Faith*).

Political prankster Dick Tuck, who had introduced himself to me earlier in the week and told me he was covering the convention for *Playboy* magazine, came over to where Ralph and I were seated.

"Hey, how ya doin'?" Tuck asked as he gingerly approached, almost testing.

"Fine," I said, equally gingerly.

"Maybe you haven't seen my first edition," he said. I had no idea what he was talking about, so I shook my head. "Here, have a look," he said, handing me a copy of a special convention-edition newpaper called *Reliable Source*. Across the top was printed: GET YOUR GREAT WALLPOSTER—FREE INSIDE. I still didn't know what it was, so Tuck said, "Open it up, go on." The newpaper was really a large poster, folded in eighths, with the printing outside. And inside: me!

The picture was a rather forlorn-looking John Dean. I doubted if Tuck knew when or where it had been taken, but I remembered. A photographer had taken it through the window of a U.S. marshal's car when I was headed off to prison. The printing on the huge poster was equally unpleasant: "Ex-creep John Dean makes the Kansas City scene. He's done his time like he oughta/Now he's working for Jimmy Carteh."

Tuck had succeeded in an effort to publicly embarrass me. But I would be damned if I'd let him have the pleasure of knowing it. "That's really clever," I told him in a chipper voice, "thanks for bringing me a copy," and I passed it over to Ralph to examine.

"You bet, John. Glad you like it. We've printed about 10,000 of 'em. They're all over the city. A real collector's item. Folks are snapping them up and hanging them all over."

"Good, it should help sell books later."

"Oh, by the way, I've mentioned *Blind Ambition* in the article about you. After you read it, come on over and tell me what you think."

The article, which claimed that I'd been sent to the GOP convention by the Carter campaign committee to "re-open old wounds," also claimed to have an excerpt from *Blind Ambition* which proved Nixon guilty long before publicly known. Tuck had merely distorted a passage from my Senate testimony, giving it a flavor of reality which caused even Ralph to ask: "Is it real?"

As Ralph studied *Reliable Source*, I got up for a walk outside the Kemper Arena. I felt terrible. The fluorescent-lit parking area and walkways around the convention arena were nearly deserted. Walking near the shadows of the building to avoid being recognized, I shaded my hurt feelings. "Well, you asked for it by coming here," I mumbled aloud to myself. "And you got it."

What had just happened with Tuck reminded me of an incident that had occurred when I was very young, one of those growing-up traumas I had not thought about since childhood. I must have been seven or eight years of age when, roller skating several blocks from our home, I came upon some boys I didn't know. "Hey, kid, come over here for a second," one of them said, "I want to show you something." He held his fist as if he were clasping some treasure. I moved closer for a look and, with all the force he had, he wound up and punched me square in the stomach. The group broke up with laughter as I doubled over on the ground, hurting too badly to cry or strike back. That was exactly how I felt as I walked silently with my thoughts outside the convention hall.

AUGUST 16, 1976—Kansas City.

Despite my best effort to avoid it, my earlier fears have moved from premonition to reality. The story *about* me is increasingly overshadowing the story *by* me.

Realistically, I can't begin to compete for the stories that could be written about this convention. Being *persona non grata* among

Republicans—particularly in their collective state of mind here—I can expect to get the crumbs that other reporters don't want.

For me to write any kind of "think piece" about this convention, I have to rely on the work of other reporters, and I could have done that by staying home. The only original story I can get out of this visit is about the atmosphere surrounding the convention, the mood, and personal reflections on the personalities of the Republican Party.

The only thing Jann is really getting from me is a lot of national media attention, since mention of me usually results in mention of *Rolling Stone*. But maybe that is all Jann wanted from the outset.

Jann Wenner was so exuberant over the press coverage I was generating for *Rolling Stone* that he decided to come to the convention and sit in the spotlight with me for a night. Even though I had refused all interviews, I learned from Mo that the television cameras were periodically flashed on me, and I knew that the print media were taking a fair share of pictures.

I told Jann that I still did not know what I would write about. I wasn't going to do a political analysis because there was very little to analyze, and, since *Rolling Stone* would not hit the newsstands until almost a month after the convention, most of the material in my article would be history.

We agreed that I should do a first-person, impressionistic piece about the mood and flavor of the convention. This would be soft news, reflective and not investigative. While I had no doors slammed in my face, nor telephones slammed down, I had been careful about whom I had gone to interview or telephone. I was not "Woodstein" at work.

After each session of the convention, Ralph and I would visit a different bar in Kansas City. It became a nightly ritual. Often we would depart a session before the herd had a chance to come pouring out, fighting for cabs. The night after Jann's visit we were heading out of the Kemper Arena when I spotted a beautiful blonde wearing outrageous attire for a political convention—a skin-tight, white evening gown—and strolling sexily across the parking lot with a group of television cameramen in pursuit. The lady was none other than Miss Elizabeth Ray.

A few days earlier I had read that she might be "covering" the Republican convention for *Genesis* magazine, but I had seen nor heard no more. Now her presence here seemed a painfully embarrassing parody of my own assignment for *Rolling Stone*. She had been hired to attract publicity for *Genesis*, and it certainly appeared that *Rolling Stone* might have given me the assignment with the same idea in mind. Elizabeth Ray could no more write an article about the convention than I could pose nude in *Playboy*. And maybe people regarded my presence here as a joke, just as they did hers.

Ralph was trying to get a closer look at what the commotion was all about, for the closer Liz got to the hall, the more people were watching. The last thing I needed was for her to spot me, and then be photographed or televised with her.

"Hey, Ralph, over here! Let's grab that cab," I shouted, and headed off on the run after a cab that was pulling out. Steadman hadn't seen me move so fast in the ten days we'd been together, but I was in a hurry to put some distance between myself and Miss Ray. We headed off for the Crown Center, which was the headquarters hotel for the Ford forces.

The hotel lobby was mobbed with young people, and the television klieg lights on the balconies framed the lobby crowd like a movie set, surrealistic and distant. Yet it was immediate, I could touch it. A contingent of Reagan supporters started chanting, "We want Reagan! We want Reagan!" Their signs identified them as Young Americans for Freedom, the right-wing youth of the Republicans. Ford's supporters whistled and booed this invasion of their headquarters. They began answering, "We want Ford! We want Ford!" If the nominating contest had been a shouting match, Reagan would have won.

I started for the bar, where Ralph was waiting, then noticed a group of young men gathered on the balcony. One of them came down the escalator, skirted the crowd, nodded a greeting to a Secret Service man at the fringe, and proceeded ahead of me. I followed and watched him size up the crowd in the bar. Then I joined Ralph.

"Ralph, this may sound strange, but I just saw myself."

"What do you mean?"

"I saw this young guy who works at the Ford White House. I could tell because I spotted his lapel pin—they all wear them for security clearance. He looked about thirty-two, the safe Brooks-

Brothers look, very self-confident. Me, five years ago. I knew exactly what he was doing, and what he was thinking when he came in here and looked around. He was reveling in being one of the President's men. I wanted to tell him it's all bullshit, trying to be somebody by association. Do you understand what I mean?"

Ralph nodded, downing his whiskey and chasing it with beer. It was uncomfortable looking at the young White House staffers, carbon copies of each other and of previous White House staffs. There was nothing I could say to them, even if I dared, for I knew that when I had been there I had had all the answers, just as they now did. I certainly had no desire to go back to all that, even if I could, and I could not.

The hours during the day, before the nightly convention sessions, were the best time to see what was happening and gather material. Delegations were caucusing, debating among themselves and receiving luminaries from both sides. I knew enough delegates from days past to have private phone conversations that embarrassed no one. Both camps were putting the final squeeze on delegates, but privately no one was predicting the outcome. Delegates were choosing sides and, as one told me, "You go with the power, and that's the President." After talking with several delegates on the house telephone at the Continental Hotel, I headed for the deserted coffee shop, ordered a salad plate, and buried myself in the newspaper.

"Excuse me, do you have any salt on your table?" a pleasant voice asked.

"Sure," I said, passing it. She was moderately attractive, midtwenties, blonde, nice figure—but nothing exceptional. I returned to reading the *Kansas City Star.*

"Excuse me, here's your salt back. Thank you."

I reached for the shaker and the middle sections of my newspaper fell to the floor. She gushed her apologies. I smiled a "that's-all-right" smile, but she continued. "Oh, I'm interrupting you, I do apologize." She wanted to talk and was making me the rude one.

"No, it's all right. No problem," I said, putting the newspaper on the table beside me.

"Are you with the convention?" she asked.

"Yes. I'm covering it."

"Oh, how are you covering it?"

"I'm a reporter."

Suddenly, she started laughing. The sweetness was gone from her voice and she barely stopped laughing as she said, "I'm really not nuts, but when you said you were covering the convention I totally misunderstood you." She kept laughing. She's odd, I thought. "Listen, you're not going to believe this—well, you may believe it—but please don't misunderstand me. When you said you were covering the convention, I thought you were a bookie or a pimp."

"Thanks," I smiled.

"Well, I'm a little tired, I guess," she said. "This town is a bitch."

"How so?"

"Well, you don't look like a cop. You're not a cop, are you?"

"No, I'm an ex-convict, as a matter of fact." I was testing for a reaction.

"No kidding," she said, perking up. "What were you in for? I did time myself."

"I was in for trying to steal part of the Constitution." She didn't understand.

"Oh, well, I did time for prostitution. I'm a hooker."

I had sensed that in the way she had flirted for the salt. While I was not the slightest interested in her services, I was interested in talking with her. I had something in common with a hooker: prison. But we had something further in common—a bad reputation. I wondered how she dealt with her soiled identity, if it even bothered her.

"Why is Kansas City a bitch?" I asked.

"Bad cops, they're mean. Now, I'm no streetwalker, but I've talked to the girls who work down on 12th Street. They say the cops are mean as hell, and their latest gimmick is sending pictures of them to the hotels around the city. They haven't caused me any trouble. They don't know who I am, since I'm from Chicago. I was also in New York City for the Democratic convention, but I work on call only. No hustling."

"Is business good here?"

"It's not bad."

"Who are your customers?"

"Well, in New York City it was mostly newspaper and TV men, but here it's been mostly delegates."

She didn't give me the details, but from our conversation I learned that she and three companions had been flown in by someone who was offering sex to the delegates. She did not receive money directly from those she visited, but was paid later—for the total number of tricks—by her sponsor. She was staying in Topeka and was being driven daily, as called, to Kansas City.

Spotting my interest in the story potential, she warned me, "These guys I work for play rough. They don't like curious people." So I asked her some less threatening questions I thought I might be able to work into my *Rolling Stone* article, such as: Who's better in bed, Republicans or Democrats? (Neither, the newsmen are the best.) What was the going rate for her services? (One hundred dollars per hour! One thousand dollars for the night!!)

She had absolutely no idea who I was and could not have cared less. She laughed and made me laugh over both my questions and her answers. Then I asked a question which she knew, from my earlier crack about being an "ex-con," was serious.

"Tell me, you ever thought of going straight?"

"Yeah, I only wish I could. But I've got no other skill. What you see is the best I've got. I couldn't begin to make the kind of money I do working in some office somewhere, although I took typing in high school. You see, I'm trying to save my money so I can send my kid, he's three, to college. After that, I'd like to get out of this racket."

"Does it ever embarrass you, being what you are?" My question was blunt, but I phrased it softly, and in a way that was not offensive.

"Sure. Not as much now as it used to, because I make a point of having no friends, other than some of the girls I work with."

"No boyfriend?"

"I can't let myself do that. But I know what you're asking. What if I met some swell fellow, and he didn't know I was a call girl. How would I handle it? Right?"

"Right."

"I've thought about that. Once I did meet a guy I really liked, and I didn't tell him. When he found out from my old pimp, who was pissed at me, it was all over, even though I wasn't working. Lots of girls who've worked have been through that very thing, and they'll all tell you, you got to lay it out right up front with your man, your kid, your friends. It may hurt, but it will hurt a lot more later if you don't. They either like you for who you are, or they don't. I don't want the whole world to love me, I don't need everyone to be my friend. I know why I'm doing this, and if others don't like me, they can stuff it."

"That sounds pretty tough."

"Why? Did you lose your lady or something for being in the can?"

"No, to the contrary. But I just wondered, that's why I asked."

The next words out of her mouth damn near knocked me off my seat: "Listen, John Dean, let me give you some advice. If you're having a difficult time being who you are, because you got caught up in that mess in Washington, it's because you are laying it on yourself. You live your life the best you know how, and remember that there's nobody on earth who's really qualified to pass judgment on you. That will come later."

Dumbfounded that she had recognized me, I was speechless for a few moments. But I appreciated what she had to say. Other than my conversations with Ralph, it was the only other enjoyable, completely relaxed exchange I'd had in Kansas City.

I needed a friend in Kansas City and found one in Ralph Steadman. This son of a Welsh miner's daughter and an English salesman was open, witty, and incredibly perceptive. He'd left school at sixteen and, before becoming a professional illustrator and, later, a political cartoonist, had worked as a rat-catcher, gardener, swimming pool attendant, and cleaner of the "wall of death" on a motorbike track. He came to the United States for the first time in 1970 to illustrate an article about the Kentucky Derby, which was being written by Hunter Thompson.

Ralph was not at all as wild or weird as his drawings. Rather, he used his sometimes bizarre style to shock people into awareness of his own distress over the decadence, corruption, and immorality that he saw about him everywhere, particularly in America.

Ralph had been retained by *Rolling Stone* to illustrate parts of the Watergate hearings. During one of the intermissions at the Ervin committee hearings, Ralph had leaped from his seat with a beer in his hand and accidentally knocked Senator Sam off his feet. He had a propensity to find himself in such situations. But Watergate had left many questions in his mind, and he was curious to talk to me about what had gone on behind the scenes.

His questions were probing and very much to the point. "What I could never figure out, John, was how you got that position at the White House at such a young age, or what kept you going in it. Have you explained that in *Blind Ambition*?"

"It's strange you should ask those questions."

"Why's that? They're obvious questions."

"I know. But, intentionally, I've not dealt with either of them in my book, other than some cursory explanations. All I said about how I got to the White House was—virtually—I was lucky. Which I suppose is, when you analyze it all, true. My editor at one point asked me where my ambition had come from. I explained that I didn't really know—which, at the time, was true, because I'd always been reluctant to look to see where it had come from."

"Obviously it must have come from your upbringing. Your parents. Undoubtedly that's part of it. Right?"

"Undoubtedly that's true." I was hesitating, for the very reason I'd hesitated with my editor: to shield myself from the pain of returning to my childhood, those years when the putty of my personality was becoming molded into the hopes and fears, the strengths and weaknesses of my character. But Ralph's warm and genuine interest gave me confidence to cross that barrier briefly to find what answers I could.

"I'm not very inclined to look back, Ralph, because while I'm sure that what happens to us as children is important, I think many adults use childhood as a cop-out for adult failures. I believe we outgrow whatever happens to us when we're children, and those who blame their parents for their fates are just rationalizing their own failures as adults."

"I don't disagree, but we certainly can understand better what motivates us by examining those early influences."

"Well, I didn't have a particularly happy childhood," I began, hardly believing I was making that confession to another person. The only person I had ever talked to about my childhood, in my entire life, was Mo. But I had never analyzed it in the context of my later behavior during Watergate.

"As I look back on my childhood now, I remember that every time my family would settle somewhere to live, and I'd develop friends to play with, suddenly we would be uprooted and have to move. We had a good middle-class existence, but my father's business forced him to move a lot. He would take over companies that needed strong management to shape them up. Once he had established administrative strength, he would be offered a better job elsewhere to do the same thing, and off we'd go. It hurt having all those childhood friendships broken up, living with a feeling of rootlessness."

"I suspect it did," Ralph nodded.

"But that's not totally it, by any means. I had a very strong father who demanded the best from both my sister and me. He was very difficult to please. Sometimes I think I have spent my life trying to please him."

"What about your mother?"

"Well, the most important thing in her life was my father. But, also, she subtly pushed him to take better jobs. I don't think my father really gave a damn about making money, other than to live comfortably. He liked to work because of the challenge, and his reward was accomplishing the job."

Ralph smiled and nodded.

"I'm boring you."

"No, please continue."

"If I had to pinpoint the source of my personal drives for ambition and accomplishment, I guess they derive both from negative and positive sources. My mother actually encouraged me to make something of my life. She had grown up in a family that was comfortably upper-middle class, until her father died, and the Depression came. While there were sufficient funds to assure that five girls and one boy had college educations, I always thought my mother felt cheated by that loss of her father, and the good life he provided, until she married my father."

"What are the negative sources?" Ralph asked.

"Reaction to my father's dominating personality. I craved his love and wanted to be the perfect little boy. As I approached my teens, my efforts to please him became an intolerable burden. I pleaded with my mother to send me to a private school, and she convinced my father. So I left home at thirteen and tried to start a new life doing the opposite of anything I thought would be typical of my father. Also, I wanted to show him—and myself—that I was as good a man as he was. That's what drove me to higher and higher jobs. In fact, the reason I chose government, instead of business, is that my father was trying to get me into business and away from government."

There it was in a nutshell, I thought: the encouragement to succeed in life by a mother who subtly suggested that I could be more than my father, and the challenge of competition with my father to be just that. It didn't take a Freudian analyst to see that this is a not untypical life pattern. Hello, Oedipus.

"How did your parents take Watergate?" Ralph asked me.

"Very well. They were loving, understanding, and totally supportive. I tried to let them know well in advance of its appearing in the news what was going to happen, tried to brace them. It also ended my competition with my father. Or maybe I've grown up a little and can see that he's really a fine man. We're closer now than ever, because when I left home at thirteen I never really went back."

My conversations with Ralph filled a lot of the time at the convention, for, by the time Ford had won the nomination, almost everyone was really paralyzed with boredom. Trying to revive the crowd, the Ford strategists screened an image-enhancing biographical film. The press gallery could not see the movie screen in the hall, but watched the film on portable television sets that many reporters had brought to their desks. I could see a picture on a set about twenty-five feet in front of me and hear the sound from the hall speakers, which was a split second ahead of what was appearing on television. The Kemper Arena was dark. The delegates were quiet. Asleep, maybe? A voice shouted from the rafters of the balcony, "Let's go home." I was with him. My mind drifted, forming its own pictures of Jerry Ford.

I remembered Ford back in the House of Representatives, in early 1966. It was my first day at the House on a new job, and Minority Leader Ford was speaking. Standing in the back of the chamber, a man who now works for Ford told me, "He's an able guy, but some say he played football without his helmet too long." That cruel joke had followed Ford for years. It didn't fit him, for when I began working for him I found him bright and an incredibly fast student of facts.

In the years that followed, I saw Ford as an unquestioning soldier and servant of the Nixon White House. I thought of the day I went to Ford to take care of a ticklish little problem in the campaign laws. Reform legislation was being debated on the floor of the House, but it didn't solve our problems on permitting corporations to make contributions to the 1972 convention. Persuading Congress to change the old law prohibiting such acts would have been difficult. I had developed a solution, and hurriedly explained the problem to Jerry Ford in the corridor just off the House chamber. I wanted to get a floor debate to reflect the different interpretations of the old law. "Got it, I'll take care of it," he answered. And he took care of it.

I remembered Ford at the 1972 convention in Miami. First, I thought of how much he'd wanted to go and the letter he had written to Nixon:

> One of the proudest moments of my life was when I had the honor and privilege of presenting you, Pat and the girls to the 1968 Republican National Convention in Miami Beach.

He wanted that proud moment again in 1972, and got it.

Ford was the chairman of the 1972 convention, and I still chuckle over his performance. I was outside the Miami Convention Hall, wandering among the Nixon trailers. The normally unflappable Dwight Chapin, who was orchestrating the entire convention from a prepared script which had been carefully calculated by Haldeman and the President, was in a rage. Dwight was always a gentleman and seldom swore, particularly in the presence of women.

But at that frustrating moment in Miami in 1972, he couldn't control himself.

"That goddamn fucking Ford is screwing us all over the lot," he sputtered at a console of telephones, earphones, and television screens. It looked like his trailer had been borrowed from the Houston space center. I asked Dwight what was troubling him. He exploded. "Ford's drunk and can't follow the script. I'm sorry. I can't talk now. I've got to call Anne Armstrong and get her to take charge of Ford. I'll talk to you later."

Now, on the dais ready to formally accept the nomination of the Republican party to be its standard bearer in the 1976 presidential race, Jerry Ford was as sober as a Sunday school teacher on Sunday morning. His acceptance speech, the usual political sermon to the faithful, ended the convention. I slipped out of the convention hall, and out of Kansas City the next morning, as quickly and quietly as I had earlier avoided the potential encounter with Elizabeth Ray.

Ralph came to Los Angeles a few days later to stay at our home while he completed his drawings of the convention. As Ralph sketched and inked away, I wrote a 15,000-word article that recounted my trip and meetings along the campaign trail, starting in Washington, on to a visit to Salt Lake City to watch Ronald Reagan in action, and ending in Kansas City. After ten days of writing and two days of tinkering at the editorial offices of *Rolling Stone* in San Francisco, we closed the article.

SEPTEMBER 20, 1976—Los Angeles.

Walter Cronkite may be the most trusted man in America— *but not by me!* He really tried to set me up today. I saw a side of Mr. Anchorman I would never have thought existed: Cronkite can be a mean son-of-a-bitch. It was a very disillusioning discovery, but, regardless of how well we think we know a public personality, we rarely glimpse the man behind the performance, as many onetime diehard Nixon-lovers can attest.

Two days ago I received a call from CBS News asking if I would do an interview with Walter Cronkite on the GOP convention. I was not particularly interested, but I called Jann to ask if he wanted me to do it, as added publicity for the article. He was ecstatic and hoped I would. I talked also with Obst and, while he cautioned me not to talk about information in *Blind Ambition*, which was soon to be released under a carefully orchestrated publicity plan, he felt the CBS exposure could only help.

I agreed to be interviewed by Walter on the condition that it would not be about Watergate or about my forthcoming book, but only about the article I had written for *Rolling Stone*, which would hit the newsstands on September 21st. That was fine with CBS News.

The next day I went over to CBS Television City, their studio complex in Los Angeles, and was taken to a small room with one chair and a television camera. I was told that Walter would interview me by satellite from New York. While I would not be able to see him, I could hear his questions through a small earphone. "This is a hell of an expensive hookup," one of the local technicians told me.

Walter wanted to talk briefly with me on the telephone, to discuss the parameters of the interview we would tape for on-the-air play: "Hello, John, this is Walter Cronkite in New York. How are you?"

"Fine, thanks."

"Did you enjoy your experience in Kansas City?"

"I don't know that *enjoy* is the right word, but the beef was certainly good."

"Agreed." He chuckled.

"Walter, I noticed at the convention that you were the only anchorperson in the TV booths (which were high above the convention floor, with large glass panels to look down on the proceedings) who stood up every time the band played the national anthem." When I noticed this during the convention, I was impressed that the man was so patriotic.

"Well, I do stand. Actually, it's a nuisance getting untangled from all the wires I'm plugged into. I never used to, until some irate viewer wrote me and chewed me out for sitting through 'The Star-Spangled Banner,' so ever since I've been standing."

McLuhan was wrong, I thought. The medium is not the message, the image is the message. Walter ended the chitchat: "I'm not going to go over my questions with you, because that's against my policy, but when is the publication of your book?"

"It's October, but we're not going to talk about that, that's my understanding."

"Have you seen Nixon personally . . . ?"

"Walter, it is my understanding that this is an interview about my experience covering the convention for *Rolling Stone*, and not about Watergate or my book . . ."

He interrupted me as quickly as I had him. "Fine, I think we've talked enough. You get wired up out there and we can begin this. So I'll be talking with you in a moment by the earphone they'll give you."

The studio lights were turned up, I was wired with a small microphone and earphone, and placed in a small, solitary chair. Beside me was a large glass window, and behind it were other technical people at control panels and monitors. I felt like a man in a 21st-century gas chamber. A little red light on the camera came on, and Walter's voice entered my ear: "John, can you hear me all right?"

"Yes, I can."

"You're coming in clear." Then he said something about "levels" to the technical people. He then asked a few innocuous questions about the convention, which were interspersed with more subchatter with other voices from the New York and Los Angeles control booths. And, then, the interview quickly deteriorated into an unpleasant confrontation that was costing CBS hundreds of dollars a minute.

"Mr. Dean," Walter began clearing his throat, "you have a book coming out in October about Watergate. Is there really anything you know that hasn't already been said?"

You rat, I thought to myself, and gave as evasive, yet provocative, an answer as I could come up with, although I was so damned mad I could barely remember his question. He proceeded to interrogate me about the book and Watergate, and I resisted by giving nonanswers. I could tell he was becoming irritated, but I was outraged by this blatant double-cross. Apparently, he had figured he'd just get Dean in there, put him in the hot seat, and get a newsbreak on his book. Cronkite had pretended to be interested in the *Rolling Stone* article just to get me to the studio. Within a few minutes, the satellite interview came to a screeching halt. Walter gave up on me, and as I disconnected the earphone I heard a lot of ugly words being exchanged between Walter and the control rooms.

"He doesn't sound very happy," I said to an embarrassed director, who popped into the little studio from the control room as I unwired myself and stepped from the chair in front of the camera.

"That's an understatement. But thanks for coming anyway,

John." We shook hands, and, as I headed out of the studio, I was thinking about how unlike the kindly Uncle Walter of the CBS Evening News Cronkite had become when his deception did not go his way.

"Sorry, but I'm not into playing little games," I told the local director of our coast-to-coast connnection. "If you had been honest, I could have saved you a lot of time and money. I didn't come here to talk about Watergate, and you knew so."

Moral of the story: even the most trusted man in America might sell his grandmother for a newsbreak.

The next day, September 21st, *Rolling Stone* was on newsstands throughout the country, and CBS News had missed the opportunity to pick up a potentially explosive newsbreak. Cronkite did not even mention, let alone use, any of the interview taped the preceding day. In the following weeks, however, many other reporters called me about the article. They had spotted a story which Cronkite had missed, and eventually broke what became known on the front pages as the "Earl Butz Affair."

The story began innocently enough at the Kansas City airport where I met several other Californians returning home after the convention. Among them were Sonny Bono and his girlfriend, Susie Coelho, whom I had met in Los Angeles. Sonny introduced me to Pat Boone, who had been a Reagan delegate. Since he had been pleased with a profile that *Rolling Stone* had published about him a few months earlier, Pat consented to give me an interview concerning his experiences as a delegate.

After breakfast, Pat changed seats with the man next to me for the interview. We were engaged in intense conversation, when Agriculture Secretary Earl Butz walked up the aisle to say hello to me. Earl and I knew each other from the Nixon years, and he was very friendly. I was one of the first people he had met in the Nixon administration, because I had had to clear him for conflicts of interest and the like before he could be appointed to his Cabinet position.

Just before Earl came up to us, Pat and I were discussing the fact that the party of Abraham Lincoln was not able to attract black voters. I had a notepad out and was scribbling furiously. When Butz interrupted, I told him that I was interviewing Pat and introduced them.

What followed was very awkward, and quite unusual. Earl launched into mini-monologues sprinkled with profanity and off-color humor on the subjects under discussion, and I continued to take notes. I thought at the time this was a strange performance on Earl's part. There was no drinking going on. There was no eaves-dropping on my part. I was in the middle of an interview with pad and pencil in my hands and Earl chose to shoot off his mouth. Perhaps the most extraordinary part of his curious behavior was the delivery of these bigoted views in raw language in front of a well-known Christian. I suspected that if we had not been at 35,000 feet, Pat Boone would have excused himself and stepped out of the plane for a while. He was noticeably uncomfortable with what was being said.

When the plane landed in Los Angeles, I saw Earl again in the baggage claim area and we had another little chat. But I did not think about his odd remarks again until I was reading my notes for the article. I decided that this was such an outrageous performance for a Cabinet officer that I would include the scene on the airplane in my piece for *Rolling Stone*, but without identifying the secretary. So I described what had happened:

> Pat Boone, Sonny Bono and a distinguished member of Ford's cabinet (who shall remain nameless, unless *he* chooses to be otherwise) talked freely about the convention on our flight back to California.
>
> Pat Boone had gone to the convention thinking, "I'll get some sun, play some tennis, swim and do a little voting in the evenings." He was wrong. The Reagan team placed him on their sales force, sending him from delegation to delegation where he could sell the Ronald Reagan he'd known for many years. Pat found this a little difficult "because the Ford people didn't want us in some places, like the New York delegation." While we winged west Pat became philosophical about his political experience in Kansas City and the future of the nation in an election year. "Both Ford and Carter are fine Christian men, so I'm not worried about what will happen this fall." But something did bother Pat about Republican politics, and we'd just begun discussing the dwindling base of the party when the shirt-sleeved cabinet member ambled over. I introduced the secretary to Pat and then asked him a question.

"Mr. Secretary, the delegates seemed very disappointed with Dole (whom Ford had selected as his running mate). He really got a lukewarm reception. The cabinet looked like they'd just arrived at a state funeral when Dole spoke."

"Oh hell, John, everybody was worn out by then. You know," he said with a mischievous smile, leaning over the seat in front of Pat and me, "it's like the dog who screwed a skunk for a while, until it finally shouted, 'I've had enough!' "

Pat gulped, then grinned and I laughed. To change the subject Pat posed a question: "John and I were just discussing the appeal of the Republican party. It seems to me that the party of Abraham Lincoln could and should attract more black people. Why can't that be done?" This was a fair question for the secretary, who is also a very capable politician.

"I'll tell you why you can't attract coloreds," the secretary proclaimed as his mischievous smile returned. "Because colored only want three things. You know what they want?" he asked Pat.

Pat shook his head no; so did I.

"I'll tell you what coloreds want. It's three things: first, a tight pussy; second, loose shoes; and third, a warm place to shit. That's all!"

Pat gulped twice.

I refused to identify Earl Butz to all who called after publication of the article. But a reporter for *New Times* (a now-defunct investigative magazine) decided that since I would not tell him, he would deduce it for himself. This reporter called every Cabinet member's office to determine who had been flying from Kansas City to Los Angeles on the day after the convention, until he discovered that Earl Butz had been on the plane. Armed with Earl's name, he called Pat Boone. He said to Pat, "Are the remarks that Earl Butz made to John Dean in front of you reported accurately?" And, unsuspecting, Pat said: "Absolutely." Well, the reporter had his story.*

On October 4, 1976, Earl Butz was forced to resign his post as Secretary of Agriculture. I was surprised by the extreme reaction to

---

*Later, I heard that David Obst had boasted of providing the tip to *New Times*. I never confronted him on the matter, for to my knowledge David never knew—but might have guessed.

his remarks, for I did not feel Earl was the racist some were saying he was. I would never have guessed that his indiscretion would cost him his job. But the campaign had reached a peculiar level where political fluff had become serious issues. Before Earl Butz cracked his joke, the major issue confronting the voters was whether or not Jimmy Carter still lusted after women in his heart, as he had confessed to *Playboy* magazine he once did.

Of course, Earl Butz need not have felt alone in singing the Kansas City blues. Singing right along with him were Ronald Reagan, Howard Baker, Nelson Rockefeller, John Connally . . . and me. The convention had given us a Republican presidential nominee with whom I had special reasons to feel uneasy. Also, it had effectively dashed my naive hopes of a career in journalism. I had unexpectedly become involved in another whistle-blowing episode with Butz. And I'd ended up receiving political ridicule from bored commentators that equaled what I had suffered at the height of Watergate. This search of a new identity, a new profession, honor—it had failed.

I had had enough. I wanted to go and hide. Yet I couldn't, for I was scheduled to begin a multi-city book tour for *Blind Ambition*. And Gerald Ford's nomination in Kansas City had set the scene for yet another political storm. Like the victim in a bizarre recurring nightmare, I would find myself again engaged in a very serious game of "truth or consequences" with a president of the United States.

CHAPTER EIGHT

When You Kick the King

My favorite country lawyer, Charles Norman Shaffer, first said it to me when he was representing me during the Senate Watergate committee hearings: "If you kick the king, you've got to be ready to kill him." At the time, Charlie was testing my readiness to testify publicly about the misdeeds of Richard Nixon. When *The Washington Post* called me in late September 1976—just six weeks prior to the presidential election—to tell me that they would be breaking a story from *Blind Ambition* about President Gerald Ford, I thought of Charlie's remark; I knew that this story would hit Ford right in the shins.

In examining advance page proofs that my publisher had "leaked" to them, the *Post* had focused on the story about now-President Ford's role as the former minority leader of the House of Representatives in blocking the first planned congressional investigation into Watergate. It was only a passing reference to Ford in the book. But it would be a major problem for him, and, I would learn, for me.

This particular shadow of Watergate had been cast four years earlier, during the 1972 presidential-election campaign. On September 15, 1972, I was meeting in the Oval Office with President Nixon and Bob Haldeman. We were relieved that only seven indictments had been handed down for the Watergate break-in that day, and everyone in the White House felt the "Watergate problem" would end with Nixon's re-election. The private White House polls showed that no one then cared about Watergate except the partisans, who'd stop harping after the election. The FBI investigation was complete, the Democratic National Committee lawsuit was under control, and the few newsmen still digging were plowing the wrong fields.

The remaining problem was Wright Patman, an obstreperous and eccentric Texas congressman who chaired the House Banking and Currency Committee. Hesitatingly, I raised this remaining nasty problem with the President, explaining the subterfuge to kill the Patman investigation. A ludicrous claim had been contrived that the hearings would violate the civil rights of the seven indicted for the break-in. The President liked the scheme, but I had explained only part of the problem to him.

The Patman investigation was pursuing the same area as the initial thrust of the FBI's investigation by tracking the large sums of money that had passed through the bank account of indicted Watergate burglar Bernard Barker. Privately, re-election committee finance chairman Maurice Stans explained that the contributions had nothing to do with the Watergate break-in, and he was telling the truth. Rather, the monies had been turned over to Gordon Liddy when they arrived after the election-law cutoff date for anonymity. Liddy, in turn, had passed them on to Barker for cashing and they had been returned to the re-election committee. But Stans was very distressed that first the FBI, and now the Patman committee, was investigating these transactions. I suspected that, although unrelated to Watergate, they were somehow illegal.

When the FBI had stumbled onto these funds the problem had worked its way right to the top. On the so-called smoking gun tape of June 23, 1972, Haldeman explained to the President that the FBI investigation was "in the problem area," and the President approved a plan to have the CIA divert the FBI's investigation. I could not tell if the President was aware of the specific nature of this "problem area." Haldeman was, and earlier the President had talked to Stans about the Patman investigation. Either on general principle or because of his specific knowledge, the President was quite anxious to block the committee investigation. But there was another problem.

White House congressional-liaison man Richard Cook had been monitoring the Patman investigation. Cook had told me the investigation would proceed, unless Republican Minority Leader

Gerald Ford stepped in to pull the Republican members together.
Ford was ignoring the matter, and was busy campaigning for Republicans for Congress.

As I sat in the Oval Office on September 15, 1972, explaining
that "Jerry Ford is not really taking an active interest in this matter
that is developing," I was repeating a message from Dick Cook.
Cook had told me that Ford was off on a campaign junket to Mid-
dletown, Ohio, where he had told the press, "I have made my own
personal inquiry, and the answers received over the past several
months were verified with the (break-in) indictments, in that I've
been assured that no one in the position of leadership were involved
(sic)." However, those in a "position of leadership" were very unhappy when I told them of Ford's inattentive attitude toward the
Patman inquiry.

"Put it down," Nixon abruptly told Haldeman, who opened his
notepad. "Jerry should talk to Widnall (the ranking Republican of
the Banking and Currency Committee) and, uh, just brace him, tell
him I thought it was (time to) start behaving." I agreed and the
President continued, "Jerry has really got to lead on this. He's got to
be really (tough)."

"Jerry should, damn it," Haldeman injected. "This is exactly
the thing he was talking about, that the reason they (the Demo-
cratically controlled Congress) are staying in (session) is so that they
can run investigations."

"Well, the point is that they ought to raise hell about this," the
President said with a clenched fist. And again, later, the President
emphasized Patman's investigation. "Well, the game has to be
played awfully rough. I don't know," he said soulfully, then paused
and turned to Haldeman. "Now, you, you'll follow through with—
who will over there? Who—Timmons, or, with Ford, or—How's it
going to operate?" The President always insulated himself in dealing
with matters such as blocking a congressional investigation or pres-
suring congressmen. However, he was anxious to know the mechanics for turning off the Patman committee.

"I'll talk to Bill (Timmons)," Haldeman answered, and made a
note on his notepad. Then he had a second thought. "I think—
yeah."

I interrupted with, "Dick Cook has been working on it."

"Cook is the guy," Haldeman quickly agreed, making a further notation.

The President didn't seem satisfied, and suggested, "Maybe Mitchell should."

Haldeman thought about it. "Well, maybe Mitchell ought to," but then asked, "Would, could Mitchell do it?"

"No," the President declared flatly, after reconsidering.

"I'll talk to Cook," Haldeman said later to resolve the problem, but the President still wasn't satisfied.

"Oh, I—maybe Ehrlichman should talk to him (Ford)," thinking Ehrlichman would be added weight to swing Ford into action. "Ehrlichman understands the law, and the rest, and should say (to Ford), 'Now God damn it, get the hell over with this.' "

Haldeman wasn't convinced Ehrlichman was the man. "Is that a good idea? Maybe it is," he shrugged.

"I think maybe that's the thing to do," the President concluded. Then to let us know the seriousness of the matter, the President said in a theatrically stern voice, "This is big, big play. I'm getting into this thing. So that he (Ford)—he's got to know that it comes from the top."

"Yeah," Haldeman nodded.

"That's what he's got to know," the President emphasized, turning to me.

"Right," I confirmed, and Nixon continued, "and if he (unintelligible) and we're not going to—I can't talk to him (Ford) myself—and that he's got to get at this and screw this thing up while he can, right?" We agreed, and the President again reminded Haldeman, "Tell Ehrlichman to get (Banking and Currency Committee member Garry) Brown in and Ford in and then they can all work out something. But, they ought to get off their asses and push it. No use to let Patman have a free ride here."

When the conversation ended I departed and waited for Haldeman to emerge from the Oval Office to make certain who was to do what. Bob said, "I'll talk to Timmons about the Patman thing. I don't think we need Ehrlichman. Bill (Timmons) can handle Jerry Ford."

The events that followed that September 15th meeting are extremely sensitive—a sensitivity caused by what vice-presidential nominee Gerald Ford later said, under oath, about his reasons for assisting in blocking Patman's hearings. At the time of Ford's confirmation hearings, November 1973, the tape of the September 15th conversation in the Oval Office was not available as a basis for questioning him. Nonetheless, the issue was raised in these hearings in the Senate by West Virginia Senator Robert Byrd, who asked Ford: "Were you in contact with anyone at the White House during the period of August through October 1972 concerning the Patman Committee's possible investigation of the Watergate break-in?"

"Not to my best recollection," Ford answered.

When Byrd pressed further, wanting to know if Ford had talked with Haldeman, Ehrlichman, me, or anyone at the White House about the Patman investigation, Ford "categorically" denied ever talking with the President, Haldeman, Ehrlichman, or me. He did acknowledge that "almost daily, during my period as Republican leader in the House, I talked with Mr. Timmons, or someone in the Legislative Liaison Office of the White House, but even in this case I do not recall any conversations concerning this particular matter."

Senator Byrd pressed, with an incisive inquiry about Mr. Ford's motivation in assisting in blocking the Patman hearings. Ford said that some Republicans on the committee had come to him and urged him to call a meeting of all the Republican members. Ford did this, and said the conversations were general discussions of how to handle the Patman hearings. Senator Byrd, who clearly felt Ford's actions were politically motivated, summarized Mr. Ford's position with some disbelief: ". . . as I understand you, any efforts that you may have contributed towards the stifling or the impeding or the blocking of such investigation by the Patman Committee was not born of your feeling . . . that such an investigation would be harmful to the President and harmful to his chances of re-election or harmful to your party . . . ?"

Ford's answer was unequivocal. "The answer is no, Senator Byrd."

Ford's role in blocking the Patman investigation was again raised at the House vice-presidential confirmation hearings by Congresswoman Elizabeth Holtzman, who said, "I understand that you as a Republican leader played a role in the stopping of the investigation plan in connection with the report by the Banking and Currency Committee investigation."

Ford began to answer, but the Congresswoman had more. "This

is not my question, Mr. Ford; let me finish. Now, I understand also from your testimony that although you met with Mr. Timmons of the White House virtually every day, you did not discuss with him these matters of the allegations in the Banking and Currency staff report and you did not discuss the White House role or White House interest in stopping the investigation by the Banking and Currency Committee; is that correct?"

After Ford and Holtzman sorted out some confusion over the question, he answered, "I did not discuss the action that I took, which was to call two Republican meetings of members of the Banking and Currency Committee, with Mr. Timmons or anybody else."

Holtzman continued. "I understand. What I wanted to ask you was, did you discuss with Mr. Timmons or with anybody else at the White House whether or not the allegations made by the Banking and Currency staff had any basis in fact or not. Did you discuss with them, let's say up to the period of November 1st?"

"I do not remember discussing those allegations with anybody on the White House staff in 1972," Ford responded.

I learned of Ford's confirmation testimony long after it had been given. It was the fall of 1975 when a reporter called me at my home in Los Angeles with a question about my Senate Watergate committee testimony.

"John, do you remember your testimony about the White House effort to block the Patman committee?"

"Yes, why?"

"Well, there are three places where you refer to 'the Republican leadership.' First, after Patman announced that he would hold a vote on October 3rd on issuing subpoenas, you testify, and I'm quoting, 'With this announcement the White House congressional-relations staff began talking with the members of the committee as well as the Republican leadership of the House.' Then later on in your prepared statement, after mentioning that Bill Timmons was among those whom Patman would subpoena, you say that Timmons 'had been working to prevent the hearings from occurring . . . through his conversations with the Republican leaders and members of the committee.' Finally, the third place you talked about the Republican leaders is when you were telling of the nose-counting efforts to block the hearings, and you testified, 'Mr. Timmons discussed the matter with the House Republican leaders who agreed to be of assistance,' etc. Now, my question is, who are you referring to when you talk about the Republican leaders?"

"I'm surprised that nobody ever asked me that question when I was testifying. I was referring to Jerry Ford, but I pulled my punch, because I didn't want to drag any more Republicans into the mess than necessary."

"That's what I figured."

"Why do you want to know?"

"Have you seen Ford's confirmation testimony?"

"Nope."

"You should read it."

A few weeks later, I was in Washington and decided to obtain a copy of Ford's testimony. Off to the Government Printing Office bookstore I went, where I tried to purchase copies of the confirmation hearings. They were out so I placed an order. That night, talking with friends, I was shown a copy of an October 1975 *Washington Monthly* article by Marjorie Boyd: "Is the President a Perjurer?"

Ms. Boyd had sifted all the available evidence and concluded:

> It certainly appears from material now on the public record that President Ford committed perjury in his vice-presidential confirmation hearings of November 1973, when he declared repeatedly and vehemently that he had not dealt in any way with the White House during his efforts to squash the Patman investigation the previous year. The only way this appearance of perjury can be dissipated, if it can be dissipated at all, is by release of the White House tapes from the fall of 1972, which are now in the possession of Philip Buchen [Ford's counsel].

I arranged to meet the next evening with Hays Gorey, the *Time* magazine reporter. Hays knows Washington politics and Watergate as well as his own children, and he was a person I could talk with about this matter. I joined him across the street from the *Time* Washington bureau offices, at the Sheraton-Carlton Hotel's cocktail lounge. Almost instantly we were huddled over a bowl of peanuts, deep into a conversation that wasn't to be shared with the stragglers remaining from the cocktail hour.

"Do you think Ford's really going to run, or is he just making noises like a candidate, so he'll not be considered a lame duck?" I asked Hays. Ford had reversed his position about not running for the presidency about two months earlier.

"I still can't tell if he's serious or not. I'm not sure he really knows himself, because I don't think he'd run if Betty Ford's health were bad. Ultimately, I think her health will decide it for him. What do your old friends over there say?" Hays asked, nodding his head in the direction of the White House.

"They say that he says he's going to run, but still they're not positive." Then, on an off-the-record basis, I told Hays about the possible Ford perjury situation. He was aware that several reporters already were looking into it.

"You think Ford did lie, then?" he asked.

"I'll say this. I know I wasn't lying when I testified before the Senate Watergate committee about Timmons's dealings with 'the Republican leadership' on the Patman investigation. If anybody had asked me who I was talking about, I would have said I was talking about Jerry Ford. In fact, I did testify that it was Ford before the impeachment committee."

Hays was slowly nodding his head.

"Although I was never present when Timmons talked with Ford in person or on the phone, I can't imagine why he would have told me he'd been talking with Ford if he had not. But I have more than just Timmons's word. I can remember when Dick Cook came in to Timmons's office and told us about how Ford was calling a meeting in Les Arends's office off the floor of the House of Representatives, to pull the Republicans together to block the Patman investigation. Dick also indicated that he had talked to Ford. And, in addition to that meeting, I had other conversations with both Timmons and Cook that involved Jerry Ford."

"That's very interesting." Hays was still slowly shaking his head from side to side. He stopped, munched on some peanuts, washed them down with his extra-dry martini, hunched closer toward me, and said, "John, it would be a hell of a story. I'd love to write it." The waitress penetrated our huddle, asking if we wanted a refill. We did, and Hays continued, "Are you going to write about this in *Blind Ambition*?"

"No, not really. I'm not sure the story fits, other than very tangentially. But I must say that it does bother me, knowing what I know about Ford now."

"I guess so."

"That's why I wanted to talk. I went down to the Government Printing Office yesterday, trying to get a copy of Ford's confirmation testimony. They were out, but while I was there I picked up a copy of the final report of the special prosecutor's office. I just wanted to make sure I had no obligation to report what I knew about Ford, more than I'd already told them. Anyway, after rereading their charter, it looks as if Ford's possible perjury is not within their jurisdiction. In fact, I don't even know if he really did commit perjury."

"Sure sounds like it, though, doesn't it?"

I nodded agreement. "You know, Hays, the prosecutor's office literally went over every inch of my Senate testimony, line by line. At one point they told me they were not investigating the obstruction of the Patman committee hearings because they considered the hearings, as well as the effort to block them, political. During discussions of those hearings, however, we did talk about the fact that I had referred to Jerry Ford. Even more interesting, however, when I testified before the House impeachment committee, I said flat-out that Ford was the one who had helped the White House block the Patman investigation. The impeachment committee was looking at the obstruction of those hearings as a possible impeachable offense. Of course, those are the same people who approved Ford's nomination."

"Your evidence is not really new, then?"

"Indeed not. But no one has noticed it. I guess it's up to the press, just as it was in Watergate, to decide what's important and what isn't. But maybe I'm wrong, maybe this is not even important to the press, and is a sleeping dog that ought to be left lying."

"Well, I'm not so sure about that," Hays said, smiling.

"Do you want to do something with this? If I go public, I'll get charged with some dubious motive for coming forward. Actually, I have no bones to pick with Ford, but I know from other reporters who have called me that this issue is lurking just below the surface. I'd like to get it cleared out before it boils into something more than it is right now."

"I think you're absolutely right."

"Hays, I think you ought to see what you can find out."

"Do you think Timmons will confirm your position?"

"No. He's going to have to deny it. I understand he signed a sworn affidavit that he had never had any contact or conversations with Ford about the Patman investigations. Cook will also deny it. He's got himself a fancy, high-paying job as a lobbyist in Washington. I saw him on an airplane a few months ago, when I was flying out of Chicago. It was a strange meeting; he looked at me, then squinted his eyes hatefully, and turned away. He's the first guy I've run into from the old Nixon White House who looked like he'd seen a ghost when I appeared. I guess he knows what I know, and it doesn't make him feel very good."

"Well, maybe I'll give him a try, anyway. You never know what will turn up," Hays said, making a note on a scrap of paper from his pocket.

"I think the way to unravel this, Hays, is to get hold of the records from either the House impeachment committee or special prosecutor's office. Because I think, probably, that Ford talked not only with Timmons and Cook but, very possibly, with Haldeman or the President himself. Jerry Ford was just too active on this issue, too enthusiastic about it, too determined to be successful in blocking those hearings, not to have been really jacked up by somebody at the White House—somebody at the top. I think if you look at the records of when Ford and Nixon had dealings, there may be evidence that they did have dealings about this time."

Hays made some more notes on his little scrap of paper. Then he asked me, "If I get some other people to speak on the record, will you go on the record on this?"

"I will."

After our meeting, Hays Gorey set to work. But he immediately and consistently ran up against a stone wall. No one would talk. After he spent a month with no progress, Hays gave up.

When editing the final version of *Blind Ambition*, in the spring of 1976, I considered adding more material on this matter, but I had already devoted several pages to showing how serious the White House had been about blocking the investigation. It had been an all-out White House effort, including my calling Treasury Secretary John Connally, at Haldeman's suggestion, for his thoughts on how to put political pressure on Wright Patman. Haldeman hoped that Connally's Texas-politics background might produce a nugget that could be used against his fellow Texan, Patman, to dissuade him from pursuing the matter. Connally indeed thought that Patman might have received political campaign contributions "from an oil lobbyist up here. I don't believe Mr. Patman has reported them, either."

In *Blind Ambition* I noted:

> Timmons, who met regularly with Jerry Ford, had explored with him Connally's suggestions about Patman. "What do you think?" I asked Timmons. "Do you think we ought to dig into this stuff? Parkinson [a re-election committee lawyer] sent me a file on what contributions these guys have reported."
>
> "Well, John, you know, this is kind of sensitive," said Timmons, "and I talked to Jerry about it. Jerry doesn't think it would be such a good idea. And, frankly, I'll tell you the problem is that, uh, Jerry himself might have some problems in this area, and so might some of our guys on the committee. I don't think we ought to open this up."
>
> "I see. I guess that scraps that."
>
> "Yeah, I guess it does."
>
> "Well, how does your head count look?"
>
> "It's gonna be close, but I think we can pull it out. Jerry and Dick Cook [Timmons's aide] tell me they're sure every one of the Republicans is lined up. They're gonna march them into that committee room like cattle, all together. Nobody's gonna be off playing golf that day. But we still need some Democrats to carry the committee. I'm working on the Southerners. I think we can get a couple."

I was well aware that even including this much additional detail would make Jerry Ford unhappy. But I decided it was very little more than I had testified to before the Senate Watergate committee, and then clarified in testimony before the House impeachment committee. These facts were already public. Besides, there was no way this could become an issue in the 1976 presidential campaign, as *Blind Ambition* was not scheduled for publication until January of 1977.

The day that I learned that the Book-of-the-Month Club, not exactly a partisan organization, had bought the rights to publish *Blind Ambition* in October 1976, and that the entire publication schedule had been readjusted accordingly, I knew that even this brief passage could cause some stir. So I was not surprised when *The Washington Post* leaked it on September 23rd—right in the heat of the '76 campaign. However, I did not expect the rapid escalation of events that followed.

The day after Earl Butz resigned, I flew to New York to be interviewed for the "Today" show by host Tom Brokaw and NBC news reporter Carl Stern, who had covered Watergate for the network. The lengthy interview was taped to begin airing on October 13th, the beginning of the official publicity tour that I would make as the author of the book.

When *The Washington Post* had published its story about the conversation I recorded in *Blind Ambition* with Bill Timmons, he was asked for a comment. As I expected, Timmons denied it, as he denied ever having talked with Ford about the White House effort to stop the Patman investigation. Veteran newsman Carl Stern immediately attacked that issue—and my credibility. It was as if, after all these years of my testimony's having held up, here might be a weak spot. More important, if my story was true, it raised questions about the truthfulness of Gerald Ford's testimony. And that was potentially a huge story.

I was confident in my knowledge and, in fact, I had not written all of which I was aware. So when Stern began pushing, I shoved right back with more details, and stated during the interview that Timmons's aide, Dick Cook, had also spoken with Ford. This, of course, made Ford's original denial even more flimsy. I did not call Ford a liar, despite the efforts of both Carl Stern and Tom Brokaw to provoke that charge.

Dick Cook nearly came unglued when he was approached by other NBC news reporters who were dispatched immediately for his comment on my interview. He refused to say anything on camera, which always raises some suspicion with reporters. Even more disconcerting to Carl Stern, who called me after I arrived back in California to inform me, was that Dick Cook had virtually pretended not to know me, let alone to have met with me about such nasty business. I told Stern that he could clear that matter up very quickly, since I had all my phone logs from the White House, and would go through them. The logs, recorded by my secretary at the time I was at the White House, had been used as unimpeachable evidence in countless Watergate proceedings. When I studied them, they showed that Dick Cook had been a regular caller, indeed he'd even been a visitor to my office.

Confronted with these facts, Dick Cook changed his tune a bit. He decided to issue a statement, more accurately a broadside against me, which revealed the fear he felt now that he was a lobbyist for the Lockheed Corporation, which had its own history of Watergate-related problems. Cook called me a liar.

Dick Cook's statement to NBC also said that my memory had been prompted in order to stimulate sales of the book, and that "despite John Dean's repeated and frantic requests, I never spoke with Mr. Ford about the need to deny Mr. Patman's request for subpoena power." Throughout Cook's lengthy statement he repeated what had become, during the days of Watergate, the standard White House defensive posture and attack on my credibility. Maybe Dick Cook forgot that this posture hadn't worked the last time.

I thought about what Cook had said, after it was reported to me in another call from Carl Stern. My immediate reaction was to bury him with hard evidence of what had happened, because I had had a chance to take a look through my files, and I knew there was evidence there to reconstruct the events. I decided against it, however. I would let him stew in his own juices, and would not escalate the debate. He knew who was lying and protecting Ford. If others should escalate this issue, I would hold my evidence closely and blow him out of the water at the right moment.

Dick Cook's calling me a liar annoyed me more than it should have, I thought. I knew why. My honesty was the only bit of public honor I had to hang on to, and I wasn't about to let him wantonly sling mud at it. Suddenly I recognized my years of passivity about public attacks. I'd been a fool. I had never made any effort to correct the record when outrageous lies to discredit me and my testimony had been orchestrated years earlier by the Nixon White House. I had crawled for cover when I had been blatantly mischarged at the GOP convention with campaigning for Jimmy Carter. Maybe it was time to forget the gentlemanly approach.

The more I thought about it the madder I got, and I headed back to my filing boxes and began digging to see what supporting material I had. I was surprised to find that I had more than I remembered. Of particular interest was a copy of the congressional resolution creating the Patman committee, which Dick Cook had given me and on which I had jotted notes from a conversation with him. Interestingly, both the Senate Watergate committee staff and the special prosecutor's office had looked at my documents, photocopied them, and returned them to me.

With these documents and my phone logs before me, I reconstructed what had happened after the meeting on September 15th, when Richard Nixon had demanded that Jerry Ford get involved in the fight to stop the Patman hearings.

Bob Haldeman, during the September 15th meeting, had pulled out his yellow pad and made the following note at the top of a clean sheet: Alongside Dick Cook's name, Haldeman noted, "Ford—brace Widnall re Patman hearings." Opposite the initial "E," for John Ehrlichman, Haldeman wrote, "*Must* get minority together raise hell re jeopardizing defendants. P. [President] can't talk to you—but it must be done." Also under "E" there was another note: "Get Garry Brown and Ford in." To the best of my knowledge John Ehrlichman was never brought into this matter. Haldeman told me that he would take it up in the morning at the regular staff meeting with Bill Timmons.

I have no personal knowledge that Haldeman did take it up with Timmons, but it seems likely that he would have done so. Certainly Timmons was interested in the matter. In fact, he was worried—for reasons that were never clear to me—about the fact that his name had been put on the list of witnesses to be called by Patman. Early in Watergate's public unfolding there had been some mistaken press coverage about one of the Watergate burglars sending material to Timmons, and it had never been straightened out in the public's mind. Actually, Timmons had not a thing to worry about. But he was highly motivated in wanting to block those hearings.

Timmons's deputy, Dick Cook, was an appropriate person to handle the matter before the Banking and Currency Committee, since at one time he had been the minority counsel to the committee. He knew the members well. Cook was principally dealing with Congressman Garry Brown of the Patman committee, who was a Michigan congressman, as was Gerald Ford. The Cook–Brown–Ford grouping represented a bunch of old friends working together on a problem. Undoubtedly, much of Cook's communication with Ford would be through Brown, who would see Jerry daily on the House floor. However, Cook had a very good relationship, independently, with Ford.

My phone logs indicated many conversations with both Dick Cook and Bill Timmons, and I was sure the logs were not complete, because often I had used the inter-office phone to reach them, and they had done the same. The logs reflected only the calls that had come in through my secretary. Dick Cook had called me on September 6, 7, 11, 14, and 29, and October 2, 6, 11, and 12. Bill Timmons had called on September 11 (twice), September 28, October 2 and 11. I'd also had meetings with both Cook and Timmons, one meeting with Cook in my office, and several meetings with Bill Timmons in his office. All of these calls and meetings involved matters concerning the blocking of the Patman committee hearings.

There was no way for me to be certain exactly how much action Cook and Timmons had generated with Ford, so I reviewed what Jerry Ford had done in the period between September 15th and November 1st, the latter date being the date the Patman committee hearings had ended. My records indicated that Ford had called and presided over two meetings of the Republican members of the Patman committee to develop strategy to block the hearings, and to try to get the Republicans to act in a unified manner.

Also, Ford had sent a letter to all the Republican members of the Patman committee just before the crucial committee vote on issuing subpoenas on October 3, 1972, telling them that it was "imperative" and of "utmost importance" that they attend the session. Timmons had told me that many Republicans were talking about taking a walk instead of voting.

My notes from a session in Timmons's office with both Cook and Timmons indicate that one of the problem members of the committee was Congresswoman Margaret Heckler. In a book I had read by Pulitzer-prizewinning journalist Clark Mollenhoff, I learned that, at the very time the Congresswoman was making up her mind on how to vote on the Patman committee, she had had a meeting with Jerry Ford. She had mentioned that she had not had time to read all the allegations the committee had against the White House, and now was not inclined to bother, since Jerry Ford had told her "the White House had assured him that Watergate was simply a caper perpetrated by Liddy, Hunt and some irresponsible Cuban-Americans." This statement by Margaret Heckler was illuminating, because Jerry Ford had testified under oath that "I do not remember discussing those allegations with anybody on the White House staff in 1972." One wonders where he got the information he relayed to Margaret Heckler.

Another series of memos I found in my file also raised questions. On September 11, 1972, I had received a memo from Ken Parkinson, one of the lawyers at the Nixon Committee for the Re-election of the President, with suggestions for counteractions against the Democrats who were pursuing Watergate. Ken discussed a series of lawsuits, ranging from a malicious abuse suit against Democratic party chairman Larry O'Brien to a libel suit that was being filed by Republican finance chairman Maurice Stans. Finally, he proposed that a complaint be filed with the Fair Campaign Practices Committee. Haldeman particularly liked Ken's last idea, and apparently it was decided at a morning staff meeting that the best people to file such a complaint would be the Republican members of Congress. So, another memo was forwarded to the congressional-relations staff instructing them to follow up.

I reported to Parkinson that his idea had been sold. A few weeks later I received a copy of the complaint filed with the Fair Campaign Practices Committee. The complaint was written on the congressional letterhead of the minority leader of the House of Representatives—Gerald Ford. The letter was dated October 5, 1972, and was signed by the Republican leadership of the Congress—Ford, Congressman Leslie C. Arends, and Senators Hugh Scott and Robert Griffin. For a man who never talked with the White House during this period, Jerry Ford certainly had a hell of an instinct for what the White House wanted done.

The next set of documents in my files were very curious, and only indirectly related to Gerald Ford. On October 16, 1972, Bill Timmons wrote me the following note:

Baron Shacklette is the administrative assistant to Chairman Patman. He is 63 years old, a lawyer, with a background which includes Army CIC, government investigator at several agencies, including GSA, and chief investigator of one of Patman's subcommittees.

I'm told he is an expert in electronic surveillance and so recognized by his bugging colleagues. I'm also informed he figured in the Goldfine case* some way.

You might want to check Shacklette out to see if he's still involved in these practices for Patman.

Nothing was done about this particular tip from Timmons. But on November 1, 1972, a few days after the very negative report of the Patman committee came out, I received a memo that evidenced White House desire to get back at Patman, however possible. In fact, I suspect this information came from the President, since it was sent to me by Rose Mary Woods, Nixon's personal secretary. The memo noted:

> During the Goldfine–Sherman Adams thing Goldfine's attorneys were holed up in a hotel room and were discussing their client's case and someone noticed an object under the door and they opened the door and squatting on the floor on the other side of the door with a pair of ear phones was Baron Shacklette and with him was Jack Anderson.
>
> This can be verified by going to the newspapers at that time.

I remember chuckling over this confidential note. Indeed, it was old news that Jack Anderson had been wiretapping early in his career, and now it was more ironic given the attacks that Anderson had made on the administration for doing the very same thing. But the significance of these notes is that they showed the disposition of the White House to attack the staff of the Patman committee.

Finally, I found, in news clippings in my files from the time, that Jerry Ford had sent a telegram to the Speaker of the House on November 1st demanding that the entire Democratic staff of the Patman committee be fired. He was charging them with improperly releasing a report of the committee's findings, which were damaging in their Watergate implications. Again, it is amazing that Jerry Ford

*See Chapter Six for a brief discussion of the Sherman Adams–Bernard Goldfine scandal.

knew exactly what the White House wanted—without talking to a soul.

It is a point of historical irony that the Patman committee hearings were closed down under White House pressure, because it was this closure that provoked Teddy Kennedy to commence his Senate investigation, and it was this Senate investigation that in turn resulted in the Senate resolution creating the Ervin committee. Perhaps had Nixon encouraged the Patman committee to go forward, it would have been the one and only congressional investigation into Watergate. Given the very limited jurisdiction of the Patman committee, Nixon might well have survived such an inquiry. There's an example of White House stupidity I wish I had recalled when I was talking to Daniel Ellsberg.

All this digging in my files managed to cool my temper. While I could not prove that Ford had committed perjury, I felt much more comfortable if push came to shove on my statements. But there was still the possibility that this accumulation of indirect evidence was leading me to the wrong conclusion. Maybe Timmons and Cook had only told me that they were dealing with Ford directly when, in fact, they were dealing through intermediaries. Bill Timmons had mentioned Les Arends's name on several occasions. Given the busy schedule that Ford kept in those days as minority leader, possibly Timmons did deal with Ford through Les Arends. Cook talked constantly about his dealings with Congressman Garry Brown, the member of the Banking committee who was being most helpful. Maybe Cook was dealing with Brown, who, in turn, was talking to Jerry Ford. While all this still would make Ford's confirmation-hearings statement more a "half-truth," it would also make it less than perjury. I wasn't absolutely sure.

The next three weeks became a frenzy of activity as I began my book tour. Each day as I traveled to television stations, meetings with magazine and newspaper reporters, or into radio studios, I would pick up bits and pieces of information about the Ford perjury question between interviews. Because I was frequently being asked questions about the latest developments, I managed to make notes in my journal on the escalating confrontation between myself and Gerald Ford.

OCTOBER 10, 1976—Los Angeles.

Two days ago Congresswoman Elizabeth Holtzman and Congressman John Conyers each wrote letters to Watergate Special Prosecutor Charles Ruff (the latest and last in the succession) requesting that he investigate Ford's possible perjury and his role in obstructing the Patman investigation. Holtzman pointed out that someone had to be lying: Ford told the Senate that he had no recollection that he had talked with anyone at the White House, including Bill Timmons, about the Patman investigation. He told the House he may have talked to Timmons "in general terms" about it. Timmons filed a sworn affidavit saying he had never talked to Ford, even in general terms, about the Patman investigation.

OCTOBER 13, 1976—New York.

The "Today" show aired. Interesting that Jerry Ford is campaigning here in New York, yet he has not issued a statement regarding the charge. If he can, I hope he will clear up the entire matter.*

OCTOBER 14, 1976—New York.

Yesterday Elizabeth Holtzman wrote another letter to the special prosecutor, based on the information in the "Today" show interview, raising the matter again.

Today I watched Ford's nationally televised press conference, and was flabbergasted! He began by announcing that the special prosecutor had cleared him of charges of misusing campaign funds, a charge which had been issued several months earlier and had been investigated for several weeks by the special prosecutor.

After that statement, reporters started grilling him on my allegation. He ducked. Then he bobbed. Then he weaved. He refused to answer their questions. Unbelievable! Rather, he claimed that the "matter was fully investigated" during his vice-presidential confirmation hearings. That's ludicrous, and every reporter in the room knew it.

---

*Years later I read an account of this day by Ron Nessen, Ford's press secretary, in which he states that Ford met with Walter Cronkite on this date. Ford told Cronkite there was no truth to my charge. Uncle Walter said Ford's word was good enough for him. The intrepid Cronkite!

This could get very sticky. I thought Ford would be able to explain all this. Instead, he's stonewalling it.

OCTOBER 16, 1976—Washington, D.C.

Special Prosecutor Ruff yesterday responded to Elizabeth Holtzman's inquiry, stating that Ford's involvement in blocking the Patman hearings had already been investigated by the staff at an earlier time. They had determined that it would be difficult to show the requisite "corrupt" intent in such political and legislative activity. With regard to the "accuracy of President Ford's testimony at the time of his confirmation," the special prosecutor said that this was not a matter "within the jurisdiction of this Office, but would, rather, fall within the general authority of the Department of Justice."

Today's newspapers and the morning television news are all carrying stories that Henry S. Reuss (now the chairman of the House Banking and Currency Committee and a very respected member of the House of Representatives) has charged Ford with "stonewalling" at his press conference. Reuss called on the special prosecutor to release the relevant Nixon White House tapes, since Ford was being evasive.

Former Watergate Special Prosecutor Leon Jaworski has charged me with withholding information. "What bothers me is, why hold a matter of this kind for several years?" And Leon concluded that I had done it intentionally for my book. Leon is such a putz!

Jaworski obviously has no idea what his office did or did not investigate. Not only was all this raised before in my testimony, but Leon's own staff went over it with me. Even more amazing, as Charles Ruff has stated, is that it was not of interest to Jaworski's office. If Cox hadn't left Jaworski a sharp staff, probably nobody involved in Watergate would have been sent to jail. The man is lucky—and so is the country—that Archibald Cox was there first to set it all up before Nixon sacked him.

OCTOBER 17, 1976—Washington, D.C.

The media types are going crazy again. They smell another Watergate. It's front-page time all over. Mo says the calls are coming in so heavily at home that she's turned the bell off on the telephone and stopped answering it.

OCTOBER 19, 1976—Washington, D.C.

Congressman John Conyers has called on Special Prosecutor Ruff to "specifically outline the basis for his decision not to investigate" Ford's potential perjury. Conyers requested that Ruff reconsider that decision.

Yesterday I talked with a Ford White House aide and longtime acquaintance. He said that my interview on the "Today" show had gotten Ford so upset he could hardly speak and, when he did talk, it was a lot of ugly invectives and expletives about me. Apparently the White House staff had to talk Ford out of publicly attacking me, telling him to play it cool at his press conference. But they never expected him to play it so cool that he wouldn't even answer the questions.

"You gave him a hell of a right cross, and Jerry's not used to being punched like that," I was told. "All this is too damn reminiscent of the old days." A statement with which I agreed.

I learned that the White House is also going to try to counterattack with an attempt to discredit my "Today" show interview by claiming I was paid by NBC to come on and say those things. "Guess who gave Ford that information?" my friend asked. "None other than Walter Cronkite, who said he had it on good authority that you'd been paid $7,500."

Congresswoman Elizabeth Holtzman yesterday wrote to Attorney General Edward Levi, requesting that he order the special prosecutor to investigate the allegations that Ford had lied. She also said that she "deeply regrets that this matter must be raised in the heated atmosphere of a Presidential election campaign," but noted that she had asked for this investigation three years ago, and nothing had been done.

Today I talked with Charlie Shaffer on the telephone. It was a vintage, circa 1973, conversation, and he seemed to be vicariously enjoying my new scrap with Gerald Ford.

"So you decided to kick another president. Are you prepared to finish this one off, too?" Charlie asked facetiously.

"Are you looking for work?" I countered.

"You got it down pat; hell, you don't need me anymore."

We bantered, and laughed a bit more, then Charlie asked, "Seriously, where is this going to go? How far? Because, if I know one thing about you, I know that you're not sticking your neck out on something that you don't know to be a fact. I also bet every

damn reporter in the country knows that, too. And a lot of the public understands it, as well. Where is this going to end, John?"

"I'll be damned if I know, Charlie. But I'll be frank and say I
could do without it."

"Bullshit, it's got to be selling a load of books."

"Well, my friend, just as there's a lot more to life than working
at a nice job at the White House, there's a lot more to life than
selling books."

OCTOBER 20, 1976—Washington, D.C.

This had to be one of the fastest investigations in history. Attorney General Levi announced that they have "carefully studied"
my interview on the "Today" show, my previous testimony before
the Ervin committee, Ford's confirmation testimony, and the de-
nials of Bill Timmons and Dick Cook. They have also checked with
Leon Jaworski to see what he might know. Conclusion: "On these
bases, it has been concluded that there is no credible evidence, new
or old, making appropriate the initiation of a further investigation."
So Levi said that was it.

Levi's position has produced outrage both in Congress and in
the media. Carl Stern tracked me down and was sputtering his disbelief. He said that NBC was going to get to the bottom of what
was going on, because he said something was astray.

I learned today that Dick Cook has backed off. On a public-
radio interview he said he "can't categorically deny" telling me he
had a conversation with Ford. "Dean might have a memo of the
conversation. I can't remember that well," he said. Finally he
stated, "I can't win a battle with John Dean and I know that. Dean
has a 100% batting average." When I learned of Cook's retreat, it
changed my attitude about this matter. I have no desire to escalate
it in any way. I had been carrying my notes from my file in my
pocket, prepared to add more detail if it were necessary. But I have
not volunteered it.

Today I gave an interview to *The Washington Star*, which will
appear on the front page. It's a verbatim question-and-answer session that won't be distorted through reportage; in doing so, I tried
to cool the matter off a bit. This is all too reminiscent of the past.
Thus, I carefully explained to the *Star* that I was certain that Jerry
Ford had no intention of covering up when he helped to block the
Patman hearings. He didn't know what we knew. (This was certainly charitable, I feel, for you had to be living in a tree in Wash-

ington in those days not to realize that the Patman investigation was into plenty of very embarrassing areas. Ford certainly knew he was not aiding the pursuit of the truth when he stopped the hearings. But I didn't say that.)

OCTOBER 22, 1976—New York.

Elizabeth Holtzman and others have charged Attorney General Levi with a "cover-up" and a "whitewash." Sounds familiar!

OCTOBER 23, 1976—Los Angeles.

I returned from New York in time to catch the final debate between Carter and Ford. About a quarter of the way into the debate, Jack Nelson, the Los Angeles Times Washington bureau chief, who had covered Watergate and knows his stuff, asked Ford if, since he had become president "because of Watergate," he didn't have a "special obligation to explain in detail your role in limiting one of the original investigations of Watergate, that was the one by the House Banking Committee. . . . Will you name the persons you talked to in connection with that investigation, and since you say you have no recollection of talking to anyone from the White House, would you be willing to open for examination the White House tapes of conversations during that period?"

Nelson's question would be hard for Ford to dodge, I thought. Yet Ford did it, albeit ineptly. In fact, as he stood there at the podium in the auditorium at Williamsburg, Virginia, before the cameras that relayed it to the nation, the President of the United States gave a blatant factual distortion.

Ford repeated again that he had testified under oath before both the House and Senate confirmation committees on the Patman matter and that the matter "was gone into by (those) two congressional committees," which overwhelmingly approved him, he noted. Of course, that simply is not a factual statement. The chairmen of both of those committees have said publicly that Ford's repeated statements to this effect are misleading, because any "clearance" of Ford was based only on information available to the committees at the time of his confirmation hearings.

Next, Ford pushed distortion to outright falsehood: "The special prosecutor, within the last few days, after an investigation himself, said there was no reason for him to get involved, because he found nothing that would justify it." In fact, Special Prosecutor

Ruff had said nothing of the kind. Ruff had said he had no jurisdiction to get involved. But Ford was implying that Ruff had cleared him.

Finally, Ford stretched his credibility to the extreme by saying: "And then just a day or two ago, the attorney general of the United States made a further investigation and came to precisely the same conclusion." To the contrary, Attorney General Levi had said he would not make an investigation, and, in fact, the evidence clearly showed he had only taken a cursory look at the problem.

Ford said that the matter should be "closed once and for all." As for the request that he have the tapes turned over, he said, "I have no right to say yes or no." That did not sound like a man who wants the tapes released. Then Ford repeated how "all the committees, the attorney general, the special prosecutor, all of them have given me a clean bill of health."

Hadn't Ford learned anything from Watergate? The man was in deep trouble, that much was clear from his answers. Here he had the perfect chance to clear himself, yet he decided to do the opposite.

The panel member who had asked the question, Jack Nelson, looked amazed as he listened to Ford's response. With his follow-up question he did not call Ford a liar, but noted nicely that his question had not been answered: "If I do say so, though, the question is that I think that you still have not gone into details about what your role in it was." And then Nelson pressed again about whether Ford would be willing to ask that the tapes be released for examination. Again, Ford ducked the question, saying that it was a matter "for the proper authorities" and repeated how everyone had investigated and cleared him.

Jerry Ford is hiding, covering up. His performance could lead to no other conclusion. Deep in the pit of my stomach, I know that we are headed for real trouble if Jerry Ford is re-elected. Given the post-Watergate atmosphere in Washington, if this question is not resolved before Election Day, the Democrats will sure as hell pursue it afterward.

OCTOBER 26, 1976—Los Angeles.

This book-touring business is absolutely exhausting. Carl Stern called while I was on the run to report that he was still in pursuit. Carl said he had filed a Freedom of Information Act request with the Department of Justice to determine the nature of the investigation they'd conducted, but, much to his amazement, the information request had been turned down on the basis of the attorney general's discretion. Unfortunately, there is nothing in the Freedom of Information Act that would enable the attorney general to exercise such discretion, and Carl plans to press on to force them to state their reasons for not providing the information to him.

The heavies are starting to move on Ford today. I read a *New York Times* article quoting Peter Rodino, chairman of the House Judiciary Committee, who had headed the impeachment probe. He rejected Ford's claim that he had been cleared on this issue by his confirmation. Buried in the article was a comment from Rodino that, while nothing could be done now, something could be done later. I don't know if I was reading into it more than was there, but the reporter was implying that this issue is headed toward an impeachment investigation. This is really getting very unpleasant.

OCTOBER 27, 1976—Los Angeles.

Banking committee chairman Henry Reuss sent President Ford a telegram stating: "Despite repeated opportunities you have still not told the public the truth or falsity of John Dean's recent allegation that one of President Nixon's White House aides, Richard Cook, talked to you about the efforts to block (the Patman hearings). Your failure to provide a specific and direct answer to the Dean charge raises new questions about your role in the obstruction of the 1972 investigation." Slowly, but steadily, the congressional machinery is cranking up. Only the defeat of Jerry Ford at the polls is going to make this issue go away.

OCTOBER 28, 1976—Chicago.

Yesterday Dick Cook released another statement saying, "I am not only willing, but anxious to state under oath the circumstances surrounding Dean's distortions regarding me in connection with his promotion of his book '*Blind Ambition.*' " Carl Stern said that NBC newsman Jim Polk has been talking with Dick Cook who has "progressively been changing his story, and tune." Apparently, Cook now says that he did meet with me on many occasions and he admits that we did talk about his approaching Ford. But he says he never in fact did meet with Ford. It looks like a two-thirds admission. Bill Timmons still refuses to be interviewed by NBC or anyone else.

Also, Dick Cook has charged NBC with "pocketbook journalism," accusing them of concealing the fact that they paid me. Obviously, Cook is working closely with the White House.

This effort to discredit my interview I doubt will work. I received the $7,500 back in January of last year, after my release from prison. It was a financial understanding David Obst negotiated to make certain there was no pocketbook journalism. For their $7,500 NBC was given the first option for the documentary rights to *Blind Ambition*. However, they waived their option on my book before I appeared on the "Today" show to eliminate the charge that I was paid for that interview. The $7,500 was a nothing issue. Obst, whom I saw last Tuesday, said that Bob Haldeman had been paid $100,000 by CBS News for his interview. (The Obst figure amounts to $50,000 more than was reported in the papers, but David has his own unique and reliable sources.)

OCTOBER 29, 1976—Chicago.

The wire services and newspapers are reporting that Attorney General Edward Levi's investigation of Ford was no real investigation at all. I was shown a copy of the article before an interview by one of Chicago's local NBC anchormen.

I felt drained by the book tour, and debilitated by the stress of the ongoing confrontation with President Ford, when I arrived in Chicago. Thankfully, it was the last stop on the first phase of my tour, and it was marked by an odd incident. Doubly odd, because it was tied to a not unrelated incident that had occurred many months earlier in Chicago. The latest incident happened at the American Airlines ticket counter in Los Angeles, as I was about to board my flight to Chicago.

"Are you John Dean?" a smiling ticket agent asked, tearing the flight coupon from the folder of tickets.

"Not the one you're thinking of," I snapped, flashing a mean look.

"You sure look like him," the man said, smiling, thinking I was playing a game.

But this was no game, and my usually placid, controlled temper came rumbling and roaring to the surface like it had been stung by a bee. "Goddamn it, you're wrong, pal, so buzz off," I barked, grabbing my ticket and heading for the gate. I was surprised at myself. I could not remember ever having been so rude.

What had come over me? I wondered. Why the outburst? How absurd of me to push this ploy of nonrecognition so far. Obviously, this man recognized me, and the ticket said J. Dean. I stopped, turned around, and went back to the counter. I said to the agent, "Please excuse me for being so rude, but I have a little problem. I wasn't very nice, and I apologize."

I had a problem indeed—but it was not so little. Over the past few months I had begun to deny my own identity consistently, even in situations where the denial was completely unnecessary. This self-camouflage had started back in the spring, before I'd gone to Washington to get background material for my *Rolling Stone* article.

On May 26, 1976, I had had a one-stop lecture in Chicago, at the West Suburban Breakfast Club, at the awful hour of 7:00 A.M. Rather than waste a trip to Chicago, I decided to visit Barry Golson, a senior editor at *Playboy* magazine, to explore my writing something for *Playboy*. After my speech I met Barry at his office in the Playboy building, where he introduced me to others on the staff. We went out to lunch and, while descending in the crowded elevator, I began feeling intensely, and disturbingly, conscious of my identity. To deal with this discomfort, I assumed what I hoped was a low profile—standing to the back of the elevator, eyes down, cleaning my glasses with my necktie. I hoped I was less recognizable without my glasses.

As I hid, I was struck by the thought that once I had wanted, more than anything else, to be someone. Now I wished I were no one, or at least not the person I had become. When the elevator door opened, I sighed with relief, for I had not been recognized.

"Oh, don't I know you?" a little gray-haired woman asked the moment Barry and I emerged in conversation into the lobby of the Playboy building.

I smiled and nodded, but secretly I shuddered. It was a half-acknowledgment that I hoped would end the matter. It did not, and she stopped me with a hand on my arm. Barry stopped, too, obviously intrigued.

This happened to me often, but in the past I had not given it much thought. It always made me wonder if it meant I was famous or infamous. I suspected the worst and thought that people might sneer, snub, or insult me, although it had never happened once. I felt at this moment that luck was running out.

Actually, at worst, people treated me quite well and, at best, even admiringly. There was fan mail; people stopped me on the street to say "thank you for telling the truth"; others requested autographs; the best tables in the best restaurants were available without waiting; and influential people extended themselves, expressing interest in my well-being. All this, of course, was pleasant, and over the years I had let down my guard. But now it was up.

I was sure this woman staring at me intently with her eyes slightly squinted and her jaw tightly clenched, would ask, "Aren't you John Dean of Watergate?" That was the usual question, and what worried me was the reaction that might follow my admission to this lady. The thought occurred that, to avoid embarrassment, I would answer, "No, but that bastard Dean, who looks like me I guess, has caused me no end of problems." Such a rude response would blunt the encounter instantly.

"Yes, indeed, I recognized you," the woman continued, but the intense look on her face had faded into a sweet and comforting smile. "Why, you're James Dean, the actor," she declared. Then, patting my shoulder, she added, "And I certainly enjoyed your last movie."

Barry Golson looked like he might explode with laughter, but he managed to contain himself, and moved in closer to hear how I would handle this case of mistaken identity.

"Thank you, that's very nice of you to say." Then I smiled, shook the hand she had extended rather demurely, and, with another "thank you," moved away.

"That was wonderful," Barry said, as we headed for Michigan Avenue. "Does that happen often?"

"Not quite like that."

"Why didn't you tell her who you are?"

As we hurried to cross the street to avoid oncoming cars, Barry forgot his question. I was glad, because I was not sure what the honest answer would be.

The ploy worked so well, however, that I tried it again, when in Washington, and I had even used it during my book tour. It had worked every time, in every situation. People are not sure they are right when they spot people they recognize only by television or newspaper pictures. We are either taller or shorter, better looking or less good-looking, than the image in their minds. Thus, the inevitable: "Aren't you . . . ?"

Three or four, and possibly more, times I had denied my identity in the past few weeks since the confrontation with Ford had heated up. Denial was becoming a practice, rather than a game. It was not that I was always concerned at the moment about some ugly confrontation, but it was a way of avoiding any discussion of the past. The absurdity of this ploy, and the extreme to which I had carried it, raised questions about my mental stability.

Here I was on a nationwide tour to promote *Blind Ambition*. Television, radio, newspapers, magazines—I was doing the works. Before this, I had toured the lecture circuit like a Chautauqua preacher, "sharing my Watergate experiences." In these circumstances I would talk publicly and unflinchingly about the worst days of my life. But as soon as I got offstage, I didn't want to be recognized or approached. And I was literally scared of harmless people. The paradox was obvious.

Was I only comfortable when it was financially advantageous to talk? No, that wasn't it. I gave lectures without an honorarium; I wrote candid and lengthy replies to inquiries, and spent long hours with reporters, researchers, and writers seeking my knowledge about Watergate. Yet, if these same people had approached me in a supermarket or at a cocktail party, I would have shied away from them. There is distance, a lack of intimacy, about these public appearances or academic encounters.

What was the explanation for my behavior? The last leg of a book tour was the wrong moment for much self-analysis. But I knew I must examine this later—stop playing the first-year psychology student with myself and find some real answers.

After a long day of book promoting in Chicago, I returned to my hotel. During the day I had called Barry Golson at Playboy, whom I hadn't seen since our luncheon the previous May, to see if he'd join me for dinner. I went to the hotel reception desk to pick up my messages: I had nothing from Golson, but there was a letter-sized white envelope with no markings except my name. I opened it and noticed immediately there was no letterhead or signature on the neatly typed sheet, which read:

WHISTLE BLOWERS DON'T LIVE LONG.
THE NEXT TOOT OUT OF YOU WILL BE THE LAST!

I froze for a moment. It was as if I had pulled a small rattlesnake out of the envelope, then realized what I was holding. Aw, shit, I said to myself. I was more annoyed than panicked, for I had had to deal with such death threats before.

I stepped over to the reception desk and erupted, demanding to know who had delivered the white envelope, which I slammed on the counter. No one knew. It had arrived before the afternoon shift had come on duty.

As the manager tried to reach the off-duty clerk, I felt a terrible heaviness bearing down on me. It was that feeling a body has at high altitudes where the oxygen is insufficient. No luck, no answer at the clerk's home. I took a deep breath and returned to my room.

I closed the drapes, which made me feel safer. I knew there was really nothing I could do about the threat. If I were to notify the police, it would be at the risk of the threat's becoming a news story, which would only increase the risk of some other nut's doing something that hadn't before occurred to him.

I took my wallet from my jacket pocket to make certain the card I had put there after the last threat was still there. It was a handwritten message with emergency names and numbers just in case anything did happen. I had put the information on the back of a coupon for a free shoeshine at the Pfister Hotel in Milwaukee.

After that cheerless check, I plopped down on the bed and stretched out to let the anxiety pass. This latest threat, I figured, had to be prompted by Ford's perjury matter.

My thoughts went over what had happened and could happen, and I felt sure, if Ford were elected, things would get very nasty. But why, in God's name, didn't he resolve it right now? I closed my eyes and tried to think how I might stop a bad dream from becoming another real, live nightmare.

The telephone beside the bed rang, as if it were attacking. Its second ring made me think for the first time in years of ripping out a

phone. I must have growled when I answered, because the unfamiliar voice said, "Hey, if this is a bad time, I'll call back."

"No, it's fine, what can I do for you?"

"My name is Robert Dimley." He explained he was a writer
based in Evanston, Illinois, who was working on "a rather unique
project."

"How'd you happen to locate me?" I interrupted.

"Well, a friend at the *Chicago Trib* told me he thought you were
staying at the Ritz-Carlton." I decided to tell the switchboard to
clear all calls before putting anyone else through, and Dimley continued, "You see, I'm putting together a service that provides up-
dates on well-known public figures like you, and well, I guess what
I'm doing really is to humanize the famous."

I didn't understand. "Sorry, come again?"

"Right, okay, you see, what I do is just a little touchy. But what
it is, I prepare and distribute current and very well-written obituaries on famous people to the papers that subscribe to my service,
and I'd like to—"

"Obituaries!"

"Right, you see, I've found that this is probably the sloppiest
area of modern journalism, since most papers and wire services put
their most inexperienced reporters on updating them. So what I do
is—"

"Listen, I'm not planning to die for a while," I protested, as
much to reassure myself as to end this absurd call. The timing could
not have been worse.

"Sure, I understand, but we never know, do we? And this way, if
you'll give me about thirty minutes, if it's convenient, we can make
sure the last words are really good, you see?"

"I'm sorry, Mr. Dimley."

He ignored my response and went on. "Like this draft obituary
on you I got from one of the papers that's interested in my service."

"Like what?"

"Well, it seems that this draft was done about a year ago, some
time in late 1975, and I must say whoever did it was trying to give
you a fair shake, but I'm not so sure it worked out that way."

"What do you mean?" The man had snagged a thread of my
curiosity.

"Okay, you see, this draft was written with the lead, 'Former White House Counsel John Dean died today,' but the obit editor changed it to read, 'Watergate Conspirator John Dean,' with a note in the margin that says, 'Dean is Watergate first and always—dead or alive!' "

"Thoughtful fellow."

"Right, exactly, that's the kind of thing that needs correcting. I want to show that public figures like you are also private figures, real people, and also get off all that morbid writing that typifies most obituaries."

It was a mistake listening to the rest of the obituary he was revising. I was sure his services would have a very limited circulation when he told me that he wanted to write me up as an "Evel Knievel of modern politics who had made a leap over the moral chasm of the Nixon years. . . ."

Before this peculiar conversation with Robert Dimley I had been fretting over the prospect of a protracted contest of credibility with a newly elected President Ford. My thoughts returned to this situation the moment I hung up. I knew I had to do something, and all I could think of was to call Hays Gorey, the Washington-based *Time* magazine correspondent with whom I'd earlier discussed it. Hays had been assigned to *Time's* editorial offices in New York City for the duration of the campaign, where he was writing, rather than reporting on the election. By the time I reached him it was late, but he was still busy at work.

"Listen, Hays, this damn thing should be resolved."

"Well, I think the election (which was only three days away) will do just that. It's still close, but our latest polls show that Carter will win."

"What if the polls are wrong? Then we'll have a president under investigation and, frankly, I'm tired of being in the middle."

"I don't doubt that you are. You know, John, what I think I might do is call Bill Ruckelshaus and lay it out to him.* Bill would

---

*William Ruckelshaus had resigned as deputy attorney general under Richard Nixon, rather than fire Watergate Special Prosecutor Archibald Cox, and was now serving President Ford as a high-level consultant and political troubleshooter.

have no part of Ford if he had committed perjury, and he's a fellow who could force the issue within the Ford camp."

"That sounds like a good idea. Thanks, Hays."

After talking with him I felt relieved. I didn't expect Hays to call back, and he didn't. But I imagined Bill Ruckelshaus demanding to know the truth and insisting that arrangements be made for someone to quietly listen to the Nixon tapes to determine if they evidenced perjury by Jerry Ford.

I don't know how long I sat on the edge of the bed that night, thinking about my conversation with Hays and the events of that day. But I sat there for a long while, as many thoughts were churning through my head—more thoughts than I can begin to recall or separate from later thoughts I would have about the little lady in the Playboy building lobby, my pushing the identity ploy, the death threat, hearing my obituary, or how close it appeared we were coming to repeating recent history.

I knew, however, that I had reached a transition point in my life. I had reached a point where I must look at myself and make decisions about my life and how to live it. I remembered a paper I had written as an undergraduate on Joseph Conrad's *Lord Jim*. I thought about Conrad's treatment of "the conscience of lost honor" and wondered if I, like Lord Jim, would never escape the mistakes of my past. Would I, as the obituary editor said, always be—dead or alive—"John Dean of Watergate"?

NOVEMBER 7, 1976—Los Angeles.

Ford lost! What a relief. I wonder if, other than a few journalists who followed Ford's handling of the potential perjury issue closely, anyone realizes how terrifyingly close we came to having another Watergate! Certainly not the same as the first—but, nonetheless, a president under attack for his alleged misconduct.

There is no doubt in my mind, after what several of these reporters have told me, that, had Ford won, he would have been under investigation for this potential perjury within a matter of days. The House Judiciary Committee did not like the treatment they were given in trying to get answers before the election. Also, Ford's behavior told them that they had hit pay dirt in pursuing it.

It is frightening to me that history has come so close to repeating itself, within such a short time. Ford, and his advisers, kept compounding the problem rather than moving to eliminate it. Maybe Ford made a mistake, or told a white lie. There's no doubt the facts show that his statements under oath raise many more questions than they answer.

It's over now. No one will pursue Ford as an ex-president. He's a nice man, harmless, and not exactly a threat to anyone. He's got lots of friends in Congress, and they will let it all fade away. Yet someday people will see that what happened with Ford shows how easy it will be to have another president under attack à la Watergate. As fresh as the memory of Watergate remains, this is the most obvious example that it has had little lasting impact.

Ford stonewalled and no doubt feels he got away with it. But had he really "gotten away with it" by gaining election, I'm sure he would have discovered that impeachment proceedings are no longer an unthought-of political device for attacking a president. The machinery has been tested and used, and a small group in the Congress will undoubtedly keep it well oiled for emergencies.

Two days before the election, when some polls still showed Ford had a shot at winning, I had had a very interesting call. A reporter from *The Washington Post* said he wanted to make a deal. (He wasn't that blatant, but he wasn't very subtle, either.)

This reporter had followed the Ford perjury story "very closely." He suspected I knew more than I had made public. He also told me that Democrats in Congress would go after Ford if he won. He said, "I'd like you to be my Deep Throat," and went on at great length about how he would protect me as his source, and even go to jail before revealing me.

"Do you think I'm crazy, that I want to create an impeachment situation, with myself as the star witness?" I asked. "Don't you think I've had enough?"

"I think you'll tell the truth," he responded, "and I think you have a duty, if Ford gets elected, to do so." We debated this more than I felt inclined to do. Then he made an offer to try to sweeten the deal and gain my cooperation.

"I don't know who Woodward's source, Deep Throat, was, but I think you could figure it out, particularly if I told you what we know inside the *Post* about Woodward's reporting."

"So what, I don't give a damn," I said, for I'd had my fill of Watergate and everything connected with it.

"Listen, you give me a little help, and I'll give you a little, it's that simple."

"Nothing is simple, and this conversation is probably a waste of your time, and mine, because Ford probably will lose, and it will be over—moot."

"Possibly, but if Ford wins, will you talk to me?"

"If Ford wins, I'll move to Tierra del Fuego."

"Will you think about it?"

"Listen, if I decide to talk to you, it won't be because I'm swapping anything. Besides, why would a colleague of Woodward's help uncover his source?"

"Woodward has not gained the love and respect of everyone here, let me assure you." Jealousy is obviously another motive of the leaker, I thought.

This conversation went nowhere. But two days after the election, this *Post* reporter called me back to say, "You were right about our conversation's being moot. But I want to repeat an earlier offer. If you ever want to explore who that source was that caused the Nixon White House so much trouble, I'd be happy to help. Why? Because I'd like to know myself, and I think you could put the pieces together."

While talking on the telephone to this reporter, I began doodling. The unconscious doodle that emerged was a name I wrote several times, and traced repeatedly with the dark, felt-tipped pen I had in hand at the moment: *Deep Thought.* I labeled the notes from these calls "Conversations with Deep Thought." Having a source within *The Washington Post*, this name seemed appropriate, for we would talk again, years later.

CHAPTER NINE

Hiding and Seeking

When we accepted Chuck Colson's invitation to a dinner party given by the producer of his movie, it didn't occur to me that such a dinner, bringing together some of the people who would be involved in Chuck's movie about becoming a "born again" Christian, would be nothing remotely like a Hollywood party, but very much like a church social.

Neither Mo nor I noticed anything that would suggest an evangelical evening ahead when we arrived at the home of Bob Munger. I knew Bob had developed the idea behind "The Omen" and had made a mint from it, which conjured up images of a far more palatial house than his modest home. Chuck and his wife, Patty, spotted us immediately and warmly welcomed us, then introduced us to the others. As we made our way around the room, meeting Chuck's friends and people associated with his prison ministry, I saw my onetime interview subject—who'd joined me a few months earlier in national news over the Earl Butz flap—Pat Boone.

"I think you know Pat," Chuck said with a smile as we approached him. Knowing Chuck's prankish sense of humor, I was sure he was secretly enjoying this encounter.

"Sure, we know each other," Pat Boone volunteered, smiling and extending his hand in greeting. Then Pat introduced himself and his wife to Mo. We all chatted for a moment, and Pat said, "I think you did the right thing in reporting the Butz story, John. But I do feel sorry for poor Earl."

"Me, too." Enough said, I thought, we've cleared the air. The conversation turned to the movie business. Chuck, cohosting as he was, informed us that if we'd like some refreshments, they were on the table over by the patio.

"I think I will," I told Mo. Although I am no longer a serious drinking man, I do enjoy a cocktail before dinner. I assumed Mo too was ready for a drink, so we excused ourselves. The table had an assortment of glasses filled with an orangish-red liquid. Mo took a glass and passed it to me. "What is it?" she asked. I didn't know. As she sipped hers, I asked, "Is it spiked?"

"Are you kidding?" she laughed. "If you think you're going to get a drink at this party, you're wrong. In fact, I don't even see an ashtray in this room, so prepare yourself and your habits for a long night."

"Jesus," I exclaimed flatly, in mild panic. No more had this blasphemy left my mouth than another guest walked over, in obvious and sincere misunderstanding of my slip of the lip, for he thought we were talking about religion. The gentleman immediately launched into an explanation of how he was a Jew, but had recently become a "born again" Christian. Mo and I smiled, nodded, and commented several times, "That's wonderful!" I wondered how he had been "born again" if he'd only just become a Christian.

Chuck Colson suddenly swept into our presence. "Want to join me for a cigarette?" he said, and headed out the large glass patio door, retrieving a cigarette from his pocket. Off to a corner of the patio we all puffed away like junior high school kids safely outside the chaperon's eye.

"Christians don't have much fun," I told Chuck kiddingly, with a big smile.

"Well, I've learned there are different standards for different groups," Chuck said, drawing his cigarette smoke down to his toes. "This is a pretty good group here. Actually, lots of Christians drink and smoke. The Bible doesn't say we can't. But some interpret it a bit stricter than others. Anyway, I don't flaunt it. If I don't abuse it, I don't think the Lord minds if I have an occasional cocktail or a smoke. But I'm fairly selective where I have them." Then Chuck changed the subject. "How've you been?"

Chuck and I had been through enough together that I wouldn't have been embarrassed telling him, "awful." However, this was neither the time nor place to talk about the sense of disquiet, bordering on depression, I felt about my life. So I shrugged off his question with, "You know how exhausting it is to do a book tour. I'm still worn out." Then I changed the subject. Mo and I chatted comfortably with Chuck and others while we waited dinner for a priest who'd lost his way to the party.

Our dinner was prepared and served by young Christian volunteers and reminded me of church-basement suppers I had attended in my youth. I was seated beside Pat Boone and next to Bob Munger, our host, who was at the head of the table. Barely had the benediction for the meal brought conversation back to the table, when Bob Munger turned to me and started.

"You know, John, the Lord came into my life and changed everything. I can't tell you how wonderful I feel. Since I've accepted Jesus, there's nothing I can't do with my life."

"That's wonderful, Bob."

"Wonderful is right. The Lord shares his love with us in so many ways. . . ." I'm afraid I tuned Bob out. While I tried to give him the impression I was hanging on every word, my attention was actually catching bits and pieces of other conversations around the table, wondering if others were talking about more interesting things. Bob must have sensed he was losing me, for he put his hand on my arm. "John, why don't you come over to Christ? You could do so much for your life, and help others, too."

Pat Boone had been observing the hard-sell proselytizing I was being given. He seemed to sense that, not only was I uncomfortable, but just about ready to tell my host to stick it in a place good Christians don't talk about. I was starting to seethe. The only offensive Christian to me is one who pushes his beliefs on others. I have spent an entire adult life working out what I believe and don't believe, and I know that I don't want my religious beliefs sold to me like plastic dishes at a Tupperware party.

Pat Boone gently dealt with the situation, passing the message that the hard sell is not always the best sell.

"John," Pat said to both of us, "I've been catching a bit of your conversation with Bob. I'm sure you can understand his enthusiasm at having found the Lord. But each of us comes to the Lord in our own way," he added, as he looked meaningfully at Bob, who sat back and began working on his dinner, instead of me.

Pat then told a story to the entire table about how, after a recent performance in Australia, he'd gotten into a taxi, and, out of the blue, the driver had begun telling him how upset he was because he'd missed seeing Pat Boone's performance; he was a big Pat Boone fan. When Pat told him who he was, the taxi driver didn't believe him. "Some fan," Pat said, and everyone laughed.

Shortly after dinner we escaped. Mo said she'd caught fragments of the hard sell I was getting, and wondered how I'd handled it. "Not well," I told her, and we drove off in the silence of our own thoughts.

Throughout the time Mo and I had courted, and when we'd lived in Washington, we'd made a practice of visiting churches of different denominations throughout the city. Mo had been raised a Catholic, gone to a Catholic school, and she, as I, had an abiding and unshakable belief in God. But seldom had we had more than a passing exchange about our religious beliefs.

It was while I was in college that I had begun reading about the foundations of other religions, and began talking with other students of different faiths, shaping my own belief that, while I was very much a Christian in my thinking, and hopefully my actions, I certainly did not believe that Christianity had a special standing in the eyes of God. What about the Jews, the Hindus, the Islamic faiths—I considered them all important, and found the more I learned of other beliefs, the more difficult it was to hold to just one belief.

"I didn't handle it well," I again told Mo to break our silence. "I shouldn't have taken offense, but I personally think it's in as poor taste to ask someone what his religious beliefs are as it is to ask him about his financial affairs, or sex life."

With this pronouncement we returned to silence for a few moments, as I searched to find my way out of the suburban hillside roads and back to the main streets, and home.

"You know, Mo, I've had it. I really have. This celebrity crap that seems to give the entire world the right to know anything and everything about our private lives is over."

"That's fine by me, but easier said than done."

"Not really. I'm not going to go anywhere or do anything where I have to subject myself to endless prying. My damn life's an open book, for all practical purposes. My private life is practically nonexistent. I think we should get out of town for a while."

I needed to hide for a time. But, being someone who can't just do nothing, the first part of packing up required a trip to the bookstore, where I loaded up with an assortment that suited my mood: Tolstoi, Kierkegaard, Abraham Maslow, and an autobiography of William Shirer—some "fairly cheerless reading," as Mo noted. With the addition of two Heathkits (electronic self-build kits) and a new soldering iron, I was ready to shut out the world—and I did just that.

For days on end I read, soldered wires to transistors and resistors, and talked with Mo, until she observed, "John, you must have really liked being in prison." Mo had busied herself as long as possible reading, completing her Christmas shopping in Palm Springs, and keeping us in touch with the outside world, as I holed up in our hideaway. But it was time to return to Los Angeles. The prospects of family and friends over the holidays seemed more enticing than threatening, so we headed home.

DECEMBER 23, 1976—Los Angeles.

The solitude has been helpful. It has provided time to understand myself and my life a bit more. For me, and I suspect everyone else, books are very useful, self-analytical tools. They add perspective by provoking thoughts that might not otherwise have occurred; they provide insights by pointing out how we all, despite our uniqueness, are much alike. Doubtless, no man or woman has ever had any experience in life so unique that someone has not been there before. Yet, I don't think there is a book I've read or a person I've met that hasn't had an idea or an experience worth knowing, when I have taken the time to really look. Also, unexpected revelations occur when least anticipated.

I had purchased William Shirer's memoirs—*20th Century Journey*—because I thought I'd enjoy his reflection on history. Indeed, this journalist has witnessed great moments, which he shares beautifully with his reader. But I got far more than I'd hoped from this memoir of a man wise in the ways of life. He not only shares history, but he shares himself.

Barely had I begun the book, when Mr. Shirer treated me to a passage from Epicurus worth remembering:

Faith in immortality was born of the greed of unsatisfied people who make unwise use of the time that nature has allotted us. But the wise man finds his life span sufficient to complete the full circle of attainable pleasures, and when the time of death comes, he will leave the table, satisfied, freeing a place for other guests. For the wise man one human life is sufficient, and a stupid man will not know what to do with eternity.

By the time I finished Shirer's book, I understood what he meant when he said he was leaving the table of life satisfied. I understood the panic of my feelings back in Chicago before the election, and I began to understand part of the underlying problem about the personal stigma and shame of my association with Watergate.

It probably first hit me with Irene's death, but I failed at the time to recognize it for what it was—the realization that half my life was over, added to the fact that I had left the first half in pretty bad shape. Not only am I frightened of what I'm going to do with the next half and whether I can really start afresh and survive financially, but even more basic is the question of how much time I have left.

Constantly, since Watergate, I have been examining my life, but I now realize that my reassessment efforts have been misdirected. I have been making a "damage study," not an evaluation of who I am and what I am going to do. I have been asking questions like, "Will people hold my past against me?" My view has been backward, not forward. And I have been dwelling on the trivial, or insignificant, too much. Time is running out, and I must come to terms with my life.

The days for fantasizing great achievements are gone. Ambitions and goals must be realistic if I want to avoid great disappointment at the end. Both years and events have provided sufficient maturity, self-awareness, and introspective honesty to determine what is really important to me. What is it that would give me the satisfaction to graciously leave the table?

What is important, John?

As clear as this question became, equally clear was the need to answer it. But I had no quick or simple answer. There were several obvious answers, such as good health, happiness, and financial security. But I couldn't say, to my disquiet, what I hoped to get out of life specifically, or what I wanted to do with the rest of my life. Years earlier, in college, I had had no idea what I wanted to do with myself; now I felt I was right back where I'd started—only with fewer options and less time to do whatever it might be.

How easy it is merely to let each day bring what it may and have events make the decision, rather than make the decision itself. I still had that old confidence that I could do anything I wanted—if I wanted it enough—but what was it I wanted? The more I thought about it, the less I knew, so I again found events affecting my short-term decisions. I told myself only careful thought and time would enable me to make that long-term decision.

With mixed feelings about the most notable coming event on my calendar, several weeks in England for more *Blind Ambition* book touring in late March and early April, I returned to our Palm Springs hideaway.

"If you're going to be a writer, you've got to write," said Jann Wenner, *Rolling Stone* publisher, who tracked me down. He wanted to discuss my doing an article on the new president, Jimmy Carter.

"I'll tell you what I'd like to explore, Jann, is what kind of impact Watergate might have on the Carter presidency." I explained that since Carter was just getting started, the best measure of how he might be affected was to take a reading of those who would be reporting on him—the Washington press corps.

These people are more important to a president than most new presidents realize, for an indispensable part of governing is communicating, and it is through these people that presidential communications are filtered. If the press was still under the spell of Watergate, and the type of reporting it had allowed them to do, this could affect Jimmy Carter. Jann agreed, and thought it worth exploring.

No sooner had I committed to the assignment and hung up the telephone, than I had serious doubts. This was becoming a pattern—a second-thought syndrome about everything. It was a new behavior cycle that had developed since Watergate. Everything called for some internal debate.

For me to write about Carter seemed about as appropriate as a defrocked Vatican priest's writing about a new pope. Yet I was curious about the lingering effects of Watergate. So I drew up a list of reporters representing a cross-section of the Washington press corps, and those who have some clout with the president and, over the next

few days, called them. Only partially had I anticipated the reactions
I would get from people I assumed preferred not to read their names
in print, other than in their own by-lines.

The first call I made was to syndicated columnists Rowland
Evans and Robert Novak, neither of whom I had ever met. They
took my call, with a surprising opening: "Thanks for calling." But I
was not sure which one it was I was talking with, for I have the same
problem keeping them separate as many do Haldeman and Ehrlichman. Nor was I anxious to find out, for I wanted to end the call.
They thought I was calling them because they were working on a
story about Senator Howard Baker, whom the Senate Republicans
were about to select as minority leader of the United States Senate.
They were incredulous that Baker could be given this prestigious
post. "Haven't people read your book?" I was asked.

It was very clear that this was not an opportune time for me to
interview them about Watergate's impact on Jimmy Carter. They
were making it very plain that Watergate was quickly being forgotten by one part of official Washington—the Republicans in the Senate—and they wanted me to provide ammunition to help stop
Baker's appointment. "Can you give us more details about what you
said in your book about Baker?"

I had said very little about Howard Baker, and Evans and
Novak had been, as best I could tell, the only reporters to notice it.
Now they wanted more about how Baker had held a secret meeting
with Nixon to discuss the Senate Watergate hearings; how I had let
Baker know I knew about that secret meeting before the formal
hearings had started, and how Baker had managed subtly to reverse
his position, first saying he'd never met with Nixon about Watergate,
then disclosing the meeting when he feared being caught in a lie.

To me, what Howard Baker had done in the Senate paralleled
Jerry Ford's activities in the House. Baker had been a soldier for
Nixon, doing his best to protect the President and, at the same time,
not get himself into a mess. I had no desire to pick a fight with either,
so I ended the conversation very quickly.

"I suggest you talk with Sam Dash," I said, to get off the hook.
I knew that Sam, as the chief counsel to the Senate Watergate committee, had found Howard Baker nothing short of a nightmare. Sam
had alluded to it in his book, *Chief Counsel: Inside the Ervin Com-*

mittee. With very little digging, I figured that Evans and Novak would realize that Howard Baker had developed an interesting ploy to deflect the true responsibility of Watergate away from the Nixon White House. Baker had cleverly raised the issue of the CIA's involvement in Watergate and had suggested, during the hearings, that it was the CIA that was really the culprit.

This was hogwash, for I knew of no evidence to support it. But, had Baker succeeded, Watergate might have become more of a mystery than it is. It was Chuck Colson, while we were serving time together, who told me how he had worked with Baker, as had others from the Nixon White House, in an effort to protect the President by obfuscating the issue. Colson said the White House had obtained just enough information from the CIA to enable it to plant seeds of suspicion. This information had been passed on to Baker, through his crony Fred Thompson, the minority counsel to the Ervin committee. Howard Baker knew how to use this information without being drawn a diagram by the Nixon White House. And Sam Dash had told me that incredible numbers of hours and dollars had been spent by Baker and Thompson "in their effort to establish CIA responsibility for the whole Watergate affair." They failed, obviously, because it simply wasn't true; thus the ploy wouldn't work.

In talking with Evans and Novak, I was amazed at their outrage that Senate Republicans would name Baker their leader. These reporters were old hands at Washington politics, and with each passing year it had become more clear that Watergate was as much, if not more, politics than morality. For the press, however, it was still, at this late date, a great story, the greatest most reporters who'd worked it would ever experience.

Clearly, Watergate was a story that was hard to let go of. That fact, as much as the more fundamental significance of Watergate, came through again and again as I talked with other reporters about what kind of relationship Jimmy Carter might anticipate with the press.

Pulitzer prizewinner Mary McGrory, then *The Washington Star's* top syndicated columnist, is a good weatherwoman of the presidential political climate in Washington. She told me the storm clouds had gathered already over the Carter White House. "I think most reporters who cover the president are very disillusioned with

Carter." "Why?" I asked. "Because of Nixon and Ford." I could understand Nixon, but wasn't sure why she had included Ford in the same breath. "The Nixon pardon jolted the press badly. We thought Ford would bring openness, goodness, and wholesomeness back to the White House. Then we got jolted. Now the press knows it's got to be on patrol." I asked how this skepticism translated to Carter, and she responded without hesitation, "Carter promised so much in his campaign, and made a big thing out of saying he'd never lie. I don't believe anybody cannot lie."

Joseph Kraft, a scholarly columnist with a world view, felt his colleagues were "suffering from lost illusions" with Carter. They felt the incoming president had promised more than he could deliver. "Maybe I'm overly suspicious, but I think Carter's honesty program is pure public relations."

David Broder, a *Washington Post* reporter whose honesty, objectivity, and fine analytical mind have earned him a Pulitzer and the widest respect of his colleagues in Washington, hit on the same point. "The press is weary of his (Carter's) rhetoric, and the expectations he's raised in talking about openness and never lying. Furthermore, the press is tired of being agents for a propaganda machine, particularly the White House press corps. In the past, many of us were lied to, and we're a bit sensitive now."

While he didn't fit in the category of others I was talking with, Bob Woodward certainly qualified as someone who might have a feel for how reporters viewed the new administration. And his perspective differed in one degree from others. Yes, there was suspicion in the press about anybody in government. But, Woodward felt, "lots of reporters are frustrated politicians, and they want to be advisers to Carter, so they write columns filled with advice. When Carter doesn't follow their advice about how to put together his administration, they get even more distressed with him." When I told Woodward in more detail what I was doing, he made a suggestion that seemed a good one—talk with Ben Bradlee, the executive editor of *The Washington Post.*

I've never met Ben Bradlee, but I have seen pictures of him; yet, as we talked, I visualized Jason Robards, who played Bradlee in "All the President's Men," on the other end of the line: "Yeah, sure, I've noticed hostility among reporters toward the White House, but I'm not sure it's any different than when Lyndon Johnson or Nixon came into office. Tell you this, though, the last time I was out as a working reporter was when Kennedy came into office, and I didn't see that kind of hostility toward him."

Bradlee echoed what I'd already heard, many times. "You've got to remember, these guys who cover the White House have been lied to a lot. It's left scars. Today, there's a reluctance to believe a president: the burden of proof has shifted." Our conversation closed with an interesting aside from Bradlee: "You know, pal, they said Nixon would ruin this town, particularly *The Washington Post*. But he put us on the map, didn't he?"

The picture was clearer than I would have thought. Unabashedly, reporters were saying that, because of Watergate—and Vietnam—the President would have to prove everything he said. That same hostility, suspicion, and doubt that had confronted Ford, from the moment he pardoned Nixon, was being transferred now to Jimmy Carter as the wake from Watergate continued to keep Washington reporters unsettled.

My last call was to Hugh Sidey, who has been watching presidents for Time-Life since 1960. While Sidey spoke from the same view as others, his insights added perspective. Sidey told me, "Carter is a lonely man who brings up visions of Nixon and Agnew. Carter is self-contained, and he does little of the normal-type consulting in making his decisions. This, of course, gives the press little to write about his decision-making process."

Sidey continued, "Carter's not a fun man. Most journalists enjoy camaraderie, which they don't find with Carter, whose ambition is very large. And his southernness, along with his defensiveness—all these things keep reporters at length from him, and this helps to produce doubts."

I did not have to mention what was most on my mind, for Sidey raised it himself. "Watergate produced a hostility and suspicion of all federal servants. The press realizes that they were slow on the draw in getting the story, and feel it can't happen again. Also the press has grown accustomed to a diet of spectaculars like Vietnam and Watergate. This, added to the fact we've been living in a time when people look for thrills, is felt by the press." In short, Carter was in trouble with the news media.

More calls, and more of the same comments, which told me that this story was so obvious, there was no story. It was clear that Jimmy Carter was starting his presidency with the negativism of Watergate to overcome, and that would be difficult. Yet, while I didn't feel I had a story worth writing for *Rolling Stone*, I had discovered something else. In digging out information about Watergate's impact, I had felt very objective. It no longer seemed as threatening poking through these ashes as it once had.

Three months went by without a note to my journal. I knew from my calendar where I was. I was hiding. I knew from the journal that I was lost, too—sorting, reading, reflecting thoughts that brought me to this entry in the journal, the evening Mo and I were packing to go to England for the book tour:

MARCH 29, 1977—Los Angeles.

What's important to me, truly most important, is at last very clear. It's sure taken a while to get to it, but if I could sum up my life—what I want it to be—I'd like to be known as:
A MAN WHO LOVED TO LEARN
AND LEARNED TO LOVE—AND LAUGH!

It is difficult to point to any single moment, or event, and declare it a turning point in life, for living is a flow, and emotional evolution is gradual. Yet, I felt very different about myself after I'd spent those months sorting out what I wanted my life to be all about.

I had gone from daydreams to nightmares; I had projected myself into fantasy to see if I liked living my wildest dreams, then gone back to the reality of preparing list after list of what I could, should, and would do with my life. All of this had now been reduced to a simple epitaph. If I could make these few words a living motto, I was certain I'd find satisfaction at the table of life.

While the sifting and sorting period had edged me toward a rather "gray funk" feeling, not quite depression, I now felt that, for maybe the first time, I had a grip on my life, a direction I wanted to take myself, an aim, a perception of what would make it all worthwhile. It was a good feeling.

As Mo and I headed off to promote my book in Great Britain, I felt excited. We flew to Washington, spent the night at the Dulles Marriott Hotel and, the next morning, boarded the Concorde and soared—three and one-half hours from wheels up to wheels down—to London. The flight matched my spirit. Only a few months earlier, when the British tour had been decided upon, I had feared it. I'd been told the British media were the toughest, and they were anxious to "have at me." Now, I relished the prospect.

We arrived at the Savoy Hotel in London about 11:30 P.M., which was only 4:30 in the afternoon for bodies that were still on USA time (somewhere between West Coast and East Coast times). Mo sensed my newfound enthusiasm for life and was more than ready to join me. So we stayed up all night, drinking and talking, and watched the sunrise on the Thames from our window.

The book tour was a blitz—well planned and well executed. We went from television tapings to radio studios, to news reporters' interviews, one day after the next for five days in London, and then by helicopter to Birmingham, Manchester, Glasgow, Edinburgh, Leeds, Bristol, Southampton, and London again—plus a quick train ride to Oxford, as well.

The Oxford visit had provided just enough time to locate one of my former White House colleagues, David Young, who had fled the United States after he squeaked through Watergate. David had been an aide to Henry Kissinger and, later, had worked with Bud Krogh in creating the infamous "Plumbers' Unit." In fact, it had been David who had labeled the operation. After an aunt asked him what he did at the White House, David had responded he was working on "leaks." And, as he tells it, the aunt asked, "Oh, like a plumber?" Well, that was about as close as he really wanted to come to describing the activities of Howard Hunt and Gordon Liddy, so he made a little sign for the door—"Plumbers' Unit"—and an inside joke became another national symbol of disgraceful presidential operations.

B. H. Blackwell Ltd. in Oxford is one of the world's greatest bookstores. I'd long known of it and, rather than sit for an hour autographing books, I would have much preferred to browse and buy. Just as the signing session was ending, a young woman approached me with a note, saying she was David Young's secretary, and he'd enjoy seeing me. I knew that there would be barely time enough for a visit, as the whirlwind was scheduled to move on. So I called David to tell him I would be back in the fall, and we could then get together.

"How's it going?" he asked.

"It could be better," I sincerely answered.

"They've been a bit tough on you, over here, I'm afraid," he said, referring to some of my press coverage.

"It's all included in the price of the book—what I have to pay, I guess. But, David, believe it or not, it doesn't bother me anymore." I meant what I'd told him. We exchanged numbers, more small talk, and agreed to stay in touch.

To visit Blackwell's without taking a look at their entire operation, which runs through several buildings, and a huge underground, shelf-filled area, was impossible. I could have spent a month there. I could have spent every cent I'd ever earn from my book buying others. But there was no time for it. I'd have to return. While looking around, however, I spotted a paperback book I thought might be interesting to reread. I took it from the shelf, but Blackwell's wouldn't let me pay for it. As we returned to London, and during the rest of the trip, I enjoyed rereading *Lord Jim.*

APRIL 10, 1977—London.

As a result of my tour, I have been on television for 2 hours and 40 minutes; radio, 5 hours and 45 minutes; had 890 column inches in newspapers and magazines, which started with a 14-hour schedule that averaged about 8 to 10 hours per day. It worked—*Blind Ambition* stormed onto the London *Times'* national bestseller list at number five, and is climbing.

The media coverage has been fair to outright pleasant. The negative coverage has not bothered me—for I've felt an increasing detachment from it. No longer do I take it personally.

The visit has been wonderful. Rather than merely being caught up in the motion, I've used the trip to learn—and have had an invaluable experience. With most every reporter, after the interview, or even during it, I've asked questions that interest me, and learned more about the workings of the United Kingdom in the past few weeks than I could have in a year of reading.

What a fortuitous selection I stumbled across at Blackwell's. Conrad's treatment of Lord Jim refreshed and illuminated the haunting problems our mistakes can create, particularly when we fail to face them, try to run from them. This read has put firmly in mind what must be next. I will build a new life to replace the old, and I must bring to a close those chapters of my life that are Watergate-related. That will be easier said than done, for I have to do another tour this fall with the paperback edition of *Blind Ambition*, plus Mo and I are scheduled for a series of meetings with the screenwriter who will adapt our Watergate story for television.

Mo and I had barely unpacked our suitcases and settled into the routine of being back home, when Watergate again began pulling at my life with almost daily calls from journalists. The reason: the Nixon/Frost interviews. British journalist, television host, and entrepreneur David Frost had spent twenty hours interviewing Richard Nixon, and had edited the material into four 90-minute shows. Reporters wanted everything from an agreement to televise me watching the show, to my coming to a television studio to do an after-air analysis, plus they had never-ending questions: What did I think of Nixon's making a million bucks from the show? Why did I think Nixon was doing it? Would he come clean at last?

While I was curious about what Nixon might do, I refused all requests to get involved, or to speculate on Richard Nixon's potential performance. Finally, when the calls reached an absurd level, I arranged for the telephone company to put in another "unlisted line," and let the answering service handle the unlisted number that every reporter in the land apparently had acquired.

MAY 3, 1977—Los Angeles.

We had a pleasant meeting with Stanley Greenberg, who will combine Mo's book and mine into a teleplay. Stanley didn't seem to be looking for information, rather he seemed to be trying to get a personal feel for who we are. While we have the right to suggest changes in the script, both Mo and I are leery of this entire project. It may have been a great mistake to sell these stories to television.

Today I had a call from a reporter who claimed to want nothing more than that I consider his observation, for he was sharing inside information he'd gathered. He said many in the media think that tomorrow night's airing of the Nixon/Frost interviews will mark the beginning of the resurrection of Richard Nixon. He said,

"John, if Nixon has dazzled Frost, and manages to pull the wool over Americans' eyes again, you must do something to keep the record straight. Unless you want all that you and your friends have gone through to be for naught."

It was clever bait, but I'll have to see what Nixon actually does. And, just as I am getting my life headed away from Watergate, I sure don't want to take it back in that direction. Nor am I the keeper of the truth on the Nixon presidency, or perceived as such, I'm sure.

Late in the afternoon of May 4th, camera-crew trucks started parking in the cul de sac we live on. When a cameraman rang the bell at the end of the drive, I walked down, opened the gate, and told him that I would not be available for any interviews, and not to bother to set up the camera. Other local stations, and the networks, were en route, he told me, so I returned to my office and typed a note.

> To the Press:
> I appreciate the fact that you have been sent to my door by the "higher powers" of the news gathering business, but I hope you will appreciate my decision not to comment on the Nixon–Frost interview tonight, or until all the sessions have been aired, or at all! So, hopefully, you will give the Deans a break and not bother ringing the bell and asking me to reconsider—for I won't!!
>
> Thank you,
> John Dean
>
> 5/4/77
> 5:00 P.M.

Having decided, ironically perhaps, to tape Nixon's interview, I set up my dictating machine near the television speaker. I'm not sure what I expected, but, when the show finally began, it was déjà vu. Nixon looked good, tanned, relaxed, a bit grayer than when president, jowls more accentuated by age—yet good. Very much in command of the situation, I thought.

Frost opened the session by throwing him a softball, suggesting Nixon characterize his role in Watergate. The question was so mushy, Nixon passed on it, stating he'd rather get into specifics.

Frost more than obliged him, immediately. The usually congenial, almost unctuous Frost transformed himself with each succeeding question from Mr. Talk Show Host to public prosecutor. Within a brief time, it was evident that David had become Goliath.

I was pleased that Frost was prepared, evidencing a solid understanding of Watergate, and even possessing information that was not yet in the public domain, although the impeachment committee and special prosecutors had had the tapes he was using to undercut Nixon's canned responses. Nixon was clearly shaken, stunned, and shocked at what was happening.

Nixon kept clinging to his argument that, while he had done certain things that might appear to others to be illegal, he, Nixon, did not have the requisite illegal intent to make them a crime. Nixon was playing on what he hoped would be Frost's nonlegal background, and, when Frost began quoting and paraphrasing the obstruction of justice statute, Nixon was on the ropes.

Suddenly, the old Nixon was all over the television screen, displaying those facial reflexes that everyone had witnessed so often before when the man was unable to handle the truth—eyelids fluttering, voice stuttering, syntax disintegrating, facial expressions frozen, smiles forced and condescending, the familiar band of sweat crowding the upper lip. He was "hanging tough," but the performance reeked of a guilty man.

I had read that Frost had not delved into questioning Nixon on Watergate until the last of his interview sessions, although he was airing the Watergate conversation first. Midway through the program, it was clear that Frost had broken Nixon on Watergate, confronted him with facts he couldn't get around, and was pushing the former president down, down, down. By the time Nixon reached the explanation of his resignation, I wondered if the watching Americans might be taking offense at this Brit pushing their former president into showing his disgrace. It was difficult not to feel sympathy for this tragic man telling of his fall.

Most viewers, I was sure, would recognize that this performance was vintage Nixon, à la the Checkers speech, who confessed, "I let down the country.... Yep, I ... I let the American people down, and I have to carry that burden with me for the rest of my life. My political life is over...." But Nixon is never out of control, so he added along the way, "Technically, I did not commit a crime, an impeachable offense. . . ."

The show closed with Nixon's greatest admission of guilt: "I made so many bad judgments," which he qualified as "mistakes of the heart," rather than of the head.

Frankly, I felt revulsion, not sympathy, by the time he had finished. What a burden, indeed, this man must carry, I thought, living his life out trying to pull the wool over the world's eyes. He's incapable of seeing himself as he is, I decided. Maybe Dr. Abrahamsen was correct.

I listened to the tape I'd made of his interview, and I realized that Nixon had admitted more than he probably realized; for, in fact, he had confessed to obstruction of justice, even if he didn't choose to call it that. Again I felt the man just isn't as smart as people think he is. He pretends to more intellect than he possesses, and the reason he doesn't see his activities as criminal or impeachable is that he's incapable of comprehending it all. He's mixed his self-serving, defensive emotions into his thinking, and it's clouded it all so badly that he'll never understand.

MAY 5, 1977—Los Angeles.

> I can't handle the thought of being quizzed *ad nauseum* by the press about Nixon's interview. Nor do I feel like sifting through all he said to straighten out fact from fiction—and what's in between. Thus, I must do something I've never done—cancel my scheduled lectures. I am mentally and emotionally unprepared for what awaits me.
>
> Just as I'm getting away from Watergate, there always seems to be something pulling me back to it. Why do I feel a responsibility to talk about it all? Why don't I just eliminate it from my life—ignore it, pretend it didn't happen—and get on with what is important, and interesting to me?

To ask myself the question in my journal was to answer it, in this instance. Immediately, I began doing everything possible to keep Watergate out of my life, launching my life in a series of new directions simultaneously. Life became an absolute pleasure. I signed up for night-school courses at UCLA, and immersed myself in studies. I added to my weekends the Evelyn Wood Reading Dynamics course, and watched my skills move from 680 words per minute to several thousand. Within the next fourteen weeks, I'd read over five hundred books—only to discover that "speed reading" is like chug-a-lugging: you get it all, but there's not much pleasure in doing it, so I soon tapered off.

My days were filled with exploration of a new business venture—magazine publishing. Jann Wenner had offered me the job of publisher of *Rolling Stone.* But it was a job I couldn't accept, since I knew that Jann, whatever he called himself on the masthead, would always be publisher. Yet, publishing fascinated me, because it involved communicating information. And I had an idea. Why not publish a supplement to the Saturday newspapers, like *Parade* magazine? But, rather than charge newspapers, give it to them free and make the revenues strictly from advertising.

Over the course of the summer, I talked with newspaper publishers, magazine publishers, met with printers, artists, writers, financial analysts, and gathered a mass of information. The idea appeared viable, but the financial projections raised higher risks than I felt prepared to take. Publishing is a tough business, and magazines start and fail daily.

During the course of my analysis of this business project, which took ninety percent of my time, I found that I was distancing myself from my past—and it felt terrific. Next, I was asked by two businessmen I knew to assist them in negotiating the sale of a major company. When I started calling others I knew in the New York financial community, I was no longer concerned about my Watergate reputation. Also I put to work my investment skill. In days past, prior to entering government service, I'd been very successful in making and developing financial investments. I quickly discovered I'd not lost the old touch.

On August 14, 1977, I was temporarily back into Watergate, with a three-week book tour for the paperback edition of my book. But this time it was different. The questions were softer, and it all felt more like a ritual, with rote responses. Plus I had fun, asking television-news producers if I could do the weather—or some other crazy presentation. Fortunately they said, "No." It all was light and enjoyable.

On several stops I was asked if I'd be interested in hosting a regular television show—or a radio program. I was flattered, but the idea of commuting regularly to San Francisco, New York, or Chicago—where the offers were made—was not appealing. The tour ended back in Los Angeles, at a radio station on Sunset Boulevard. After being interviewed by KIQQ's public services director, a pleasant young fellow named Carl Goldman, I was ready to shelve Watergate indefinitely.

"Would you be interested in doing a radio show?" Carl asked me, as I turned off the automatic pilot for responding to questions from his interview. I was standing at the door of the studio, ready to leave, but this time thought I'd explore the reason behind this not unflattering inquiry. "Why do you ask?" I questioned.

"Well, our general manager, Pat Shaughnessy, would like to talk with you if you have any interest," Carl explained.

I did, and after several weeks of discussions, it was decided that I would host a daily, three-minute show called "The Right to Know." The show would deal with current political and social issues. I agreed to commence immediately on our return from a vacation in England, although, not to lose time, I also lugged a hefty recorder with me so that I might start getting interviews while Mo and I traveled.

The *Queen Elizabeth II* was enormous, a far larger ship than either Mo or I had anticipated. We had been invited to make an Atlantic crossing as guests of the Cunard lines, if we presented the other passengers with an informal lecture about Watergate. Not only did this arrangement provide passage for the Deans, but for two guests as well, and we'd invited Morgan and Louise, friends we knew would be fun traveling with.

We boarded the *QE 2* in New York harbor and, after being shown our spacious staterooms, we immediately headed for the deck to see the wonderful skyline of New York as the ship headed to sea. Mo and Louise chatted and strolled, while Morgan and I excitedly explored this magnificent ship. As we headed from the bow toward the stern, Morgan stopped, put his hand to his mouth, and said, "Oh, my god, I don't believe it."

"What is it?" I asked, not sure what was happening.

"You're not going to believe this. I can't believe it. But we're in for one of the most incredible weeks at sea ever, if what I see is what I believe."

Morgan was smiling from ear to ear, and trying to look inconspicuous. "Come over here," he said, leading me to a vantage point where we would not be seen, but where I could see a group of men talking. "If I'm not mistaken, I think that's Bebe Rebozo, Nixon's best friend," Morgan said, pointing to the group, who now had their backs to us as they looked over the rail toward New York City.

"Baloney," I quipped. Morgan was many years my junior, and, while he was very politically sophisticated, he also loved to play games. "Come on, let's look around," I said and headed on, taking one last glance at the men. "Holy shit, it is Rebozo," I exclaimed, barely believing my own eyes. "It's also Robert Abplanalp." And then it flashed before me: "You know, Morgan, with Rebozo and Abplanalp on board this ship, it's possible Nixon's here, too. Those are Nixon's two closest companions. You're right, this is going to be a hell of a week at sea."

The huge *QE 2* suddenly felt very small. This voyage had more than the potential of being interesting; it might get ugly. Rebozo would probably rather be anywhere in the world than on the same ship as I, particularly since I was there to tell passengers about Watergate. I decided to deal with the situation immediately.

"Watch this," I told Morgan. I headed across the deck to where Bebe and Bob Abplanalp were hanging over the rail, viewing the city. As I approached, Abplanalp turned, so I went over, reintroduced myself, and shook his hand, asking, "How are you?" He responded very pleasantly. A few feet away, Bebe turned to see who his friend was talking with.

"Hello, Bebe," I said, and extended my hand. By reflex, Bebe extended his hand, but I don't think it had immediately registered who I was, or what was happening. "I just wanted to say hello, and let you gentlemen know I was on board, and that I'm lecturing on Watergate, as well."

"Oh, that's interesting," Abplanalp said, evidencing surprising sincerity.

Bebe looked stunned. It had taken only a second, but now he recognized me, and he had turned ashen. He began sputtering—his mouth was working but nothing was coming out—until finally he managed to say, like a choking man, "I, I, d. . .d. . .don't have any, anything to say." He shook his head and abruptly turned his back on me, looking back out toward the city.

"Nice seeing you, Bebe," I said to his back, as politely as I could. Then I shook hands again with Abplanalp and walked away.

Morgan could barely contain himself. "That was great, absolutely wonderful. Rebozo looked like he was having a coronary; he turned gray, absolutely gray. I was waiting for him to faint and fall overboard."

I was glad I had confronted the situation, for now I felt free to move about the ship and completely enjoy the trip. Only once again did I see Rebozo, who managed to stay out of my sight, but I did have a brief encounter with a third member of the Rebozo–Abplanalp group, author Victor Lasky. I learned from the Cunard people that Abplanalp was holding a board meeting for one of his companies on the *QE 2*, which explained the group's presence. Nixon was not on board.

When Victor Lasky learned I was giving a lecture on Watergate, not only did he show up, but he insisted that he be permitted to give a lecture himself, since he'd written a quasi-authorized Nixon apologia of Watergate—*It Didn't Start with Watergate.*

Victor did his best to disrupt my lecture, which had filled the *QE 2* auditorium to capacity, to the delight of the Cunard people, who had never had that happen before. But Victor was no problem. I invited him on the stage, but he didn't want to appear with me. So I let him blow off from the audience, until the audience was sure they weren't interested in him. And they weren't. When the Cunard staff later arranged for and announced a Lasky lecture, only a handful of people showed up.

The cruise was a delicious way to go to Europe. We ate, drank, danced, read, and relaxed our way across the Atlantic, then vacationed with friends during the six-week stay in England. We visited with Ralph Steadman and his wife, with David Young, and with many other friends. Also, I began interviewing people for my radio show, which was scheduled to begin when we returned home.

"The Right To Know" would deal with any political or social issue I wanted to get into. While in London I interviewed a British civil-defense expert who told me that civil defense was useless against nuclear attack; the manager of a punk-rock group who explained the political and social significance of punk; an expert on terrorism; the head of Playboy's London casino, who told me about Arab gamblers; and I interviewed several experts on tax fiddling (cheating) in England, to mention but a few. I wanted the radio show to be wide ranging.

When I returned home, I learned that creating, writing, interviewing for, and narrating a daily show was an all-consuming activity, even with a full-time assistant. But I loved it, and began cranking out shows on everything from teenage alcoholism to the congressional "Koreagate" scandal. Although the syndicators were having problems finding a sponsor, they were pleased with the reception the show was getting from stations throughout the country that were signing up to carry the program.

I avoided the subject of Watergate, and the Nixon White House, totally. That was past, and I was living in the present. Then Bob Haldeman's book about Watergate, *The Ends of Power*, named Fred Fielding as Deep Throat. I felt I should do something.

Fred Fielding had been more than my deputy at the Nixon White House, he'd been one of my closest friends. We'd shared good times and tough times, and, when Watergate became a part of my daily life at the White House, it had strained both our friendship and working relationship. At first I had talked openly with Fred about Watergate, and we'd worked on it together, as we did so many matters that came through our office. However, when I realized the direction Watergate was headed, I stopped talking with Fred. From the day I was asked to find out about raising hush money for the men arrested at the Watergate complex, I knew the cover-up was headed toward criminal activity. There was no reason to draw Fred into the mess I'd found myself a part of.

At the time, Fred was annoyed and upset with me. Later, when he realized I had protected him—and the others on my staff—from the facts of Watergate, he was appreciative. I knew Fred had not had it easy in convincing investigators and reporters that he knew nothing, but I knew he knew nothing about Watergate. And I was sure that the name Deep Throat, courtesy of Bob Haldeman, would be a most unwelcome appellation, since it all but made Fred a liar. I called Fred to talk with him about how he was going to deal with the situation.

Fred said he had learned several weeks before publication that Haldeman had named him Deep Throat. "An old friend, a reporter, called me," Fred explained. "He'd seen an advance copy and wanted to know if I'd give an exclusive interview. I was quite taken aback by the whole thing."

I asked why he thought Haldeman had named him.

"I've got no idea why he'd name me." And then, with the old Fielding wit, he added, "Everybody in the world knows it was Hal Holbrook."

Fred explained what I knew well, that he didn't have access to the information that Deep Throat possessed; however, he felt he had something even more important going for him: "I'm fortunate that I've got evidence that'll show I couldn't be Deep Throat. When I learned what Haldeman had done, I reread Woodward's book, and one of the most critical conversations he had with Deep Throat was on January 24, 1973. As it happened, you'll recall, I was out of the country, in South America on government business, from about the 22nd of January until the 27th or 28th. I've been looking for my old passport, which will have the evidence stamped right on it."

We talked about how he'd proceed if and when he located his passport. I suggested he take it over to Hays Gorey, at *Time* magazine. I told him Hays had had a continuing interest in the Deep Throat story and, if he could prove it to Hays, *Time* magazine would certainly shoot down the Haldeman allegation. Fred agreed.

Understandably, Fred was angry with Haldeman's dragging him back into Watergate. "And another thing about his book that I guess I shouldn't be surprised about, but I was," Fred noted, "is that he has nothing good to say, nothing positive to offer, about anyone he discusses—except himself." Somewhat bitterly, Fred observed, "Haldeman may have made his mark in history, but it certainly isn't as a historian."

I told Fred that I was going to try to uncover the identity of Deep Throat. "If anyone can do it, I think I can. I've been gathering bits and pieces over the years, and now is the perfect time to do it. I can use the radio show to release my findings." And I would begin, I decided, by calling the keeper of the source.

Bob Woodward was surprised to hear from me, and not particularly enthralled when I told him why I was calling. "I never thought you'd become a plumber," he noted sarcastically. But he agreed to let me record our conversation for my radio show and, while I didn't think he'd give me anything new, it was a chance to get him nailed down a bit tighter:

DEAN: First, why have you refused to name "Deep Throat," and, second, why do you not even want to talk about it at this late date?

WOODWARD: The reason I'm not willing to name who it is, is obvious; namely, I gave my word that I wouldn't until I was released from that, and I haven't been released from it. The reason I don't want to talk about it is . . . this may be of some interest. About a year ago I was talking to Pierre Salinger, who was John Kennedy's press secretary, and the question of sources came up, and I asked him to identify the five or six most devastating leaks of the Kennedy administration. He did, and I said, "Even now, fifteen years later, have you learned the source of even one of those leaks?" He said, "No, I haven't, and I'd give my left arm, even at this late date." I guess the point is, even traditionally, the names of those sources don't come out unless you've got somebody like Daniel Ellsberg, who was anxious, and proved, to be identified as the source.

DEAN: Most people would think though, Bob, that Deep Throat was a positive source, and can't understand why he'd hide from it.

WOODWARD: I think a lot of people would think that he'd done a good thing, a noble thing, and a lot of other people would think of him as a rat, as a fink. You, yourself, who sort of came out of the closet, if you will, and said what was going on, lots of people have different reactions to you, and it's not always positive, right?

DEAN: That's very true.

WOODWARD: Same problem this person has, and he's . . . and I'm willing to say he's roughly between the ages

of 20 and 80, who has a career, or who thinks he has a
career in government or some other profession and, accordingly, doesn't want to subject himself to that debate,
and the mixed reactions people would have to him.

DEAN: Bob, one more thing. I said, very early on, that
I didn't believe there was a Deep Throat, that it was a
multiple source. You've gotten the word to me, and you've
said to others, that that's absolutely not true, that there is
a Deep Throat. Is that correct?

WOODWARD: That is correct. There is a Deep Throat,
and it's one person.

Although Woodward had not dropped any new clues, time was
running out to use this material as a timely radio show. After several
weeks of intense investigation, I was both surprised and startled at
what I'd turned up. Not only did I feel close to the answer, but I felt
I might even have solved the mystery. Still, I needed to do much
more checking to be positive.

I decided I would proceed to do two radio shows on this subject.
I would keep them nonspecific as to where Deep Throat had worked,
and not name my prime candidates. From Woodward's writings, I
had to assume that Deep Throat fancied himself a spy type, with all
that business of flower pots for signals, secret markings in *The New
York Times* for meetings, making Woodward use two cabs for traveling to meetings, then meeting in an underground garage. I would
give enough in my show to provoke a news story to let Deep Throat
know that I was in pursuit.

Shortly after I recorded the Deep Throat shows, I received bad
news. Pat Shaughnessy, the president of the company that was syn-
dicating my program, told me that he was still having difficulty finding a sponsor, despite the fact the show was being carried by eighty-
five stations, and in most of the top markets. But Pat said no sponsor
was interested in either the show, the time available from stations
carrying the show, or anything connected with it.

"Is it me?" I asked.

"I've wondered myself, but honestly, John, I don't think it is.
We're getting (advertising) time from the stations, and it's a good

lineup. The sponsor could take the time and not be connected with you or your show. It's just one of those things in this syndication business." Pat assured me that he still believed in the show, that the stations—primarily rock stations carried the show, to my surprise, and Pat's—loved it. But if a sponsor weren't landed soon, we'd have to call it quits. I agreed, since the show was costing Pat money, and I wasn't making any until he made it.

To help land a sponsor, Pat suggested I give a few speeches to advertising groups, so they could get to know me. While the series of speeches didn't land the needed sponsor, the last one I gave, in Minneapolis, Minnesota, on March 22nd, made all the work that had gone into doing the show worthwhile.

I'd completed the speech and was about to check out of my hotel and return to Los Angeles, when I noticed the desk clerk was smiling. He had looked at my credit card as he was about to make an imprint. It was, I was sure, the old game of recognizing me. Sure enough, he couldn't contain himself, and, as he handed me the bill to sign, he asked, "Are you *the* John Dean? From 'The Right to Know'?" I could have kissed him. For the first time in many years, I wasn't "John Dean of Watergate."

Nor was I John Dean of "The Right to Know" much longer, either. On May 5, 1978, we folded the show. No sponsor, nor prospect of one. I regretted its ending; I had enjoyed it, even though I'd not made a cent. In fact, I had turned down speeches and other jobs to work on the show, and I had not had any real income for many months. Pleasantly, however, I did not feel that I had been a failure. To the contrary, the radio show had done well on the air; but, more important, it had taken my life a great distance from Watergate and the past. The only problem, which was not unsubstantial for me, was, what would I do with my life now?

CHAPTER TEN

Through Others' Eyes

The scene was frighteningly clear in my mind, since I had imagined it many times. Short of a nuclear holocaust, it was, without doubt, the worst thing that could happen to the United States Government. Millions of Americans would be in their homes watching the president deliver his State of the Union address to a joint session of Congress. Suddenly, their screens would go blank. People would flip the dial and would find the same message repeated again and again: DUE TO TECHNICAL DIFFICULTIES. . . . Within minutes, the world would learn that those "technical difficulties" had changed history forever.

Terrorists had managed to set off a small, high-powered bomb during the State of the Union address. The leadership of the country had been annihilated: the president, the vice president, the speaker of the House, the membership of Congress, the Cabinet, the Joint Chiefs of Staff, and the Supreme Court.

From this opening scene, the story I envisaged would center around those who would try to fill the leadership and power void—a story of how our nation might survive such a blow, a look at the nation's raw powers in a troublesome conflict which the laws of succession were inadequate to remedy. I wanted to write this fictional horror because I feared it could happen: I saw the annual ritual of gathering the nation's leaders in one place as dangerous—even foolish. A dramatic story, showing the possibility and consequences of such an event, even if fiction, might prevent it.

I spent several weeks devising a plot, developing characters, and then writing an opening chapter for the proposed novel, along with an outline of the rest of the story. I mailed the package off to my publisher with high hopes that my life would soon be that of the political novelist. I had thought about alternatives to writing, like contracting an executive search firm to see if my skills might be marketable, but I was still very sensitive about my past and not yet ready for the potential of rejection I feared in pursuing that course.

Soon, I heard from my publisher through Alice Mayhew, who had edited *Blind Ambition*. Alice was intrigued by the novel's story, but said, "I don't think you should be writing fiction. Your audience wants facts from you." She also explained that fiction writing is a tricky business, and asked, "Why do you want to write fiction, anyway?"

"Because the Deans need to eat," I said.

Alice then said that I could get a far larger advance for a nonfiction book, since I was "untested as a fiction writer." Again, she emphasized that my audience was a nonfiction audience. Why didn't I think about doing a book "on the presidency, or some other aspect of Washington," where my background and knowledge would be very helpful?

The more we talked, in this conversation and those that followed over the next few days, it became clear that my knowledge of Watergate was still my most employable asset. I agreed to prepare an outline of a book looking at the aftermath of Watergate, and the consequences it had had on everything from my life to presidential politics.

The initial enthusiasm I felt for the project derived in no small way from my interest in financial survival, which was certainly sufficient to prepare an outline that would garner a handsome book advance. While I did not relish the prospect of continuing to make a career out of Watergate, I was very curious to see what I might find in examining its impact on others. I knew only too well the lingering effects Watergate had had on my own life, and what I knew told me that a decision to further relive it was unwise. I had told myself, after leaving the White House, that I would never again work on anything I found distasteful, even if I went broke. But, when you're near broke, it's amazing how tastes can change.

To begin, I used a part of my advance to hire a research assistant, Auriel Douglas, to go to the Beverly Hills and Los Angeles public libraries and dig out all that had been written about Watergate's aftermath. Barely had Auriel begun her work when I had a request from a friend to prepare a summary of facts and law in a complex antitrust case, if I could "take the time." It was the first good excuse I had not to work on the book, so I jumped at it, while Auriel continued her research.

Three months later, when I'd completed the antitrust case summary and been paid well for the work, fate flashed another smile. An investment I'd made years earlier proved worth more than I'd ever anticipated. It was money enough to make the addition to our home Mo had wanted for years. The next thing I knew, I had another excuse not to work on the book, for I'd made myself the *de facto* foreman on our construction site. This was great therapy. As a college student I'd worked on home construction and was a decent carpenter in my own right. As construction progressed, I found myself working with a hammer instead of a typewriter.

Soon half a year had passed without my coming close to producing the book I was committed to write within a year. I knew I had to get to work—this time on the book. Thus began a lengthy and fruitful inquiry into the impact of America's worst scandal.

I headed first for the University Research Library at UCLA, where I immersed myself for weeks on end, poring over materials Auriel had suggested I read—both academic and popular-press analyses of Watergate's effect on the courts, the Congress, the presidency, lawyers, businessmen, and the general public. After filling my head, and countless file folders, with information, data, theories, and opinions, I began scheduling interviews with those who had given these subjects considerable study. I also began lecturing to facilitate traveling to such places as Yale, MIT, the University of Syracuse, and the University of Chicago, where political scientists, psychologists, sociologists, even anthropologists were teaching, and, far more important to me, researching the subjects I was examining.

Within a few months I had read enough, seen enough, and heard enough to prepare half a dozen doctoral dissertations on

Watergate's impact on the law of the land, the "system," and the American public. Most important, though, was that I succeeded in reaching several well-founded conclusions.

Watergate did not result in any significant new laws, nor did it create any landmark court decisions. While Congress did enact reforms in federal political campaigning, proposals which had been introduced long before the Nixon abuses surfaced, the only significant statute to emanate directly from Watergate was the Ethics in Government Act of 1978, which requires annual financial statements by some 14,000 high-ranking government officials. The law created an Office of Government Ethics to monitor this disclosure nightmare and resolve conflicts of interest—real or apparent—within the executive branch.

But the most interesting provisions of the law, which was hotly debated but adopted, was the procedure whereby the Department of Justice (which is under a president's control) can be bypassed, and the courts can appoint a special prosecutor to investigate alleged wrongdoing by the president, vice president, Cabinet members, and other high officials of the executive branch. In other words, never again would there be a repeat of the shocking "Saturday Night Massacre"—named for that unpropitious moment when Richard Nixon fired Watergate Special Prosecutor Archibald Cox, then substituted his own man, the ready-to-please Leon Jaworski.

I did not realize that Watergate had provoked a minor epidemic of prosecutions against all sizes and shapes of government malfeasance—federal, state, and local. The Justice Department reported on February 10, 1977, that federal grand juries had been busy: there were 63 officials indicted in 1970, 160 in 1971, 208 in 1972, 244 in 1973, 291 in 1974, 255 in 1975, and 337 in 1976. At first blush, it might be perceived that government officials had become more careless and corrupt in the wake of Watergate, rather than more careful and honest. In fact, it was the post-Watergate prosecutorial vigor that accounted for the increased indictments. More money and increased effort had joined forces in the U.S. attorney's office to investigate government corruption.

Watergate also produced a flood of civil litigation, a fact of which I was all too painfully aware. At one time I had been personally sued in no fewer than twenty different civil cases, with potential damages against me of over $400,000,000! I had enough civil suits going to keep a good-sized law firm busy for at least a decade. I can only surmise that anyone who sued the government, alleging that this or that Watergate-related activity had infringed his rights, assumed that I, too, was involved.

It was a costly nightmare. While the government, through the civil division of the Justice Department, represented me in many of the actions, others they did not. The suits consumed long hours of pulling together the facts and locating the necessary documents to establish that I was not part or party to these alleged injuries. I spent more time and money defending myself against these actions than I did on my own criminal misconduct in Watergate. And, because I had no involvement whatsoever in these official misdeeds, the nuisance of repeated litigation was bitter to stomach. Perhaps the only advantage was that it allowed me to observe firsthand how the courts have dealt with this plethora of civil litigation, which, on balance has been with surprising fairness.

The closest Watergate has come to producing landmark law is *United States v. Nixon*, the President's case before the Supreme Court to resolve whether or not he had to turn over the tapes of his Oval Office conversations. It's a case that will stimulate law-journal articles for years to come. In short, the court ruled that the president does have a presumptive "privilege" to withhold information from the other branches of government, based on his need for confidentiality in dealing with his top aides, but that "executive privilege" can be overridden by the needs of the criminal justice system.

The court's decision distressed many legal scholars, who would argue that "executive privilege" is a myth to begin with. But the Supreme Court has now acknowledged that it does indeed exist. Although, since Richard Nixon's presidency, it has seldom been invoked, it's there—and surely future presidents will use it. And not necessarily legitimately.

During my dealings with lawyers, in the aftermath of Watergate and in periodic visits to law schools to lecture, I have had a recurring conversation. During the Senate Watergate hearings, Senator Herman Talmadge happened to notice a list I had prepared, while still at the White House, of all the people I thought were criminally involved in Watergate. The Senator asked me why there were stars (actually, I'd intended asterisks) beside some names and not others. I responded: "After I did the list—just my first reaction was there certainly are an awful lot of lawyers involved here. So I put a little asterisk beside each lawyer (because I thought) how in God's name could so many lawyers get involved in something like this?" Over the years I have often been asked if I ever found the answer.

In talking privately with other lawyers, and with law school professors and deans, I did, I believe, find the answer to this question. First, most lawyers graduate from law school with very little knowledge and understanding of criminal law. Second, lawyers are instilled with a competitive spirit to take either side of a case and win it for their client. In short, they can be whores (and good ones) with ease. Third, law schools used to emphasize acquiring legal skills at the expense of providing the sort of training that places legalistic zeal within perspective and balances it with such important considerations as fidelity to simple justice and the public good. I found that, because of Watergate, law schools and bar associations are taking time to provide training that makes it very unlikely that lawyers will be at the center of the next Watergate—for they certainly will have been taught the meaning of professional responsibility and legal ethics. My only concern, after sitting in on one law school ethics course, is that the professor teach and not "preach."

Since the day Richard M. Nixon announced he would resign the presidency, August 8, 1974, it has been proclaimed by almost everyone—members of Congress, judges, government officials, historians, political scientists, news reporters and commentators, just about anyone who followed Watergate—that "the system worked." This observation, which was first offered with sighs of relief, has echoed through the years until it has become a statement of fact, an unquestioned assumption of truth.

For many years I too accepted this analysis without question. A president guilty of wrongdoing had been removed from office, which resoundingly reinforced the fundamental principle of our nation that no man is above the law. The courts and the Congress had emerged during Watergate as Constitutional coequals to the president, checking and balancing one another, just as our founders had designed.

It was while I was still in prison, in one of those late-night conversations with my neighbor, Joey, the former Mafia hitman, that I was first prompted to second thoughts about *how* the system had worked.

"Let me ask you something, Deano," Joey began, and, the way he was scratching his head and frowning, I figured he had given this question a good deal of thought. "What would have happened if Nixon had told everybody to go fuck themselves, you know, that he wasn't turning over no damn tapes, nothing?"

"He probably would have been impeached for obstructing justice by withholding vital evidence," I responded.

"Bullshit, no way. You can't tell me that, 'cause it just wouldn't have happened. I ain't no specialist in politics, but I've known guys in the Congress, and I know that unless a case had been made against Nixon, there ain't no way that he could have been removed. And since he had all the evidence, unless he gave it to 'em, there weren't no case."

It wasn't the most articulate analysis, but, the more we debated the point, the more compelled I was to agree with Joey. Here was a man, a Mafia top dog, who had spent his life "beating the system," and he'd done it successfully until he had decided, voluntarily, to retire. Joey's point cuts right to the core of the assumption that the system worked: it worked because Nixon let it work. It was never really tested.

"I'll tell you this, Deano. If me and my onetime former associates had been counseling Nixon, and giving him a little hand here and there, he would have been like a pig in shit—a little dirty and smelly, but nobody would have touched him."

It was when I was visiting a friend in New York, a lawyer long active in the American Civil Liberties Union, that I found myself again thinking about this question of how the system had worked during Watergate. It was early summer, 1979, and Watergate Judge

John Sirica had just published a book about his trials and tribulations. The book, *To Set the Record Straight*, had irritated a lingering sore spot in my lawyer-friend—Sirica's handling of Watergate.

"I am delighted that Judge Sirica has written his book," my friend began at dinner, "because too many people have forgotten, or ignored, what went on in his courtroom. The other morning I saw Sirica on an early morning talk show. He was introduced as 'one of the heroes of Watergate,' and 'the man who made the system work.' We all like to talk about the system working during Watergate, but no one is really looking at what this judge did. What he did is terrifying—to me, almost as troublesome as what Nixon was doing at the White House, and I don't say that lightly or easily."

My friend believes, with ample justification, that Judge Sirica operated a modern-day Star Chamber during Watergate, with "judicial horrors" that equaled the "White House horrors" in their intrinsic impropriety. More specifically, it is the precedent of Sirica's actions that worries not just my friend, but many who are sensitive to the civil liberties and rights of all Americans, even Watergate burglars.

During the trial of the men who were arrested for illegally breaking into the Democratic headquarters, John Sirica was not only the judge, but the prosecutor and jury as well. He grilled witnesses, and all but accused them of lying (when, in fact, they were telling all they knew, and the truth, as Hugh Sloan well remembers). He goaded the U.S. attorneys on how they should handle their case, when he did not have all the facts, and repeatedly committed errors that in normal circumstances would have been reversible by a higher court.

After these men were convicted, either by pleading guilty or by a jury that surely felt the judge's wrath, Sirica chose to bludgeon the defendants in his personal extrajudicial search for the truth. Accordingly, he handed out "provisional" sentences of thirty-five to forty years to these first-time offenders, with the understanding that their sentences would be reduced if they cooperated with the Senate Watergate committee and the federal grand jury that was still investigating Watergate.

Those who have paused to study John Sirica's behavior during

Watergate are, understandably, troubled. From the political left to
the right, liberals and conservatives alike have spoken. To wit, an
editorial in the *Saturday Evening Post*, July/August 1979, made the
following observation on Judge Sirica's judicial tactics:

> He used torture and the obvious threat of it to extract testimony
> from the very guts of those who stood before him. Was it tor-
> ture? Indeed it was; 40 years is a lifetime. These men had no
> money; they had wives, and children, and honor. They believed
> themselves to be Cuban patriots and friends of the American
> government.

At the other end of the periodical spectrum, *The New Republic*
offered a review of Judge Sirica's memoir, and a reminder of his
actions, written by Joseph Rauh, Jr., a prominent Washington labor
lawyer active in the Americans for Democratic Action. Rauh, who
expressed grave concern about Sirica's activities during Watergate,
was equally concerned that they had been approved by a higher
court.

Rauh says that "there was no warrant for Sirica to go beyond
his proper judicial role," and the fact that his actions were approved
by the Court of Appeals was "more a commentary on anti-Water-
gate hysteria than a justification for Sirica's misuse of judicial
power." Rauh finally notes that this same hysteria caused the spokesman for the ACLU, "the greatest civil-liberties organization in the
history of the nation . . . to applaud Sirica's conduct. But all of this
cannot alter the end-justifies-the-means philosophy that surrounded
Sirica's actions."

It is true—the system did work! But with the passage of time,
thoughtful people are looking more closely at how it worked, and not
finding great satisfaction in what they discover.

For me, the most nagging question has been what I felt, from
my study of the impact of Watergate, was surely the most important
of all questions: How did Watergate affect the people of this country? It was the question I first, and always, raised with the many

academics I visited, or interviewed by telephone, during late 1978 and early 1979.

It did not take a university study to establish that public confidence in government reached a low ebb during Watergate, or that public distrust and alienation toward government grew as a result of this national disgrace. But it was not until I began sifting through the data myself (everything from Gallup, Harris, and Roper public-opinion polls to even more comprehensive information collected by the University of Michigan), and discussing it with political scientists, that I discovered the trend toward public disillusionment in government had long preceded Watergate. Since 1964 there has been a steady loss of public faith in government and its leaders. Clearly, Watergate gave this downward curve in confidence an extra boost, the wrong way.

But what did this widespread disillusionment among nine out of ten Americans mean? Had Watergate wrought some permanent damage on our democracy, a governmental system that is premised on the participation of the governed? Would future historians look back on those of us involved and say that, because of our public misconduct, we had created a situation that made the nation ripe for capture by fascists or Communists, or worse? Knowing that most people are apathetic about government, not even concerned enough to vote, I was sure I was worrying about problems that very few others cared about. Yet I did. These questions of the new public disposition were of utmost concern to me, equal to my own feelings of personal shame—and not unrelated to it.

The answers I found are both reassuring and disquieting. On some questions I was anticipating even worse than I found; others better than I discovered. Again, I tried my best to dissociate my own notions, preconceived or otherwise, from my inquiry. I wanted honest answers. I needed to know.

The writings of University of Massachusetts, Amherst, sociologist James D. Wright represent the position I found, and believe, to be a fair consensus of the academics and others who have studied the implications for a nation whose millions upon millions of inhabitants have tuned out and turned off their interest in government. Professor Wright does not see this discontent lending itself to a takeover by demagogues of either the right or left, the reason being that the disenchantment "has touched every group in the society more or less equally." It would be difficult, nay, probably impossible, for some new leader to find a sufficiently powerful constituency to back a takeover.

Professor Wright feels—and, based on my research, his feelings are shared by a host of his professional peers—that:

> The only reasonable prediction about short- or long-term consequences of the recent trends is that the level of political apathy will continue to rise in the society. Political participation, never remarkably high in American politics, will, I expect, sink to all-time lows through the coming decade, especially if neither major party can come up with a Presidential candidate able to rekindle popular confidence. From certain points of view, some of them quite prominent among academic theories of American democracy, decreased participation might seem a good thing; according to these theories, apathy is a sign of basic contentment with the *status quo*. My view, however, is that increased apathy would only signal a further de-democratization of a political system that is already excessively responsive to the interest of those at the top. . . .
>
> The probable net effect of increasing discontent, then, is to intensify the existing unequal distribution of scarce social, political and economic resources in the society, to heighten still further the disparities between the higher and lower social strata, to increase that portion of democratic opinion which drops out of the basic political process. In all probability, we will not experience some heightened sense of mass vigilance, but on the contrary, an increased nonconcern with the comings and goings of political elites. Increased apathy, in short, will remove yet another constraint on the behavior of the political leadership; it will make another Vietnam, another Watergate, not less likely but more.

Many of the political scientists, sociologists, psychologists, and historians I spoke with recommended I visit the National Opinion Research Center (NORC) of the University of Chicago. I was told that they had sifted through a lot of the public-opinion findings and feelings on Watergate, and could probably answer some of my questions. On May 3, 1979, I was in Chicago on business, with available

time, so I called NORC. My call was directed to Ms. Julie Antelman, who suggested I meet the next morning with Dr. David Garth
Taylor.

The University of Chicago evokes pleasant memories for me. I
had an aunt who worked for the head of the divinity school for years,
and when I was ten I used to visit her office on weekends. My parents then lived in Evanston, and she lived with us. At ten I wrote my
first book—a fifty-page western novel—which Aunt Elizabeth typed
for me on weekends in her office, as I watched.

It was these memories that made me all smiles as I entered the
campus offices of the NORC, where I was taken to Dr. Taylor's
book-laden office and introduced. Garth Taylor reminded me of a
short-haired Jann Wenner. But the comparison ends with appearance. This Ph.D., who teaches at the university, has a long string
of academic credentials and studies. Much of what he said was very
representative of what other social scientists had told me, but he'd
done a bit of extra digging in his analysis of Watergate's long-term
effects.

He handed me a study that he and his colleagues had prepared.
"Take a look at pages 25 and 26. It's our conclusion," he said. I
flipped through the document, as instructed, and read the following:

> The Watergate prosecutions and Congressional committees cer-
> tainly had their impact on the public trust—particularly on the
> governmental agencies and incumbents most directly involved
> in the scandal. But the overseeing and investigating activities of
> the Congress, the press and citizen action groups such as Com-
> mon Cause would have been pursued with much less vigor (and
> funding) if the credibility and legitimacy of these groups had
> not already been established by the changes in public trust
> which were taking place before the early 1970s. A falling rate
> of confidence was both a cause and an effect of the Watergate
> era. In a social structural sense, a decline in confidence, such as
> the change which occurred before the Watergate era, creates a
> need for social institutions (i.e. investigative bodies, Congres-
> sional commissions) which monitor and "expose" the workings
> of government, business, or whatever institutions are losing
> credibility. One of the consequences of monitoring and ex-
> posure, however, is a continued fueling of the sense of a lack of
> trust in institutions. An indirect effect of a decline in confi-

dence, then, is the creation of new institutions which act so as to ensure a continued lower level of confidence.

"Fairly gloomy prognosis," he quipped as I looked up.

"Indeed it is," I answered. "It's pretty damn distressing. Tell me this, if you can. How long will this impact be felt?"

"There's really no way to say."

"Well, what could change the circumstances?"

"It seems, based on our study, that this matter of confidence in institutions, like government or business or the media, is cyclic, so it will change when the cycle does, but we don't know the length of the cycles. There is, however, the fact that a big event can occur that will divert attention away from the present situation, and confidence will be restored."

"Like a war, maybe?" I interjected.

"Exactly. This question of people's confidence in institutions doesn't really fit into neat categories, say by race, religion, rural-urban, and the like. It cuts every which way. There is some kind of psychological process going on here that affects everybody. It's almost like some sort of genetic reaction people have—some people trust, some people don't."

"Have you seen any studies that indicate what, if any, long-term or maybe even permanent impact Watergate might have had on the American people? Obviously, for some, it was a trauma, so I assume it affected them somehow."

"The opinion researcher can't really answer the question. If any pollster tells you he can, he's lying, because you'd have to have data going back to World War II, and we don't have it. Maybe the clinical psychologists can help you."

"I plan to talk with them, as a matter of fact."*

"Without that data, going back, it's hard to say what permanent effect Watergate's had. And, as far as the reliable data we have, going back to 1972, it's difficult to separate Watergate from other big events, like Vietnam, race relations, ERA, and women's rights."

Based on all the studies and information I had uncovered, it did

---

*I did speak with several clinical psychologists and was unable 1) to uncover any studies on the psychological impact of Watergate, or 2) to get anything other than speculation that Watergate had probably affected public trust in the presidency, but not necessarily permanently.

not appear that Watergate had inflicted any mortal injury on the American psyche, although it certainly hadn't helped it. Yet, there was evidence in several of the studies of serious trouble ahead for one segment of public opinion, and a very important segment— young people.

Political scientists have established that it is during childhood, during those formative years between eight and twelve, that we develop many of the fundamental feelings we hold toward government, for it is at this time that we first become aware of our political system. Studies conducted of children in this age range during Watergate (1973 and 1974) do not bode well for the future.

Even before I met personally with Yale political scientist F. Christopher Arterton, I had read a conclusion from one of his studies: "The effect of Watergate has been to transform the president from a positive, morally good symbol (for young people) into a negative object to be affectively and morally rejected." In a subsequent study Professor Arterton found the problem had had a long-range impact and, when I visited with him in late 1978, he said, "Probably more than anyone else, young people have taken the brunt of negative impact from Watergate."

The tragic element of these findings is that those attitudes and beliefs, that transformation of the image of the president from benevolent to malevolent, cannot now be corrected in those who were children during Watergate. It is these young people who must one day regenerate the political process, but, when those who were eight, nine, ten, eleven, and twelve during the height of Watergate come of age in the 1980's, the nation will have a damaged resource to draw upon. Thus, one of Watergate's most devastating negative impacts has yet to be fully felt.

By the time I'd finished my survey, I was again weary of my immersion in Watergate. As I had proceeded with the study of Watergate's wide-ranging implications, I had continued to involve myself in business and investments. I'd always had a touch with real estate, so I spent a lot of time looking for investment properties. Friends in varying businesses, aware that I was no longer consumed by a daily radio show, began requesting that I do quasi-legal/business consulting for them.

Following my work on the antitrust case, another friend, in charge of acquisitions for a large conglomerate, had requested that I do studies on a number of companies he was considering acquiring. I began taking on more and more of this type of work. I enjoyed the challenge of sorting and sifting through complex legal-accounting-business operations, and the financial rewards for my efforts were substantial. The more I made from these activities, the more active I became in pursuing them, and the less interested I grew in government and politics. No longer had I much enthusiasm for Watergate—or a book about it.

By the fall of 1979, my commitment to a study of Watergate's impact had dissolved. My energy and interest were concentrated on my consulting work, investment analysis, and the decision I'd made to create a new organization that would develop and produce radio programming. I'd enjoyed my foray into radio and had learned just enough about the business to see its potential. I decided that I would maintain a low profile in the radio business, which would primarily produce special music programs with big-name recording artists; I would serve as the chief operating officer behind the scenes. The organization would start modestly and build on its own income. This is not to say that I ignored Watergate entirely, for I couldn't. But my journal entries relating to it became fewer and with greater intervals between.

AUGUST 8, 1979—Los Angeles.

This morning's *Los Angeles Times* had a feature article marking the "fifth anniversary" of Watergate, for it was five years ago tomorrow that Richard Nixon gathered his staff and loved ones about him in a final, sad farewell.

The newspaper's analysis of Watergate-five-years-later was interesting, the premise being that it is "neither gone nor forgotten." The article was by Jack Nelson, who is the L.A. *Times* bureau chief in Washington. Jack is one of those unsung reporters of Watergate. He was there when Woodward and Bernstein were plugging away, one of the few reporters who, early on, grasped the significance and potential dimensions of the break-in. Nelson's quizzing of Jerry Ford, pressing him about his potential perjury during the presidential debate, was further evidence of his grasp. What Jack Nelson writes about Watergate, I find worth reading.

Nelson's article corresponds with my own findings that "Watergate has left a poisonous residue of bitterness and mistrust in the wellsprings of American political life—reducing the ability of Presidents to meet their responsibilities and damaging the basic relationship between the people and their government."

Jack also noted President Carter's recent speech, which most people ignored. Carter has obviously felt the impact of Watergate on his own presidency, which prompted him to give a tough sermon to Americans about the crisis in confidence that exists in this country, noting, "We regarded the Presidency as a place of honor—until the shock of Watergate."

SEPTEMBER 30, 1979—Los Angeles.

Only some five years after Nixon was forced from office for his Watergate politics, the significance of those events appears to have dwindled considerably. The L.A. *Times* today reprinted a rather startling poll, which they recently completed. According to the *Times'* findings, "three-fourths of Americans say they would consider voting for a presidential candidate 'who sometimes bends the rules to get things done.' "

That's the kind of poll that could encourage Richard Nixon to run again for president. Well, so much for "post-Watergate morality." In fact, that about sums it up for Watergate—nobody really gives a damn!

The cynicism I felt was based in bitterness. For years I had been motivated by, and attached to, the idea that Watergate had had some positive results, that it had had a cleansing effect on politics and provided a real education to the public. I could find self-respect in my efforts to tell people what had really happened, thinking my doing so served a larger, and important, purpose. Like many of the myths that had grown up around Watergate's significance, this was my own private myth, which was all but destroyed by the L.A. *Times* poll.

Other than an occasional lecture, or a few futile bursts of energy stimulated by inquiries from the editor of my book, I removed Watergate from my thoughts. Daily life became business—radio programming and business consulting.

In late 1980 I took on the job of selling a sizable European concern—a corporation doing about $300 million in annual sales—which had been inherited by an American. The transaction became entangled in complex litigation, and unraveling it became virtually full-time work. At the same time, the radio-programming business was growing, and each quarter became better than the prior.

In 1981 I expanded from radio into television and movie production as well. The blend of these activities, while exhausting at times, was satisfying. I would one day be interviewing a music superstar and then writing a show around him. The next day, I'd be wading through three feet of financial documents, or depositions, or annual sales figures from my consulting work, which would bring me into contact with businessmen around the world. Then I'd turn to a new movie script.

Watergate was in my past now. And, working in these new, nonpolitical fields, people seemed to ignore my past, for business is the here and now—today and tomorrow. Success brought not only financial reward, but a new self-image. For years I had imagined that a new life would begin for me at a particular moment, in a recognizable way. It wasn't until this new life was well under way that I was able to appreciate how quietly it had begun and how surely moved forward. I discovered I could indeed start over and make it, for I had.

I didn't know if I'd ever write the book I had agreed to take on: I was prepared to repay the publisher if it came to that. I had studied Watergate's impact through the eyes of others and discovered the consequences—as well as the answers to the questions that had once worried me. But best of all, my life was no longer either directly or indirectly controlled by Watergate, for no longer was my only asset the mess I'd been so much a part of. I felt free, as if I was edging out of the shadow of my mistakes at last. While the past still weighed on my conscience, I tried to ignore it. But Watergate, I would learn, has a life of its own, and we were destined to meet up again. Again I would find myself challenged by the remaining mystery—who was Deep Throat?

CHAPTER ELEVEN

The Resurrection

With some success I had buried Watergate by bulldozing the past with the present. That old bromide, "out of sight, out of mind," had almost worked. But I sensed Watergate's return even before the media began heralding an official resurrection. I knew that June 17, 1982, would mark ten years since the Watergate break-in, and each passing month was bringing me closer to the decade past. Although I was sure time had softened its impact, I had never been able to drive a stake through the heart of the monster, and I wondered if the inevitable reunion would be another haunting experience.

By November of 1981 I had already received four requests to participate in the "tenth anniversary" of Watergate. Two magazine editors had requested I write articles on the subject of Watergate-ten-years-later. Another had requested an interview. Finally a television producer had tracked me down with a proposal of a documentary looking back on the significance of Watergate.

As the years distanced me from the events of Watergate, and gave greater balance to my perspective, the clearest truth I could see was that, of the many things it was, it was above all else a media event. As such, it was only fitting that the media jump on this irresistible opportunity to round up the Class of '72. It was an excuse for them to have at it again—despite the fact that they had celebrated the "fifth anniversary" less than three years before.

267

FEBRUARY 5, 1982—Los Angeles.

It's building steam. The tenth anniversary is going to be everything from feature newspaper and magazine articles to television
shows. I've had two dozen calls, and, from what each caller says,
they all realize their competition is going to do something on the
anniversary, so they can't be left out of the action. I even heard
from one caller that CBS is talking about rerunning the "Blind
Ambition" movie.*

Amusingly, several of the calls have been from reporters, editors, and producers who have taken me to task in the past for
"cashing in on Watergate." Now they want to kiss and make up.
It's awful how these people will degrade themselves to get a story.

Today I was struck again by the thought that the media invented me, made me a public person, when I would far rather have
done what I had to do, in testifying about the White House years,
in private, and have experienced my shame outside that pitiless
spotlight of publicity I was forced to remain in throughout Watergate. It is because I am a publicly known quantity that I am now
being summoned by the media.

When they want me, they say, "You're a good writer and could
give us a hell of an article. We'll pay you top dollar." Or, "You make
a good impression on television. You're one of the most articulate of
all those involved." Smoke, smoke, smoke—right up the old behind. Yet these same people will turn around and attack me if I
decide on my own to write an article or book, and appear on television to discuss it.

Individually, people in the news media are some of the brightest, most likable people in the world. Collectively, they can be an
uncontrolled, undisciplined, unfair mob—and, if they could see

---

*When the show had first aired in May 1979, and Mo and I had, for the first
time, seen our lives during Watergate portrayed, it was as if we were eavesdrop-
ping on the lives of strangers. The only personal reaction we felt had been at the
truly awful depiction of Mo, who had been presented as relentlessly bitchy, boring,
bored, and on the verge of breakdown.

The second airing, surprisingly, proved a mentally taxing, and emotionally
wrenching, experience. For three days and nights we were transported back in time
to feel the strain, unpleasantness, and despair of all that had gone so terribly
wrong, and wondered what friends, family, and those unknown millions of viewers
thought of the way "our story" portrayed us.

themselves from my vantage point, I think they would have to admit it!

FEBRUARY 16, 1982—Los Angeles.

This tenth-anniversary thing is threatening to get out of hand. For the past several days a producer from CBS-Los Angeles has been calling, insisting I give him an interview. "We want to bring our camera to your office, shoot you at work, and have you tell us what you've been doing since Watergate. Nobody's quite sure what you've been up to the past few years."

The fact that I didn't wish to do an interview made no difference—he was sending a crew anyway. I tried to explain, nicely, that I did not want to drag my present business into Watergate, that I have a lot of wonderful people working for me who shouldn't have to be burdened with this nonsense, that "I try to maintain a low profile," since we deal with a lot of major music artists who might not want to be identified with me in the context of Watergate.

Despite my request, CBS sent a camera crew. They set up outside the office and commenced filming. Suddenly my business associates understood what it was to be imprisoned by the press, for they didn't want to venture out and be quizzed. That this was a total invasion of my privacy was irrelevant to CBS, who not only filmed the office, which is a very identifiable, refurbished old house on the edge of Hollywood, but made the location very clear.

POSTSCRIPT : *April 5, 1982.* It's only been a few weeks since CBS ran the film on the office. We've been barraged with kook calls, and we were burglarized. They cleaned out the studio, two word processors, typewriters, video equipment, cameras. Estimated loss—$50,000. Insurance will cover less than half. Thank you, CBS!

As the phantasm of Watergate loomed nearer, I found myself being forced to think about Watergate anew: what perspective should it be viewed from ten years later? Given the magnitude of the event in recent history, I was relatively certain I could predict much of what "could" be said, and what "would" be said. For me, it became a question of what "should" be said. And that was very clear, just as it was clear I would have to say something.

Very little, in relation to all else that has been said about Watergate, has focused on the impact that the event had on the media, and vice versa—the impact of the media on Watergate. Yet this relationship is as much a part of the history as the involvement of Nixon himself. To explain Watergate without explaining the role of the press is an incomplete, even distorted, report. While a few academics had written about the role of the press, and several of the books that emerged in the wake of Watergate had touched on it, in reality the story had never been told. Because it was the news media that were putting Watergate back on the agenda for national attention, I felt that my ten-years-later perspective should include the story of the media vis-à-vis Watergate.

This was not a story, however, that the media themselves would be very likely to focus on. Reporters, editors, and television news producers do not much fancy self-analysis, and, while subtle self-congratulations and a sharing of war stories would be in order, a hard, critical look at what the media had done, how well they had done it, and how they had been affected was unlikely.

In thinking about how I might stimulate this kind of media self-analysis, I instantly thought about my old, elusive friend, the mysterious Deep Throat. Revelation of his identity—the man who lives in history as the ultimate "unidentified source"—would do just that. I had let the fellow rest in anonymity after my radio shows, for I lost interest and lacked the time necessary to complete my investigation. Uncovering Deep Throat again seemed like a great idea, for it could force an examination of the media's true role in Watergate.

The dimensions of the Deep Throat mystique had helped bolster what, to me, was a myth about the media and Watergate. His continued secrecy lent its own credence to the widespread impression of millions of Americans that today, as during Watergate, vigilant reporters were watching out for their interests, and, should any public official even think about crossing the line of propriety, he would soon be found out by an enterprising reporter.

The myth that the news media in general, and *The Washington Post* through the Pulitzer-prizewinning efforts of Woodward and Bernstein in particular, uncovered the Watergate affair became embedded in the public's perception with the release of the movie, "All the President's Men." When I visited lecture halls throughout the country I repeatedly discovered that this is taken for granted, as fact. Because it could be considered poor form for me to confront this issue head on, I had not. But when I was scheduled to join Bob Woodward in a lecture at the University of Massachusetts shortly before the tenth anniversary of Watergate, I decided it was an opportune time to state the facts as I knew them.

It has always been evident to me that the fact that Watergate was discovered at all—that it became known that the men under Liddy's direction had entered the Watergate complex—was an accident. First, there was the bungling of the tape on the door, which the security guard discovered by pure chance. When he telephoned for the police, another accident occurred. The call went out for a patrol car to investigate the burglary in progress, but there were no patrol cars in the vicinity of the Watergate building. There was, however, a car containing undercover vice/drug-squad officers, who were about to take a coffee break. They told the dispatcher that they would check out the call, and proceeded to the Watergate office building. When these nonuniformed policemen pulled up in front of the Watergate in their unmarked car, Liddy's lookout man across the street in the Howard Johnson's Motor Lodge saw them, but they did not look like policemen, so he gave no alert. Thus, a second accident resulted in the arrests of the burglars.

The next morning the city editor of *The Washington Post* assigned Woodward and Bernstein to the story. It is not necessary to proceed story by story through *The Washington Post* to make the point; but, as someone who was in the White House at the time, I can say without equivocation that *not one story* written by Woodward and Bernstein for *The Washington Post*, from the time of the arrest on June 17, 1972, until the election in November 1972, gave anyone in the Nixon White House or the re-election committee the slightest concern that "Woodstein" was on to the real story of Watergate.

Occasionally, as I presented this information from a podium on April 22, 1982, I looked over at Bob Woodward to check his reaction. He did not appear surprised at all to hear what I was saying. So I continued, explaining to the audience that there had been very little Watergate reporting before the election. I told about my meeting a few years earlier with Senator George McGovern,* and how he had tried to make Watergate a campaign issue, but neither the press nor the public was interested. I cited the study that Professor Edward Jay Epstein had conducted, showing how the press had mishandled Watergate and was falsely claiming credit. Finally I presented figures I had found in the *Columbia Journalism Review* (July/August 1973), which showed that, of the 433 reporters in Washington who could have been assigned to cover the Watergate story, only fifteen were actually assigned. Watergate, before the election, was a nonstory, ignored by most of the papers and covered by television news little beyond the extent of repeating *Washington Post* headlines, and involving none of the networks' vast investigative resources.

Woodward had once told me that, after Nixon's overwhelming election victory, he and Carl did not think they would ever write another story about Watergate. They weren't the only ones who stopped writing about Watergate. After the election, there was almost no Watergate reporting at all.

Only one story was published that caused any real concern. It was an article written by Seymour Hersh of *The New York Times*, on January 14, 1973. Hersh reported that the men arrested at the Watergate were receiving "hush money," thus suggesting a cover-up. This story hit home! It had everyone concerned, and folks in the White House and at the re-election committee were on the wall. But it was killed when the men arrested at the Watergate appeared the next day in Judge Sirica's courtroom, and the Judge asked them about the *New York Times* story. They denied it, which was a lie, but it killed the story.

No, the press never cracked the case. Only Sy Hersh came close. It was later, in the spring of 1973, when the story had all but disappeared from the news, that the entire mess fell apart. It started crumbling with L. Patrick Gray's confirmation hearings to become director of the FBI. Watergate collapsed of its own weight—because it was a complex criminal conspiracy and all the key conspirators were unhappy to find themselves a part of it. It wasn't until Water-

*See Chapter Six.

gate had begun to disintegrate in full view of the public that the press began treating it as a major story.

What happened to those hundreds of reporters assigned full time to cover the White House, who totally missed the biggest story to occur in Washington in many decades? Many of these reporters live on handouts; they are fed each day like barnyard animals with bits and pieces from the White House press room. This satisified some of them. Others had their sources within the White House and throughout the administration. And these sources were telling them that Watergate was nothing, that the *Post* was overplaying it all, and that nobody of any consequence was involved; i.e., they were being fed the cover-up line.

Because so many "big name" reporters missed the Watergate story, which had to be a professional embarrassment to many of these very able and learned journalists, they later reacted with anger and distrust of those they were covering, as I discovered when I talked with a representative cross-section of these reporters at the outset of Jimmy Carter's presidency. No longer were a president and his top advisers given the benefit of the doubt in carrying out their duties, but they were presumed to be doing wrong until they proved otherwise. An angry news media had shifted the burden and presumptions of propriety in high office because of Watergate.

Jimmy Carter's candidacy and presidential campaign were designed to appeal to the public "anti-Washington" feelings in the wake of Watergate. Most political pundits and pros felt that Carter was elected because of the mood of the country after Watergate—that Watergate actually elected Carter. I think the facts also show that Watergate was Jimmy Carter's undoing, as well, and that he was the third president to lose his job because of Watergate, thus following Nixon and Ford.

During Carter's single term in office the news media moved from vigilant to vigilante. It was Richard Nixon who had always complained that the news media, with their unchecked powers, had it in for him. But it was Jimmy Carter, who did not complain, whose presidency was in fact decimated by some of the most sensational, overhyped, distorted, and unfair reporting in the annals of modern journalism. Post-Watergate reportorial zeal haunted the Carter presidency from its first day until its last.

Before the new Carter administration had even found its way into its new offices, the rumblings about Bert Lance began. Slowly and steadily they built, with the press feeding the investigation into Lance's past banking practices, and the investigation, in turn, feeding the press. Finally, in the fall of 1977, it exploded into what appeared to be a first-rate scandal. To read the papers and listen to the newscasts, it sounded like Carter's best friend, and closest adviser as director of the Office of Management and Budget, was little more than a con man who had built up a personal fortune in the banking business through devious wheeling and dealing, and that Jimmy Carter's campaign had been the beneficiary of these dubious dealings. On September 15, 1977, Bert Lance appeared before televised hearings to explain his personal financial affairs to the Senate Governmental Affairs Committee, and I wondered if we were going to have another Watergate-type set of hearings, with this the opening round.

On September 21, 1977, an emotionally distraught President Carter announced at his nationally televised news conference that Bert Lance was resigning. Carter appeared near tears when he said, "Bert Lance is my friend. I know him personally, as well as if he was my own brother. I know him without any doubt in my mind or heart to be a good and an honorable man." From the news coverage it sounded like Bert Lance was on his way to jail. And when the coverage of Lance continued after his tarring and feathering in Washington, I began to think, as I am sure others did, that President Carter himself might become tainted by what the press had now dubbed "Lancegate."

Barely had "Lancegate" subsided, with not so much as a scintilla of evidence that President Carter had done anything improper or, for that matter, that Lance himself had done anything other than what was the custom and practice of many small, rural bankers, than the press was onto Carter White House top staffer, Hamilton Jordan. This time it was barroom etiquette, for, according to a February 19, 1978, *Washington Post* story, ole Ham had turned up in a singles' bar and, after downing a beer and two "Amaretto-and-creams," had spat his drink down the blouse of a young lady, who in turn had slapped his face. Soon, others in the media were examining Jordan's social life, and the evening news was telling us that he had behaved boorishly at a dinner party two months earlier, when he allegedly had tugged at the bodice of an ambassador's wife and expressed interest in seeing "the pyramids." Ham Jordan was clearly a target of the press, but, after issuing a 33-page denial, and after someone put a leash on the man at night, he was safe for a while.

The scandal-hunters moved on and in July of 1978 found new bounty and another scandal, which the official labeler of Carter scandals, William Safire (the Nixon speechwriter and apologist who had gone to work for *The New York Times*), called "Pillgate." This involved another close friend of the President's, Dr. Peter Bourne, whom Carter had brought to the White House as his special assistant for health issues. Between the lines of the rather sensational coverage this little incident created, it appears that Dr. Bourne was overly solicitous of the well-being of his aides, for he was caught writing a prescription for methaqualone (Quaalude) to a fictitious name. Since "ludes" are rumored to be aphrodisiacs, this suggested the potential of a sex scandal in the staid Carter White House.

The "Pillgate" affair ended quickly, and with little satisfaction for those looking for wrongdoing. No sex scandal. Dr. Bourne resigned, explaining he had used the fictitious name to protect the White House aide from publicity, since he had recommended this potent sedative for medical, not sexual, reasons. While all this prompted a police investigation, Dr. Peter Bourne and all involved were cleared of any misconduct. And another notch was added to the guns of those in search of scandal.

During these early efforts to unearth scandal, it should be noted that, in a much broader view of the Carter presidency, Carter was enjoying some of the worst press coverage of any recent president for everything he did, or did not do. He was in a "no win" situation, for to read the headlines of those who wrote about him was to read that he had no chance.

Far more serious charges of scandal in the Carter administration made headlines in late summer, 1979. The owners of a popular New York City nightspot, Studio 54, were arrested for tax evasion and, in an effort to lighten their liability, they charged that Hamilton Jordan had been snorting cocaine in their discotheque. Jordan de-

nied the charges, and had witnesses to back him up. The charge
triggered an investigation by the FBI pursuant to the 1978 Ethics in
Government Act. And once all this was leaked to the press, the investigation became increasingly public.

Amidst the still continuing reports of the latest pretrial developments in the criminal action pending against Bert Lance, and the
flow of bad news for the Carter White House about whether Ham
Jordan did or did not "do coke," new headlines of even more scandal
broke: 'COVER-UP' CHARGED IN INQUIRY ON VESCO. On August 28,
1979, the foreman of a federal grand jury claimed that Carter's Justice Department was blocking a probe into an allegation that Ham
Jordan and Charles Kirbo, the President's old friend, adviser, lawyer,
and informal member of his administration, were part of a scheme to
prevent the extradition of Robert L. Vesco.

Vesco—a name right out of the Watergate era, and back on the
front pages. There were about a half-dozen federal indictments out-
standing against Vesco, who had fled the country rather than face
trial. Vesco was accused of looting and misappropriating the assets
of the I.O.S. Ltd. mutual fund, and of having made a $200,000 ille-
gal campaign contribution to Richard Nixon, among other crimes.
Now it appeared that Vesco had somehow gotten his tentacles into
the Carter White House.

During these days of headlines reminiscent of Watergate (SPE-
CIAL ATTORNEY NAMED TO PROBE JORDAN DRUG CASE; PERJURY BY A
CARTER AIDE IS ALLEGED IN FEDERAL INQUIRY INTO VESCO CASE;
etc.), I was giving an occasional lecture. Often, at the outset, I would
ask the audience, based on their news reading or listening, how they
felt about these charges. Not surprisingly, the overwhelming majority were convinced the charges were founded on fact and evidenced
serious misconduct and wrongdoing in the Carter White House. Yet,
with the passage of a few months, and completion of the investigations, no evidence of misconduct or wrongdoing was discovered. As
late as the week before the tenth anniversary of the Watergate
break-in, I asked fourteen students, whom I met with in a private,
graduate-level seminar studying the presidency, what had happened
to Bert Lance. Nine students said he had gone to jail, and the other
five had no idea. In fact, Bert Lance was never convicted of any
wrongdoing.

The most serious charges of misconduct, which involved Carter personally, along with his White House counsel, his attorney general, his top national security adviser, and even his wife, arose at a time when it was certain to have the worst effect, during his 1980 campaign for re-election. This final, and most serious, charge of scandal was called "Billygate."

From the start of the Carter presidency, "First Brother" Billy Carter had been a willing fool, and total tool, of the news media to embarrass the President. Billy, clearly suffering deep emotional difficulties in dealing with his older brother's success, managed to make a jackass of himself regularly. From urinating in public to endorsing "Billy Beer," his hijinks earned him top dollar and constant national press attention. He would do anything and say anything, and, as they say in the business, it all made "great copy."

But by midsummer of 1980, Billy Carter was no longer a laughing matter. He was in deep trouble for having accepted a $220,000 loan from the Libyan government, for whom he conducted a goodwill campaign, and for failing to (but later begrudgingly agreeing to) register as required under the Foreign Agents Registration Act. The odor of scandal arose over the fact that the White House, through First Lady Rosalynn Carter and national security adviser Zbigniew Brzezinski, had helped bolster Billy's credibility with the Libyans. Then questions arose about possible special treatment given Billy by Attorney General Benjamin Civiletti, and the intervention of White House counsel Lloyd Cutler to assist Billy in his wrangling with the Justice Department.

The story would not go away. Tidbit after tidbit trickled out and into the headlines; soon the Senate was calling for an investigation, and the FBI was investigating the White House and even the attorney general. It became a major story: daily headlines, cover stories on the national magazines, and specials on television.

Finally, President Carter apparently recognized the need to open up totally or be ruined by innuendo, and he held an hour-plus, prime-time news conference in an effort to defuse the issue before the Democratic convention. The President's openness, supported with a formal 13,000-word report, including 99 pages of official government documents and the President's own diary entries, helped. But the news media refused to let go. Despite the findings of no official wrongdoing, three days before the 1980 election a bit of enterprising journalism uncovered a Justice Department report on Billy's relationship with the government of Libya, which alleged that the President had failed to cooperate in the investigation of his brother's activities. The report also was highly critical of Carter's attorney general, Mr. Civiletti.

The presidency of Jimmy Carter was whipsawed in a continuing Watergate backlash, a news-media McCarthyism in search of scandals that did not exist and witch hunting where there were no witches. While history may not write that Jimmy Carter would have succeeded without these problems, since his presidency was clearly beset by many others, will historians appreciate how much of his time was deflected from concentrating on the important issues facing the country because his administration was repeatedly and falsely charged with wrongdoing? Presidents do not issue press releases about the diversions adversely affecting their ability to govern, nor do they want to reraise it when later writing memoirs, yet, as someone who has been there, I know that it is matters such as these that make presidents and their staffs toss and turn at night, and misdirect their energies during the day.

In the wake of Watergate the news media unfairly smeared the Carter presidency, painting it with repeated false charges. While some reporters will discuss the unfair treatment that Jimmy Carter received, most will not. Yet, many surely recognized what they were doing and why. Unfortunately for Jimmy Carter, that recognition came with his defeat. And with Ronald Reagan's election, a new attitude emerged.

Why there was a change of feeling is not clear. Shortly after Reagan's inauguration, I shared a lecture platform with syndicated columnist Jack Anderson, who specializes in nastiness toward any and all White House incumbents. I had noticed that Anderson had become very gentle with Reagan, so before we went out before the audience I asked him why he and so many of his colleagues were being so nice, nicer than usual even during the "honeymoon" period accorded most presidents.

"The press was tough on Carter, no doubt about it," Jack said. "It's not good to be negative all the time, so I think Reagan's going to get a break. Enough time has passed since Watergate, and Reagan seems like a decent fellow, so he shouldn't have the same problems Carter did." Another reporter, after the assassination attempt on Reagan, told me, "After what Reagan's been through, there was no way the press could jump on him. So what has happened is that slowly, because of the passage of time, we're getting back to a normal relationship between the press and the president."

These were the kinds of facts I thought should be brought out and discussed during the tenth-anniversary media reexamination of Watergate. Too often history judges presidents in the isolated context of their four or eight years in office, ignoring the residuals they inherited from their predecessors. But new presidents do not start anew. They are a part of the flow of history, and Jimmy Carter arrived on the muddy shores of the Potomac during the still-receding tide of Watergate. It was a time when muckraking was easily supplanted by mud throwing.

Before my scheduled visit with Bob Woodward at the University of Massachusetts, I had reviewed my earlier "paper investigation" of Deep Throat, hoping Bob might drop a clue. I knew much more than I had reported in my radio shows. And as the tenth anniversary of Watergate approached, I was determined to make a serious effort to solve the Deep Throat mystery. Over the years I had amassed considerable material on the subject, and I was sure that a quick review would be helpful in completing the puzzle.

Back in 1978, when my initial search for Deep Throat had begun in earnest, I had read and reread *All the President's Men*, preparing elaborate and detailed index cards for every bit of information in the book relating to Woodward's friend. In the process, I had relied on several working assumptions for my search.

First, I was inclined to accept Woodward's word for it when he told me—as he had Hays Gorey and others—that his source was a single person, not a composite character. Thus I assumed there really was a Deep Throat.

Second, I did not think, from my reading of Woodward's and Bernstein's book, that Deep Throat was as omniscient as some felt he was. But, based on what he appears to have known, I concluded he was probably either someone in a high position, or someone in a unique position to get information.

Third, whoever it was clearly had access to the FBI's investiga-

tion of Watergate, for much of Deep Throat's information was minutiae and gossip about the investigation, rather than hard or major
facts explaining the full dimensions of Watergate. But, obviously,
Woodward's source was following the progress of the Watergate investigation on a regular basis, with access to information on a regular basis, and seldom did Deep Throat appear to have information
before the FBI had it.

Based on these assumptions, I had prepared a chart of potential
operating bases for Deep Throat within the executive branch, which
Woodward states is where his source was located. The chart listed:
the White House, the Department of Justice, the United States attorney's office, the FBI, and the Secret Service. I knew that many
people felt that Deep Throat might have been a CIA operative. But
the CIA did not, at that time, have easy access to FBI information,
for during J. Edgar Hoover's tenure the two agencies had grown
hostile to one another. Nor did the CIA have access to "inside"
White House information, as did Deep Throat. From my own knowledge, I was ninety-nine percent certain there were no other places
within the executive establishment, apart from the five agencies
listed on my chart, that had access to the information relating to
Watergate.

The next step had required many more hours than I had anticipated, but the extra effort was vital. I had sought to ascertain, as
closely as possible, the time that Woodward had received information from Deep Throat. This was done, in part, by a close reading of
All the President's Men, for the authors in most instances supplied
the dates, although not always directly. In other instances, I found
the dates by reviewing the actual Washington Post articles Woodward and Bernstein had written. Fortunately, I had saved almost all
of the Post articles.

The most important step of this earlier investigation had been
determining who "could" have had the information that Deep
Throat gave Woodward at the times Woodward says he received it.
To make this determination, I had proceeded index card by index
card with the summaries of information that Deep Throat had
passed to Woodward. On the back of the card I placed the names of
those I knew, from my own knowledge, had the information. Next, I
read the testimony of anybody I felt could add insight, for I had

collected the testimony of numerous people in many of the countless investigations connected with Watergate. These ranged from testimony before the Senate and House investigations of abuses in the FBI and CIA, to numerous confirmation hearings, to testimony before the Senate Watergate committee that I had never read. The effort was productive, for I found nuggets about who knew what—and when.

As I went over this material in my files, much of which I had forgotten, I was soon reexperiencing the revelations of countless clues, and thinking again about the names of people who could have been Deep Throat, some of whom I knew well, others not at all. I prepared a master list of the names—there were over one hundred! However, if my assumption was correct that Woodward was being truthful in saying it was one person, then I knew my list of candidates would be narrowed as I crossed off any name that did not appear on every index card; i.e., if Deep Throat was one person, his name would have to be among those who I thought could have known a particular fact at the time Woodward said he'd learned it, and his name should appear on every card. After this process, my list was down to thirty-five names—and limited to five agencies: Justice, the U.S. attorney's office, the FBI, the White House, and the Secret Service.

To limit the candidates further, I took note of what Woodward had said about the habits of Deep Throat; i.e., he smoked, drank Scotch, knew literature well, acted like a spy with his secret moves, and was clearly a nocturnal person, with their many pre-dawn meetings. While I didn't know all the people on my list well enough to be certain, this information did eliminate a few who clearly had to be disqualified if Woodward was being truthful.

I looked at my list of candidates again:

JUSTICE DEPARTMENT: Carl W. Belcher
Richard K. Burke
John C. Keeney
Laurence S. McWhorter
Henry E. Petersen
Harold Shapiro

U.S. ATTORNEY'S OFFICE:

Donald E. Campbell
Seymour Glanzer
Earl J. Silbert
Harold Sullivan
Harold H. Titus, Jr.

FBI:

Thomas E. Bishop
Charles Bowles
W. Mark Felt
L. Patrick Gray III
David D. Kinley

WHITE HOUSE:

Stephen Bull
Alexander P. Butterfield
Kenneth W. Clawson
Charles W. Colson
Leonard Garment
David Gergen
Alexander M. Haig, Jr.
Richard A. Moore
Jonathan C. Rose

SECRET SERVICE:

Lilburn "Pat" Boggs
Charles Bretz
Roger Schwalm
Louis Sims
Alfred C. Wong
Raymond C. Zumwalt

How different this list was from any others, I thought, since the general public would recognize almost none of these names. Aside from Henry Petersen, Pat Gray, Mark Felt, and the men from the White House and U.S. attorney's office, none of these names had ever received more than a passing reference in the media, if that. Yet everyone on my list "could" have been Deep Throat because each "could" have had the information Deep Throat gave Woodward. But the distance between *could* and *did* was great, and the list was still very long.

I decided I would attempt to narrow my candidates with an abbreviated continuation of my investigation, i.e., I would focus on the first and last reported conversations that Woodward had with Deep Throat.

According to the book, *All the President's Men*, the first contact Woodward made with Deep Throat was on June 19, 1972. Bob made two calls and, on the first call, "his friend said hurriedly that the break-in case was going to 'heat up,' but he couldn't explain and hung up." When Bob called "his government friend" later that same day to ask for advice, he was told that "the FBI regarded [Howard] Hunt as a prime suspect in the Watergate investigation for many reasons. . . ."

While Woodward reported this as the first contact in the book, I hadn't forgotten that the movie had played this initial contact far differently. In the movie, Redford (*qua* Woodward) had alluded to the fact that his friend had helped him with information relating to the shooting of Governor George Wallace in Laurel, Maryland, so he implored his friend to help again.

I had also discovered in *The Great Coverup*, a book by Barry Sussman, Woodward's editor at *The Washington Post*, a similar allusion to the Wallace shooting and Deep Throat's connection that preceded Watergate by almost a month. Sussman wrote:

> On May 15, 1972, hours after George Wallace was shot in a Laurel, Maryland, shopping center just sixteen miles from the center of the District of Columbia, we at the *Post* still had not learned the name of the man who shot the Alabama governor. Woodward mentioned to me that he had "a friend" who might be able to help. It was the first time I remember hearing Woodward speak of his "friend" [who, Sussman explains, was later dubbed "Deep Throat"].

With a trip to the library, I was able to dig out the *Washington Post* article of May 16, 1972, written by William Greider, which not only had the assailant's name, but the charges against him:

> Police immediately arrested a blond young man identified as Arthur Herman Bremer, a 21-year-old busboy and janitor from Milwaukee, Wis. He was charged by state authorities with four counts of assault with intent to murder and was arraigned in Baltimore on two federal charges. One of the federal charges

was interfering with the civil rights of a candidate for federal
office, a provision of the 1968 Civil Rights Act. The Wallace
second charge was for assaulting a federal officer; one of the
four people shot at the rally was (a) Secret Service officer.

I also discovered at the library that Woodward had stayed with
the Wallace story. On May 17, 1972, he wrote a front-page article,
with Jim Mann, reporting how Bremer had followed Wallace for
weeks, an article in which it is difficult to determine if Woodward
received help from "his friend." But the article Woodward prepared
with Hedley Burrell, for the front page of the May 25, 1972, *Post*,
strongly suggests Woodward had inside help.

The Toronto Star had released a story, on May 24th, stating
that Canadian officials believed that Bremer was "stalking" President Nixon during his visit there on April 13 to 15, 1972. The Woodward article, picking up from *The Toronto Star*, reported that
"Federal sources here confirmed yesterday that Bremer has been
traced to Ottawa and appears in crowd photographs taken by U.S.
agents of the throngs that assembled to greet Nixon there on Parlia-
ment Hill" during Nixon's visit. While this information could easily
have been obtained by any reporter, what follows looks like Woodward had a very good source:

> In Washington, federal sources said that Bremer had been
> positively placed in Ottawa during the President's visit, but they
> said that there was no evidence that Bremer was "stalking"
> Nixon. . . . Overall security for Nixon's visit was generally con-
> sidered to be the tightest in Canadian history. . . . In addition,
> federal sources said that some of the notes later found in
> Bremer's car indicated that he had recently been in Canada. . . .
> A reliable federal source close to the investigation termed "in-
> credible" the picture of Bremer's travels being assembled by
> federal investigators.

Woodward's article proceeds to list a host of these locations,
which also appear to have come from someone close to the investigation. These George Wallace shooting stories suggested that Woodward's friend worked for the FBI, which was conducting the
investigation, or the Secret Service, which was closely following the

investigation. The other possibility was that he worked in the White House and was able to get information from the FBI or Secret Service. And the White House had been extremely interested in the Wallace shooting.

Woodward's later reference, during the height of his reporting on Watergate, to his earlier stories relating to the Wallace shooting suggested the direction I should head.

My reading, and rereading, of Woodward's Watergate articles now paid a dividend. I remembered how he had mentioned something I'd not understood at the time. The article was written for the June 21, 1973, *Post*, reporting on the revelation that Howard Hunt had been instructed by Chuck Colson to visit Bremer's apartment in Milwaukee within hours after the Wallace shooting. Woodward had not discovered this story from Deep Throat; rather, it had been leaked from the Senate Watergate committee after Hunt had told them about the episode. But the story had caused Woodward to return to his pre-Watergate reporting on the Wallace story. On June 21, 1973, Woodward provided this flashback, and dropped what could be a useful clue in my search for Deep Throat:

> Within hours of the Wallace assassination attempt, a White House official was asked by the *Washington Post* about the identity of the governor's attacker. During a subsequent conversation that evening, the official raised the possibility of Bremer's connection to leftist causes and the campaign of Sen. George McGovern, through literature found in his apartment. . . .
>
> One White House source said that when President Nixon was informed of the shooting, he became deeply upset and voiced concern that the attempt on Gov. Wallace's life might have been made by someone with ties to the Republican Party or the Nixon campaign.
>
> If such a tie existed, the source said, the President indicated it could cost him the election, which was then less than six months away.
>
> "The President was agitated and wanted the political background on Bremer," the source said.

Were these comments passed on by Deep Throat? Was the "White House official" asked by the *Post* about the identity of Wallace's attacker Deep Throat, as Sussman suggests? Or was the source of these stories Chuck Colson, which is suggested by the book, *All the President's Men*? It wasn't clear. But what was very clear was that all these Wallace stories appeared to have come from the White House, not Justice or the FBI. And the White House would include the Secret Service, for the Service would have had that kind of information about Bremer, as well as the White House reaction to the attempt on Wallace's life. Also, if Deep Throat was in the Secret Service, Woodward could use the amorphous, and anonymous, reference to "White House official" or "White House source" without disclosing, or correctly identifying, his true Service source. Indeed, these people from the Secret Service were assigned to the White House, so they fit the description. Woodward could also call them "federal sources," or "sources close to the investigation," and still be correct.

One line, in particular, in Woodward's June 21, 1973, story rang another bell that pointed again toward the Secret Service—the comment about "Bremer's connection to leftist causes and the campaign of Sen. George McGovern."

I knew firsthand that, at the time of the Wallace shooting, the spring of 1972, the Secret Service had it in for George McGovern. They felt he was nothing less than a Communist, and they were doing their best to make sure the world found out about it. This fact had escaped any real public attention, although it had come up during my testimony before the Senate Watergate committee. The Senate committee's report, which had run 1,250 pages, mentioned it in one page, noting that not only had I been given politically damaging information about Senator McGovern, but the Secret Service had also passed on information suggesting McGovern's ties to Communists to others on the White House staff, as well.*

The Secret Service had always been high on my list of places where Deep Throat might work, because it was the Secret Service that first alerted the White House to the arrests of the men at the Watergate complex. Within hours of the arrests, Lilburn "Pat" Boggs, assistant chief of the Secret Service, had called Jack Caul-

---

*See the Final Report of the Select Committee on Presidential Campaign Activities, U.S. Senate, June 1974, p. 148.

field to tell him that James McCord had been among those taken into custody. Boggs also called John Ehrlichman at Caulfield's suggestion. Alfred Wong, the special agent in charge of the technical security division at the White House, and an old friend of McCord's—in fact the man who had recommended McCord to Caulfield when Jack was looking for a "security man" for the Republican National Committee and the Committee for the Re-election of the President—was one of the first to alert the White House to the fact that Howard Hunt's name had surfaced in the investigation. Wong called Alex Butterfield.

The Secret Service had been plugged into the Watergate investigation from the very first moments, and probably had remained plugged into it throughout. The Service had liaison with the D.C. police, the U.S. attorney's office, the FBI, and the Justice Department. Also, the Service was both directly and indirectly involved with the re-election committee, as a concomitant of their protective functions for the President. No one outside the President's own handpicked aides could know more about his thinking, his reactions, or the activities within the White House, than the Secret Service—for they are everywhere. Like lamps, they just stand there, never very far from anything and everything. They hear it all, just because they're there, and the president and his staff forget they are there.

The Secret Service during the Nixon years knew more about what was going on than in any other administration, before or since, for they installed the secret listening devices on the President's telephones, and in his Executive Office Building office, at Camp David, and in the Oval Office. They were responsible for changing the tapes and making sure the system worked. It is not impossible for me to believe, having come to know many of these agents, that they did from time to time listen to the tapes—and hear firsthand what the President of the United States and his staff were doing.

There also was a strong possibility that Bob Woodward could have come to know, and befriend, one of these Secret Service agents when he was in the navy. Not many people knew that Woodward had worked at the White House during the Nixon years. Very little had been published about Robert Upshur Woodward, who was born in Geneva, Illinois, on March 26, 1943. But another of his editors at the *Post*, metro editor Leonard Downie, Jr., who wrote a book entitled *The New Muckrakers*, reported that, after Woodward graduated from Yale in 1965, he entered the navy pursuant to an ROTC commitment.

Woodward served his first two years as "an officer aboard the presidential flagship for communications, which was a carrier fitted out to become a floating White House in case of emergency." Next, he was assigned to a new guided missile ship, and moved his first wife to California, where the ship was based. Because of the Vietnam war, Woodward's enlistment was extended to a fifth year, and he was transferred back to Washington as "a communications liaison officer between the Pentagon and the White House," while his wife stayed in California, where she had enrolled in school; they were divorced after his discharge from the navy in 1970.

It appears that Woodward arrived at the Nixon White House in 1969, and was there until 1970 working as a Pentagon liaison officer, carrying pouches back and forth. It would have been a perfect occasion to meet someone on the White House staff or in the Secret Service. I used to see these people meeting and mingling in the cafeteria in the EOB regularly. Also, the Secret Service's White House offices are very near the offices made available to the military couriers. It all fit, very nicely. The question, however, was, who in the Secret Service would be the most likely candidate to be Woodward's "friend"?

It was time to check my elimination process against the last conversation that Woodward reported with Deep Throat, to see what it uncovered. That last conversation, reported on page 333 of *All the President's Men*, was very short and simple: "one or more of the tapes contained deliberate erasures." This message from Deep Throat was passed to Woodward in a garage somewhere in Washington the first week of November 1973. Woodward and Bernstein reported in their book that, after receiving it, Carl "began calling sources at the White House. Four of them said they had learned that the tapes were of poor quality, that there were 'gaps' in some conversations. But they did not know whether these had been caused by erasures." They also observed that the story they wrote anonymously quoted Deep Throat's remark that there were gaps of "a suspicious nature" that "could lead someone to conclude that the tapes have been tampered with."

Quoting Deep Throat, even anonymously, was unusual, for, according to Woodward's early statement in the book regarding the ground rules with Deep Throat, he had agreed never to do so. Thus, I was curious to find the article. To my distress, I didn't have it, so I had to return to the library and dig it out. But the near-blinding process of searching microfilm was worth it.

The November 8, 1973, *Washington Post* had a front-page headline that read: TAPES HAVE PUZZLING GAP. Sharing this headline were two articles, one by George Lardner, Jr., about Nixon's secretary, Rose Mary Woods, discovering a gap, and another by Woodward and Bernstein. Their article referred to "White House sources" and quoted the Deep Throat revelation, noting:

> Of five sources who confirmed that difficulties have risen concerning the quality of the tapes, one said the problems "are of a suspicious nature" and "could lead someone to include (sic) that the tapes have been tampered with."
>
> According to this source, conversation on some of the tapes appears to have been erased—either inadvertently or otherwise—or obliterated by the injection of background noise. Such background noise could be the result of either poorly functioning equipment, erasure or purposeful injection, the same source said.

Not only did Deep Throat say much more in the article than was mentioned in the book, but Woodward was, again, identifying his friend as a White House source. This certainly could be the Secret Service, but it could not be Justice, the FBI, or the U.S. attorney's office by any interpretation. The substance of Deep Throat's remarks points to someone who had listened to the tapes, or who had spoken with someone who had listened. Indeed, the article notes, "The four other sources disputed that there is anything suspicious about the deficiencies and insisted the tapes are marred only by technical problems that can be satisfactorily explained in court." Of course, Deep Throat was correct and soon the rest of the world would learn of the infamous 18½-minute gap on the tape of the conversation between Bob Haldeman and Richard Nixon on June 20, 1972 (three days after the Watergate break-in). But it is important to note that Deep Throat had this information at least a week to ten days before it became widely known. In fact, when Deep Throat gave this information to Woodward, according to *The Final Days*—Woodward's and Bernstein's second book on Watergate and their report on this time period—very few people knew it or could have known it.

In *The Final Days*, Woodward and Bernstein reconstructed the events surrounding the discovery of the erased tape in detail. According to this account, the President and his new chief of staff, Alexander Haig, had told Nixon's in-house Watergate lawyer, Fred Buzhardt, of a gap, with buzzes, early in October 1973, after Rose Mary Woods reported to the President that she had accidentally erased a portion of a tape. But none of them felt there was anything to be concerned about, because they didn't believe the problem tape was among those subpoenaed to be turned over to Judge Sirica.

According to this account of the period, none of the White House staff had heard the tapes except the President, Haldeman, Steve Bull, Rose Mary Woods—and the Secret Service. Buzhardt was not permitted to hear the tapes until November 14th and he immediately discovered the 18½-minute gap—filled with buzzes and sounding much like Deep Throat had described it to Woodward some six to seven days earlier. Thus Woodward's source had to be either someone who had heard the tape or someone who had been told of its condition—and this was a very small group: Nixon, Haig, Woods, Bull, and possibly Haldeman—or someone who was very close to one of these people or closely connected with the tapes, like the Secret Service.

Without a doubt, I could make a very strong case that Woodward's friend had to be on the White House staff or in the Secret Service. And my list of Secret Service and White House candidates was rather limited, possibly too limited. Still, flushing Deep Throat from the group would be very tricky, for I still had little more than my analysis and hunches to go on.

At last the scope of what I was onto began to take form in my mind, and inherent in it was a very unpleasant implication. To see the Secret Service surface as the source of the greatest leak in presidential politics would mean serious problems: more investigations, further public scrutiny of a government agency, and a greater dissolution of trust in the institutions of government. Yet, if I was correct about the man who had guided Woodward through the shoals of Watergate reporting—if he was in fact a Secret Service agent—the world should know it. If a president can't trust those who have been entrusted with his life, who, by necessity, must have proximity to him, his family and his staff, then the system must be changed.

The next potential hit me like a bolt, and I wondered why it had taken me so long to see it. Had Deep Throat tipped Woodward about the existence of a taping system in the Nixon White House, the secret that would, more than any other single revelation, change history? In short, had Deep Throat killed the Nixon presidency?

Again, I reread the section of *All the President's Men* in which Woodward asserts that it was indeed Deep Throat who had first mentioned Alexander Butterfield's name. Then, in May 1973, Woodward himself mentioned Butterfield to a member of the staff of the Senate Watergate committee (undoubtedly his friend, Scott Armstrong, whom Woodward, I'd heard, had talked the committee's chief counsel, Sam Dash, into hiring.) Reading this section now, it was tempting to read between the lines. It was very possible that Deep Throat had tipped Woodward—given him just enough to push for Butterfield's being called before the Senate committee staff.

Woodward's problem was that he could never have reported the existence of the system, or written about it even indirectly, without the risk of compromising his source. The taping system was the best-kept secret at the Nixon White House, with only Bob Haldeman, his deputy, Larry Higby, Alex Butterfield, Butterfield's replacement in the spring of 1973, Steve Bull, and a few in the Secret Service who installed and maintained the system, knowing about it.

In *All the President's Men*, Woodward, perhaps frustrated by his inability to disclose what he knew, tries to take credit for bringing Butterfield to the attention of the Senate Watergate committee. Maybe he couldn't reveal the information he had without giving away the identity of his source, so he found another way to bring it out. He's gone as far as he can go. Maybe, under Deep Throat's guidance, Bob had really brought down the President of the United States. Even if Deep Throat had merely told Woodward to push for Butterfield's interrogation by the Senate committee, hoping they would stumble into the taping system, as they did, the results were the same.

This was an entirely new slant on explaining the unraveling of Watergate. The stakes in uncovering Deep Throat seemed suddenly to have escalated tenfold. Care and caution were called for. Rather than rush to any judgments, I would have to check and recheck my facts. There was still a lot of work ahead in building a case for which of my candidates was Deep Throat.

It had been ten years since Deep Throat first started giving information to Woodward about Watergate. I had narrowed the field to the White House and Secret Service. I'd moved to the edge, but I needed to do more than an armchair analysis if I was going to uncover Deep Throat's identity. I was scheduled to travel to Washington, D.C., in early April, so I decided to meet with my own special source from *The Washington Post*—"Deep Thought"*—with the hope of expediting my inquiry.

APRIL 3, 1982—Washington, D.C.

I spent four and a half hours with Deep Thought at his suburban Washington home, and I'm not sure what to make of it.

We began with Woodward's coverage of the George Wallace shooting. Deep Thought says that (*Post* metropolitan editor) Harry Rosenfeld had told Woodward to go out to Laurel, Maryland, the scene of the assassination attempt, but that Woodward was not particularly interested in doing so, and managed to hang around the office looking for a better assignment. Apparently, when Woodward discovered that the *Post* was having difficulty learning the name of Wallace's assailant, he went to another editor, Barry Sussman, and volunteered his assistance. This follows what Sussman wrote in his book, but Deep Thought has added a new wrinkle.

Deep Thought says there were half a dozen reporters working on finding out who Wallace's assailant was, and he is not at all sure that Woodward, through his "friend," ever came up with the name.

---

*Deep Thought, for the record, is not to be mistaken for anything other than what he is: a composite character. Deep Thought is actually two people, two excellent sources within *The Washington Post*. Both have been told that I am referring to them by this pseudonym, but neither is aware that the other has been my source. Using two sources with similar information and insights proved invaluable in double-checking on information, tips, and leads. I named my source Deep Thought because both men are very careful, cautious, thoughtful individuals. I thank them both.

He believes the *Post* got the name from Ken Clawson (the former *Post* reporter who was working at the White House at that time), but Deep Thought quickly added that he "just wasn't sure at all on that point." He was sure, however, that Woodward managed to stay on the Wallace story because he was coming up with solid information that no one else had.

Deep Thought told me that Woodward was very close to Barry Sussman during Watergate and suggested I talk with Sussman, who might be willing to talk, since he and Woodward had had some sort of falling-out. Deep Thought knew all the Watergate players at the *Post* well—Sussman, Woodward, Bernstein, Rosenfeld, Bradlee, and Leonard Downie (another editor), and he was very knowledgeable about how the *Post* had handled the story.

Deep Thought does not believe "Woodward's friend," as he calls Deep Throat, was a very big deal at the *Post*, that he never produced any great leads, or tips, "certainly not early on." His information was only used as a "reassurance to Ben Bradlee and other editors later on in Woodward's reporting," and much later than the book *All the President's Men* would suggest. But this is only his impression.

"You know, Woodward had to write up memos, internal memos, on most of his information," Deep Thought told me, "and I've looked at some of them." Based on his reading of these memos, which reported firsthand what Bob had learned from his "friend," my source, Deep Thought, claims, "Woodward's friend was used principally to confirm stories, not as the original source."

I asked Deep Thought if he knew who Deep Throat was. He smiled. He stroked his chin a couple of times, and asked me, "Do you think I should?" I didn't know what kind of game he was up to, so I said I had no idea. "Actually, I may be the only person in Washington who has never really given a damn who Woodward's friend is." He proceeded to explain that he thought that "Deep Throat" was some of the greatest hype since "Bob Feller started selling Wheaties." According to him, the entire fallout of Watergate on *The Washington Post* had "damn near ruined the paper," especially when everyone was wondering who would play whom in the movie. "Everyone around the paper actually was starting to believe the *Post* was as uniquely good, moral, and noble as we were portrayed in the Hollywood version of the story."

Deep Thought appeared genuinely distressed. "Do you think we should be proud of the fact that our reporters used tactics that

we would have lambasted the White House for, like harassing people, pulling their telephone records illegally, and invading the secrecy of the Watergate grand jury?" Deep Thought also said, "It's
a goddamn lie in *All the President's Men* that we had two or three
sources for every story. Often we went with one. You can't run any
newspaper in the world on a two-source basis."

Eventually, I got the conversation back to who Deep Thought
believed Deep Throat might be. "I don't know, and, as I told you, I
don't really care. If I had to speculate, I'd say I lean toward the
FBI. But I've never really tried to analyze it. Let me tell you this,
though. I think there are a bunch of people at the *Post* who now do
know who Woodward's friend was. It happened during the Janet
Cooke flap."*

During this embarrassing time for *The Washington Post*, Deep
Thought told me, many people began to wonder if Deep Throat
might have been a fiction. Ben Bradlee apparently insisted that he
be told the identity of Woodward's friend at that time, to make sure
that the *Post* not be totally humiliated and, indeed, tarred and
feathered for the greatest journalistic fraud of all time. "I think
several people learned about Woodward's friend at that time,"
Deep Thought speculated. Then he made a surprising offer.

"Tell you what, I'll sniff around for you, see what I can come
up with. While I'm not interested in blowing the whistle on Woodward's source, I know a couple of *Post* reporters who might be willing to help you do just that.

"Tell you something else," Deep Thought added at another
point in our conversation, "Woodward told several of us, when he
was working on his book, that he had deliberately disguised the
presentation of Deep Throat to throw people off the track. So don't
read that book as all fact about his friend."

Deep Thought and I parted on an interesting note. "I kind of
hope you do reveal Woodward's friend, because, while I think the
Post did a hell of a fine job of reporting on Watergate—and we
were almost the only reporters in the world interested in pursuing
the story—I also think it's time the world knows that we were skat-

---

The Washington Post was awarded a Pulitzer prize in 1981 for a story written by a *Post* reporter and edited by assistant managing editor Bob Woodward,
which turned out to be a bogus story. Janet Cooke, the reporter, had been hired on
a phony resumé, and then wrote a woeful tale of a young black child that was pure
fiction. Woodward, as her editor, had let the story go to print. It was a bleak episode in journalism, and a terrible embarrassment for the *Post*.

ing on very thin ice. Woodward's source was wrong on a lot of things. What I'm saying is, the *Post* took some big risks on Watergate—and won. But it should be in perspective for history."

My session with Deep Thought did little more than lend moral support to my effort to pursue Woodward's friend. Certainly no new clues had emerged from this session. To the contrary, it was clear that even those who were familiar with Woodward's reporting during Watergate had little real knowledge about his best source. The fact that Deep Thought believed it was someone in the FBI, someone "close to Pat Gray," simply did not fit. There was too much information from Deep Throat about the inner workings of the White House, the mood at the White House, how various White House people had reacted to *Washington Post* stories. Such information had to come from someone "inside" the White House, and that precluded not only the FBI, but the Justice Department and U.S. attorney's office as well.

Deep Thought's remark about Woodward's deliberately distorting the portrait of his friend in his book made me wonder if it was possible to use anything in the book as a reliable clue. And if I could not—how could I unravel this mystery? At one point in our conversation Deep Thought had advised me to rely on my own instincts. "You know all the possible players. Follow your hunches." He was probably right. I would only be able to glean so much from *All the President's Men*—and *Washington Post* articles—and the rest would have to come from developing other sources and pursuing my hunches.

Based on the book and the *Post* articles, I was now fairly certain that Woodward's source had been on the White House staff or in the Secret Service. I was proceeding on two tracks, but if I was going to complete this inquiry before the June 17th anniversary date, I'd have to pick one track or the other. There wasn't time to run out both.

What did my hunches tell me? My strongest instinct had always been that Deep Throat was a composite character, a fiction. Despite these feelings, I believed that Woodward was an honorable person; thus, if he claimed it was one person, I accepted that fact— as fact. My next hunch placed that person on the White House staff—but the quick check of my top candidates had put them out of the running. Based on my analysis of who could have known about the 18½-minute erasure on the court-subpoenaed tape during the first week of November 1973, I had narrowed the White House candidates down to Alexander Haig and Steve Bull. The others who were privy to the buzz on the tape were very unlikely—Nixon, Rose Mary Woods, Fred Buzhardt, and Bob Haldeman. I later had dismissed Bull because he would not have been in a position to learn about the FBI's investigation, and Haig because he had been out of the country at the time Woodward had a very important conversation with Deep Throat: October 9, 1972.

I knew I was not the only one who had a strong hunch that Deep Throat could have been Alexander Haig. Only a few months earlier a *Time* magazine reporter, John Stacks, had stopped by my office to discuss this possibility. Stacks had told me that he and Sandy Smith had been quietly investigating this prospect and wanted to know my reaction, since they understood that I too was working on this question. I had told Stacks at that time that the records indicated that Haig had been in Paris with his boss, Henry Kissinger, on October 9, 1972, and was thus unavailable for a vital pre-dawn rendezvous with Woodward.

Haig had been a long and strong hunch that had not borne out during my initial check. But, given Deep Thought's admonition about not treating Woodward's depiction of events as fact, I wondered if I should look at Haig again. Logic alone should have directed me that way, but I was following hunches, plus curiosity, and these were leading me right toward the Secret Service. Besides, I knew that others had looked at Haig and had not been able to make the case, so I was more inclined to plow where others had failed to look. After all, this was as much a process of elimination as anything else; if I didn't succeed in finding Deep Throat in the Secret Service, then at least one more location for Woodward's friend would be eliminated.

On April 20, 1982, I shared a lecture platform with E. Howard Hunt, at noon, at Fordham University. I came in from California; Howard, from his home in Miami. We had appeared together once before, several months earlier, so we chatted about family as we were driven from the airport to the school. In lecturing, Howard tries to justify his role in Watergate; I never have, nor do I feel this possible, so we talk about it from far different perspectives.

After an uneventful lecture, Howard decided to fly the Eastern shuttle back to Washington with me, where he could catch an early flight to Miami. High in the sky over the eastern coast, in a conversation that was simply conversation with another passenger who happened to be Howard Hunt, Howard unknowingly dropped a clue about the identity of Deep Throat that would, for a while, send me off on a wild-goose chase, but not a useless one, for I would pick up many more clues along the way. And, I was a willing victim, for this was the Secret Service clue I'd been waiting for.

"The other day I was reading *Smithsonian* magazine," Howard said casually, then asked, "Do you get it?"

"I used to. I dropped my subscription about a year ago. But it's a fine publication."

"It is, isn't it?"

I nodded, and Howard rambled on about some article he'd read. I barely listened, until he said, "I also saw in that issue that Al Wong has gone to work for the Supreme Court. He's the marshal. Did you know him?"

Mentally, I bolted upright. Holy cluster of cows! How had I missed that fact? My mind began clicking thoughts like a slot machine lining up jackpot bars. Howard had pulled a mental lever that started bells ringing and lights flashing in my head.

I gathered my composure. "Yeah, I knew Al. But I hadn't heard that he'd left the Secret Service. Sounds like he got himself a nice job, though," I answered as coolly as possible.

"Yep, he sure did," Howard said, and went on talking about something else.

I could barely wait to get off the flight. Not since the early stages of my search for Deep Throat had I found a more titillating clue.

Alfred Wong had long been one of my prime candidates. As a Secret Service agent at the White House, he had overseen installation of the presidential taping system, and had been none too happy about doing so. The significance of his new job rested on an irresistible "coincidence": Woodward's third book, *The Brethren*, was all about the Supreme Court. The first book ever to probe the secret inner workings of the high court, it had obviously been written with the aid of a solid inside source. If Al Wong had moved to his new job as marshal of the Supreme Court before, or about the same time that, Woodward had started researching *The Brethren*, then Al Wong might just deserve to move to the top of my steadily narrowing list.

At Washington National Airport I said goodbye to Howard and thanked him for "some very stimulating conversation," a comment which made him frown in wonderment. Then I rented a car and hurriedly drove to the first phone booth I could find—a gas station on the edge of Alexandria, a few miles from the airport.

I called Mo. "Listen, dear, I'll hold the line, but I want you to go to the bookshelf in the den and bring a copy of Woodward's and Armstrong's book, *The Brethren*, to the phone. I want you to check the foreword and tell me when Woodward says he started to work on the book."

When Mo returned to the phone, she confirmed that Woodward and Armstrong had started on the book in 1976. Next, I telephoned the Supreme Court and asked the operator for the marshal's office. A secretary came on and, in answer to my question (though I was an unidentified caller), told me that Al Wong had served as marshal of the Court since late 1975.

Absolutely unbelievable! I thought to myself, as I stood stunned and staring at the telephone. By the time I'd moved a few hundred feet back to my rental car, my head was filled with so many thoughts, I just sat motionless behind the wheel sorting through them.

Al Wong. The pieces fit together so easily—almost too easily, I thought. Wong was the man who had recommended James McCord to head up security at the re-election committee. Al Wong was the Secret Service agent in charge of the technical security division, which would give him liaison with the D.C. police and the FBI, a perfect place to keep track of the Watergate investigation. Al Wong was the man in charge of the presidential taping equipment, the one who installed the system and monitored its operation. Al Wong had never had to testify, as his appearance had always been blocked by Nixon under some mysterious privilege, "performing protective functions for the President."

I had several appointments the following day regarding my production business, and preparing for them was also important. I would not have time to do anything with the Wong lead, so I forced myself to put the mental brakes on and get back to the business that provides my livelihood. Also, I would be meeting with Bob Woodward in two days, for he and I would fly together to our joint lecture at the University of Massachusetts on April 22nd. Woodward, like Howard Hunt, might just drop a tidbit that would cement it all. I would have to wait to see if and how all this might fit together.

Bob Woodward was late arriving at the gate for our flight to Hartford. Luckily, the ticket agent knew who I was and, when I said I was flying with Woodward, he recognized that name also, and blocked two seats for us on an oversold flight. I'd not seen Bob for several years. We'd visited, and had dinner together, when he was in Los Angeles on a book tour for *The Brethren.*

I liked Bob too well to set him up, for I didn't think he would do that to me. So I let our reunion and conversation take its natural course, from what we were doing, to family, mutual friends, politics, how we'd handle the lecture together, and all the little conversational tangents that fell between.

When we arrived at the campus of the University of Massachusetts, we separated for the dinner with the students before the lecture. The lecture was fun: I took on the reporting of Watergate; Bob talked about journalistic responsibility in general; then we spent about an hour answering questions. The banter between us was so good, many might have thought we'd rehearsed for years. Exhausted, we were driven back to Hartford, where we retired about midnight, immediately on returning to the motel. Both of us had early flights in different directions in the morning.

APRIL 22, 1982—Hartford, Connecticut.

Before I go to sleep, I should make just a few notes about my conversations with Bob Woodward. We spent twelve hours together. I did not really probe or push him on Deep Throat, but he did drop a few clues.

Before we were about to be taken to the U. of M. campus, I stopped by Bob's room to go with him to the lobby, where we'd

meet the students. We talked about the lecture, and he suggested
we ask each other questions. I said, "Fine," then jokingly added,
"Like, why don't I ask you who Deep Throat is?" Bob chuckled,
and said, "I hope you're not still one of those who doesn't really
believe I had such a source."

"No, not me. I believed you when you told me several years
ago. In fact, I think I know who Deep Throat is." I was bluffing,
but it must have worked.

Bob looked over at me, a little startled at my confident tone
and statement. "Well, I guess a lot of people at the *Post* know who
he is, but he doesn't want to be identified, even at this late date." I
sensed that Bob was saying, "Don't try to put me in a tight spot
tonight on this question," but I also felt he was fishing, wondering if
someone at the *Post* had told me who Deep Throat was.

"No Deep Throat tonight," I said. "We'll save that for another
time and place." He smiled, and we were off.

Driving back to the motel, after the lecture, we were both
tired and relaxed. I felt Bob had enjoyed our joint effort. I knew I
had, far more than most lectures. It was late, about 11 o'clock, and
the two of us were spread out in the back seat as our student hosts
piloted us along the highway. We began talking further about
Watergate, comparing notes, and the conversation evolved to the
accuracy of some of Bob's and Carl Bernstein's reporting. I said
that some of the information in *All the President's Men* had proved
wrong. We were talking about this when Woodward said, "Is that
story about Pat Gray marching over to the White House and virtually blackmailing Nixon into appointing him director of the FBI
correct?"

"No, not really." Gray had been acting director, and it was
Attorney General Richard Kleindienst who had gone to bat for
Gray.

"Got that story from a source at the White House, usually a
pretty good source," Bob lamented, and the conversation moved on.
According to *All the President's Men*, that source was Deep
Throat, so Woodward confirmed that Deep Throat was not at the
Justice Department or FBI, but rather the White House, which
certainly could include the Secret Service, and, more particularly,
Al Wong!

As close as I felt I was, I knew I had more very delicate work
ahead. There was no way that I would have time to surface Deep

Throat on or before the tenth anniversary of Watergate. Also, I would need help. It would be hard for me to do the digging around Washington to confirm my findings, without other reporters getting wind of it and scooping me.

I had talked earlier with a Washington-based private investigator and, although he had good sources and was a very resourceful (and honorable) practitioner of his profession, it would take me a long time to educate him. Another reporter, someone who had covered Watergate and already done work on the Deep Throat question, was what I needed—and Hays Gorey was at the top of my list.

MAY 25, 1982—Los Angeles.

No longer do I feel that the resurrection of Watergate means a return of my nemesis. While it won't be pleasant to have the past dredged up, I feel less shame and more curiosity about how the media will handle it.

I have agreed to appear on the "Today" show, from Washington, on June 17, 1982—the tenth anniversary. Returning to Washington will enable me to meet with Hays Gorey to discuss the final pursuit of Deep Throat. Also, I can better measure how the media handles their reexamination of Watergate ten years later. But there is no way I can complete my Deep Throat inquiry before the "anniversary"—unfortunately!

In planning a trip to Washington to determine if Wong was Woodward's friend, I thought about others who might be of assistance to Hays and me—people with their own sources, which would be far different from those any reporter would have. The one name that kept coming to mind was Pete Kinsey, the extremely able lawyer who had worked for me at the White House—and then worked as a top aide to Senator Lowell Weicker. It was Pete who had been kind enough to pick me up at Fort Holabird the day I was released from prison. Pete and I had stayed in touch over the years, and I'd watched his private law practice blossom.

"Pete, how would you like to help me uncover Deep Throat?" I asked, as we settled in at our table for dinner at Chadwick's in Old Town, Alexandria, Virginia.

Pete did a double take, smiled, and said, "I'd love it."

"I want to hire you," I said, handing him a dollar bill. "Now you're on retainer, and anything and everything I tell you I consider privileged." It was not that I had to worry about Pete's keeping a confidence, but with lawyers it's such nice insurance to hire them, thus binding them contractually and ethically to silence. With that formality out of the way, I explained what I'd uncovered and how I'd done it. There were couples seated on both sides of our table, so I spoke in hushed tones. Occasionally both Pete and I found ourselves taking side glances to make certain I wasn't being overheard.

"Al Wong," Pete said reflectively, when I had finished. "It sure fits."

"It fits on paper. But whether it fits in fact, I don't know. Let's go back to Barry's house, where we can talk more openly."

We returned to a former neighbor's house in Alexandria, Virginia, where I had once lived and was now staying, and settled in at the dining room table that, over the years, had become my office away from home. Pete sipped a can of beer as I explained what I thought I had to do to corroborate my analysis that Alfred Wong was the right man. Pete had some ideas on how he could help, but wanted time to check a couple of things.

The next day Pete joined Hays and me for lunch. We met at the favorite place of many of Washington's high and mighty—The Palm, with its walls filled with caricatures of the people who frequent it, and run the country. We were given a private booth in the back, where Joseph Califano's* caricature looked over my left shoulder as I sat with my back to the wall, Pete on my left, Hays on my right. There was a wonderful feeling of irony about discussing one of Washington's best-kept secrets in such a public place.

"I think I've found Wong's home address," Pete reported. "It was in the 1977 Congressional Directory, but did not appear in sub-

---

*Joseph Califano is a well-known Washington person. A former general counsel of the army and White House staffer during the Lyndon Johnson administration, during the Carter administration Joe left his lucrative law practice with Edward Bennett Williams to become Secretary of Health, Education and Welfare. More recently he served as Alexander Haig's lawyer during Haig's confirmation hearings, and, as we were lunching, he was working in the congressional investigation of drug abuses in the Congress.

sequent years. He, at one time anyway, lived at 8517 Hunter Creek Trail in Potomac, Maryland. I don't know if he's still there."

"Last night I reread your material on Deep Throat," Hays interjected, "and it's very convincing. The case on paper certainly looks like you've got the right man."

Hays's reassurance was comforting, because, as close as I felt I was, I also felt there was a considerable distance to go before establishing it as fact. How to do that eluded me. As lunch progressed I shared this concern. Neither Hays nor Pete had any solution, so we proceeded to discuss how we might work from what we did know to fill the void.

"You know, if Woodward paid Wong it could be a crime," Pete noted matter-of-factly at one point in our conversation. Both Hays and I looked over at him with unconcealed astonishment. That prompted Pete to say, "I got into that with the Paula Parkinson case.* The Criminal Code, Sections 201, 203, and 208. Paying or giving something of value to a government official for a favor can get you and the official five years in the pokey."

"You mean to say that paying a source could be a crime?" Hays asked, incredulously.

"If it involved an official act. That's the question."

"How'd you resolve it in the Paula Parkinson case?" I asked. "Did you argue that sex with her had no value?" We all laughed, breaking the tension.

"Impossible, if you've ever seen her. That's what the boys at Justice said. But they never charged her," Pete added with a big grin.

I asked Pete to take a closer look at that criminal statute and the statute of limitations. I was not particularly interested in either Woodward's or Wong's (or any other of the candidates who could be Deep Throat) going to jail, if Woodward had paid his friend.

Hays soon moved the conversation and planning session on to my meeting with a friend of his—one of Washington's best investigators. Hays said he had talked to his man at some length by phone. "He doesn't know if Wong smokes cigarettes or drinks Scotch," as Woodward had described Deep Throat, Hays said.

---

*Paula Parkinson, who had posed nude for *Playboy* magazine, had made headlines with revelations about her use of sex for lobbying.

"But does he think Wong could be our man?" I asked.

"He has doubts about that. But he does agree that it's a possibility. He's probably reserving an opinion until he sees what you've got, and I can't say I blame him. You're looking down an alley here that very few people have traveled."

The lunch ended with an agreement that I would call Hays and Pete in two and a half hours, to see how they had progressed.

I stopped at the corner drugstore, purchased a map of Montgomery County, Maryland, where Bob Woodward had first worked as a reporter, and headed off for Al Wong's house—or at least where he had lived in 1977. Driving through northwest Washington, through those neighborhoods where I had spent my first years out of college, I thought again how this city had once held nothing but unending potential for me, how I'd watched others fulfill their ambitions and climb the power ladder—become important, powerful people. It was a city filled with the ambitious, and, knowing many of them as I had over the years—including myself—I wondered if fulfilling ambitions was not more important to most of them than governing the country.

By the time I found Al Wong's house in suburban Maryland, I had concluded that it was a sad but true fact of life that those who come to Washington with pure motives—those who want to make this country run a little better for the good of all, the ideologues with noble intentions—do not fare very well. To succeed, you have to be pliable. "Go along to get along" had never been etched in stone on any monument or building in Washington, but it was an indelible truth that all who made it understood.

Al Wong's house was comfortable looking, certainly not palatial, but above the standard of most men who had spent a lifetime on the government payroll. I studied it carefully, noting that the blinds were pulled, and that behind the large columns that flanked the front of the Georgian-style, two-story home was the alarm horn of a sophisticated security system. For a man who was a security professional, that was no surprise.

Heading back to town, with absolutely no conclusion to be drawn about Mr. Wong from this trip, I decided I must cut this process short—confront Al Wong personally.

That night Pete and I huddled again to plan a strategy. We talked by phone several times to Hays, and, finally, all three of us agreed that confronting Wong seemed the best way to bring the matter to a head. But before seeing Wong, I would meet with Hays's friend, the investigator.

"I have access to a suite at the Hay-Adams, which would probably be the best place," Hays suggested. "Your coming to the office would raise a lot of questions with curious *Time* reporters." The Hay-Adams Hotel is right beside *Time* magazine's offices on 16th Street, and right across Lafayette Park from the White House. The meeting was set for eleven o'clock the next morning.

For reasons I can't myself understand, I arrived at a parking garage off 16th Street, and at 10:45 A.M. I walked to the Sheraton-Carlton Hotel, up the block and across the street. There I waited until 11:15 for Hays and his friend to meet me in the lobby, then called his office. He was gone. I waited. At 11:30 I looked at my watch. Where in hell are they? Then it dawned on me—I was in the wrong hotel. This mistake was as dumb as the mistake I'd made during my testimony about where I'd met with Herbert Kalmbach. I have a mental block about the names of Washington hotels.

I proceeded on to the Hay-Adams, called Hays on the house phone, and cracked him up when I told him what I'd done.

The suite was elegant, furnished in a subtle Danish-modern style, with a postcard view of the White House across Lafayette Park. Hays introduced me to his associate and friend, whom I'll call the Investigator. He had once spent a lot of time tracking Deep Throat with Hays. They'd never cracked the case.

We got right to the reason for our meeting, and I told Hays's friend I was convinced that the Deep Throat leaks had to have come from the White House.

"You're right," the Investigator said, "and that could include the Secret Service." This man had sources everywhere: the FBI; Justice; the CIA; the Secret Service; the White House. He was a pro who'd spent a lifetime developing his sources.

The Investigator was surprised that I knew Woodward had once spent time at the Nixon White House, for he'd missed the book by *Washington Post* editor Leonard Downie, in which this information had appeared. He already knew it from his own sources. "You know, Woodward was carrying some heavy secrets, stuff from the secretary of navy's office, to the White House," the Investigator said. "And that's the key. That's where he had to have met his friend," he emphasized.

I told him I agreed, and that was why I thought it was someone in the Secret Service, for that would have been an opportune time. As Hays had suggested, the Investigator seemed almost at pain to agree that was possible; but it was very possible, he conceded.

We talked for about an hour. The Investigator felt I could be on the track, but wasn't sure. He kept repeating, however, that the key was: Whom did Woodward meet when he was delivering those pouches of information from the secretary of the navy to the White House? I had hoped that my visit with the Investigator might spark his interest in helping me. But Hays told me that he was deeply involved in an investigation of his own, which precluded that possibility. We'd have to go it on our own, and the next step would either be a big step forward, or eliminate another candidate from my list.

When I called Al Wong at his office in the Supreme Court the next morning, and told his secretary who was calling, I was put right through.

"Al, this is obviously a voice from the past. How are you?"

"Fine, John. How are you?"

"Good. Listen, Al, I have something extremely important I need to talk with you about. Can we meet for lunch?"

"I've got to leave the office at 1:30, so. . . ."

He was hedging, so I added urgency to my voice. "It's very important, Al, or I wouldn't ask."

Lunch was out, and he didn't want me coming to his office, so he suggested we meet outside the Court building. I would wait for him on the street corner across from the underground garage entrance behind the Supreme Court building. (It would have been more fun, of course, had my number one suspect suggested we meet *in* the underground garage, since this was part of Deep Throat's *modus operandi*. Nothing so tidy was to occur, I guessed.)

At noon a small, maroon foreign car pulled up the ramp of the

Court's garage to the street, with the balding head of the diminutive marshal behind the wheel. I waved; Wong stopped and picked me up on the street. He looked about as pleased to see me as if I'd been selling herpes. After his subdued greeting, he asked, "Where to?"

"Let's just see if we can find a spot around the corner."

As he drove off, he asked, "What's this all about?" I began telling him, but I wanted to watch his reaction, so when I saw a spot where he could park, I suggested he pull over. He did.

"Al, I've got information that you were Bob Woodward's source, Deep Throat!"

Wong blinked, looked straight ahead, and sat gripping the steering wheel. When he finally looked over at me, his expression asked, "Why are you doing this to me?" Then he said, "Tell me more."

I proceeded to take him, step by step, through evidence that would point toward him: the information about the Wallace shooting; the fact that Woodward had worked at the White House as a Pentagon courier; that Woodward's third book had come from inside the Supreme Court, where he now worked; and a tidbit I had picked up the preceding day—that he had been seen talking to another reporter from *Time* magazine after the existence of the tapes was revealed.

Wong stopped me only once during the ten or so minutes it took to give him this summation of evidence. He seemed surprised that Woodward had had access to the White House. "I didn't know that, but I can check it. His name would probably still be on the computer down there." I tried to judge his reaction to everything I said. When I finished, he denied he was Woodward's source, but he appeared burdened by the evidence I had.

"I didn't know the Wallace-shooting information. That would probably have come out of the intelligence division (of the Secret Service)," he said, shaking his head. He admitted that he'd met with a *Time* magazine reporter. "Yeah, after Butterfield testified about the tapes every reporter in town wanted to talk to me, but I didn't tell them anything." As for Woodward's Supreme Court book, he claimed, "Woodward and his associate, Scott Armstrong, were up here, sure, but I told them I couldn't and wouldn't talk to them. And I didn't."

"Where did they get all that inside information?" I asked.

"As best we can figure out, from law clerks. Those guys come and go. And they're not very loyal, either. Which surprises me for lawyers, who I always thought were not supposed to talk about what they did."

It wasn't what Al Wong said, as much as the way he said it, that persuaded me that maybe the paper analysis that led to him was wrong. To loosen him up, in hopes of getting more, I told him I didn't really believe it was he, which was, by now, the truth.

Al's car was like a sauna, so I suggested we get a little air. As we walked along one of the streets behind the Supreme Court, Al was much more relaxed.

"You know that Trudy's up here with me," he said. Trudy Brown (Fry) had been in charge of the sensitive files at the White House, plus liaison with the FBI for security clearance. Trudy had worked for Alex Butterfield, and Wong's mention of her name convinced me all the more that he was hiding nothing. Trudy could have been in a position to learn from the FBI about the Watergate investigation, and she also knew about the political people on the White House staff and at the Committee for the Re-election of the President. Trudy's knowledge, and Al's, clearly could have added up to Deep Throat's knowledge.

Either Al Wong was being very artful in handling me, or he was not Deep Throat. My feeling was the latter, and I was glad I'd confronted him. It might have severely disrupted his life had I made my case on paper and named him. Yet proving he wasn't Deep Throat could be tough, for he'd given me no solid evidence he wasn't. Just as finding out who Woodward's friend was required not only information but instincts, so did knowing who was not his friend. All my instincts now told me it was not Wong.

I asked Wong if he would assist me by looking at what Deep Throat had given Woodward. Al wasn't thrilled at this prospect, but he agreed to assist. From my own research, plus my conversation with the Investigator, I had solidly eliminated the U.S. attorney's office, the Justice Department, the FBI, and now I needed to eliminate the Secret Service. Wong could help.

Over the next few days I moved through Washington like a tornado, and later learned that I had sent some people in the Secret Service heading for shelter as I wound my way through the city, and

had meeting after meeting with agents. Also I was able to put together how Woodward and Scott Armstrong had gotten their information about the Supreme Court. After a hectic week, I knew the
following:

—Al Wong could not have been Deep Throat because he had
moved from the White House, as head of the technical security division, to the headquarters office by November 1973, and custody of
the Nixon tapes had been taken away from the Secret Service and
transferred to Al Haig in July of 1973, following Alexander Butterfield's Senate testimony. This made it almost impossible for Wong—
or anyone in the Secret Service—to tell Woodward (as his friend had
done) that the tapes contained "deliberate erasures."

—Talking both with retired Secret Service agents, and with
those still active, a picture of the Service emerged that made it very
remote as the base from which Deep Throat might have operated.
As one agent said, "We're basically cops. Politics causes us problems, so most guys don't get involved." While some agents pointed
fingers at others as potential candidates for Woodward's friend, none
of those singled out bore out, for they all established to my satisfaction that they did not have—nor could they have had—access to the
information Deep Throat possessed.

—Al Wong, in giving me his best analysis of whether or not
anyone in the Service could have known what Deep Throat knew,
explained that he had kept the men in TDS in compartments, so that
none could have had access to the information. Nor was it likely any
of them had listened to the tapes. "The tapes were a nuisance, a
burden, and no one had the time or the inclination to listen to them,"
he explained, very persuasively.

—Finally, I was able to learn from several good sources where
and how Woodward and Armstrong probably obtained their information for *The Brethren*. The bulk of the material, I was told, had
come from something called "The Brennan Diary." Justice Brennan
has his law clerks prepare a detailed account of what goes on within
the court. This "diary," an internal chronicle of the court for many
years, deals in varying length and detail with cases. For example, the

Bakke "reverse discrimination" case is reported in over fifty typed pages. Because so few of Justice Brennan's law clerks have worked on the diary over the years—and some clerks have had a two-year stint with the Justice—it is very unlikely that Woodward got the diary from a law clerk, for such a source would have been too easily identified. Several "well-informed" sources believe that Justice Brennan himself made it available to Woodward. Brennan, I was told repeatedly, is not antimedia, like Chief Justice Burger. He is known to talk to reporters "informally" and "off the record" regularly.

In addition to the Brennan Diary, Woodward had, I learned, had the use of material from Nina Totenberg, a reporter with National Public Radio, who has a close personal friendship with Justice Potter Stewart. Also, to a lesser degree, reporter Anthony Lewis of *The New York Times* provided information and insights to Woodward.

Although Woodward and Armstrong say they conducted hundreds of interviews, my sources said this accounted for only a small percentage of the information in the book. Also, my sources believed that about five percent of the book was pure speculation. None of them felt Al Wong had provided anything.

Hays and Pete were a little down as I prepared to return to California—empty-handed. "We're back to square one," Hays said. I was disappointed, too, but I felt we were a long way from starting over. My list had once consisted of over a hundred names. This trip had been useful in paring it down to one remaining location in the executive branch. Given the time, effort, and information we had uncovered about the whereabouts of Woodward's friend, it was now fairly certain that he must have been on the White House staff. This would be an advantage, for it would be far easier for me to run down information on my former colleagues than to battle the bureaucracy in the other places in government we had been searching. Thus, while disappointed, I was still encouraged that it was possible.

CHAPTER TWELVE

Looking for Woodward's Friend

Before me were nine names, former members of the Nixon White House staff who I felt "could" have had the information that Deep Throat gave to Bob Woodward. There was no way to know this for certain, because people who work at the White House develop many and widespread relationships with people throughout government. Plus they develop relationships with others on the White House staff itself—and through all these personal channels flow hard information, rumor, and gossip.

The sub-rosa information network that flows to and from the White House is vast and complex. It would be impossible for me to know who knew precisely which bit of information, and when. Yet each of the names I had placed on my list was there for a reason that I felt qualified him as a possible nominee for Woodward's most secret and celebrated source.

The list had originally been prepared in 1978, when I'd first sorted through all the information about Deep Throat. Now that I had eliminated every agency except the White House as the venue from which Deep Throat operated, I was studying anew the list and my notes about why I had selected each as a candidate. The time had come to narrow the list to the most viable candidates.

Chuck Colson was tuned into almost everything at the Nixon White House. He certainly knew all about the Wallace shooting; he knew about Howard Hunt and Gordon Liddy in general; and he

311

knew much about the Watergate investigation in particular. One special bit of information that Deep Throat had given Woodward had resulted in my including Chuck. On October 9, 1972, Deep Throat revealed that John Ehrlichman had told Howard Hunt to "leave town." Ehrlichman has always denied this, but I was the one who passed this order on to Hunt, and I did so in Ehrlichman's office, while Colson was present.

But Chuck Colson did not seem a very likely Deep Throat. He was too loyal to Nixon, and too deeply involved in many of the notorious activities to have risked playing the double-agent role. Also, he had received too much unfavorable press coverage from Woodward and Bernstein to be such an important source; while Deep Throat may well have been the subject of negative stories by Bob, which would facilitate the cover, I doubted this would necessitate the degree of bad press Colson had actually received. As I reflected on the unique information about Ehrlichman's ordering Hunt out of town, I had to acknowledge that this tidbit had moved well into the area of gossip by the time Deep Throat gave it to Woodward, which was almost five months after it had happened. Any number of people could have heard it by that time.

Alexander Butterfield certainly "could" have known what Deep Throat knew, but, over the years since I'd first placed him on my list, I had talked many times with Alex, and I knew for a fact that he did not have the necessary knowledge. In fact, Alex and I had renewed our White House friendship in the past year, and I knew he was as curious as I about Deep Throat's identity. In trying to assist me with the investigation, Alex had given me invaluable background information about certain people whom he knew far better than I.

Leonard Garment had made my list for several reasons. When I had dug out all the articles that Bob Woodward had written for the *Post* prior to Watergate, I discovered a lot of articles about doctors profiting from Medicaid, violations of the 1972 federal price and rent freeze—stories from the District of Columbia that struck me as the sort of goings-on Len Garment would have known about. Had Len tipped his friend to get him started as a cub reporter at the *Post*? I wondered. Another persuasive element was that Len fit my image of the perfect Deep Throat, for if there ever was a keeper of the moral and ethical code at the Nixon White House, Garment had the keys. He was an honorable man, a person with a true conscience about what was right and wrong. His outrage over Watergate could have driven him to leak.

While nothing had changed my impression of Garment, I had never been able to find a clue—anywhere—that he had much information about Watergate until the spring of 1973, when he took over my post as Counsel to the President. While I could not keep Len's name in a primary candidacy for Deep Throat, neither could I simply remove him.

Dick Moore, like Woodward a Yale man, was another difficult potential to pin down, for he "could" have passed the information that Deep Throat did. Dick had worked at Mitchell's Justice Department before moving to the White House, and could easily have had a conduit to information about the investigation. Dick also spent a considerable amount of time at the re-election committee after Watergate, trying to help solve the public relations problems. Given his relationship with Mitchell, Mardian, and La Rue at the re-election committee, he could have been aware of the investigation. He was also involved in working with Dwight Chapin on the Segretti matter, when that story broke. But Dick never struck me as a man who would play both sides of the street as Deep Throat had, nor, given his age, could I imagine him meeting with Woodward at pre-dawn or all-night meetings. He was a very weak candidate, at best.

Ken Clawson, because of his former relationship with the *Post* as a reporter, plus the fact that he had covered the Justice Department and FBI while working at the *Post,* was early on my list. But in the time since I had placed him there, I had learned that his new-found hatred of his former employer was unending. Ken was burned by his former colleagues, and had never forgiven them. I did not think it likely that he had hated them and helped them simultaneously, and for this and other reasons I had stricken his name.

David Gergen, as another Yale graduate and a known source to Woodward, had automatically gone on my list. However, Taylor Branch, who was as able an investigator as could be found, had concluded that Gergen was not likely. When Taylor had confronted him, Gergen had not proved he wasn't Deep Throat, but he had made a persuasive case. Taylor's findings convinced me I could remove him from my list.

Jon Rose was a remote possibility whom I'd included because he'd stopped me outside the White House within a few weeks of the Watergate break-in to tell me he'd learned something about where the Watergate burglars might have purchased their electronic bugging equipment. He'd displayed a surprising degree of interest. And when I later learned that he too was a Yale graduate, it gave him a sufficient potential tie to Woodward for inclusion. Also, Jon's father, Washington lawyer Chappy Rose, later became a behind-the-scenes consultant to the White House, following the unraveling of the cover-up in the spring of 1973. Therefore Jon could have had access to Deep Throat-quality information. He would have to remain on the list until I found a reason to disqualify him.

Alexander Haig was a true insider at the Nixon White House, one of those bureaucrats who knew bits and pieces of everyone's business and what was going on. He worked the gossip grapevine like a master, so he certainly "could" have known. All I knew about Haig was what I'd picked up while working at the White House, and, although my earlier check of his whereabouts had shown he was out of the country for a vital meeting, given the information that my source, Deep Thought, had shared about deliberate distortions of fact in *All the President's Men*, I couldn't remove Haig from my list without learning more about the man.

Steve Bull had taken over Alexander Butterfield's job at the White House. Before that he'd occupied an office on the opposite side of the Oval Office, and had been the president's top "gofer." Like the Secret Service, Bull was always around; thus he could have been privy to much information. Steve was also considered a gossip while I was at the White House, but whether that propensity extended far enough to include reporters, I could not tell. I would have to keep Bull on my list for a while.

My list was considerably shortened: Len Garment, Jon Rose, Al Haig, and Steve Bull. But how could I be sure I had not accidentally eliminated the real Deep Throat? Also, I had never resolved how to deal with little-known assistants and secretaries, and, based on what I had learned about Woodward's and Bernstein's investigative style, these people were not unimportant. Bernstein had told their editor, Leonard Downie:

The thing is to work from the bottom up, finding secretaries, clerks, and middle-level aides. They're people without the vested interests of their bosses, and very often you will get a much better version of the truth from them than you would get from their superiors or the target you're after.

Although my best estimate had reduced my list to four, when I thought about what Bernstein told Downie, I had to ask if maybe that list should be a thousand and four. I thought again about how Carl and Bob had described Deep Throat's position in the executive branch as "extremely sensitive." Could that describe a clerk, secretary, or middle-level aide? Only if the person's boss had an extremely sensitive position.

I felt mired in quandary and uncertainty. I needed to get off paper and back on my feet. This was going to take a lot more digging. And suddenly it all seemed a bit overwhelming.

Why was I doing this? I scanned the voluminous notes I had compiled in my hunt for Woodward's friend. Was any purpose other than my own curiosity served by uncovering him? Was I only trying to embarrass *The Washington Post* and Woodward—some subtle retribution for their aggressive pursuit of Watergate?

I considered what it was I was doing. Clearly, at one level it was a game—purely the unraveling of a mystery for the sake of the solution. Testing myself against the odds. A bit of the "hey-look-at-me-I've-done-it" syndrome. But there was more to it than that, for I had always found it unsettling that Deep Throat's information was taken for fact by so many people. I had no desire to contest either the *Post* or Woodward. But I knew from traveling the country to lecture that, of all the books about Watergate, probably the best-read—and most-read—book, particularly by young people on campuses, was *All the President's Men*. Many times I'd been asked questions that had come directly from Deep Throat's misstatements of fact, and I had told Bob Woodward that I was bothered by this when we'd met in the spring at the University of Massachusetts. I believed that only the disrobing of his friend would resolve both the errors and why they were there.

While much of the information Bob received from his friend

was right on target, some of it was a distortion or an exaggeration. But there was also information that was terribly wrong. Looking again at his reported conversations, I made note of those that still bothered me:

—On September 17, 1972, Deep Throat told Woodward that Bart Porter was deeply involved in Watergate, equating Porter's involvement with that of Jeb Magruder. This is not true.

—On October 9, 1972, Deep Throat told Woodward that "much of the [Nixon forces-inspired] intelligence gathering was on their own campaign contributors, and some to check on the Democratic contributors—to check people out and sort of semi-blackmail them if something was found . . . a very heavy-handed operation." This is not true, and never have I seen any evidence from all the hearings, investigations, and reports to support it.

—On October 9, 1972, Deep Throat further stated that John Mitchell had conducted his own investigation after Watergate, and what he found "astounded even him." Woodward's friend also said, "Howard Hunt, of all the ironies, was assigned to help Mitchell get some information." This is not only false, it's ludicrous.

—On October 9, 1972, Woodward's friend told him that the "November Group," which handled the advertising for Nixon's re-election in 1972, was one of the "undercover operations." This tidbit has, over the years, caused problems and anguish, and necessitated a lot of explanations for some of those who joined the November Group. It was not an undercover operation of any sort.

—Also during this October 9th visit, Deep Throat told Woodward that, "You can safely say that fifty people worked for the White House and CRP [Nixon re-election committee] to play games and spy and sabotage and gather intelligence." This figure of fifty political espionage agents would be repeated in story after story. Yet, as Professor Epstein noted after studying the *Post's* reporting of Watergate, "the putative fifty other Donald Segrettis have never been found."

—On January 24, 1973, Deep Throat included Chuck Colson

among those behind the Watergate break-in. Tons of investigative evidence, even books by Hunt and Liddy, do not support this "information."

—In late February 1973, Woodward's friend told him that L. Patrick Gray had secured his nomination to director of the FBI by virtually blackmailing Nixon, implying that "all hell could break loose if he wasn't able to stay in the job permanently and keep the lid on." This never happened, and even Woodward had doubts, since he footnoted the conversation to indicate it might be incorrect. I told Woodward this was wrong in the spring, when he said he'd gotten it from a usually reliable "White House source," and told him it had been then-Attorney General Richard Kleindienst who had pushed for Gray's nomination.

—During that same February 1973 conversation, Deep Throat explained that wiretaps (later called the "Kissinger taps") on newsmen were the work of an "out-of-channels vigilante squad" of wiretappers. According to Woodward's recounting of the conversation, "[Deep Throat] explained that the wiretapping had been done by ex-FBI and ex-CIA agents who were hired outside of normal channels." Today we know the FBI installed and oversaw those wiretaps for Kissinger and the President. The "vigilante squad" has never surfaced in any of the investigations—to my knowledge.

—On April 16, 1973, Deep Throat was able to tell Woodward that Bob Haldeman and I were out of the White House, "for sure." Yet the tapes of the Oval Office conversations show that it would be several weeks before that "for sure" decision would be made.

—On May 16, 1973, Deep Throat summarized the status of Watergate for Woodward, with more collective inaccuracies than in all their preceding conversations, to wit:

He said I had talked with Senator Howard Baker, who was "in the bag completely," reporting back directly to the White House. I never had such a meeting with Baker; rather, Kleindienst and Nixon himself met secretly with Baker.

He said the President "threatened" me with jail if I revealed any national-security information. This never happened.

He said Caulfield told McCord, "Your life is no good in this country if you don't cooperate." This never happened, although apparently some investigators believed this true.

He said there was a problem raising money for the cover-up, so they (Haldeman, Ehrlichman, the President, Dean, Mardian, Caulfield, and Mitchell) "started raising money on the outside and chipping in their own personal funds. Mitchell couldn't meet his quota and . . . they cut Mitchell loose." This never happened, nor anything resembling it.

He said, apparently "these guys in the White House were out to make money and a few of them went wild trying." This has always mystified me, as it has investigators who later asked me about it. It's not true.

It was also at this May 16, 1973, meeting that Deep Throat had warned Woodward that "everyone's life is in danger," that the CIA was conducting "electronic surveillance," and that Woodward had better watch himself. These warnings seem rather exaggerated in hindsight.

These glaring gaps in the reality of the events of Watergate simply did not comport with Woodward's assessment of his friend. Woodward claimed that "Deep Throat never tried to inflate his knowledge or show off his importance. He always told rather less than he knew." Bob believed that "Deep Throat would never deal with him falsely." I wondered if Woodward still felt the same about his friend, now that the facts were out.

Identifying this misinformation both piqued my curiosity about who had provided it and rekindled my interest in setting the record straight. While I had not resolved whether I should look for someone high in the White House, or low—I felt one further bit of investigation might further help me narrow the field.

In reviewing all of Deep Throat's information, it was evident that he clearly had knowledge of what was happening inside the White House and the FBI. Feeling I had to check and recheck everything, I had made a list that evidenced this unique knowledge:

FACTS FROM FBI AND WHITE HOUSE

"The FBI regarded Hunt as a prime suspect in the Watergate investigation for many reasons. . . ." (*June 19, 1972*)

"During the summer, he had told Woodward that the FBI badly wanted to know where the *Post* was getting its information." (*Summer 1972*)

"Both the FBI and the White House were determined to learn how the *Post* was getting its information and to put a stop to it." (*September 17, 1972*)

"The story about Mitchell's aides had infuriated the White House." (*September 17, 1972*)

"The Nixon White House worried [Deep Throat]. 'They are all underhanded and unknowable,' he had said numerous times." (*October 9, 1972*)

"Remember, you don't do those 1,500 [FBI] interviews and not have something on your hands other than a single break-in." (*October 9, 1972*)

"Deep Throat had access to information from the White House, Justice, the FBI and CRP [Nixon re-election committee]. What he knew represented an aggregate of hard information flowing in and out of many stations." (*All the President's Men, p. 138*)

"Deep Throat confirmed what the reporters' other sources had hinted. The FBI's and the grand jury's investigations had been limited. . . ." (*October 9, 1972*)

Publication of Senator Eagleton's drunk driving records were "somehow tied into Hunt and the White House." (*October 9, 1972*)

Referring to information about the fifty Segretti-type agents: " 'It's all in the files,' Deep Throat said. 'Justice and the Bureau know about it, even though it wasn't followed up.' " (*October 9, 1972*)

" 'Chapin took it close in and there's a lot of tension,' Deep

Throat explained. 'That's to put it mildly—there's tension about Haldeman.' " (*October 21, 1972*)

"Deep Throat described the Haldeman operation." (*October 27, 1972*)

"The reporters tended to doubt that someone in [Deep Throat's] position would be so cavalier toward matters affecting Richard Nixon or the Presidency itself." (*All the President's Men, p. 242*)

" 'The White House knows it, the FBI knows it.' [Deep Throat said, regarding Colson's and Mitchell's involvement in Watergate]." (*January 24, 1973*)

"The White House, [Deep Throat] said, was developing plans to make sure no congressional investigation could succeed." (*January 24, 1973*)

"Our President has gone on a rampage about news leaks on Watergate. He's told the appropriate people, 'Go to any length' to stop them. . . . At a meeting, Nixon said that the money left over from the campaign, about $5 million or so, might as well be used to take the *Washington Post* down a notch." (*Late February, 1973*)

"Deep Throat's message was short and simple: one or more of the tapes contained deliberate erasures." (*First week of November, 1973*)

A close study of this information, which Woodward reports in *All the President's Men*, shows that it is basically correct and appears to be based on fact. Clearly it would have to have come from someone "inside" the White House who had good access to the FBI. Yet, much of this information could also be supposition, and, every time I reviewed what Deep Throat had said, I was nagged by the feeling that he was a composite, or that the authors had stretched their source to appear to be more than he (or she) might have been.

I had to ask myself if those who had been in the White House during the "final days" of the Nixon presidency, some of whom had told me that the picture that Woodward and Bernstein painted was an exaggeration, were correct; I wondered whether this might not be true of *All the President's Men* as well. In reading Raymond Price's account of his days at the Nixon White House, I'd been surprised at the outrage he had focused on *The Final Days*. Ray, a mild-mannered speechwriter, and former newspaper editor, exclaimed, "The old-fashioned respect for literal truth has been subsumed by the new fashion of reaching for 'intrinsic' or 'symbolic' truth." Ray's reading of *The Final Days*, as one who was there, raised the caveat that I felt about *All the President's Men*:

> Woodward and Bernstein's *The Final Days* is breathlessly hailed as true by those who want to believe it true. Its authors invent thoughts which they place in people's heads, words which they place in people's mouths; they boast of having interviewed 394 people, and maintain that every word of their book is true because they include nothing unless confirmed by at least two "sources." What this means is that if two people have heard the same rumor, they weave a story around it, wrap it in manufactured detail and sprinkle it with quotation marks, and present the story as fact. "Journafiction," Bill Safire aptly called it. "Crap," *The New Republic*'s John Osborne called it. "Trash," Richard Nixon called it. Who were the 394? The authors don't tell us. Rather, they artfully contrive to convey the impression that their sources were the principals whose actions, words, and thoughts they purport to describe, rather than admitting that it was gossip from second- or third-hand sources, embellished by the authors. . . . Parts of the book are true, parts are not; but the artful interweaving of fact and fiction does a disservice not only to the record but also to the concept of truth itself.

Returning again to my newly gleaned list of Deep Throat's unique information, and keeping in mind Bob's assurance that his source was one person who knew all this, I asked myself which bit of information would have been the most difficult to know. Which morsel was most closely held as an inside secret? And proved correct, too? The answer, it seemed to me, was the tip that Woodward received in the first week of November 1973—the fact that "one or more of the tapes contained deliberate erasures."

Earlier I had scrutinized the events surrounding the revelation of this information. Unlike some of the misinformation that I discovered had never found its way into *The Washington Post*—but only into Woodward's and Bernstein's book—this fact had been printed by the *Post* on November 8, 1973. It had been correct; almost two weeks later the White House admitted there was an eighteen-minute, fifteen-second gap on one of the tapes, which sounded like it had been deliberately erased.

By focusing on exactly who in the White House knew this information, I hoped I could narrow my list to the most viable of candidates. Fortunately for the purposes of my inquiry, the revelation of this gap had caused such an uproar that the special prosecutor had demanded a hearing to determine who had caused it or how it had happened. While they had never found the answer, I knew that in the process they had determined who was aware of its existence, and when. That was the information I needed to convincingly narrow my list of Deep Throat candidates. I had to learn who on my list had this knowledge by the first week of November 1973—when Deep Throat had given it to Woodward.

First I read the book written by those who had conducted the investigation into the gap: *Stonewall*, by Richard Ben-Veniste and George Frampton, Jr., the former lawyers from the prosecutor's office who headed the investigation and conducted the hearings. I then studied *Not Above the Law*, by James Doyle, the reporter who had been in charge of press relations for the Watergate prosecutors, and *The Right and the Power*, by Leon Jaworski. All had written about the gap, as had Richard Nixon in his memoirs, and, of course, Woodward and Bernstein in *The Final Days*. From all these accounts, plus the newspaper clippings from *The New York Times* and *The Washington Post*, I reconstructed who had known what, and when.

It appears that in July 1973, after Alexander Butterfield revealed the existence of the Nixon taping system in his Senate Watergate testimony, the custody of the tapes was given to Alexander Haig, who had become chief of staff at the Nixon White House. Special Prosecutor Archibald Cox had subpoenaed a number of the tapes, and, while it was not certain what the White House would do, some preparations were made to learn the contents of the tapes, for

Nixon was considering providing verified summaries in lieu of releasing the actual tape recordings.

On September 29, 1973, Rose Mary Woods was at Camp David trying to transcribe the June 20, 1972, tape for Nixon's use. Steve Bull had obtained the tapes from Haig and, after checking the subpoena, had queued the tapes up for Rose on the tape recorder. On October 1, 1973, back at the White House, and using a different machine than the one she had used at Camp David, Rose ran into a problem. She went into Nixon's EOB office, according to Nixon's own account, and told the President that "she thought she might have caused a small gap in the Haldeman part of the June 20 tape." Nixon reassured her this was no problem, because he did not believe the Haldeman part of the conversation had been subpoenaed.

Nixon then "called Haig in and told him what had happened," and they "checked with Buzhardt to make sure that [Nixon] was right"—that the damaged tape had not been subpoenaed. There is no evidence in Nixon's memoirs that Buzhardt was told about the damaged tape, but it is certainly a fair inference to make that he, too, learned about the erased portion of the tape at this time. Rose Mary Woods believed she had accidentally destroyed only about five minutes of the Haldeman–Nixon conversation.

It is easy to understand how the significance of this erased conversation got buried for several weeks, for all hell began breaking loose around the White House. The Yom Kippur War broke out in the Middle East. Agnew was forced to resign. Nixon selected Ford as his replacement. On that same day, October 12, 1973, the Court of Appeals ruled that Nixon must turn over the subpoenaed tapes. Plans were concocted in mid-October to give summaries of the tapes to the near-deaf Senator John Stennis for verification. Cox was fired on October 20th for refusing to accept a compromise on the tapes. On October 25th an unprecedented military alert was put into effect because of the Middle East crisis. And on October 30th Buzhardt informed Judge Sirica that two of the subpoenaed conversations had never been recorded, and thus could not be turned over to the court.

I was still living in Washington at the time the world learned of the missing tapes, and, because one of the missing conversations was an important exchange between Nixon and myself on April 15, 1973, I suspected foul play. I had friends at the White House, and I knew they were suspicious also. One told me that Nixon, who had claimed to Buzhardt only to have a "Dictabelt" (dictated notes) of that conversation, had even suggested dictating a *new* Dictabelt to replace the "lost" one! This was later repeated by Woodstein in *The Final Days*. But these rumors were swirling only around the issue of "missing" tapes; no one whom I talked with during that first week in November had heard that any tapes had been "erased."

The knowledge that one or more of the tapes had been erased was limited to a very select few: Richard Nixon, Rose Mary Woods, Al Haig, and Steve Bull. Probable knowledge extended to Bob Haldeman and Fred Buzhardt. By this time Buzhardt and Len Garment were very close, thus Len may have been told of the erasures as well. In turn, Len was close to Chappy Rose, and could have told him, and Chappy could have told his son, Jon. All of these people very likely had knowledge that at least five minutes of a conversation had been destroyed.

I looked again at the four remaining names on my list of Deep Throat candidates: Leonard Garment, Jon Rose, Alexander Haig, and Steve Bull. This latest bit of "homework," while it had not served to eliminate any one of these names from consideration, had at least confirmed that all four names did belong in the running.

I sat for many long moments, sifting the complex elements of the information before me. Over and over, a single name pushed its way to the fore. I considered certainty of knowledge versus probability of knowledge; I considered the intricacies of access to information; I considered the totality of what I knew about Deep Throat's methods and personality. Endless hours of research began to merge with intuition, yielding no absolute proof, but far more than a mere inkling or suspicion.

Alexander Haig, without a doubt, was my top candidate. Some of the others who were privy to the knowledge of the erased tape could be eliminated out of hand—Nixon and Rose Woods. Buzhardt didn't qualify because he had not been at the White House long enough; Al Haig had only brought his pal Buzhardt over from the Pentagon in the summer of 1973. Garment, Bull, and Jon Rose would have to remain on this list, for they could have known—and probably did.

Finally, my list of candidates pared down to a workable few, I was ready to return to Washington, where I could search for more clues and, I hoped, eliminate names, or, even better, get the sort of solid information that might make my case for me—ending the mystery that was becoming a saga.

I arrived in Washington on Sunday, September 12, 1982, and called Hays Gorey. We agreed upon a plan of attack. Hays would free himself of normal duties to work with me. He would locate Woodward's 1972 apartment; we would visit it and former neighbors to see what we could learn. Hays would talk with friends of his at *The Washington Post.* I would visit with my own secret source and "friend," Deep Thought. I was really counting on him this time.

His arms folded on the table, Deep Thought sat quietly as I acquainted him with a summary of my investigation: how the Secret Service had been conclusively eliminated; who had been on my original list of White House contenders; how I had reduced that list to four remaining possibilities. Although he was most interested in how Woodward and Armstrong had put together *The Brethren,* he appeared to be experiencing vicarious delight in the whole investigative process. When at last Deep Thought asked how I planned to proceed with "plumbing my former White House associates," I explained the biggest dilemma facing me.

"I'm down to just four names, which doesn't sound like much of a problem, considering the number I started with. But you know and I know that it could take weeks to check them out."

Deep Thought said nothing at first, his eyes focused intently on some far-off point. I wondered if he was deliberating whether he *could* be of assistance to me, or whether he *should.* The silence seemed ominous.

"Maybe I can help," he offered at last, his conflict apparently resolved. "I've heard that Ben Bradlee believes there is a way—one way—to figure out who Deep Throat is."

"Really?" I gushed, as I felt a rush of blood coursing through my body.

"I can't give you his exact words, because I've never talked with

Ben about this, but I can, on good authority, as we say, give you the substance. Apparently Ben believes that if someone looked at who had access to the information, and then looked at who was out of town on the dates in question, that alone would resolve it. Ben feels, I guess, that when Deep Throat was unavailable, Bob and Carl didn't get very much."

"That's very interesting. But that's exactly what I have been doing."

"I know. But I think it tells you something else. Or at least that's what I read."

"What?" My mind refused to grasp the possible significance of what my "friend" was saying.

"*Bradlee is also saying that it's someone important enough to have done a lot of traveling—someone whose travels could be documented by an outside party.*"

This was the best, most solid tip I'd had in all the years I'd been pursuing Woodward's friend. In my estimation, it was as good as a clue from Woodward himself, since Bradlee actually knew Deep Throat's identity. It also solved the one remaining problem of how to figure out where to focus my attention.

Only one name fit what I started calling the "Bradlee Riddle," and that was Alexander Haig. No one would know about, or be able to trace, the travel of the others who might have known about the erased conversation—Garment, Bull, and Jon Rose. The Bradlee Riddle also eliminated all those little-known secretaries, clerks, and middle-level aides. At last my list had been distilled to just one name—a name that had, ironically, qualified as one of my earlier, instinctive prospects. But could Al Haig really have been Woodward's secret friend?

Immediately after my visit with Deep Thought, and excitedly, I called Hays to tell him about the Bradlee Riddle and the almost inescapable conclusion that it pointed toward Al Haig.

Hays said, "You remember, of course, that Haig was *Time's* top candidate, until you told [John] Stacks that it wasn't possible."

Hays was right, I had turned *Time* off of Haig. "Things have changed since then. Maybe we'd better take a closer look. Haig certainly fits the Bradlee Riddle."

"He sure does," Hays said emphatically.

We agreed that we would continue to follow out all our leads, talk with people who knew Bob, look for new clues, new sources, anything and everything that might help. In the evenings, I would start piecing together material on Haig to see if it fit. Before long I felt very much like what I had become—a detective. My time in Washington was primarily devoted to gathering information, and once back home I would sort and sift, and try to fit pieces of the puzzle together. Hays agreed to follow up in Washington.

The test I had developed was simple, although finding the information to complete it was anything but. There were six elements to the test:

First: Was there any evidence that Woodward and Haig had met prior to Watergate, since this relationship appeared to have existed before that time?

Second: Where was Haig when Woodward and his friend were said to be meeting? While I could not accept everything in Woodward's book as literal truth, I certainly had to accept the bulk of it. Thus Haig would have to appear to have been available for the conversations Woodward claims he had with his friend on the dates he says he had them. I already knew that Haig had been out of the country on one such date, October 9, 1972, but I would have to see what the records indicated of his whereabouts on the other key dates.

Third: Did Haig have the character and personality of someone who would leak explosive information to Woodward?

Fourth: Did Haig have access to the information that was given Woodward, i.e., information known specifically to the White House and FBI?

Fifth: Did Haig have unique access to information that only a few people had, i.e., were there more instances like that involving the knowledge of the erased tape?

Sixth: Was there evidence that Deep Throat had continued as a source for Woodward, and did Haig fit that category?

Alexander M. Haig, Jr.—indeed a fascinating prospect, I thought. But what did I really know about the man? Although Haig was a well-recognized public figure, very few people really knew him well. His public image was that of "the soldier," the general who served his president with unquestioning loyalty. I knew enough about Haig to know that this image did not always mesh with reality. The Al Haig I knew was a clever, ambitious bureaucrat, a known "talker" whose principal loyalty was to the advancement of his own career. I knew reporters to whom Haig had leaked; and I had watched him, while I was at the White House, adroitly straddle the politically treacherous gap between the Haldeman–Ehrlichman camp and the Kissinger camp. Haldeman loved to share with some of us the latest "Kissinger gossip" he'd gotten from Haig; and friends on the National Security Council would tell me the latest "Haldeman gossip" *they'd* gotten from Haig. Al Haig, I knew, was experienced in the workings of Washington in general, and of the White House in particular.

Even though the real Haig was unknown, from my personal dealings and observations I did know that Al's habits and demeanor jibed with any number of the descriptions that Woodward had so enticingly planted about Deep Throat, for Al smoked, drank, worked long and unusual hours, was a nocturnal type, enjoyed intrigue, and had a flair for the dramatic. I'd even seen Haig, when drinking coffee at his desk, "wipe his mouth inelegantly with the back of his hand"—just as Woodward had described.

The picture of Haig in my mind fit well enough, and, as Hays had agreed, he certainly met the Ben Bradlee qualification, for Al was sufficiently visible to know when he was in Washington, and when not. But I needed to learn a lot more about Haig, for my perception of him may have been unfairly jaded by the fact that I knew he had spent considerable energy as White House chief of staff trying to discredit me as a witness against Nixon. I would have to put him to the test.

First question: Could I establish a prior Haig-Woodward connection?

Based on personal knowledge, extensive phone conversations with former colleagues, and a review of the available documents, I was able to arrive at a conclusion to this first test that was based on what I believed was reasonable conjecture, if not proof positive. The key obstacle to a clear and easy answer was the time factor. Thirteen years had gone by since Woodward was carrying high-level secrets between the secretary of navy and the White House in his role as a Pentagon courier. Alexander Haig had been made a deputy to Henry Kissinger at about the same time, and it was not inconceivable that their paths could have crossed. If a friendship had developed between them, and if Haig had been Woodward's source, then I was safe in assuming that Watergate had forced them to be careful about being seen together ever after.

I spoke with several people who had served on the staff of the National Security Council with Haig, and none could remember a specific connection between Haig and Woodward. Many expressed surprise at learning of Woodward's job with the Pentagon, and all agreed that it was very possible the two could have met at that time.

Following a lead I had been given by Hays Gorey's friend, the Investigator, I asked another former NSC staff man, who had been working in the Nixon White House at the time, if he could tell me specifically to whom Woodward would have delivered his secret documents. His answer was unequivocal: "Al Haig, in the Situation Room." This information was stronger than any speculation that "their paths could have crossed."

I remembered Al Haig from those days, and he was far from the imperious figure he would later become. His style was to come across as "one of the guys," but only when he was *with* the guys. Given the fact that Haig himself had once been a Pentagon courier to the White House, he might have felt a unique bond with Woodward. And knowing what I did of Bob Woodward, it did not seem likely that he would have been unimpressed by the White House, or opposed to establishing a friendship with a pleasant young army colonel like Al Haig.

The information that Woodward had in all probability delivered his documents specifically to Al Haig was very interesting. I felt I had some pretty strong evidence, but nothing solid on this first phase of my test. And certainly nothing to disqualify Haig.

Second question: Could I account for Haig's whereabouts?

The next task in putting Alexander Haig through the test required days of digging for information that is hard to find. I had to determine, based on the best available information, if Haig had been in Washington on the dates Woodward met with his friend. Unfortunately, this test was also contingent on my being able to pinpoint, from my reading of *All the President's Men*, the exact dates in question. This I was able to do, but not without great difficulty.

According to *All the President's Men*, Woodward had had contact with Deep Throat on at least thirteen different days. References are made in the text to two other "meetings"—a second meeting in the summer of 1972, and one in December 1972—but no information is given about the information that was imparted on those occasions. I concentrated, then, on the dates when disclosures allegedly had been made:

1. Monday, June 19, 1972. Woodward placed two afternoon telephone calls to his "friend."

2. Summer 1972. No date or form of contact is given. The reference to information given to Woodward "during the summer" is included in the passages surrounding a September 16, 1972, conversation between Woodward and Deep Throat.

3. Saturday, September 16, 1972. This was an afternoon phone call placed by Woodward.

4. Sunday, September 17, 1972. Another telephone call placed by Woodward.

5. Monday, October 9, 1972. Woodward and Deep Throat met in an underground garage from 1:30 to 6:00 A.M. Woodward initiated contact.

6. Saturday, October 21, 1972. Woodward had signaled his friend for a meeting the preceding day, but Deep Throat had not shown up. Deep Throat initiated this meeting, which took place in the underground garage at 3:00 A.M.

7. Friday, October 27, 1972. Woodward initiated contact for this 3:00 A.M. meeting in the underground garage.

8. Wednesday, January 24, 1973. The text does not indicate who asked for the meeting, or at what hour the two of them met. It was a garage meeting, and, if it took place after midnight, then technically the meeting date would be January 25th.

9. Late February 1973. When Woodward asked for this meeting, he journeyed to the underground garage only to find a note from Deep Throat suggesting that they meet at 11:00 P.M. the following night in a bar on the outskirts of Washington. (The date in this instance is particularly difficult to pinpoint. The text reveals that on February 26th, "Woodward was off for a few days in the Caribbean." A later passage states that "Woodward returned from the Caribbean later that week." Since "that week" went from Sunday, February 25th, to Saturday, March 3rd, it would appear that Woodward did not return from his trip until around the first of March. However, the text also places Woodward at the opening of Pat Gray's confirmation hearings, which began on Wednesday, February 28th. Because Woodward's meeting with Deep Throat *preceded* the Gray confirmation hearings, or so says the text, I will assume that they met in "late February 1973.")

10. Monday, April 16, 1973. This was a Woodward-initiated telephone call.

11. Thursday, April 26, 1973. Deep Throat phoned Woodward at the *Post* at 9:30 P.M.

12. Wednesday, May 16, 1973. Woodward and Deep Throat met in the underground garage at 11:00 P.M. The book does not say who requested the meeting.

13. First week of November 1973. Woodward and Deep Throat had, according to *All the President's Men*, an underground garage meeting that Woodward requested. (I have great difficulty believing this, for two reaons: First, because the message from Deep Throat "was short and simple: one or more of the tapes contained deliberate erasures." This fits the characteristics of previous phone-call messages: one piece of information, succinctly presented. Second, because of the urgency of the information and the politically explosive repercussions that were to ensue from it, it seemed to me quite unlikely that Woodward had accidentally called a meeting. It is far easier to suppose that Deep Throat had a plum that, for his own reasons, he had to pass on to Woodward.)

Having ascertained as best I could the dates on which Woodward and Deep Throat had met, I turned my attention to Alexander Haig's whereabouts on those dates. This enterprise proved even more difficult than the first. Although every possible nugget of information was mined on this subject, short of getting an interview with Haig's personal valet, it was impossible to say conclusively where Haig had been on all the meeting dates.

Focusing on the week before and the week after each meeting, I combed *The New York Times*, *The Washington Post*, the *Los Angeles Times*, and all the "Watergate books" that made mention of Haig. I studied Nixon's memoirs, Kissinger's memoirs, the Haig biography—everything I could get my hands on. While some sources established that he definitely *was* in Washington on a couple of dates, and that he was in Washington shortly before or after other dates, the important point, I felt, was that I could establish that he was *not* in Washington on only one date: October 9, 1972.

On October 9, 1972, Woodward had a session with Deep Throat that he and his editors would later believe gave them a true handle on the dimensions of Watergate. According to *All the President's Men*, the meeting was prompted by the fact that Carl Bernstein and Barry Sussman were having trouble making sense out of what they had learned about Donald Segretti. Carl had received a tip from a government lawyer, on September 28th, that someone had tried to recruit a friend of his many months earlier for a dirty-tricks operation against the Democrats. Bernstein had tracked down this friend and, three days later, was given the name of the man who had tried to recruit him: Donald Segretti. On Friday, October 6th, Bob Woodward had done something he rarely did, take a weekend off. He had gone to New York City. On Sunday the 8th, Bernstein and Sussman decided to call Bob and discuss the story on Segretti they were putting together. Bob did not think what they had was very strong, and suggested they wait. He would return and arrange to check the facts with Deep Throat. According to Woodward's account of the conversation with Deep Throat, his friend "would not talk specifically about Segretti's operation."

Barry Sussman presents a similar account in his book, yet there is one important difference. Sussman had written, of this meeting Woodward had with Deep Throat in the early hours of the 9th, that "sometimes, at moments when Deep Throat was particularly angry, he gave more than just general assistance, as he did when Woodward asked him about Donald Segretti." Very odd.

The *Washington Post* stories that followed Woodward's October 9th meeting with Deep Throat employ the usual mask of anonymous officials. Earlier I had gone through every Deep Throat-based story in *The Washington Post* to see how they had referred to him, and it ran such a gamut that it was not a clue. He was called a "source close to the investigation," a "federal official," a "federal source," and, later in their reporting, he was even referred to as a "White House source." It is easy to see why those who have checked this have concluded Deep Throat was a composite character. In discussions with Deep Thought I came to understand that these descriptions often were applied without thought, sometimes by different editors who had no idea who this person was, and other times deliberately by Carl or Bob to camouflage their source as best they could.

Yet with this Segretti story, which ran in the *Post* on October 10th, there is a rather unique attribution to the sources, for the article notes, "Asked by the Washington *Post* to discuss Segretti, three FBI and Justice Department officials involved in the Watergate probe refused. At the mention of Segretti's name each said—in words of one—'That's part of the Watergate investigation.' One of the officials, however, became angry at the mention of Segretti's name and characterized his activities as 'indescribable.'"

Questions: If Deep Throat would not discuss Segretti, as Woodward says, and if the FBI and Justice Department would not discuss him, as the story says, where did the information come from? Is it possible that Woodward made it up? Or pulled together bits from earlier conversations with his friend? And how could an editor, who never asked Bob who his source Deep Throat was, later write that Deep Throat had provided them with material about Segretti? None of this was clear.

As I had discovered earlier, this October 9th meeting had other problems, for Deep Throat also allegedly told Woodward that the Nixon forces were investigating their own contributors, and that John Mitchell had conducted his own post-break-in investigation with Howard Hunt's help. Both pieces of information are totally false. But the biggest bit of misinformation to come from this meeting was the revelation of the so-called Canuck letter.

At the height of the 1972 presidential primary campaign in New Hampshire, the *Manchester Union Leader* published a letter from an alleged Paul Morrison of Deerfield Beach, Florida, claiming that Democratic candidate Senator Edmund Muskie had laughed at an aide's use of the ethnic slur "canuck." The letter led to an anti-Muskie editorial in the Manchester newspaper, which many felt hastened the decline of Muskie's faltering campaign.

During the long October 9th meeting, Deep Throat told Woodward that the "Canuck letter" was a "White House operation." Later that day Carl and Bob learned from another *Post* reporter, Marilyn Berger, that Ken Clawson had boasted to her of having written the letter. Clawson had once been a *Post* reporter himself. Miss Berger was asked to confront Clawson with the fact that the *Post* was doing a story on the letter and would report his claim. Clawson then tried to retreat from his boast.

There is an inside story to this episode, for I had talked with Clawson, and I knew he was telling the truth in saying he'd not written the letter. What the *Post* did not know was that half a dozen people within the White House had claimed to have written it. It was a joke; no one in the White House really believed that anyone among them had had anything to do with it. But since it had been so hard on Muskie, many wanted to pretend they had been his undoing.

When Clawson told me what had happened, and that the *Post* would claim they had learned from "federal investigators" that the letter was engineered by a White House aide, I called Acting FBI Director Gray. I had by this time read a great number of FBI "302's," internal Bureau reports which Gray had provided me and which contained raw information about the FBI's investigation. Why had I not been shown this information, I asked. Gray did not know, and said he would get back to me. He did call me later, explaining that "the reason you did not know this is because the FBI did not know it. We have nothing on the 'Canuck letter,'" he told me.

I remember feeling stuck, for I knew if I passed this information along to Ken Clawson, he would feel compelled to use it in his own defense. But the last thing we needed just before the election was information that the White House was monitoring the FBI's investigation. I called Clawson to commiserate, and asked him why in the world he had made such a statement to Marilyn Berger.

"You don't have to tell me it was dumb, I know that. I'd had a few drinks and was trying to impress the lady. You know how that can happen, don't you?" I sure did. But what burned Clawson most was the fact that the *Post* was going to say that he was in her apartment when he made the statement. "It was all innocent as hell, but it won't read that way. It's really a low shot. They're trying to stick it to me for coming over here. What a bunch of bastards!"

The *Post* ran their story, attributing the information partly as having come from "law enforcement sources," and, in a later story, to "federal agents who investigated the Watergate bugging." The other attribution was to Marilyn Berger. Ken Clawson was the victim of a non-story story.

More to the point, however, recalling all this made me wonder how Deep Throat could have delivered so much misinformation on October 9th. I thought I should check further to see if anything had ever come out on the Canuck letter that might support Deep Throat's claim that it was a "White House operation." I looked in the Senate Watergate committee report and discovered that they had never been able to learn anything. The committee's counsel, Sam Dash, reported the same thing in his book. The reason they could not find anything was that it never happened as Deep Throat described.

The more I studied this October 9th meeting, the more I began to question whether it might be pure fabrication. Could that explain the degree of misinformation that had emerged from this session? Possibly the best explanation of this meeting was that it was designed deliberately to throw a tracker like myself off Haig's scent, since Haig was clearly out of the country on this date. Perhaps Bob could justify such tampering with events as necessary to protect his source.

As so often happened when sifting through all this evidence, I paused again, wondering if I were tracking a great hoax. I knew that almost every name that seemed a viable candidate had one or more problems. It would not be difficult to make a very strong case that, based on *All the President's Men*, absolutely no one could be Deep Throat. But Al Haig had far more going for him than any other candidate, and the October 9th meeting had, in my own mind, taken on a certain taint. So I put aside my doubts and pushed on, curious to look at the Bradlee Riddle and meeting dates from another angle.

Inherent in Ben Bradlee's clue is that when Woodward was unable to contact Deep Throat, his stories about Watergate were few and far between. I decided to look at what had happened right after the November 7, 1972, election, for I remembered well that *The Washington Post* had very little to report about Watergate at that time. The first thing I discovered was that Al Haig was out of Washington a great deal. On November 9th, Nixon sent Haig to Vietnam for further peace discussions with President Thieu. Haig returned by the 12th of November. Then he was off to Paris with Henry in early December. Back again on December 9th. Then off again by December 19th, when Nixon dispatched Haig back to Saigon.

In this post-election period, Woodward did notify his friend that he was moving out of his apartment (late December), but he was not getting much from his friend at this time. And he was under pressure to do so. Ben Bradlee was demanding follow-up stories. As explained in *All the President's Men*, "Sussman told [Woodward and Bernstein] he detected a lot of pressure for a story—any story, as long as it was good; something that would take the heat off the *Post* and put away the notion that the paper had been promoting George McGovern's campaign." This would be exactly the kind of dry spell for Carl and Bob that might prompt Bradlee to say that if you look at who could have been Bob's source, and who was traveling when, you can figure out who Deep Throat was.

Although Al Haig would leave the White House and go back to the Pentagon for several months after the peace settlement in Vietnam was reached (January 21, 1973), he remained very close to Nixon, as evidenced by Nixon's own diary, and to others on the staff, and would appear to have been available for the periodic meetings that Woodward would have with his friend early in 1973: January

24, late February, April 16 and 26. Later, on May 4, 1973, after Haldeman's resignation, Al Haig returned to the White House as Richard Nixon's chief of staff.

Throughout the months Haig was out of the White House, he remained close enough to know what was going on, and close to the FBI as well. (Few people know that when Haig returned to the Pentagon in early 1973, he became involved in developing a virtual "war plan" that would employ the U.S. Army in solving the problems at Wounded Knee. It was Haig who arranged for all those M-16 rifles and other weapons to be supplied to the U.S. marshals and FBI agents who were battling the small band of Indians protesting the treatment they received from the government. Al Haig is another character for Marlon Brando's movie on the subject.)

While there were some minor problems, and I certainly was handicapped in that I did not have access to Al Haig's diary, I was satisfied I had done everything possible to establish his whereabouts. From all I could gather, Haig appeared to have been available to meet or talk by telephone with Woodward with only one verifiable exception: October 9, 1972, and this had been a meeting that did not bear scrunity well. On balance, I felt that Haig had not been disqualified by this test either. But what of my next test? Was Alexander Haig the type of person who would leak on a president he pretended to serve?

Third question: What sort of light could be shed by an examination of the character and personality of Alexander Haig?

This was not a question that needed answering in my own mind, because, based on everything I knew about the man, I had no difficulty believing that Al Haig was capable of duplicitous and self-serving behavior, or of "leaking," either. Rather, I felt an obligation to examine this question "for the record." Others who had worked with Haig had written books in which the general had come under close inspection. Since they knew Haig better than I did, I looked to see what they had to say about him.

Bill Gulley, who was director of the military office in the White House under four presidents, was in a good position to monitor the

snowballing of Haig's White House power and prestige during the
Nixon years. In *Breaking Cover*, Gulley gives an often colorful account of this period.

> Kissinger's faith in Haig was such that he never worried about
> his ass being covered while he was off on his secret negotiations,
> flying all over the skies of the world. He was confident that loyal
> old Al Haig was back in the White House, passing his messages
> on to the President and protecting his, Kissinger's, position.
>
> Meanwhile, what's really going on back at the ranch is that
> loyal old Al Haig sees the golden gates will open for *him*,
> now. . . . Suddenly, he has Access To The President. . . .
>
> What Haig realized—because not only is he smart, he's
> shrewd—was that Richard Nixon did not consider himself to be
> the pupil of Henry Kissinger. He considered himself to be the
> mentor of Henry Kissinger. So Haig gave Kissinger's messages
> a tilt. He did a little editing here and a little rephrasing there,
> making a suggestion that this or that point might fall in line
> better with the President's view of what should be done, rather
> than Kissinger's. . . .
>
> At the same time, he found a way to make use of Bob
> Haldeman. He began to tell him little, intimate tidbits of gossip
> about Kissinger. . . . Kissinger was hot copy, and everybody
> wanted to be let in on the inside story, a story nobody but Haig
> could give out. So he began to use it as valuable currency, and
> he bought Haldeman's support with it.

Even more interesting in viewing Al Haig as Woodward's potential "friend," however, is Gulley's analysis of why Haig decided to
depart the White House staff in the fall of 1972. He maintains that
"Haig's eyesight is superb where his own self-interest is concerned,
and when Watergate loomed on the horizon, I think he saw what
might be coming and started making plans to get the hell away. . . ."
Gulley says that Haig came back to the White House as chief of
staff, when Nixon asked him to do so, because it would make him
"Somebody."

Next I read what former Vice President Spiro Agnew had written about the role Alexander Haig had played in forcing Agnew's

resignation. Evidently it had been a job that Nixon had been unwilling to do himself.*

In his memoir of the time, *Go Quietly . . . Or Else,* Agnew says:

> The American people should know that in the last hectic year or more of his residence in the White House, Richard Nixon did not actually administer all the powers of the presidency. As I have stated earlier, it was General Haig who was the de facto President. Haig had the power of the bureaucracy at his command, and the Washington insiders knew he was standing there behind Nixon, pulling the strings. Haig had direct connections with the C.I.A. and the F.B.I. and every other agency. For four years he had been Henry Kissinger's chief deputy with clear access to all the government; his power extended into any agency he chose. The very survival of the Nixon presidency was threatened.
>
> Many who are familiar with General Haig's career are convinced that a man does not, in only a few years, climb through the upper echelons of the army—from a one-star to a four-star general's rank—to be the President's top civilian adviser, without being totally self-centered, ambitious, and ruthless. I believe that this man who jumped so easily from general to civilian back to general had placed himself in the position where he took actions far exceeding the proper authority of White House staff personnel. He apparently felt that the President, because of the Watergate pressures, was incapable of making the right decisions, so the general probably made them in his name. Mr. Nixon did not have the stomach to confront me openly, so it is logical to conclude that Haig took over and determined how to force me to get out. I believe that by using the "escalation theory" after my California speech, he deliberately influenced Nixon to acquiesce in the decisive move against me: the threat to play nasty—and dirty.
>
> I am also convinced that Haig desired not only to move me out, but in due course, after someone else had been brought into

---

*Later, when Nixon had decided upon Gerald Ford as Spiro Agnew's replacement, he had made Haig get on the telephone line and give the news to Ford. It would seem that Nixon preferred not to deliver even *good* news himself.

the vice-presidency, to move Mr. Nixon out, too. I really think
that by this time, Al Haig already knew enough about the dis-
crepancies in the tapes—and the truth about Nixon's involvement in the Watergate cover-up—to be convinced that
eventually the President himself must go. And Haig did not
want me in the line of succession.

Spiro Agnew obviously does not play a lot of golf these days
with Al Haig. Perhaps on the surface not the most creditable source,
Agnew was nonetheless a former vice president, and he had had
memorable and close dealings with General Haig.

I needed not only more objective information, but simply much
more information, and found it in a new book, *Haig: The General's
Progress*, written by Roger Morris, who had served on Lyndon Johnson's National Security Council and then stayed on at the request of
Henry Kissinger. Morris, who knew Haig well, resigned his post in
1970 in protest over the bombings in Cambodia. His entire book
could be used to support this third test question; I found the text
littered with examples relevant to my inquiry. In general terms, Morris describes Haig as "Smooth, sometimes pandering, and rarely
critical in person with his succession of demanding chiefs," then goes
on to say that "he can be coarse and acidly contemptuous of the
same men out of their presence."

Morris establishes that a formidable alliance was forged between Haig and Haldeman,* despite Kissinger's loathing and distrust of the White House inner circle. The alliance, however, was
good for the sort of gossip Kissinger enjoyed:

> From his discreet forays upstairs at the White House, Haig
> brought back news of the rise and decline of a presidential
> counselor like Pat Moynihan, or later, more ominously, of the
> creation of Ehrlichman's plumbers and the fulminating obses-
> sion with internal security and domestic espionage that would
> bring down the government.

---

*According to Morris, Haig would later refer to his friend Haldeman as
"that criminal."

More revealing than the above statements, however, was the example Morris gave of the dichotomy between the public and the private Haig:

> [At the same time that Haig was] dropping in on Haldeman or dutifully sitting in as the "man of action" in Nixon's speech-writing, [or] while chatting respectfully with the presidential night stroller [Nixon], Haig in private with the NSC staff referred to Haldeman and Company as "those shits," to Nixon as "our drunk," and joked savagely—a variation on the Kissinger refrain—about Nixon's "limp wrist" relationship with businessman and White House "intimate" Bebe Rebozo.

But if anyone had doubts about Al Haig's ability to turn on Richard Nixon, the story carried in the December 5, 1976 *Washington Star* evidences more than mere disloyalty at a time he was proclaiming his fealty to the man. According to the *Star* article, two months before Nixon resigned, Haig allegedly ordered the army's Criminal Investigations Command to conduct a secret investigation into any Nixon connections with huge cash contributions from countries in the Far East. What, specifically, did Haig want? According to the chief investigator, Haig wanted to know if Jack Caulfield and Tony Ulasewicz had traveled to the Far East and brought money back to Nixon. Haig also wanted to know if Nixon had ever been mixed up with organized crime. What did the investigator report? "I concluded that [Caulfield and Ulasewicz] probably had gone to Vietnam, and I considered there were strong indications of a history of Nixon connections with money from organized crime." To my knowledge, Al Haig had never commented on his actions in calling for this investigation. But it took little imagination to figure out what he might have done with such information, had he been trying to force Nixon from office. It also took little imagination to appreciate that a man who would institute a secret criminal investigation against the president would have little trouble being the instrument of his ruin.

While I could only speculate about Haig's motives in supplying Woodward with information, there could have been many. The most obvious motive might have been pure disgust with the amateurishness of many of the Watergate-type activities. From the Ellsberg break-in to the Watergate break-in, Liddy and Hunt botched everything. Haig, from his relationship with the National Security Council and the CIA, knew how the pros operated—and supported the justification that such activities were in the best interests of the nation. Another motive might have been self-protection, since Al Haig appears to have been aware of what the Plumbers were doing, and may have known how they were doing it. He could have been steering Woodward, and the media in general, away from activities we still don't know about.

Shortly before I testified before the Senate Watergate committee, in June 1973, a very strange thing happened. John Lindsay conducted an interview with me and turned it in to *Newsweek*. On June 18, 1973, *Newsweek* reported that I had told investigators of a White House-concocted plot to murder Panamanian dictator Omar Torrijos. I had never told Lindsay anything of the sort, for I'd never heard of such a plot, but *Newsweek* spelled out in detail what I would have to say:

> Dean's story is that the Administration suspected high Panamanian Government officials of being involved in the flow of heroin from Latin America into the U.S., and were also concerned about strongman Omar Torrijos's uncooperative attitude toward renegotiating the Panama Canal treaty. Thus, in Dean's telling, some officials found a Torrijos hit doubly attractive. The contract, he said, went to E. Howard Hunt, later a ringleader in the Watergate break-in; Hunt, according to Dean, had his team in Mexico before the mission was aborted.

When I read this in *Newsweek* I was flabbergasted, and called John Lindsay to protest. He said he knew I had never said such a thing to him, and he hemmed and hawed, much unlike himself. Someone had forced the story on him, he insisted. It was all very strange, and soon a bit frightening, for, with the appearance of this story, the government insisted that I have U.S. marshals to protect me around the clock. It was as if whoever had leaked this story had subtly put a hit squad on me.

Where and how did *Newsweek* get this information? Over the

years I have learned very little. Lindsay did confess later that it had come from the White House, not to him, but to another reporter or editor at *Newsweek*. It had apparently been planted by someone who feared I knew about it and would be testifying to such knowledge publicly; in leaking it the White House had tried to soften the impact of its discovery. The White House was mistaken, but it certainly caused me to wonder whether this might be representative of the kinds of secret activities that the White House, and perhaps Deep Throat, wanted to keep from the rest of the country.

In speculating about Deep Throat's possible motives in giving information to Woodward, I also had to keep in mind that, if the man's motives were not sinister, but *noble*—if he believed the future of the nation was at stake—then an examination of Deep Throat's character and personality would necessarily take on a different slant. I looked again at *All the President's Men*, and found a passage that seemed to sum up the authors' assessment of this question:

> [Woodward and Bernstein] had speculated on the reason for Deep Throat's piecemeal approach; they had several theories. If he told everything he knew all at once, a good Plumber might be able to find the leak. By making the reporters go elsewhere to fill out his information, he minimized his risk. Perhaps. But it was equally possible that he felt that the effect of one or two big stories, no matter how devastating, could be blunted by the White House. Or, by raising the stakes gradually, was he simply making the game more interesting for himself? The reporters tended to doubt that someone in his position would be so cavalier toward matters affecting Richard Nixon or the Presidency itself. *More likely, they thought, Deep Throat was trying to protect the office, to effect a change in its conduct before all was lost.* [Italics added.]

Maybe Woodward and Bernstein were right. I did not find it hard to believe that Deep Throat had acted out of conscience and not malice. In fact, I suspected that most people would prefer to believe this. Nor did I find it hard to believe that Alexander Haig could have given Woodward information because of a strong belief that it was the right thing for the country. In my mind, Alexander Haig had the sort of character and personality that would qualify

him as the greatest source of all time no matter what his private
motives. This part of the test, the personality profile, he clearly
passed.

*Fourth question: Did Haig have access to the information that
Deep Throat had given Woodward?*

Alexander Haig joined the Nixon administration as a military
adviser to the National Security Council in 1969. He was one of the
first aides Kissinger hired. Haig had learned the ways of Washington
and government well when he had worked at the Pentagon as an aide
to Joseph Califano, who was working for the secretary of army in
1963. Roger Morris writes that one of Haig's 1963 duties grew out
of the ill-fated Bay of Pigs invasion of Cuba:

> In 1963 he dealt directly with the aftermath of the invasion and
> missile crisis on the working staff of a special Defense Depart-
> ment group created by [Secretary of Defense] McNamara and
> chaired by [Secretary of Army] Vance to formulate a "long-
> range policy toward Cuba."

Morris says that part of that policy included approval of the covert
CIA "boom and bang" sabotage campaign against Cuba, and "one
of the CIA saboteurs in those raids was Eugenio Martinez," who
later became much better known for his involvement in the Watergate break-in.

There is good reason to speculate, based on this information,
that Al Haig has known E. Howard Hunt since 1963, for Hunt was
deeply involved in the Bay of Pigs as one of the CIA's top men and
remained involved with men like Martinez after their unsuccessful
mission. I wondered whether Haig, in addition to Chuck Colson,
might have been one of Hunt's sponsors? On one occasion, back in
1971 at the White House, I personally had seen Hunt and Haig
emerge from a meeting together, in deep conversation. They paused
in the hall and conversed in hushed tones. At the time, I thought
nothing. Now I had to wonder.

In 1964, when Joe Califano was moved into the office of the Secretary of Defense, along with his boss, Cyrus Vance, who had been made deputy secretary, Al Haig moved with them. There, Morris reports, he was given the added function of "a liaison or simply a courier, carrying the views of the civilian defense secretaries both to the Joint Chiefs and to the Johnson White House." In 1965 Haig studied at the Army War College, then did a tour of active duty in Vietnam, after which he was returned to West Point, where he had graduated. It was from West Point that Haig had moved to Kissinger's staff at the Nixon White House.

Initially, Alexander Haig's job with Henry Kissinger was very similar to the one he had performed for Califano—a paper pusher and receiver of documents. He was not a front-office man, but rather worked in the bowels of the White House basement, the Situation Room. But Haig knew how things worked, and he quickly plugged himself into both the vast Washington bureaucracy, and, most relevant to my inquiry, the FBI.

Roger Morris, who was there at the time, says:

All the [FBI] reports came routinely each day to Haig, who from the outset was NSC liaison with the FBI. . . . An FBI agent attached to the NSC staff reported to Haig on internal security matters. . . .

Later, when everyone scrambled [because of Watergate and its fallout] to avoid responsibility, to present themselves as innocents caught in unseemly circumstances, no investigating body understood—and Haig never admitted—that from January 20, 1969, he was the sole executor of the busy, ongoing NSC–FBI liaison, the "staff man" for wiretaps. . . .

In further checking this point about Haig's relationship with the FBI, for it was vital that Deep Throat have a long-standing relationship to have obtained the information he appears to have possessed, I turned to Bill Sullivan's book, *The Bureau: My Thirty Years in Hoover's FBI*. Much to my surprise, in Sullivan's description of his relationship with Al Haig, when Haig was telling the FBI which newsmen and White House aides to wiretap, as Nixon and Kissinger tried to uncover leaks, Sullivan said: "I had never met Haig" before that time. In my earlier conversations with him (*Chapter 3*), I had the impression Sullivan and Haig were old friends. That was one of the reasons I'd long suspected Al as Deep Throat.

But a bit more searching gave a different picture. Apparently Sullivan was protecting his old friend when he wrote his book, for Haig himself, in testifying before a closed Senate committee hearing about Kissinger's role in the wiretapping, stated:

> I must say I have known Mr. Sullivan for a number of years. I knew him at the Military Academy [West Point]. He used to come up and lecture. I worked with him when I worked for Secretary McNamara. On a number of occasions I had a lot of contact with the Bureau, and he is a man of the greatest patriotism and has been under great strain. I consider him a friend and I have great confidence in him.

It was clear that Al Haig, by his own admission, had a longstanding relationship with the FBI. It appeared the kind of relationship that would enable him to keep abreast of the Watergate investigation without anyone's really knowing—aside from his sources in the FBI.

Fifth question: Did Haig have unique access to information that only a few people had?

Much of the information that Deep Throat knew was known by many people. While it is impossible to know who might have whispered secrets to whom, thus broadening the circle of knowledge, working logically two particular bits of information that were given to Woodward by his friend easily point to Al Haig.

On March 5, 1973, *Time* magazine broke a story that the White House had wiretapped newsmen and White House aides in an effort to track down leaks. The White House denied the story was true, although it was true. *Time* had cracked this case, but they could not learn from their sources in the FBI and Justice Department who had been bugged. The records of the taps had been removed by Bill Sullivan, and passed by Bob Mardian to the White

House. When the *Time* story broke, the records were in John Ehrlichman's safe.

When Woodward met with his friend in late February, shortly before Pat Gray's confirmation hearings, Deep Throat was able to tell Bob that Gray had been aware of these wiretaps and that the work was done by an "out-of-channels vigilante squad." This last piece of information could have been a deliberate effort to mislead Woodward, since it was not true. Deep Throat also gave Woodward the names of two people who had been tapped: "Hedrick Smith and Neil Sheehan of *The New York Times*." It is the revelation of these names that is the extraordinary information.

I found it interesting that, first, Deep Throat could state flatly that Gray knew about the taps, when he was also saying this was not an FBI operation, and when the Watergate special prosecutor would be unable to prove that Gray knew after an intense investigation with the full resources of the FBI, Justice Department, and several years of digging. Second, the only people who knew the names of those who had been tapped at the time the information was given to Woodward were Richard Nixon, Henry Kissinger, John Ehrlichman, John Mitchell, Bob Mardian, a very small group in the FBI, Bill Sullivan,* Mark Felt, and the man who gave the FBI the names—Al Haig.

When you add to this the scarcely known secret that was given to Woodward about the "deliberate erasures" on the court-sub-poenaed tape, Haig passes another test that uniquely qualifies him as the most likely person to have been Woodward's friend.

Sixth question: Was there evidence that Deep Throat had continued as a source for Woodward, and did Haig fit that category?

The last reported meeting that Woodward had with his friend in *All the President's Men* was that crucial conversation in which he

---

*Bill Sullivan, as reported in Chapter 3, had told me that he believed Hoover had leaked this information to Nelson Rockefeller, who in turn had told Pat Coyne. But Sullivan never told me or suggested that Hoover had leaked the actual names of those who were wiretapped.

was told of the "deliberate erasures." That meeting allegedly occurred the first week of November, 1973. Yet Bob and Carl continued to report on Watergate for many more months, and,
presumably, Bob continued to receive information from his friend. I
decided I must review all of the subsequent *Washington Post* stories
by Woodward and Bernstein to look for information that would appear to have come from Deep Throat, but, more important, that
could be known by very few people—but certainly by Al Haig. I
discovered forty-five more Watergate articles by "Woodstein," and,
while the sources were clear in some cases, in most it was impossible
to determine if the "informed source" or "White House source" was
Deep Throat or someone else.

Yet it was more than Haig's unique access to particular information that made him a compelling candidate. When Woodward
and Bernstein wrote *The Final Days*, Al Haig emerged as a hero,
although others who were also there during those days saw Haig
much differently. Years ago I had been told that Woodward had
made several trips to Brussels during the time he was working on
The Final Days. Of course, NATO Chief Haig was then in Brussels.
Personally, I can't imagine how anyone could read *The Final Days*
and *not* conclude that Haig had been a primary source. But it was
the final aspect of this last test that produced the most convincing
evidence that Haig was the one.

When I looked to see what, if anything, Bob Woodward might
have had to say about Al Haig in recent years, I was incredulous.
When Bob returned to *The Washington Post* after his leave of absence from working on *The Brethren*, he became a metropolitan editor. That's where he was when President Reagan nominated Al Haig
to become his Secretary of State.

Shortly before Haig's Senate confirmation hearings, I remember saying to Alice Mayhew, the Simon and Schuster editor who had
worked on all of Bob's books, "Woodward ought to have a field day
with Haig. He certainly knows enough about him." Alice agreed.
But I had never paid attention to what in fact Bob *had* written—
until now.

On January 15, 1981, at a time when there was considerable
renewed controversy over Haig's role in the Nixon White House,
Bob Woodward wrote an editorial-page column arguing that the

Senate committee considering Haig's nomination should not try to obtain the White House tapes of his conversations with Nixon as chief of staff. Citing everything from the Supreme Court's tape decision to practical considerations, Woodward was all but giving his official blessing to Reagan's nomination of Haig. Careful not to call Haig "the hero" of Watergate, Bob's column was just the kind of boost Haig's nomination needed at that moment. After all, here was one of the most knowledgeable Watergate reporters in Washington, in effect saying, "Haig's okay." Yet anyone who was familiar with Haig's actions during his tenure as chief of staff at the Nixon White House, had to know that his performance raised serious questions. (See Roger Morris's book, for example, where he tells of Haig's destroying documents as a final gesture before vacating the White House after Richard Nixon's resignation.) And even as favorable as *The Final Days* was to Al Haig, it still raised questions.

Hays Gorey had been working right alongside me in my effort to determine if Haig was Woodward's friend, and after we discussed the boost that Bob had provided Haig's nomination, Hays made a few more calls to friends. The information he picked up shed further light on the Woodward–Haig relationship.

"Woodward is a real *quid pro quo* reporter," one source told Hays. "He's not the kind of reporter who goes to bat for anyone without a reason, but if he's gotten something from a source, he'll fight tooth and nail to pay him off." Another journalist told Hays, "The reason Al Haig makes all the sense in the world as Deep Throat is that he loves all that dramatic, secret kind of shit that Woodward was put through." Adding further, "You know as well as I do, Hays, that you don't have to meet your sources in garages. It's vintage Haig to do so," concluded this reporter who had covered Haig himself.

Hays's calls picked up something else, more Woodward reporting on Al Haig. Hays's source told him that Woodward had obtained a copy of a "talking paper" that Haig had prepared for a meeting with President Reagan, which had been published in the *Post* without attribution to Woodward; then the man asked, "Do you remember back in January and February (1982) when everyone in town was talking about Haig's being unbalanced, maybe a bit crazy, that he'd been somehow mentally affected by his heart-bypass operation?" Hays said he did. "Well, a lot of us thought this was pretty serious information on the rumor mill, and not all of it unfounded." Hays learned that Woodward had looked into it, but what he did was quell the rumor and give another solid assist to the embattled Secretary of State.

On February 19, 1982, Woodward wrote a front-page *Post* article based again on his penetration of the innermost circle of the world of Al Haig. This time Woodward had obtained notes of Haig's meetings at the State Department with his closest advisers. Column inch after column inch of "unvarnished Haig," the Secretary of State at work, a man in control, solid grasp of issues, delicate perceptions of foreign affairs, thoughtful remarks about President Reagan—it was exactly what Haig needed to quiet the rumors in Washington at the time and take the wind out of the sails of those (undoubtedly in the Reagan White House) who were campaigning for his removal by feeding the city with gossip.

I was back in California and going over my notes on Al Haig when I suggested to Hays that he try and talk with someone close to Haig, for surely Haig must know that many people think he's Woodward's source. I long ago realized that Woodward's friend would never come forward on his own. Indeed, Bob Woodward had hinted to me, when I had interviewed him back in 1978 for a radio show on Deep Throat, that the world would never learn his source's identity.

Hays reached someone who had been very close to Al Haig at the State Department.* His source acknowledged that Al knew that a lot of people thought he was Woodward's source, but he denied it. He would occasionally joke about being Deep Throat, but Hays's source felt that "Al Haig would rather be shot at dawn by a firing squad than say anything that would hurt a president." I wondered if he knew about Haig's call for a criminal investigation of Nixon. Doubtful. Hays's source said he knew that Woodward had traveled to Brussels to meet with Haig on *The Final Days*, "a couple of times," but Haig told him he had never met with him. Both Hays and I thought it odd that Woodward would return for nonmeetings. Finally, Hays's source said they had never tracked down the source

*Haig resigned as secretary on June 25, 1982.

of the leak to Woodward of the notes of Haig's State Department meetings.

I decided to make one last call to check out Al Haig. I had found the Roger Morris book very helpful and a good read. Had the Senate confirmation committee dug into Haig's past as deeply as had Morris, a former colleague of Al's on the National Security Council, Haig might still be answering senators' questions.

My questions to Morris about whether Haig had known Howard Hunt (Morris said he'd not had the time or resources to check) and about his liaison responsibilities to the FBI and CIA yielded unexpected fruit. "I'll tell you this, John," Roger said, "as I was pulling this material together, it occurred to me several times that Al Haig could be Deep Throat."

I thought about all I knew about Al Haig personally, what I had learned, that a lot of *Washington Post* insiders felt he was Woodward's friend, that Hays's colleagues at *Time* magazine had placed Haig at the top of their list, and, but for that October 9th meeting, that the evidence seemed incredibly persuasive. I felt I was too close to my own investigation, so I put it aside for a few days and busied myself with the work that pays the bills each month.

The brief break added some perspective, but it also raised more rather unpleasant questions in my mind. Ben Bradlee says he has been told by Woodward who his friend was, or is. Could Woodward have given Bradlee a false name? Has Bradlee ever talked to this person, or checked to see if he really could have been Deep Throat? Has Bradlee checked the dates? Very doubtful. Unless Woodward had been truthful with Bradlee, the Bradlee Riddle would be worthless.

I reviewed and re-reviewed the now voluminous notes from the work that Hays, Pete Kinsey, and I had done during the past several months. We had talked to a lot of people about who might be Woodward's friend. And over the years I had amassed a sizable file. Either by myself, or through others, I had been able to reach into the FBI, the CIA, the Department of Justice, and the Secret Service. I obtained information from people who had served in the Nixon White House, on the National Security Council, plus people associated with potential candidates for Woodward's friend after they had left government or gone on to other places within the government. I had looked at Bob's sixth-floor balcony, where he had once signaled his mysterious friend, tracked down people who had lived in his building, The Webster House on P Street, as part of my pursuit. Also I had uncovered the names of everyone who lived in his neighborhood while he was living there, and a list of who had which offices in the Brookings Institution, from which you can see Woodward's old apartment building. I had obtained information from people who knew Bob at the Pentagon (1969–70), looked at the articles he had written for the *Montgomery County Sentinel*, where he first worked as a reporter, and everything he had written for *The Washington Post* prior to Watergate. I had discussed with people who had worked with Bob on his books how they were put together, from the original outline for what would become *All the President's Men* through *The Brethren*. I had been able indirectly to obtain information from an ex-wife, and from girls he had dated, particularly those who had worked at the Nixon White House. I had also acquired a considerable amount of information about Woodward from his journalistic colleagues, many of whom had spoken freely.

I thought about others who had been named Deep Throat by people who might know: John Ehrlichman had nominated Henry Petersen; Bob Haldeman had named Fred Fielding, and then retracted it when he found he was dead wrong—but neither Haldeman nor Ehrlichman had given it very serious thought. What I found most compelling, and again caused me to pause, was the rather impressive list of extremely knowledgeable, careful people who did not believe there was a Deep Throat, rather that he was a fictitious composite:

Sam Dash, former chief counsel of the Senate Watergate committee.

David Obst, Woodward's agent, who watched the evolution of *All the President's Men* and *The Final Days*.

Taylor Branch, who had worked on *All the President's Men* and then conducted his own investigation into Deep Throat.

Alice Mayhew, Woodward's editor on all his books.

Professor Edward Jay Epstein, who had studied Woodward's Watergate reporting in depth.

Others who over the years had expressed their doubts after

looking into the matter included Pete Kinsey, several who worked in the Watergate special prosecutor's office, as well as lawyers in the U.S. attorney's office. The majority vote of those most knowledgeable was clearly against any one person. But I had tried, despite my own instincts, and considerable evidence that supported the disbelievers' conclusion, to give Woodward the benefit of the doubt. Accordingly, I reached several conclusions*:

Deep Throat, as he is presented in *All the President's Men* (both the movie and the book), is a distorted, near-fictional character, and not a true picture of who Bob was dealing with. This was done either to protect his source, to dramatize the character, or through carelessness. And I have serious doubts about the accuracy of the dates and places of the meetings between Woodward and his friend.

I am willing to accept, however, that Bob had one particular friend in government who helped guide him, and in turn *The Washington Post*, in their more than commendable work of reporting on Watergate. Together they all changed history, for if Woodward had not had this friend, the *Post* might not have stood alone in sticking with the story, until they got the real story.

I believe that Woodward's friend had very mixed motives in helping him, some good and some not so good. It is clear he had hard information on minor details, but speculated on larger facts, and provided a lot of misinformation in the process.

I believe that Bob Woodward's friend was and is Alexander M. Haig, Jr., for the many reasons I have stated.

When I reached these conclusions, I knew that I had not proved unequivocally that Alexander Haig was Deep Throat. I was not sure anyone could "prove" who Deep Throat was—except Woodward or Deep Throat himself. The case lacked the crucial "smoking gun."

*My conclusions are indeed just that—mine. Neither Hays Gorey nor Pete Kinsey, nor anyone else who assisted me, had access to all the information I had assembled, nor were they part of the final process that brought me to my conclusions. Both Hays and Pete, and the many others, agreed to assist me because they felt that the resolution of the Deep Throat question was not without its historical significance—an important fact that should be known, and a fascinating mystery to be solved.

But I did feel I'd made a very compelling case, and I decided that, while I could not expect Haig to confess, if I was correct in my assessment, fairness required that I tell him of the conclusion I had reached.

Hays Gorey and I decided to contact Haig through an intermediary, tell him of my conclusion, give him the basis of my case, and ask him to refute my findings if they were wrong. This contact was made on Sunday evening, October 24, 1982. Hays and I sat back, awaiting an immediate rebuttal. Twenty-four hours passed, and we heard nothing. Then forty-eight hours. On the third day an answer came.

Alexander Haig strongly denied that he was Deep Throat. He also stated that he could prove he was not, but he refused to say how he could do so.

What sort of proof might this be? I wondered. There could be none, I thought, except to reveal absolutely that someone else was Deep Throat.

Because the evidence I had accumulated pointed toward Haig—his knowledge of the erased tape and the names of the newsmen who had been wiretapped, his long-standing relationship with the FBI, his general and intimate knowledge of the Nixon White House—it also raised the possibility that Deep Throat might be someone closely associated with Haig, someone close enough to have moved with him from job to job, or traveled with him. It was even possible that Haig had not leaked information himself, but had sanctioned someone else's doing so.

So many permutations were possible, but none seemed as likely to me as the conclusion I had already reached: that Alexander Haig was himself Deep Throat. My thoughts were drawn back to *All the President's Men*, where my search had begun:

> Woodward [had once] wondered if his friend was intentionally flirting with the danger of being discovered. Did Deep Throat want to get caught so he would be free to speak publicly? Was there a love-hate dialectic about his government service? Woodward started to ask, then faltered. . . . Someday it would be explained.

Hopefully I have moved us to that day.

Epilogue

What began as a very personal journal has now evolved into a book. No longer is it clear to me where the journal ends and the book begins. They have become one and the same. But I do know the story has ended.

In searching for Deep Throat I found more than the person I believe was Woodward's source; I discovered more of myself. The energies and enthusiasms that marshalled my efforts were rationalized in the beginning by personal curiosity, a desire to set the record straight, and the pure and simple challenge of it. Yet the overriding, and unstated, reason had to be that I hoped my revelation would prompt people to read what I had to say in this book. And that was important to me for more than commercial reasons.

Yes, any author hopes his book will sell well. But most authors—and I can assure you this one will so attest—also want to believe that their books will be read. While I cannot speak for others who write, I know there is a special reason I have those hopes with this book—and they relate to the loss of honor, the degradation of dignity, the guilt and shame that so justly has attached to those of us involved in the misdeeds of Watergate.

Those of us branded for life by Watergate have, each in our own way, had to bear this labeling. With great interest I have watched my former colleagues and associates to see how they have dealt with it. What I have observed breaks down as follows:

355

The Stonewallers. Richard Nixon and John Mitchell have continued to "tough it out," and, while they admit that some sordid things occurred and that they may have made mistakes, they do not consider their actions to be any worse than those of their predecessors, and certainly not criminal. They have never told but a fraction of what they know.

Nixon and Mitchell were the oldest of those involved in Watergate, and fell the furthest. Given their ages, it is perhaps understandable why they have taken the stands they have; for them it was too late to start anew. But I have often wondered if, in quiet moments of solitude, perhaps when reading a magazine that provokes a memory of a reputation that could have remained untarnished, they are truly comfortable with the facade of false honor to which they now cling.

The Modified Limited Hangouters. John Ehrlichman and Bob Haldeman have chosen to admit some of their mistakes, but both these men subtly, and at times not too subtly, twist the facts to make the case that they were basically "victims," that it was everyone else who was up to no good. Just as the jury that convicted them did not buy their arguments, from what I can tell neither has the rest of the world.

Both John and Bob were once proud men, a pride earned by accomplishments and work that brought them to the top of government. They're also intelligent men and must know that their terribly tattered public images go unmended. John Ehrlichman has dealt with this by proclaiming that he's different now—to wit a new beard, new residence, and new wife. Bob Haldeman has simply lowered his profile. Both, to me, appear to remain troubled by their past, for neither has found a sure answer for dealing with its lasting presence.

The Redeemed. Chuck Colson and Jeb Magruder have committed their lives to Christ: Chuck with his prison ministry, and Jeb as an ordained Presbyterian minister. As "born again" Christians, these two men have very successfully replaced disgrace with grace. Their conversions are heartfelt, sincere, and proof positive that a soiled identity can be cleansed by the greatest of powers.

In many ways I feel envy over the way Chuck and Jeb have made themselves better persons from their mistakes. At the same time I feel happy for them, that from the low points of their lives they could discover a calling that exemplifies all that is best in life. I have read what they have written about finding their way to God; I've talked with them both, and I know it's no publicity stunt.

The Low-Profile-on-with-Lifers. Most of the younger men involved in Watergate have done their best to "disappear" and get on with their lives. Bud Krogh was able to get back his license to practice law, as was Donald Segretti. Bud practices in Seattle and Don in Orange County, California. They avoid the press, but not to the extent that David Young does, who moved to Oxford, England, where he runs an international business consulting service. David will go out the back door if a reporter comes in the front. Dwight Chapin has regained success by working for former Nixon big-time contributor, Clement Stone. Dwight publishes a magazine: *Success.*

None of these former friends denies his wrongdoing, yet none has made a career of his mistakes. Rather all seemed to take the attitude that the best course was to admit their mistakes, take their punishment, and then set to work to put their lives back together. Over the years I have sometimes thought that they might have been wiser than I. They waited until Watergate fell apart and splashed them. When the prosecutors said, "You're dirty," they went through the process quickly and felt cleansed. For years, Watergate has been behind them. I didn't wait, yet I do not regret my role in pushing the mess over the brink.

Others who appear to fit into this category fell there because they were not in high-level positions, thus their mistakes would appear less egregious: Herb Kalmbach, Jim McCord, and the Cuban-Americans Hunt and Liddy used as burglars.

Soldiers of Misfortune. G. Gordon Liddy and, to a lesser extent, E. Howard Hunt wear Watergate as a badge of honor. From all I have learned of these former agents of espionage, they feel not the slightest twinge of disgrace over their conduct. Liddy was performing the work of his fuehrer, and for Hunt it was merely another spy mission. Their mistakes are but embarrassments—a botched job. Liddy has pushed his pride to the extreme, for he trivializes the unsettling realities of Watergate as a big joke in a road show that brings people into lecture halls as if they were visiting a carnival. The Wild Man of Borneo doesn't disappoint either, with tales of those he should have murdered, and graphic details of how he should have done it. Liddy quotes Nietzsche, not Conrad—for lost honor is not something a real man experiences, in Gordon's view.

Suffice it to say that none of these approaches or solutions was tried by me. But I do know I have been able to regain my self-esteem, and not by ignoring the past or running from it, as I tried for a while. Rather by facing it, by examining it, and, most important, by talking about it—openly and honestly. Obviously, I am neither a psychologist nor a philosopher. Yet I do know that I have no hesitation in sharing what I have found to be true: When you make a mistake, and it's the kind that can haunt you, the only course is to admit it, then understand why you made it. While this will not remove the stigma, it does give you back your self-respect. Stated a bit differently, I find honor in sharing the rest of my story.

At the front of this book I placed quotes from Lewis Carroll and Thomas Hardy, for, when I came across them, they said so well what experience had taught me. As Lewis Carroll so perceptively wrote in *Through the Looking-Glass*, it is easy to forget, for time and distance soften the horrors of moments past. The Queen is right in saying, "make a memorandum of it," which is what I have done, first with my journal, now with this book. For I too believe, as Thomas Hardy wrote, "If way to the Better there be, it exacts a full look at the Worst."

I have also thought often, in working on this book, of the note that Joseph Conrad wrote in June 1917, with the publication of *Lord Jim*, in which he addressed "the acute consciousness of lost honor" in his central character. Conrad said:

> Such a consciousness may be wrong, or it may be right, or it may be condemned as artificial; and, perhaps, my Jim is not a type of wide commonness. But I can safely assure my readers that he is not the product of coldly perverted thinking. . . . He was "one of us."

Acknowledgments

When I finish reading a book I often find myself turning back to the front to see what I can learn about how the book was assembled, for, being an author, I know that authors alone do not produce books. Because I feel that all those involved in bringing *Lost Honor* into book form should be acknowledged, and not "hidden" in the front where they get passed over, I have saved what I feel most important until the last.

This book became a reality because of the enthusiasm and interest of Stratford Press and Harper & Row. Working with Stratford Press has proved to be a delight. They are a small publisher with an organization, efficiency, and professionalism that results in their many big successes. And I hope I have given them a book that will add another bestseller to their growing list. *Rolling Stone* has been gracious in allowing me to draw from the materials I supplied them in covering the 1976 Republican National Convention; and my reflections on the experience of being imprisoned were first shared with the readers of *Newsweek's* "My Turn" column.

My appreciation is due Digby Diehl, whose editorial assistance served as a catalyst during my first attempt to bring this material together into a book. Also, Auriel Douglas freed me of long hours of searching through libraries for information about what others had discovered of Watergate's impact.

Invaluable critical reading of the manuscript was provided by Igor Stalew, Carl Goldman, Jeffrey Pill, and Mo.

In writing this book I discovered the magic of a word processor, which saved not just days and weeks, but months. The entire manuscript was produced on a TRS-80, Model III. And the person who did that was (and is) far more than a secretary, but an extremely intelligent, perceptive lady who not only can spot a misspelling before I've made it, she also has a questioning mind that makes certain everything makes good sense. Without DeeDee Evelove Parker's quick mind, and equally fast fingers at the word processor, it would have taken another year to complete this book.

It is the editor of a book who really has the task of bringing everything together and making it work. While no editor can make more of a book than an author can provide, my editor certainly made sure that I provided all I could to this book. When I decided only a few months ago to publish this book, it placed incredible pressure on all involved to make it happen by the target publication date of November 1982. No one has been under greater pressure, and performed with more professionalism and skill, than Ellen Shahan Hattman, my editor.

Assisting Ellen have been Carla Honig and Craig Kitson. But it has been Ellen herself who has tirelessly gone over every inch of this book in each stage of its evolution. For everything that works, I give her credit; and for anything that doesn't, I must take responsibility. Because there is no end to the nice things I can say about Ellen and her work on this book, I feel that the last words are the least I can do:

Thank you, Ellen.

Index

ABC, 154
Abplanalp, Robert, 241–42
Abrahamsen, David, M.D., 121–27, 238
Adams, Sherman, 138, 201, 201fn
Adcock, Gene, 10–11
"Adventures of the Mind," 158
Advise and Consent (Drury), 54
Aesop's Fables, 42
Agnew, Spiro, 128–30, 137, 231, 323, 338–40
Alexandria, Virginia, 3, 298, 301
Alice's Adventures in Wonderland (Carroll), 161
All the King's Men (Warren), 54
All the President's Men (book) (Bernstein and Woodward), 15, 30, 32–34, 78, 84, 93, 244, 279–81, 283, 286, 288–89, 291, 293–96, 300, 314–22, 328, 330–33, 336, 343, 347, 352–54
"All the President's Men" (movie), 77, 83–84, 92–94, 132–33, 230, 270, 283, 293, 353
American Civil Liberties Union (ACLU), 255, 257
American College of Psychoanalysis, 123
Americans for Democratic Action, 257
American Indian Movement, 88–89, 337
American Program Bureau, 17
American Psychiatric Association, 121, 123
American Scholar, The, 137
American University, 53–55
Anderson, Jack, 201, 278–79
Annenberg, Walter, 107, 131
Antelman, Julie, 260
Arends, Leslie C., 192, 200, 202
Armstrong, Anne, 178

Armstrong, Scott, 31–32, 291, 298, 307–10, 325
Army War College, 345
Arterton, F. Christopher, 262
Ash, Roy, 109
Associated Press, 99
Attorney, U.S., 280–82, 287, 289, 295, 308, 353

Baker, Bobby, 138–39
Baker, Howard, 130, 184, 228–29, 317
Barker, Bernard, 186
Bay of Pigs, 344
Bayh, Birch, 103
Becker, Ernest, 89–90
Belcher, Carl W., 281
Bellevue Hospital, 123–24
Ben-Veniste, Richard, 322
Berger, Marilyn, 334–35
Bernstein, Carl, 2fn, 15–16, 30–34, 71, 77–80, 83–84, 93–94, 127, 133, 263, 270–72, 279–80, 288–90, 293, 300, 312, 314–15, 320–22, 324, 326, 332–34, 336, 343, 348
Between Fact and Fiction: The Problem of Journalism (Epstein), 83–84
Beverly Hills, 85, 87, 140
Beverly Hills Public Library, 139–40, 251
Bhagavad-Gita, 130
Bible, The, 222
Bishop, Thomas E., 282
Blackwell, B. H., Ltd., 233–34
Blind Ambition (book) (Dean): xiii, 167, 179–80, 228; book contract for, 16–19, 38; book tour for, 184, 196, 202, 208, 210–13, 223, 227, 232–35, 239–40; with

361

Blind Ambition (Dean) (*Cont'd*)
  Taylor Branch, 91–92, 94–95; as cause of
    Ford testimony controversy, 185, 195–97,
    204, 206, 209; editor of, 91, 94–96, 132–
    33, 174, 250, 265; publisher of, 50fn, 94,
    132, 174, 250; rights to, 210; television
    movie of, 235, 268, 268fn; writing of, 31,
    37, 50, 50fn, 60–61, 63, 65, 75–76, 85,
    87, 91–92, 94–97, 99–100, 118, 132, 174,
    192, 194
"Blind Ambition" (television movie), 235,
    268, 268fn
Boggs, Lilburn (Pat), 282, 286–87
Bono, Sonny, 181–82
Book-of-the-Month Club, 195
Boone, Pat, 181–83, 221, 223–24
"Born Again" (movie), 221
Boston University, 28
Bourne, Dr. Peter, 275
Bowles, Charles, 282
Boyd, Marjorie, 191
Bradlee, Benjamin C., 93, 132, 230–31,
    293–94, 325–28, 336, 351
Branch, Taylor, 91–92, 94–95, 100, 117,
    133, 313, 352
Brandeis University, 124
Brando, Marlon, 87–90, 161, 337
Breach of Faith (White), 166
Breaking Cover (Gulley), 338
Bremer, Arthur Herman, 283–86, 292–93
"Brennan Diary," 309–10
Brennan, William, 309–10
Brethren, The (Armstrong and Woodward),
    297–99, 307–10, 325, 348, 352
Bretz, Charles, 282
Brezhnev, Leonid, 112, 128
Broder, David, 230
Brokaw, Tom, 196
Brookings Institution, 122, 352
Brown, Garry, 188, 198–99, 202
Brown, Trudy (Fry), 308
Bruce, Charles Delane, 114–16
Brussels, 348, 350
Brzezinski, Zbigniew, 277
Buchanan, Pat, 131
Buchen, Philip, 191
Bull, Stephen, 282, 290–91, 296, 314, 323–
    24, 326
Burbank Studios, The, 77, 93
*Bureau: My Thirty Years in Hoover's FBI,
    The* (Sullivan), 345–46
Burger, Warren, 310
Burke, Richard K., 281
Burrell, Hedley, 284
Butterfield, Alexander P., 60, 60fn, 282,
    287, 291, 307–09, 312, 314, 322
Butz, Earl, 181–84, 196, 221
Buzhardt, Fred, 290, 296, 323–24
Byrd, Robert, 189

Califano, Joseph, 302, 302fn, 344–45
Cambodia, 340
Camp David, 59, 75, 106, 287, 323
Campbell, Donald E., 83, 282
"Candidate, The" (movie), 78
Canuck letter, the, 334–35
Carroll, Lewis, 358
Carson, Johnny, 117
Carter, Billy, 277–78
Carter, Jimmy: administration of, 228–32,
    264; 273–79, 302fn; presidential cam-
    paigns of, 103, 154, 156, 166–67, 182,
    184, 197, 207, 216, 273–74, 277–78;
    press treatment of, 273–79; White House
    staff of, 274–78
Carter, Rosalynn, 277
Case Western Reserve, 41
Caulfield, John J. (Jack), 66–67, 70–71,
    119, 286–87, 317–18, 341
CBS, 178–81, 268–69
CBS Evening News, 178–81, 210
CBS Television City, 179
Central Intelligence Agency (CIA), 45, 64,
    70, 111, 121, 131, 136, 146, 157, 186,
    229, 280–81, 305, 317–18, 339, 342, 344,
    351
Chapin, Dwight L., 79–83, 177–78, 313,
    319, 357
Chappaquiddick, 4
"Checkers speech," 237
Cheney, Richard, 147
Chennault, Anna, 72, 72fn
Chennault, General Claire, 72fn
Chesen, Dr. Eli S., 121, 123
Cheshire, Maxine, 166
Chicago Tribune, 215
Chief Counsel: Inside the Ervin Committee
    (Dash), 228–29, 335
Citizens for Muskie, 82
Civil Rights Act (1968), 284
Civiletti, Benjamin, 277–78
Clawson, Kenneth W., 282, 293, 313, 334–
    35
Coelho, Susie, 181
"Cold War," 63–65
Colgate University, 53
College of Physicians and Surgeons, 124
Colson, Charles W. (Chuck), 8, 8fn, 9, 25,
    25fn, 130, 221–23, 282, 285–86, 311–
    312, 316–17, 320, 344, 356–57
Colson, Patty, 221
Columbia Journalism Review, 272
Columbia University, 124
*Coming to Power: Critical Presidential
    Elections in American History, The*
    (Schlesinger), 139–40
Committee for the Re-election of the Presi-
    dent (CRP), 8fn, 186, 195, 200, 271–72,
    285, 287, 298, 308, 313, 316, 319, 334

Common Cause, 260
Congress, U. S., 54, 106, 109–10, 136–37,
    142, 144–46, 153, 156–57, 177, 187, 206,
    218, 249, 252, 254–55, 260, 302fn
Congressional Budget and Impoundment
    Control Act (1974), 145–46, 156
Congressional Directory, 1977, 302
Congressional Quarterly, 97
Connally, John, 104–05, 128–29, 131, 184,
    194–95
Conrad, Joseph, 217, 234–35, 358
Constitution, U.S., 120, 144–45, 153, 171,
    255
Conyers, John, 203, 205
Cook, Richard, 186–88, 192, 194–99, 202,
    206, 209–10
Cooke, Janet, 294, 294fn
Court of Appeals, 79, 251, 323
Court system, *see* Judicial branch
Cox, Archibald, 204, 216fn, 252, 322–23
Coyne, Pat, 69, 69fn, 347fn
Cramer, William, 55
Crime and Punishment (Dostoevski), 26
Criminal Code, the, 303
Criminal-code-reform bill, 56–57
Criminal Investigations Command, 341,
    350
Cronkite, Walter, 178–81, 203fn, 205
Cuba, 344
Cunard line, 240
Cutler, Lloyd, 277

Daily Variety, 86
Dash, Samuel, 228–29, 291, 335, 352
Dean, James, 212
Dean, John W., III: alleged Nixon love let-
    ters, 101–02, 112–17; *All the President's
    Men*, at screening of movie of, 92–94;
    Blind Ambition, see *Blind Ambition*;
    book proposal on impact of Watergate,
    250–52, 257, 262–63, 265; and Taylor
    Branch, 91–92, 94–95; and Marlon
    Brando, 87–90; business ventures, 239,
    250–51, 262–63, 265, 299; in Chicago,
    210–17, 226; childhood, 35, 167, 174–76,
    260; college, 53–55, 305; cooperation
    with government investigation of Water-
    gate, 18–21, 120, 198, 318, *see also*
    testimony, and Watergate, government in-
    vestigation of; as Counsel to the
    President, 38, 45, 50, 58, 59–60, 64, 66–
    71, 74–75, 96, 106–09, 118–20, 144, 170,
    174, 177–78, 185–87, 216, 243, 301,
    312–14, 317–18, 334–35, *see also,*
    Nixon, Richard M., White House
    staff; death threats, 29–30, 213–14, 217,
    342; and Deep Thought, 218–19, 292,
    292fn, 293–96, 325–26; Deep Throat, in-
    vestigation of, 2–5, 33, 49, 66, 76, 94–95,
117, 132–33, 164–65, 219, 244–46, 265,
    270, 279–92, 292fn, 293–310, 311–53,
    353fn, 354–55; as diarist, xi–xii; effects
    of Watergate on, 1, 4–6, 13–14, 18–21,
    23–24, 26, 28, 38, 75, 86, 96–97, 102,
    165, 173, 184, 211–14, 217, 226–27, 235,
    238, 247, 250, 253, 263–65, 267–69, 301,
    355, 358; and Daniel Ellsberg, 61–66; in
    England, 233–35, 242–53; "Final Day,
    The," 127–31; first marriage, 20, 55, 57;
    Ford testimony controversy, 185, 190–97,
    202–06, 208–10, 213–14, 216–17; and
    Barry Goldwater, 18, 52; and Hays
    Gorey, 3–4, 191–94, 216–17, 302–06,
    310, 325–27; government protection of,
    30, 342; House Judiciary Committee,
    55–57, 177; job offers, 13–15, 50, 97,
    211, 239–40; and Joey, the Mafia hit
    man, 24–26, 64, 255; journal as basis of
    book, xi–xii; journal entries, 1–3, 12–13,
    19–20, 23, 33–34, 38–39, 42–43, 49–50,
    75–76, 83–84, 86–87, 92, 100–01, 119,
    132–33, 153, 156–57, 164–65, 167–68,
    178–81, 203–10, 217–18, 225–26, 232,
    234–36, 238, 263–64, 268–69, 292–95,
    299–301; Justice, Department of, 57–59,
    138–39; and Irene Kane, 42–43; in Kan-
    sas City, 160–73, 176, 178; law practice,
    55; law school, 55; law suits, 253; lec-
    tures, 16–17, 21–22, 28–29, 32, 34–39,
    41–50, 50fn, 75, 100, 102–04, 120, 213,
    238, 240–42, 247, 251, 264, 270–72, 276,
    278–79, 296–97, 299, 300, 315, 342–43;
    loss of license to practice, 13; military
    school, 18, 51–53, 176; movie proposal,
    97, 100, 119–21; Nixon 1968 presidential
    campaign, 57; obituary, 215–17; and
    David Obst, 15–17, 28–29, 31–32, 35–
    38, 61–65, 77–80; parents, 52–54, 174–
    76; Playboy mansion parties, 84–85; and
    the press, 2, 9–11, 13, 16, 28–29, 31, 35,
    39, 41–42, 47–50, 53–55, 99–101, 113,
    135, 140, 148, 160–62, 165–69, 178–81,
    183–85, 190–91, 193–94, 196, 202–06,
    208–10, 213, 215–16, 218–19, 228, 233–
    36, 238–39, 267–69, 301, 342; prison, ex-
    perience of being in, 7–9, 12–13, 23–26,
    171; prison homecoming, 9–11, 13;
    prison, release from, 5, 9, 96, 301; radio
    program, 240, 242–44, 246–47, 263, 265,
    270, 279, 350, *see also,* "Right to Know,
    The"; and Robert Redford, 77–80; as re-
    porter for *Rolling Stone* magazine, 50,
    119, 135, 142, 144, 147–56, 160–62,
    164–72, 178–84, 211, 227–28, 232; role
    in the Watergate cover-up, 8, 21, 45, 66–
    71, 74–75, 108, 118, 159, 171, 175, 185–
    90, 195–201, 216, 243, 253–54, 271–72,
    297, 313, 317–18, 334–35; September

Dean, John W., III (*Cont'd*)
15, 1972 meeting with Nixon, 185–88,
198; and Ralph Steadman, 161–70, 173–
76, 178, 242; and William C. Sullivan,
68–75; testimony, 19–20, 33, 41, 44, 48,
61–62, 75, 86, 142, 167, 185, 190–93,
195–97, 206, 268, 286, 328, 351; visits
the set of "All the President's Men," 77–
80, 93; and wife, Maureen, xii, 10–11,
14, 16–18, 20–24, 26–28, 34, 39, 42–43,
60, 77–79, 84–85, 89, 91, 93, 95–97, 99–
100, 102, 141, 221–25, 232–33, 235, 240,
268fn; wiretaps, 66–70, *see also* Wiretaps, Leaks, FBI, and Sullivan, William
C.; and Bob Woodward, 31–34, 244–46,
271–72, 279, 299–300, 315, 350
Dean, Maureen (Mo), xii, 10–11, 14, 16–
18, 20–24, 26–28, 34, 37, 39, 41–43, 49,
60, 76–79, 84–85, 89–91, 93, 95–97, 99–
102, 118, 141, 148, 151, 168, 175, 204,
221–25, 232–33, 235, 240, 251, 268fn,
298
"Deep Thought," 218–19, 292, 292fn, 293–
96, 314, 325–26
"Deep Throat" (movie), 128
Deep Throat: 2fn.; candidates, 31, 48, 67,
94–95, 119, 133, 243–44, 246, 281–82,
291, 295–304, 306–10, 311–15, 322,
324–30, 332, 335–54; clues, 30–31, 34,
66, 76, 93–94, 164, 244–46, 279–99,
302–03, 305–09, 311–53, 353fn, 354; as
composite, 47–48, 132–33, 246, 279,
293–95, 300, 320–21, 333, 352–33; identity, implications of, 2–3, 34, 48–49, 84,
117, 132–33, 243, 245–46, 270, 290–92,
315, 318, 353fn, 355; identity, mystery
of, 30–34, 47, 93, 132–33, 218–19, 245–
46, 265, 270, 279–82, 286, 288, 290–95,
300, 302, 304, 309–10, 311, 314–15, 318,
321, 324–26, 333, 335–37, 350–54; investigation of, 2–4, 48–49, 66, 76, 94–95,
117, 132–33, 164–65, 219, 244–46, 265,
270, 279–92, 292fn, 293–310, 311–353,
353fn, 354–55; motives of, 84, 219, 312–
13, 320, 327–28, 332, 337–44, 347, 353,
354
Defense, Department of, 110, 344
de Gaulle, Charles, 54
Democratic National Convention: *1964*, 72;
1976, 177; *1980*, 277
Democratic National Committee, 118, 186,
256
Democratic Party, 71–73, 81–82, 103, 140,
150, 172, 187, 195, 200–01, 208, 218,
316, 332, 334
Dewey, Thomas, 73
Dimley, Robert, 215–16
Directors' Guild, 92
"Dirty tricks" against campaign opponents,
81–83, 316, 319, 332–34

Doheny, Edward, 137
Dole, Robert, 183
Dostoevski, 26
Douglas, Auriel, 251
Downie, Leonard, Jr., 287–88, 293, 305,
314–15
Doyle, James, 322
Duke Law School, 122
Durham rule, 126

Eagleton, Thomas F., 154, 319
Ehrlichman, John D., 25, 66–67, 80, 89,
105–06, 109–10, 130, 138–39, 147, 188–
89, 198, 228, 287, 312, 318, 328, 340,
347, 352, 356
Eisenhower, Dwight David, 51–52, 54, 60,
73, 129, 138, 155
Elections, *see* Presidential campaigns
Ellsberg, Daniel, 61–66, 75, 123, 202, 245,
342
Ends of Power, The (Haldeman), 243–44
Epicurus, 225–26
Epstein, Edward Jay, 83–84, 272, 316, 352
Ervin committee, *see* Senate Watergate
committee
Ervin, Sam J., Jr., 46, 174
Escape from Evil (Becker), 89–90
Esquire, 133
Ethics in Government Act of 1978, 252,
276
Evans, Rowland, 228–29
Executive branch, 30, 109–10, 144–46,
156–57, 249, 252, 254, 278, 280, 291,
310, 311, 315
"Executive privilege," 253, 298
Exner, Judith Campbell, 114, 116

Fair Campaign Practices Committee, 200
Fall, Albert B., 137
Farrow, Mia, 46
Federal Aviation Administration (FAA),
60fn
Federal Bureau of Investigation (FBI): 88,
111, 130–31, 146, 157, 272, 276–77,
284–87, 300, 305, 313, 317, 320, 327,
334, 337, 339, 345–47, 347fn, 351, 354;
Deep Throat in, 132, 165, 282, 294, 295;
use of, by presidents for political purposes, 70–75, 136, 139, 317; Watergate
investigation, 82, 186, 279–81, 283–84,
287, 289, 298, 308, 318–20, 327, 333–35,
337, 346; *see also,* Watergate, government investigation of; wiretaps, 66–71,
317, 345–47, *see also,* Leaks, Sullivan,
William C., Wiretaps
Federal Communications Commission
(FCC), 130
Feller, Bob, 293
Felt, W. Mark, 67–68, 282, 347
Fielding, Fred, 31, 243–44, 352

"Final Day, The," 127–31
Final Days, The (Bernstein and Woodward), 15, 31, 94, 127, 290, 320–22, 324,
 348–50, 352
Fitzgerald, F. Scott, 84
Following the Equator (Twain), 136
Ford, Betty, 192
Ford, Gerald: administration of, 146–47,
 156–57, 185, 192, 218, 230–31, 273; in
 House of Representatives, 177–78, 185–
 87, 189, 191, 199–202, 228; pardon of
 Nixon, 46, 103, 143, 230–31; 1976 presidential campaign of, 103, 141, 143, 147–
 48, 154–56, 164, 169–70, 176, 178, 182–
 84, 192, 195–96, 203, 207–09, 214, 216–
 19, 264; role in blocking Patman investigation, 185–204, 203fn, 206–09;
 testimony controversy, 191–93, 196, 202–
 10, 214, 217–18, 264; as vice president,
 323, 339fn; vice-presidential confirmation
 testimony, 188–91, 193, 196, 200, 203–
 04, 206–07, 218; White House staff of,
 95, 144, 146–47, 157, 169, 181–84, 191,
 203fn, 205, 216fn
Foreign Agents Registration Act, 277
Fordham University, 296
Fort Holabird, Baltimore, Maryland, 8, 8fn,
 9, 301
Fort Worth Star-Telegram, 31
"Fox and the Hedgehog, The," 41–42
Frampton, George, Jr., 322
Freedom of Information Act, 208–09
Frost, David, 121, 235–37

Gahagan, Helen, 63–64
Gallup poll, 258
Garment, Leonard, 282, 312–14, 324, 326
Genesis (magazine), 169
Gentle Tasaday, The (Nance), 90–91
Georgetown Law School, 55, 112
Gergen, David, 95, 133, 282, 313
Glanzer, Seymour, 83, 282
Go Quietly . . . or Else (Agnew), 338–40
Goldfine, Bernard, 138, 201, 201fn
Goldman, Carl, 240
Goldman, William, 93
Goldwater, Barry, 18, 52–54, 121
Goldwater, Barry, Jr., 18, 52
Goldwater, Mrs. Barry, 18
Golson, Barry, 211–13
Gorey, Hays, 2–4, 133, 191–94, 216–17,
 244, 279, 301–06, 310, 325–26, 328–29,
 349–51, 353fn, 354
Government Ethics, Office of, 252
Government Printing Office, 191, 193
Grant, Ulysses S., 137
Gray, L. Patrick, III, 31, 272, 282, 295,
 300, 317, 331, 334–35, 347
Great Coverup, The (Sussman), 283, 333
Great Gatsby, The (Fitzgerald), 84

Greenberg, Stanley, 235
Greider, William, 283–84
Griffin, Robert, 200
Gulley, Bill, 337–38

Haig, Alexander M., Jr.: 328, 337–38, 340–
 43, 350; as aide to Kissinger, 69–70, 296,
 314, 327, 328–29, 335–36, 338–40,
 340fn, 341, 344–47, 351; as chief of
 staff, White House, 282, 290, 296, 309,
 322–24, 328, 337–39, 339fn, 340–41,
 348–50; as Deep Throat candidate, 282,
 296, 314, 324, 326–30, 332, 335–51,
 353–54; early career, 44–46; "Kissinger
 wiretaps," role in, 69–70, 345, 354; as
 NATO Chief, 348; at Pentagon, 336–37,
 344; as Secretary of State, 302fn, 348–
 50, 350fn, 351; role in Vietnam war
 peace talks, 296, 314, 327, 335–36
Haig: The General's Progress (Morris),
 332, 340, 340fn, 341, 344–45, 349, 351
Haldeman, H. R. (Bob), 8fn, 64, 75, 80,
 81–83, 104, 106–08, 110, 118–19, 127–
 31, 138–39, 147, 177, 185–89, 194, 198,
 200, 210, 228, 243–44, 289, 291, 296,
 317–18, 320, 323–24, 328, 337–38, 340,
 340fn, 352, 356
Harding, Warren G., 137
Hardy, Thomas, 358
Harris, Fred, 103
Harris poll, 258
Hayes, Rutherford B., 139–40
Hays, Wayne, 148, 150
Heckler, Margaret, 199–200
Hefner, Hugh, 84–85
Hemingway, Ernest, 87
Herblock, 130
Hersh, Seymour, 272
Higby, Larry, 291
Hiss, Alger, 63
Hoffman, Dustin, 71–79, 93
Holbrook, Hal, 94, 244
Hollywood, 77–78, 221
Hollywood Reporter, The, 86
Holtzman, Elizabeth, 189–90, 203–05, 207
Hoover, J. Edgar, 63, 66–67, 69–73, 247fn,
 280
House Armed Services Committee, 106
House Banking and Currency Committee,
 185–204, 206–09; *see also*, Patman com-
 mittee
House Impeachment Committee, 65, 97,
 120, 192–95, 209, 237, 281
House Judiciary Committee, 55, 209, 217
House Oversight and Investigations Sub-
 committee, 146
Hughes Aircraft, 43
Hughes, Howard, 92, 130
Humphrey, Hubert, 82
Hunt, E. Howard, Jr., 36, 62–63, 111, 131,

Hunt, E. Howard, Jr. (*Cont'd*)
200, 233, 283, 285, 287, 296–99, 311–12,
316–17, 319, 334, 342, 344, 351, 357
Hunt, Gerry, 101–02, 112–17, 132

Internal Revenue Service (IRS), 118, 130
Investigations, government; *see* Watergate,
government investigation of
Investigative journalism; *see* Press, the
Investigator, the, 303–06, 308, 329
I.O.S. Ltd., 276
It Didn't Start with Watergate (Lasky), 242

Jackson, Henry (Scoop), 82
Jaworski, Leon, 204, 206, 252, 322
Johnson, Lyndon Baines, 56, 70, 72, 72fn,
106–07, 138–39, 155, 231, 302fn, 340,
345
Johnson Library, Lyndon Baines, 106–07
Jordan, Hamilton, 274–76
Judicial branch, 252–57
Justice, Department of, 24, 58–59, 66, 74,
89, 111–12, 130, 132, 139, 153, 157, 165,
204, 208–09, 252–53, 276–78, 280–81,
286–87, 289, 295, 300, 303, 305, 308,
313, 319, 333, 346–47, 351

Kalmbach, Herbert W., 8, 8fn, 9, 106, 305,
357
Kane, Irene, 14, 21, 39–40, 42–43, 226
Kansas City, 135, 141, 144, 159–65, 167–
73, 178–79, 181–84
Kansas City Star, 162, 170
Keeney, John C., 281
Kemper Arena Convention Hall, 162, 167–
68, 176
Kennedy, Edward, 4, 156, 202
Kennedy, John, 72–73, 82, 114, 116, 136,
155, 231, 245
Kennedy, Robert, 72, 136
Kentucky Derby, 113
Kierkegaard, 225
Kinley, David D., 282
Kinsey, Pete, 9, 301–05, 310, 351, 353,
353fn
KIQQ, 240
Kirbo, Charles, 276
Kissinger, Henry, 65–66, 69, 89, 105, 107,
110, 128–29, 131, 147, 233, 296, 317,
328, 332, 336, 338–41, 344–47
"Kissinger wiretaps," *see* Wiretaps
Kleindienst, Richard, 31, 57–58, 138–39,
300, 317
Knievel, Evel, 216
"Koreagate," 243
Kraft, Joseph, 66, 230
Krogh, Egil (Bud), Jr., 67, 110, 233, 357

Labor, Department of, 130
Laird, Melvin, 31

Lance, Bert, 274, 276
Lardner, George, Jr., 289
LaRue, Frederick C., 313
Lasky, Victor, 242
"Last Tango in Paris" (movie), 88
Lawyers, 254, 302, 308
Laxalt, Paul, 142
Leaks, 33, 61–63, 65–71, 73–74, 76, 82, 84,
123, 164, 219, 233, 245, 290, 305, 313,
317, 320, 328, 337, 343, 345–47, 347fn,
354, *see also,* Wiretaps
Legislative branch, *see* Congress, U.S.
Lemberg Center for the Study of Violence,
124
Levi, Edward, 205–10
Lewis, Anthony, 310
Libya, 277–78
Liddy, G. Gordon, 61–63, 111, 131, 154,
186, 200, 233, 271, 311, 317, 342, 357
Lincoln, Abraham, 181, 183
Lindsay, John (mayor), 11
Lindsay, John (reporter), 2, 11, 143–44,
153, 160, 342–43
Lockheed Corp., 197
Lord Jim (Conrad), 217, 234–35, 358
Los Angeles, 9–13, 42–43, 49
Los Angeles Times, 18, 115, 207, 263–64,
332
"Lou Grant" (television series), 78

McCarthyism, 278
McCord, James W., Jr., 131, 287, 298,
317–18, 357
McCulloch, William, 55–56
McGovern, George, 148, 152–56, 272,
285–86, 336
McGrory, Mary, 229–30
McLuhan, Marshall, 179
M'Naghten rule, 126
McNamara, Robert, 344, 346
McWhorter, Laurence S., 281
Mafia, 15, 24–25, 64, 116, 150, 255
Magruder, Jeb Stuart, 8, 8fn, 9, 316, 356–
57
Making of the President(s), The (White),
166
Manchester Union Leader, 334
Manhattan Project, 109
Mann, Jim, 284
Mardian, Robert C., 66–67, 69, 313, 318,
346–47
Marine Corps, U.S., 106
Martinez, Eugenio, 344
Maslow, Abraham, 225
Massachusetts Institute of Technology, 251
Mayhew, Alice, 91, 94–96, 132–33, 250,
265, 348, 352
Medicaid, 312
Menninger Clinic, The, 123
Meredith, Scott, 114–16

Meyer, Larry, 2
Miami Beach, 177–78
Miami Convention Hall, 177
Missel, Renee, 119
Mitchell, John N., 57–58, 64, 66, 80, 104, 137–39, 188, 313, 316, 318–20, 334, 347, 356
Mollenhoff, Clark, 199
Montgomery County Sentinel, 352
Moore, Richard A., xi, 31, 83, 282, 313
Morgan, Edward L., 110
Morris, Roger, 340, 340fn, 341, 344–45, 349, 351
Morrison, Paul, 334
Morton, Rogers, 146
Movie industry, 77–80, 85–87, 97, 222, 265
Moynihan, Pat, 340
Munger, Robert, 221, 223
Murray State University, 102
Music Corporation of America, (MCA), 108
Muskie, Edmund, 81–82, 334

Nance, John, 90
Natchitoches, Louisiana, 47
National Commission on the Reform of Federal Criminal Law (1967), 56–57
National Council of Social Studies, 102
National Enquirer, 99, 101, 112–13, 115–17, 132
National Opinion Research Center (NORC), 259–60
National Public Radio (NPR), 310
National Security Council (NSC), 67, 110, 145, 328–29, 340–42, 344–45, 351
NATO, 348
NBC, 2, 13, 16, 196–97, 205–06, 209–10
Nelson, Jack, 207–08, 263–64
Nessen, Ron, 203fn
New Muckrakers, The, (Downie), 287–88, 315
New Republic, The, 1, 257, 321
New Times, 31, 183, 183fn
New York Academy of Medicine, 123
New York Post, 50fn
New York Times, The, 1, 34, 61, 86, 99, 127, 209, 272, 275, 310, 322, 332, 347
New York Times Magazine, The, 127
Newsweek, 1, 2, 11, 118, 121, 130, 143, 160, 342–43
Nietzsche, 89, 358
Nixon, Patricia, 22–23, 177
Nixon, Richard M.: xi, 10–11, 17, 32, 42, 46, 62, 69fn, 74, 86, 89, 97, 119, 127, 132, 138–39, 143, 167, 179, 235–37, 241, 255, 264, 270, 276, 284–85, 300, 317, 320, 321, 328, 336, 338–39, 339fn, 341, 343, 347, 356; administration of, 19, 21–23, 34, 36, 57–61, 73–75, 89, 104–06, 108–09, 111, 136–37, 139, 145–46, 153–

57, 181, 185, 189–91, 193, 201, 216, 216fn, 219, 229–31, 243, 253, 255–56, 271–73, 275, 280–82, 285–93, 295–97, 300–01, 305–06, 308–10, 311–14, 316–25, 329, 334, 337–39, 339fn, 340–44, 346–47, 355–57; alleged love letters, 101, 113–17, 132, 132fn; alleged plot against Daniel Ellsberg, 61–62; Cold war mentality, 63–65; and John Connally, 104–05; Dean meetings with, 65, 185–88, 198; early years in government, 122; FBI used by, for political purposes, 139, 317, 345, *see also* FBI, Wiretaps, Sullivan, William C., Leaks; Frost interviews, 235–38; and Patricia Nixon, 22–23, 177; ordered wiretaps, 66–70, 73; memoirs of, 322–23, 332, 336; pardon of, by Ford, 46, 103, 111, 143, 230, 231; personality, analysis of, 22–23, 63–65, 116–27, 238; as portrayed by Dean in "The Final Day," 127–31; 1968 presidential campaign of, 57, 72fn, 81, 177; 1972 presidential campaign of, 81–82, 104, 118, 148, 154–55, 157, 177–78, 186, 189, 195, 200, 271–72, 276, 285, 298, 308, 313, 316, 319, 332, 334–36; presidential library, plans for, 105–08, 127; presidential protection, policy of, 60, 287, 298, *see also* Secret Service; public opinion of, 46, 104, 153; reforms, plans for, 107–12; resignation of, 237, 254, 263–64, 341, 349; retirement fund, 46, 106; role of, in Watergate cover-up, 65–67, 70, 75, 118, 122, 138–39, 185–90, 194, 198, 201–02, 204, 228, 237–38, 252, 255–56, 289–90, 296, 298, 317–18, 322–24, 340–41, 345, 347, 356; role of press in bringing down, 34, *see also* Press, the; second inauguration, 59, 60, 108; *Six Crises*, 105, 129; as vice president, 52; White House staff of, 8fn, 28, 38, 45, 57–60, 60fn, 64–66, 69–71, 73–75, 80–82, 94–95, 104–11, 118–19, 138–39, 144, 147, 157, 186, 189–90, 194, 198, 200, 209, 233, 243, 271–73, 275, 280–82, 285–93, 295–97, 300–01, 305–06, 308–10, 311–14, 316–25, 327–29, 334–339, 339fn, 340–44, 346–49, 351–52, 354–57
Nixon vs. Nixon: An Emotional Tragedy (Abrahamsen), 121–26
Northwestern State University, 47
Not Above the Law (Doyle), 322
Novak, Robert, 228–29
November Group, 316
NSC, *see* National Security Council

O'Brien, Lawrence F., 118–19, 200
Obst, David, 15–18, 28–29, 31–32, 34–38, 47, 50, 61–65, 77–80, 91, 97, 100, 119, 178, 183fn, 210, 352

Office of Management and Budget (OMB), 274
"Omen, The" (movie), 221
"On the Waterfront" (movie), 88
Osbourne, John, 321

Panama, 342
Panama Canal Treaty, 342
Parade (magazine), 239
Parkinson, Kenneth W., 195, 200
Parkinson, Paula, 303, 303fn
Patman committee: 185–204, 206–09; report of, 190, 201
Patman, Wright, 186
Pentagon, 288, 307, 324, 329, 336, 352
"Pentagon Papers," 61
Petersen, Henry E., 31, 281, 352
Plain Dealer, The (Cleveland), 39, 41
Playboy (magazine), 151, 166, 169, 184, 211, 303fn
Plumbers' Unit, 62, 233, 340, 342–43, *see also* Watergate burglars, Wiretaps, Leaks
Poff, Richard, 56
Polk, Jim, 209
Porter, Herbert L. (Bart), 316
President Nixon's Psychiatric Profile (Chesen), 121
Presidential campaigns: *1948*, 73; *1956*, 73; *1960*, 82; *1964*, 72, 121; *1968*, 57, 72fn, 81, 177; *1972*, 8fn, 81–82, 104, 148, 154–55, 157, 177–78, 185–87, 189, 195, 200, 271–72, 276, 285–86, 298, 308, 313, 316, 319, 332, 334–36; *1976*, 103–04, 119, 135, 141–43, 147–48, 154–56, 160–72, 176, 178–85, 192, 195–97, 203, 205, 207–09, 214, 216, 217–19, 264, 273–74; *1980*, 277–78
Press, the: 9–11, 13, 33–34, 48, 141, 143–44, 148–49, 152, 164, 181, 193, 227, 230–31, 235, 244, 246, 268–70, 273, 278–79, 294fn, 299, 303, 310, 317, 320–22, 345, 354; coverage of the Carter administration, 227–32, 273–79; coverage of the Ford testimony controversy, 192–94, 196–97, 202–10, 203fn, 217; coverage of the 1976 presidential campaign, 135, 141, 144, 147–48, 154–55, 160–70, 172, 176, 178–79, 181–85, 192, 203, 207–08, 216, 218; coverage of Watergate, 2fn, 3, 30–31, 34, 41, 44–46, 53–55, 66–67, 71, 78–80, 82–84, 93–94, 132–33, 143–44, 173–74, 186, 193, 196, 198, 229, 231, 243, 254, 260, 263, 270–73, 280, 282, 285, 288, 291, 293–95, 299–300, 303, 312, 314–16, 319, 322, 332–36, 342, 348, 352–53; impact of Watergate on, 49–50, 143–44, 156–51, 227, 229–32, 254, 267–79, 293, 299, 301; as having "cracked the Watergate case," 4, 83–84, 271–73; and "investigative journalism,"

30–31, 49–50, 80, 113, 115, 119, 136, 144, 168, 183, 218–19, 245, 272, 274–75, 278, 294, 294fn, 314–15, 321; and "pocketbook journalism," 210; and Watergate tenth anniversary, 1–5, 267–70, 279, 301
Price, Raymond, 321

Queen Mary, 18
Queen Elizabeth II (of England), 155
Queen Elizabeth II (ocean liner), 240–42

Rauh, Joseph, Jr., 251
Ray, Elizabeth, 148–53, 168–69, 178
Reagan, Ronald, 103–04, 142, 144, 154, 156, 169, 178, 181–82, 184, 278–79, 348–50
Rebozo, Bebe, 106, 241–42, 341
Redford, Robert, 77–80, 83, 93, 283
Republican National Convention: *1972*, 177–78; *1976*, 119, 135, 141–42, 147, 160–72, 176, 178–84, 197
Republican Party, 8fn, 45, 53, 56, 71, 73, 82, 103, 112, 135, 141, 150, 155, 160, 165, 167–69, 172, 178, 182–84, 186–87, 189–92, 195, 199–200, 228–29, 285, 287
Reuss, Henry S., 204, 209
Right and the Power, The (Jaworski), 322
"Right to Know, The," 240, 242–44, 246–47, 270, 279
Robards, Jason, Jr., 93, 230
Rockefeller Commission on Intelligence Activities, 97
Rockefeller, Nelson, 69, 141, 184, 347fn
Rodino, Peter, 209
Rolling Stone (magazine), 50, 119, 135, 144, 147–49, 156, 160–61, 168–69, 172–73, 178–82, 211, 227, 232, 239
Roosevelt, Eleanor, 72
Roosevelt, Franklin Delano, 70, 72, 136
Roper poll, 258
Rose, Chapman, 314, 324
Rose, Jonathan C., 282, 314, 324, 326
"Rosemary's Baby" (movie), 46
Rosenfeld, Harry M., 292
Rosenman, Howard, 97, 119
ROTC, 288
Royster, Vermont, 137
Ruckelshaus, William D., 216, 216fn, 217
Ruff, Charles, 203–05, 208
Rumsfeld, Donald, 147

Safire, William, 118–19, 275, 321
St. Elizabeth's Hospital, 123
Salinger, Pierre, 245
San Clemente, 106, 128, 143
Saturday Evening Post, 158, 257
"Saturday Night Massacre," 252, 323
Saxty, Dick, 99
Schiappa, Jerry, 55

Schlesinger, Arthur, Jr., 139
Schreiber, Taft, 108
Schwalm, Roger, 282
Scott, Hugh, 200
Scott, Sir Walter, 139
Sears, John, 142
Secret Service, 66, 70–71, 130–31, 164, 169, 280–82, 284–92, 295–98, 300, 305–09, 314, 325, 351
Securities and Exchange Commission (SEC), 130, 157
Segretti, Donald H., 81–83, 313, 316, 319, 332–33, 357
Select Committee on Intelligence, 136
Select Committee on Presidential Campaign Activities, see Senate Watergate committee
Senate Armed Services Committee, 106
Senate Committee on Governmental Affairs, 274
Senate Watergate committee (Ervin committee), xi, 31, 46, 60fn, 97, 112, 136, 141, 145–46, 156, 174, 185, 190, 192–93, 195, 198, 202, 206, 228–29, 254, 256, 260, 281, 285–86, 286fn, 291, 309, 322, 335, 342, 346, 352
Shacklette, Baron, 200–01
Shapiro, Harold, 281
Shaffer, Charles Norman, xii, 8, 30, 185, 205–06
Shaughnessy, Pat, 240, 246–47
Sheehan, Neil, 347
Shirer, William, 225–26
Shriver, Sargent, 103
Sidey, Hugh, 231
Silbert, Earl J., 48–49, 83, 282
Sims, Louis, 282
Simon and Schuster, 50fn, 94, 132, 348
Sinatra, Frank, 13
Sinclair, Harry, 137
Sirica, John J., 8–9, 255–57, 272, 290, 323
Six Crises (Nixon), 105, 129
Sloan, Hugh W., Jr., 256
Smith, Hedrick, 347
Smith, Sandy, 296
Smithsonian (magazine), 297
Stacks, John, 3, 296, 326
Stans, Maurice H., 106, 186, 200
State, Department of, 73, 110, 350–51
State of the Union Address, 249–50
Staunton Military Academy, 18, 51–53
Steadman, Ralph, 160–70, 173–76, 178, 242
Stennis, John, 323
Stern, Art, 51
Stern, Carl, 13, 16, 196–97, 206, 208–09
Stevenson, Adlai, 73
Stewart, Potter, 310
Stone, Clement, 357
Stonewall (Ben-Veniste and Frampton), 322

Strachan, Gordon C., 110–11
Studio 54, 275
Success, 357
Succession, laws of, 249
Sullivan, Harold, 282
Sullivan, William C., 66–75, 100, 136, 345–47, 347fn
Supreme Court, 79–80, 249, 253, 297–98, 306–10, 349
Sussman, Barry, 283, 286, 292–93, 332–33, 36
Syracuse University, 50fn, 251

Talmadge, Herman, 254
Taylor, Garth, 260–61
Taylor, Telford, 158
"Teapot Dome" scandal, 137
Telegraph (London), 162
Thompson, Fred, 229
Thompson, Hunter, 160, 173
Thieu, Nguyen Van, 336
Torrijos, Omar, 342
Tilden, Samuel J., 140
Time (magazine), 2–4 passim, 30, 66–68, 70, 96, 133, 191, 216, 244, 296, 305, 307, 326, 346–47, 351
Time-Life, 231
Times (London), 234
Timmons, William, 143, 147–48, 187–96, 198–203, 206, 209
Titus, Harold H., Jr., 282
"Today" Show, 2, 196, 203, 205–06, 210, 301
Tolstoi, Leo, 225
Toronto Star, The, 284
Through the Looking-Glass, 358
To Set the Record Straight (Sirica), 256–57
Totenberg, Nina, 310
Truman, Harry, 73, 136–38
Tuck, Dick, 82, 166–67
Twain, Mark, 136
20th Century Journey (Shirer), 225–26

UCLA, 251
Udall, Morris, 103
Ulasewicz, Tony, 341
Uncle Tom's Cabin (Stowe), 54
United Airlines, 9–10
United States v. Richard Nixon, 253
University of Chicago, 251, 259–60
University of Florida, 81
University of Massachusets, 258, 271, 279, 299, 315
University of Michigan, 258
University of Virginia, 29, 34–37, 47
United Press International (UPI), 99

Vance, Cyrus, 344–45
Vesco, Robert L., 276

Vietnam war, 61, 63–64, 72fn, 231, 261, 288, 296, 336, 340–41, 345

Walker, Bob, 17, 28–29, 34
Wallace, George, 94, 283–86, 292–93, 307, 311
Walters, Barbara, 149
War Powers Resolution (1973), 145, 156
Warner Bros., 77
Warren, Robert Penn, 54
Washington, D.C., 1–5 passim, 48, 51–59, 87, 136, 140–41, 143–44, 146, 148–51, 153, 156–58, 211, 229, 231, 250, 273–74, 284, 287, 292, 298, 301–02, 304, 308, 325, 328, 330–32, 336, 344, 350
Washington Fringe Benefit, The (Ray), 148–150
Washington Monthly, The, 191
Washington National Airport, 298
Washington Post, The, 1, 2, 2fn, 15, 28, 31–32, 34, 48, 71, 77, 82–83, 86, 93, 130, 132, 166, 185, 196, 218–19, 230–31, 270–74, 280, 283–89, 292, 292fn, 293–94, 294fn, 295, 300, 305, 312–13, 315–16, 319–20, 322, 324, 331–36, 348–53
Washington Star, The, 206, 229, 341
Watergate affair, 22, 26, 42, 97, 100, 117, 127, 136–38, 140, 148, 176, 179–81, 197, 200, 213, 217, 226, 233, 235, 237, 241–44, 250, 255, 272, 276, 280, 315, 317, 327, 329, 338–39, 345, 349, 352, 355, 357; break-in, 1–2, 82, 154, 185–87, 189, 200, 256, 267, 271, 283, 286–87, 289, 314, 316, 319, 334–35, 342, 344, 357; burglars, 118, 185–86, 198, 200, 243, 256, 271–72, 286–87, 297, 314, 319, 342, 344, 357; cover-up, 21, 28, 34, 66–71, 75, 83–84, 122, 139, 159, 185–204, 206–09, 228–29, 236–38, 243, 252, 254, 256, 271–73, 280, 287–90, 312–14, 317–24, 327, 335, 340, 342–43, 348–49, 356–57; fifth anniversary of, 263–64, 267; government investigation of, 18–19, 21, 48, 82–84, 93, 100, 112, 120, 145, 185–87, 189–204, 206–09, 218, 228–29, 252, 254–57, 260, 272, 279–81, 283, 285–87, 290–93, 296, 298, 308–09, 311, 313, 316, 318–20, 322–23, 333–35, 346–47, 357, see also, FBI, Patman committee, Senate Watergate committee, House impeachment committee; impact of, 1–5, 23, 26, 46, 49–50, 74–75, 80, 97, 101, 103–06, 108, 111–12, 136, 139–40, 142–47, 153, 155–58, 218, 227–32, 250–58, 260–65, 261fn, 267–74, 278–79, 290, 293, 355–57, see also Press, Public opinion, Congress, Executive branch, Judicial branch; lessons

of, 4, 23, 254–55; public opinion of, 45–46, 80, 102–03, 136, 155–56, 186, 257–62, 261fn, 270–73, 282, 313, 315, 355; tenth anniversary of, 1–5, 267–71, 276, 279, 292, 295, 301; theories of the cause of, 63–64, 100, 122–23; "Watergate guys," 8, 8fn; White House tapes, 45, 60fn, 118, 131, 186, 189, 191, 204, 207–08, 217, 237, 253, 255, 287–91, 296–98, 307, 309, 317, 320–24, 327, 331, 340, 348–49, 354
Watergate (Hotel Complex), 1, 243, 256, 271, 286
Weicker, Lowell P., 141–42, 145–46, 301
Welch & Morgan, 55
Welles, Sumner, 72
Wells, Brian, 99
Wendell, Rupert, 112
Wenner, Jann, 119, 135, 149, 152, 168, 178, 227, 239, 260
West Point, 345–46
White, Cliff, 118
White House, 58–59, 106, 137, 280, 311; see also Executive branch, presidents by name
White, Theodore, 166
Widnall, William B., 187, 198
Williams, Edward Bennett, 118, 302fn
Wiretaps: 65–73, 76, 123, 136, 200–01, 287, 317–18, 345–47, 347fn, 354; "Kissinger wiretaps," 65–71, 76, 317, 345–47, 354
Wong, Alfred C., 282, 287, 297–310
Woods, Rose Mary, 46, 201, 289–90, 296, 323–24
Woodward, Robert U., 2fn, 15–16, 30–34, 47–48, 66, 71, 77–80, 82–84, 93–95, 127, 132–33, 218–19, 230, 244–46, 263, 270–72, 279–81, 283–94, 294fn, 295–301, 303–10, 311–22, 324–38, 342–43, 346–55
Woodward, Fran, 31
Wooster, College of, 53, 55
Wounded Knee, 88–89, 337
Wright, James D., 258–59

Yale University, 95, 133, 251, 262, 288, 313–14
Yom Kippur War, 323
Young Americans for Freedom, 44, 169
Young, David, 233–34, 242, 357
Young Peoples Socialist League, 44

Zeibert, Duke, 151
Zeigler, Ronald L., 28, 66–67, 131, 143
Zumwalt, Raymond C., 282